Abbas Kiarostami's Cinema of Life

Abbas Kiarostami's Cinema of Life

From Homework *to* Like Someone in Love

Julian Rice

ROWMAN & LITTLEFIELD
Lanham • Boulder • New York • London

Published by Rowman & Littlefield
An imprint of The Rowman & Littlefield Publishing Group, Inc.
4501 Forbes Boulevard, Suite 200, Lanham, Maryland 20706
www.rowman.com

6 Tinworth Street, London SE11 5AL

Copyright © 2020 by The Rowman & Littlefield Publishing Group, Inc.

All rights reserved. No part of this book may be reproduced in any form or by any electronic or mechanical means, including information storage and retrieval systems, without written permission from the publisher, except by a reviewer who may quote passages in a review.

British Library Cataloguing in Publication Information Available

Library of Congress Cataloging-in-Publication Data

Names: Rice, Julian, 1940– author.
Title: Abbas Kiarostami's cinema of life : from Homework to Like someone in love / Julian Rice.
Description: Lanham : Rowman & Littlefield, [2020] | Includes bibliographical references and index. | Summary: "Abbas Kiarostami's Cinema of Life focuses on this major filmmaker's opposition to war, his eclectic spirituality which opposes orthodox Islam, and the symbolic texture of his cinema which is more attuned to poetic than philosophical interpretation. It is one of only a few English language books on Kiarostami's films, and the only to cover the most-up-to-date films and consider the Iranian context of Kiarostami's films, with a focus on content and continuity of the individual films."—Provided by publisher.
Identifiers: LCCN 2019057120 (print) | LCCN 2019057121 (ebook) | ISBN 9781538137000 (cloth) | ISBN 9781538137017 (epub) | ISBN 9781538171240 (pbk)
Subjects: LCSH: Kiarostami, Abbas—Criticism and interpretation. | Motion picture producers and directors—Iran—Biography. | Motion pictures—Iran—History.
Classification: LCC PN1998.3.K58 R53 2020 (print) | LCC PN1998.3.K58
LC record available at https://lccn.loc.gov/2019057120
LC ebook record available at https://lccn.loc.gov/2019057121

For
Carol, Noah, and Robyn
and for
Ethan and Jack

Contents

Acknowledgments	ix
1 The Seeds of War	1
2 Kiarostami and Religion	17
3 Saving the World	49
4 War as Suicide	63
5 Obscuring the Soul	79
6 Prefer the Present	99
7 Save the Children	137
8 A Mother Grows Up	145
9 Dream a Little	167
10 The Manly Game	199
11 The Soul of Art	221
12 It's a Jungle Out There	245
Further Reading	267
Index	269
About the Author	281

Acknowledgments

I would like to thank Stephen Ryan, former senior editor for arts and literature at Rowman & Littlefield, for his ongoing encouragement and expert guidance. I am also indebted to editorial assistant Dina Guilak for formatting assistance and to production assistant Catherine Herman for refining important details in the text. Their help was augmented by the careful work of copyeditor Niki Guinan and proofreader Henry Lazarek, to both of whom I am also sincerely grateful.

Permissions to quote from the following works have been granted by their publishers:

In the Shadow of Trees: The Collected Poetry of Abbas Kiarostami by Abbas Kiarostami, translated by Iman Tavassoly and Paul Cronin, copyright © 2016 by Sticking Place Books. Used by permission of Paul Cronin, Sticking Place Books, New York.

The Expanse of Green: Poems of Sohrab Sepehri by Sohrab Sepehri, translated by David I. Martin, copyright © 1988 by Kalimar/UNESCO. Used by permission of Cambridge University Press, Cambridge, England.

The Conference of the Birds by Farid Ud-Din Attar, translated by Afkham Darbandi and Dick Davis, copyright © 1984 by Penguin Books, Ltd. Prologue and Epilogue translated by Dick Davis, copyright © 2011 by Penguin Books, Ltd. Used by permission of Penguin Books, Ltd., London, England.

Chapter One

The Seeds of War

At a time when the world is lapsing into varied forms of national fervor and environmental neglect, no artist has more to tell us about the insanity of war and the value of the natural world than the late Iranian filmmaker Abbas Kiarostami. And yet in *Sight & Sound*'s 2012 poll of the top 250 films of all time, only *Close-Up* (1990) was included, at number 42.[1] A great deal has been written about Kiarostami since the end of the 1990s, when he was acclaimed as the person of the decade by *Film Comment*. In its poll of 124 critics, scholars, filmmakers, and distributors, such luminaries as Geoff Andrew, Michel Ciment, Adrian Martin, Laura Mulvey, Bernard Tavernier, and Serge Toubiana put Kiarostami at the top of their list. Robin Wood wrote that Kiarostami's "subtle, complex, oblique art develops further with every film,"[2] and David Bordwell praised *Through the Olive Trees* (1994) as "deeply moving" and "formally adventurous," putting Kiarostami on a par with Eisenstein, Ozu, Dreyer, and Renoir: "[Kiarostami seems] to be reinventing the history of the cinema . . . without any postmodernist bad faith—instead, a spontaneous sense of human integrity."[3]

For an overview of Kiarostami's biography, career, and the international response to his films, the two best English-language studies continue to be Mehrnaz Saeed-Vafa and Jonathan Rosenbaum's 2001 *Abbas Kiarostami* and Belinda Coombes's 2005 translation of *The Cinema of Abbas Kiarostami* from Alberto Elena's 2002 Spanish original.[4] My book includes chapters on Kiarostami's output after *Ten* (2002), the last film Elena covered and the only one even mentioned (by one critic) in the 2010 *Film Comment* poll, probably because *Certified Copy* (2010) was completed too late to be included.[5] Readers are encouraged to consult the films discussed in this book in their presently available formats. The major films on DVD with English subtitles are *Where Is the Friend's House?* (1987), *Close-Up, And Life Goes*

On (1992), *Through the Olive Trees, Taste of Cherry* (1997), *The Wind Will Carry Us* (1999), *ABC Africa* (2001), *Ten, Shirin* (2008), *Certified Copy*, and *Like Someone in Love* (2012). *The Traveler* (1974) is on the *Close-Up* DVD; *The Report* (1977) is on the *Certified Copy* DVD; *Homework* is on "The Koker Trilogy" DVD; *Ten on Ten* (2004) is on the *Ten* DVD; and *Roads of Kiarostami* (2005) and *Rug* (2006) are on the *Shirin* DVD.

In a 1997 interview at Cannes, where *Taste of Cherry* won the Palme d'Or for Best Film, Kiarostami remarked, "It's not conscious, but now that one can see all my films as a body of work it seems that they all talk about the same things. Someone once said that every filmmaker basically makes only one film in his lifetime, but he cuts it down and offers it in cinematic installments to his audience over a period of time."⁶ Now that we can see the rest of

Figure 1.1. Abbas Kiarostami in a publicity photo for *Taste of Cherry*. Zeitgeist Films/Photofest.

Kiarostami's films more than twenty years later, we can see that even the ones he made in Italy and Japan carry through a unified vision, but in order to understand that continuity in ways that most other interpreters have neglected, we must consider the historical and cultural context that helped to shape his process. Born on June 22, 1940, Kiarostami was indelibly imprinted by the civil violence of the 1979 revolution and the agonizingly protracted Iran-Iraq War. These events shaped his view of the world much as the similarly protracted and useless Vietnam War shaped those of his generation in the United States.

In 1965 America involved itself in a Vietnamese civil war in order to prevent the Communist North from taking over the whole of the country because, according to the so-called domino theory, stopping the spread of Russian and Chinese influence anywhere in the world was crucial to national security. The result was a complete takeover of the country by the North, accompanied by an ignominious American withdrawal in 1973 following eight years of staggering carnage. In addition to 58,000 Americans, the military dead totaled 254,000 South Vietnamese and 1,100,000 North Vietnamese and Viet Cong. The "collateral damage" included 430,000 South Vietnamese; 65,000 North Vietnamese; 300,000 Cambodian; and 62,000 Laotian civilians. An additional 42,000 Vietnamese and 20,000 Laotians were subsequently killed and continue to be killed by land mines and other undetonated explosives.[7]

The eight-year Iran-Iraq War was equally unnecessary and horrific. It began in September 1980, when Saddam Hussein invaded a province of southwestern Iran on the pretext that the region was historically part of Iraq but more pertinently because it contained a great deal of oil. By 1982 Iran recaptured the area, and for the next six years, the war was an atrocity-filled standoff. Estimates peak at approximately two million soldiers and civilians killed on both sides. The war was fueled by other countries, with Saudi Arabia contributing arms-buying power to Iraq between 1982 and 1988 to the tune of $72 billion, with which Saddam purchased weapons from Spain, France, and the United States. Ironically, the United States also covertly armed Iran to release hostages held in Lebanon and in return for Iran's withdrawal from the war against the American-backed Contras in Nicaragua. Iran also received military assistance from Russia, China, and North Korea.

Having made the strategic error of spreading his forces too thin, Saddam proposed a complete withdrawal from Iranian territory in June 1982 and announced that he would sue for peace. Ayatollah Ruhollah Khomeini not only refused the overture, but he also called for an Iranian invasion of Iraq that would end only when Saddam's regime was replaced by an Iranian-style Islamic republic. Saddam's initiatory attack and Khomeini's furious continuation made it clear that neither leader cared about the human cost of his power lust. Finally, in July 1988, with the war in stalemate and heavy war-weariness among civilians, especially in Iran, Supreme Leader Khomeini reluctantly accepted a UN resolution that sent both countries back to the territory they had held when the war began. The ayatollah expressed his deep displeasure with this outcome in an address to the nation: "Happy are those who have departed through martyrdom. Happy are those who have lost their lives in this convoy of light. Unhappy am I that I still survive and have drunk the poisoned chalice."[8]

Khomeini's distaste for peace underlies a statement by expatriate Iranian filmmaker Mohsen Makhmalbaf upon Kiarostami's death: Though he "gave the Iranian cinema international credibility his films were unfortunately not seen as much in Iran" because, Makhmalbaf implies, "he was a man of life, who enjoyed living and made films in praise of life."[9] To understand the impact of this statement, it is helpful to briefly review the historical basis of patriotic martyrdom in Iran, a narrative to which several of Kiarostami's films and poems are strongly averse.

After Muhammad died in 632 CE, some of his followers thought the new caliph should be his cousin and son-in-law, Ali ibn Abi Ṭalib, because the prophet had no male heirs. However, at a meeting in Medina, the majority of Muslim leaders present selected Abu Bakr, a close associate of Muhammad, to lead the community. When Abu Bakr died two years later, the succession was marred by violent conflict. Bakr's assistant, Umar ibn al-Khaṭṭab, became the second caliph, only to be assassinated by a Persian slave in 644, while his successor, the third caliph, Uthman ibn Affan, was killed by rebels in 656. At this point Ali, who had been both a hero in Muhammad's military victories and the seminal scholar to whom the prophet dictated the Koran, finally assumed the caliphate, which many thought he preeminently deserved, Muhammad having said of him, "I am the city of knowledge, and Ali is its gate."

Tragically for his followers, the Shias, whose name means "partisans of Ali," the revered leader was assassinated in 656 at the behest of the Syrian Umayyad dynasty, whom the Shias refused to accept. Finally, in 680, the Shiite forces under Ali's son Al-Husayn ibn Ali were defeated at Karbala in modern-day Iraq in a battle that came to define the religious identity of the Shia and the national identity of Iran.[10] Though not divinely inspired himself, Husayn became the second great Shiite martyr, the successor in holiness to his father, whom Shias believe to have been designated by God through Muhammad as Islam's first legitimate imam. Thereafter, the male descendants of Ali were successively revered until the disappearance of the twelfth, who never died but remains hidden "in occultation" until he returns as the Mahdi on the Day of Judgment, when he and Jesus Christ will wage triumphant war against the false messiah known to Christians as the anti-Christ.

This "Twelver" faith has been the dominant theology of Iran since the Persian Safavid dynasty established Shia Islam as its state religion in 1501.

And throughout the intervening centuries, an angry sense of injustice has dominated Iran's religious culture and motivated its ongoing jihads against Sunni rivals in the Middle East. The government's intense animosity toward Israel since the 1979 Islamic revolution also has an infrequently remarked religious basis because Ali's most memorable battlefield exploits occurred in a siege of the Jewish stronghold of Khaybar at a time when Muhammad was engaged in battles against Jews and pagans for political and economic supremacy in Mecca and Medina.[11]

Shias comprise only 10 percent of Muslims worldwide, and Iran differs from other Islamic countries in having become a theocracy under the "ayatollahs," an honorific for the most distinguished of imams who rule for life after being chosen by an elected body of scholars and clerics. Khomeini and his followers rode a tidal wave of social resentment against the shah's westernized monarchy with the promise of divinely ordained equality under sharia law. As a persecuted minority in Sunni countries, particularly Saudi Arabia, Shiism has always thrived on an energy of resentment, which helped to fuel the 1979 Iranian revolution. The movement's will to persist against initial setbacks was mythically energized by the legendary prowess of Ali at the battle of Khaybar and especially the heroic martyrdom epitomized by Husayn ibn Ali and his followers at Karbala in 680. The Karbala defeat is celebrated as a spiritual victory every year during the Ashura holiday through self-flagellation and emotional recitals of Husayn's brave death. But far from being confined to Ashura, the nation's identification with Ali and Husayn has been celebrated uninterruptedly for centuries, despite westernizing efforts during the shah's regime to dilute it.[12]

The Iranian national anthem exhorts the "believers in justice" to heed the imam's "message of independence [and] freedom imprinted on [their] souls," and to follow the path of the "Martyrs [whose] clamors echo in the ears of time, enduring, continuing, and eternal."[13] These sentiments lie behind the willingness of untrained and unarmed conscripts to advance in human waves during the Iraq War. While Iraqi conscripts described being beaten into military submission and witnessing executions for retreat or disobedience, many Iranians enthusiastically entered combat. Thirty-five years later, one of them recalled his spiritual patriotism despite being ordered to clear mine fields by running into them:

> We loved Imam Khomeini, and when he gave the order to defend the country, we were happy to answer his call. All my generation went—and I think we went with joy. We were just young kids with Kalashnikovs and grenades—which we didn't even dare to use at first because a lot of us were afraid to throw them! We didn't even have bread! The logistics were terrible. But that obligation [to Khomeini] was so strong it covered everything. You're getting shot at, killed. Sometimes they cannot find your body. It's in pieces. And then you see that it's an unequal war—all you have is yourselves and the other side

has everything—bunkers, artillery, air force. When you do not have weaponry you have to break the enemy line with your body. Even the barbed wire—sometimes we couldn't cut it, so we would throw ourselves upon it with our bodies so others could pass over us. Our casualties went up and up. Sometimes seventy, eighty, ninety percent of our units were destroyed. The first time I saw a grenade strike the earth I lay on the ground for several minutes, I was so afraid. But in time hundreds of grenades were coming—and I didn't mind. You adapt and get used to war. You start to recognize which bullet is passing you and which bullet is in front of you. You become more professional.

But despite permanent injuries—plastic knee joints and a bullet lodged in his hand—this veteran felt that his nation's religious revolution was a cause worth dying for: "I think it was beautiful. It was a very elegant moment. I would rather die in that moment than live after the war. It was so nice."[14]

Nothing about the war was nice for Kiarostami. Though some of his work shows a passionate commitment to social justice, he did not participate in the revolution and later remarked that he never wanted to see blood running through the streets again.[15] In a rare direct reference to the revolution at the beginning of *Close-Up*, he has a former fighter-pilot-turned-cab-driver refer to an incident at the Lavizan Air Force barracks when shah loyalists fired on deserting comrades as a way of saying that postrevolutionary society has turned against the poor, personified by his real-life antihero, Hossein Sabzian.[16] Kiarostami expressed his hatred of war covertly in *Taste of Cherry* and *Shirin*, but in several brief poems, he could not have been more direct:

> One hundred obedient soldiers
> entering the barracks.
> Moonlit night.
> Disobedient dreams.[17]
>
> The commander's uniform
> in the closet
> was consumed by moths.
>
> Commander
> and commanded
> Both injured.
> Both hungry.
> Both reluctant.
>
> The soldier who blew the trumpet
> did it badly.
> The sharp tongued commander
> hurled invectives
> during morning parade.[18]
>
> The soldier who placed his fingers in his ears

> While the artillery was firing
> lost his fingers
> and his ears
> and his eyes
> in the blink of an eye.
>
> Injured soldiers
> Wandering.
> Groaning and bloody.[19]

Kiarostami edited his 1989 documentary *Homework* to expose the intimidating effects of militant Shiite theology on children and families. Initially hired as a graphic designer in 1969, Kiarostami went on to make short and feature-length films for Kanun, the Center for the Intellectual Development of Children and Young Adults, until 1988: "We were supposed to make films that dealt with childhood problems. At the beginning it was just a job, but it was the making of me as an artist."[20] During his tenure at Kanun, Kiarostami must have reflected on the relationship between the personal lives of the children he filmed and the disconnect in the larger society between people who address each other on the street as "brother" and "sister" but do not treat each other as family: "Once you are unable to solve your internal problems, they pour out into the streets. I certainly believe these intra-family relationships and problems are social problems—as the partners [at home], a husband and a wife, leave home every morning and become members of society."[21]

Ostensibly a documentary about the education of first- and second-graders, Kiarostami's editing gives the title a resonance that applies to the nation as a whole. Thirty years later, in his final feature, *Like Someone in Love*, he has a retired Japanese police inspector praise his former sociology professor for a book that examines the "topic of violence in society." Later in the same film, the professor corrects a college student's confusion of Charles Darwin with Emile Durkheim, who wrote an exemplary sociological essay on suicide, a trope that applies to humanity collectively in Kiarostami's later work.[22] *Homework* is an early version of how the filmmaker envisioned the genesis of fear and anger in early childhood. It is also part of an ongoing look at what children learn outside of or in spite of school, notably portrayed in such films as *The Traveler*, *And Life Goes On*, *The Wind Will Carry Us*, and *Where Is the Friend's House?*

Homework's beginning is deceptively pleasant. A long, irregular procession of briefcase-carrying children in bright winter jackets, all happy and smiling, saunters past Kiarostami and his crew. Several ask what the film is about, and an adult voice is heard asking if it's a feature film, to which Kiarostami replies, "No, it's more like a documentary, but you can't tell until the film is made." More kids come up, and the director asks if they've done their homework. One boy teases the others, "My homework's better than theirs!" These initial shots show older children unperturbed by the assignments that younger children are afraid to discuss later in the film.

Another adult voice asks if this will be a sequel to *First Graders* (1984), a previous Kiarostami documentary he saw on television. Again, the reply is evasive: "It's not clear yet. We'll see when we get into it. It's based on impressions. We're just starting today. I came across a problem when I was helping my own son with homework." Then he adds a comment that proves to be retrospectively pointed, not just about the parents of these children, but also about power relationships in the whole society extending up to Khomeini: "*Homework* is supposed to be for kids, but adults are even more involved, so I thought I'd bring a camera to see what's going on. It's not a movie in the usual sense. It's more of a research project."

The camera cuts to a large group of boys entering the school courtyard, where their vocal cacophony is abruptly silenced by a sharp whistle. The camera cuts from a close-up of the colorfully clad children to an aerial shot in which they have been reduced to tiny dots massed against nearby mountains in a symbolic grayness, where only the students and a line of trees are black. The camera returns to the courtyard, where an older boy and male adult stand facing the rows of students who begin to shout in unison, "Islam is victorious! Down with the East and the West!" The line immediately locates the children in the center of a hostile world, perhaps alluding to non-Shiite enemies in light of the Koranic passage: "Unto Allah belong the East and the West, and whithersoever ye turn, there is Allah's countenance" (Koran 2:115).

Then the teacher shouts, "Say your prayer!" eliciting a profession of loyalty to Ali, the first legitimate imam, who, as the husband of Fatima, Muhammad's daughter, resided with the prophet: "Oh, Allah! Bless Muhammad and his household!" The camera then moves behind a black-robed woman at left-center, the one female figure in the image, a disciplinarian who foreshadows the abusive mothers later mentioned by the children (in contrast to Fatima), as the students recite the overture to all Muslim prayers: "In the name of God, the merciful, the compassionate."

The rest of the prayer puts the children in a metaphysical plight that reflects the social and familial plight that their interviews reveal. Each line is spoken by the leader and then repeated by the group: "By the declining day. Lo! Man is in a state of loss. Save those who believe and do good works. And exhort one another to truth." This is repeated with the variation "exhort one another to endurance." Then the whistle blows, and the children run in place. The adult voice chants, "One and two and three and four," and the children respond, "Two and three and four and five!" When they switch from running in place to jumping up and down, the prayer becomes more militant: "The warriors are victorious. Three and four and five and six. Saddam's followers are doomed." The cycles of numbers keep overlapping, reducing the children to anonymity and potential cannon fodder: "One and two and three and four, two and three and four and five, three and four and five and six, Saddam's followers are doomed. Muslims are victorious!"

The last part of the prayer decisively separates the Iranian nation from the Sunni Saddam, most of whose troops ironically were Shiite. But the more immediate tragic irony is in pushing these vulnerable children to emulate only the warrior side of Ali rather than Ali, the transcriber of the Koran. Each of the leader's rhetorical shouts triggers the same response. The endearing faces of the school-bound children in the opening scene have now visually and vocally become a Pavlovian mass: "The first imam?—Is Ali!—Lion-hearted one?—Is Ali!—Conqueror of Khaybar?—Is Ali!" The mass begins to break up, and the students are shown from various angles entering the school in single file. The chant of those still in the courtyard continues, even though the students now shown in close-up as they pass the camera flash individual smiles. At this point, the whistle heard in the background no longer matches the image. The contrast establishes the thematic difference between social conditioning and individual sensitivity that the children retain before the conditioning finally reduces many of them to the mindlessly aggressive adults described in the subsequent interviews.

Just before the interviews begin, a woman's voiceover reports that, on the third day of shooting, the Kanun team received 526 of 856 questionnaires that had been sent to parents asking how pupils did their homework:

> More than 37 percent of the parents couldn't help their children due to illiteracy. Of the literate parents, a large percentage couldn't help their children because they were too tense, busy, exhausted, or impatient. Many parents had been asking the teachers to excuse them from the responsibility of helping their children with their homework. Through the interviews and questionnaires, we got to know the children who had special circumstances.

Interviews with the children themselves reveal that many had been slapped in the face or beaten with a belt and had never heard the word *encouragement*.

Sitting at a table with his cameraman beside him, Kiarostami elicits and later edits in responses that make the children's reports of personal violence part of a much larger picture. One boy reports that his family attends the cinema every Thursday. In a movie that particularly impressed him, he saw men fighting in a boat. Instead of answering directly when Kiarostami asks if fighting in a boat is a good thing, the boy vividly recalls what he saw: "Two Iranians are sitting in a boat, and two Iraqis come to try to capture them. One of the Iranians gets smart and says you can't beat me, and he pushed one of them. Then he cut the man's head off and threw him into the sea." Kiarostami asks if he liked this. The boy says yes and goes on: "Then the place where he—" but Kiarostami interrupts, saying, "Wait, listen. You like fighting in films?" to which the boy replies, "I like it if it's in the war."

Apparently, the boy finds cinematic violence comforting because it frames and distances the violence he has witnessed at home. When Kiarostami asks if he likes fighting at home, too, the boy says no and describes the conflict between his mother, who is his father's second wife, and his stepmother, who is the first wife and lives downstairs. When Kiarostami asks if they fight each other, the boy hesitates for a long time: "Sometimes they tease each other and argue." Kiarostami asks if this upsets him. "Sometimes my mum beats her up." Then Kiarostami asks if he is glad his mum is stronger. The boy answers indirectly by describing an internecine war that parallels the national one: "My stepmother has a son who's done his military service. My dad takes their side, and my grandpa takes my mother's side. My grandpa is the strongest, even stronger than my dad. In a fight the other day, the first wife's father came, and her son came and beat my mum. Then my cousin came and beat up my [half-]brother who, was beating up my mum."

Though the boy says he liked that, he doesn't like the constant general fighting because he's "not old enough to fight yet." When Kiarostami asks if he will fight when he grows up, the boy answers with a question of his own: "Don't they fight at the front?" His reply conflates the government narrative of noble martyrdom with the primal hostility he has known at home. Kiarostami answers, "The fight at the front is different. It's war." The boy asks, "What's the difference?" Kiarostami repeats, "The fight at the front is different. It's war." The boy says, "The difference is that we must kill." Another first-grader who displaces his personal rage into fantasies of war reports that his second-grade brother is supposed to help him with his homework but beats him up instead. His mother also beats him with a belt. When asked what he wants to be when he grows up, he says a pilot so that he can kill Saddam. Like most citizens of nations engaged in patriotic wars, he imagines the enemy nation's leader to be the cause rather than just a symptom of the universal conflict he already knows.

The physical destruction the boy mentions transparently describes the mental state of the "house" where he lives: "Saddam is cruel because he destroys houses. He ruins them." And the boy's subsequent fantasy of an alternative future is so pointedly symbolic that Kiarostami might have written the dialogue himself: "And if Saddam is dead by then, what will you be?" After a long pause, the boy says, "The ones whose heart doesn't work, who go to the hospital and lie down to have an operation."—"You want to operate on them and be a physician?"—"Yes, a pilot and a physician, both."

In a brief intercut to the children with their jackets open later in the day, once again shouting "Islam is victorious. Down with the East and the West," the black-robed woman is shown walking forward between the rows of students. She reaches toward one of them, but before we know why, the camera cuts to a close-up of a child uncontrollably crying at the interview table. He is desperately afraid to face the filmmakers alone and is calling for his friend because apparently, in the absence of a loving relationship with his parents and teachers (as in the 1987 feature film *Where Is the Friend's House?*), he has transferred his need for affection to a peer. Kiarostami dismisses him temporarily and brings in the friend, "Why is he so afraid?" The friend cannot explain the boy's home life and seems to improvise an answer: The teacher beat them with a ruler, and when the ruler broke, she replaced it with a cane. So the boy thought Kiarostami might have a hidden ruler.

In fact, it is the harsh rule-bound society that has traumatized some children more than others. The camera cuts back to the students lined up in the courtyard as a male teacher chants, "Oh Allah, bless Muhammad and his household!" The households of most of these children, or at least the ones Kiarostami has chosen to show, appear not to be blessed. The household of the prayer is that of Muhammad, Ali, and Fatima. The teacher's voice continues, "Boys, this is Fatima Day, as you all know. We all know Hazrat Fatima, may God bless her soul, daughter of the holy prophet, wife of Hazrat Ali, God bless his soul, the first imam of Shia Muslims. I'm going to sing a song you all know."

Just before he starts to sing, we see a startling close-up of a boy whose face is covered by a black scarf as if he were a militant martyr. The image synchronizes with the song's first phrase as the man and the children begin together: "In the rose garden of the martyrs." The sequence of image and word implies that all the children who have been individualized in close-up interviews are now potential martyrs in the Shia war against Saddam. As they sing, the children are shown swinging their arms back and forth over their hearts in unison, but the voices of some apparently less-obedient children in the background show that not all may be ready to martyr themselves at Khomeini's call.

The edited emphasis on Fatima is ironically appropriate at this point. She represents all things that the parents, the school, and the society are not. Like Christianity's Mary, she is the queen of Heaven, known during her lifetime for sharing her father's compassion for the poor and for interceding on behalf of suffering innocents like the children in *Homework*. Her presence in a film about educating children is powerfully ironic because the rose garden in the song represents the potential blossoming that seems so unlikely for the children in the film. When Fatima was a little girl, a wind miraculously blew four seeds into her hand as she walked in the desert. She planted them and watered them with her saliva and morning dew, and they produced four bushes, each carrying roses of a different color—white, red, blue, and gold. They represented the virtues that would combine in her and that she would inspire in others: white for spirituality and healing, red for spontaneity and creation, blue for discernment and service to others, and gold for restoring equality and promoting peace.[23]

This poetic allusion that Kiarostami probably did not plan (though he knew he would shoot on Fatima Day) perfectly contrasts with a conversation between himself and an educated parent who inveighs against the rule-bound nature of the education system and, by implication, of the society as a whole. He says that in England, for example, the homework assignments are creative projects, including handicrafts and composition. Education experts in Japan, he says, have noted that rote homework assignments of the sort used in Iran caused the suicide rate among children to rise, but in Iran the "kids are under great pressure, [and while the] teachers are trained to handle this at home, we don't know how to deal with it and dump our frustration on them." The result will be an "indignant, surly, and defensive generation susceptible to every mental problem [and] with so much pressure and unhappiness, we'll end up with a generation devoid of creativity, capable only of copying."

Many of the man's views coincide with those of Kiarostami in *Where Is the Friend's House?* and *The Traveler*: "Kids should be left to themselves at home. Otherwise they will build up natural pressure against the education system. They should be allowed to be naughty, to rebel, and develop their own ways of resisting rules and regulations." He often argues with his wife about whether their child needs to get the highest grade. She insists that their son should be the top pupil in every subject, but he describes his child as talented in music and art but not in "subjects like history, which require memorization." Last, and with conclusive emphasis, he does not approve of all subjects, "even literature [being] taught from a religious perspective," and he predicts that the twenty-first century will be different.

After a brief shot of the panicky boy still crying for his friend, the scene returns briefly to the courtyard, where some unintended humor provides a promising sign that the school's effort to robotize the students has mostly failed. After the kids begin another war chant, Kiarostami suddenly cuts the sound, explaining in voiceover, "In spite of the great care taken by the authorities to run the ceremony properly, due to the children's mischievous manner and lack of comprehension, it was performed inappropriately. Out of respect for the ritual, we opted to delete the sound from this section of the film." But the visual images humorously reverse the meaning of the words, instilling hope that the creative spontaneity traditionally associated with the nurturing Fatima and called for by the anonymous parent may not be universally quelled.

In the expressionistic ambience that the silence creates, some boys properly stare ahead as they swing their arms up and down, marching in place but going nowhere. Others march but start to look around, while still others do not march at all. A boy in a white sweater stands still and just pats his heart repeatedly. Another reaches over to tweak a boy in the adjoining row. After a minute and twenty seconds of subversion intensified by the artificial silence, the sound returns, accentuating Kiarostami's sympathy with "naughty" boys who resist authority.

Kiarostami's inclusion of his interlocutor's protest against teaching everything from a religious perspective informs the film's extraordinary final scene. In it the director's editing expresses a vision evident throughout his later work of God as a creative source rather than a political enforcer. Except for a brief profile shot at the beginning, Kiarostami's questions have been accompanied only by an image of the camera lens. Here, as if he were making a personal statement, he replaces the lens with his own face. First, he calls back the fearful boy. Then he brings in his friend to stand behind him. Shifting back and forth from one foot to the other, the boy denies that he is still afraid but then wavers when Kiarostami asks if he can send the friend back to class: "No. Yes, yes, I'm sorry, I'm sorry, I'm sorry." The friend leaves, and the boy begins to cry again, Kiarostami asks, "Shall I call him back?" Waving his finger in the air pathetically, the boy says, "Yes." When the friend returns, Kiarostami tells him to stand close behind the first boy, and now again, as the director speaks, we see only the camera.

Still waving his index finger in the air as a sign of supplication and clearly wanting to end the interview, the boy says his religion class is about to start. Kiarostami asks if he knows the answers. "No," he replies, none of them. The boy just wants to get away from Kiarostami, whom he perceives as another threatening authority figure. He starts to get upset again when Kiarostami catches him in contradictions: "Did you prepare for the lesson?"—"I did."—"Do know the questions?"—"No."—"Is that why you want to go?"—"Yes." As soon as Kiarostami tells the friend he can leave again, the boy tearfully protests, "No, I go first. Then he goes." When Kiarostami promises he will let the boy go if he tells them why he is afraid of them, the boy inadvertently voices his fear of resisting any adult: "I don't want to miss religion class."

Coming full circle, Kiarostami and the boy are shown again, separated by the desk just as he was separated from his subject in the first interview. After so much misery, the ending is unexpectedly moving and beautiful. When Kiarostami asks him if he remembers any of his religious lessons, he says he can recite the prayer "Oh Lord." As the boy speaks, we see only the camera lens rather than the director, as if to say that viewers can receive the ending however they wish: "Oh Lord! Oh thou, Lord of beautiful stars. Oh thou, Lord of colorful cosmos. O thou who created Venus." At this point, soft orchestral music replaces strident voices in the hall. The music gets louder as the boy proceeds, creating a genuinely spiritual moment, a paean to creation rather than authority: "Thou who created the moon and the sun, all the mountains, hills, and oceans, the beautiful and colorful trees, beautiful wings for the butterfly, nests for the birds, happiness, games, strength, eyes for us to see, snow and rain, heat and cold. We're all created by you, oh Lord. You granted all I wished for. Fill our hearts with happiness and joy."

As the music continues to swell, the boy's voice cracks, as if he were involuntarily moved. Just before the end, the camera backs up slightly so that both the boy and his friend are illuminated in the dark frame. With this expressionistic chiaroscuro highlighting their individual love, choral voices join the music, auguring a redefinition of the individual in relation to the nation and nations in relation to each other. As the final credits roll and the music becomes stirringly loud, the image of the boys remains as a still photograph, which, in spite of everything, affirms the constancy of cosmic love.

The credits' final words read, "This film was made in February 1987 at Shahid Massoumi School for the Institute of Intellectual Development of Children and Young Adults." In retrospect, the words are ironic because Kiarostami was obviously not guiding the children in a direction the country's Islamic guides approved. In a 2005 interview, he revealed that he cut the sound during the playground chant to appease objecting religious groups and that the film was banned in Iran for three years after its initial release and thereafter shown only to adults: "After I made *Homework* I was forced to leave Kanun because they disagreed with the film."[24] Eventually, Kiarostami would have to leave the country to make films, though he continued to live there.

NOTES

1. "*Sight & Sound* 'Greatest Films of All Time' Top 250 (2012 edition)," updated February 27, 2013, https://www.imdb.com/list/ls008765885/.
2. Robin Wood in "*Film Comment*'s Best of the Nineties Poll: Part One," *Film Comment*, January–February 2000, https://www.filmcomment.com/article/film-comments-best-of-the-90s-poll-part-one/.
3. David Bordwell in "*Film Comment*'s Best of the Nineties Poll: Part One."
4. Alberto Elena, *The Cinema of Abbas Kiarostami*, trans. Belinda Coombes (London: Saqi, in association with Iran Heritage Foundation, 2005); Mehrnaz Saeed-Vafa and Jonathan Rosenbaum, *Abbas Kiarostami* (Urbana: University of Illinois Press, 2003).
5. "The 50 Best Films of the Decade So Far," IndieWire, http://www.indiewire.com/2015/02/the-50-best-films-of-the-decade-so-far-266754/9/.
6. "Abbas Kiarostami Full Interview Cannes 1997 (English Subtitle)," posted by Waleed Khaled, January 8, 2015, video, 18:41, https://www.youtube.com/watch?v=F9l_KD96E_M.
7. "Vietnam War," Wikipedia, updated January 3, 2020, https://en.wikipedia.org/wiki/Vietnam_War.
8. "Iran–Iraq War," Wikipedia, updated January 3, 2020, https://en.wikipedia.org/wiki/Iran%E2%80%93Iraq_War. See also the Editors of Encyclopædia Britannica, "Iran-Iraq War," *Encyclopædia Britannica*, updated September 15, 2019, https://www.britannica.com/event/Iran-Iraq-War; History.com editors, "Iran-Iraq War," History.com, updated August 24, 2018, http://www.history.com/topics/iran-iraq-war; Efraim Karsh, "Iran–Iraq War (1980–1988)," *Encyclopedia of Modern Middle East and North Africa*, Encyclopedia.com, December 25, 2019, http://www.encyclopedia.com/history/asia-and-africa/middle-eastern-history/iran-iraq-war.

9. Quoted in Andrew Pulver and Saeed Kamali Dehghan, "Abbas Kiarostami, Palme d'Or-Winning Iranian Film-Maker, Dies Aged 76," *Guardian*, July 4, 2016, https://www.theguardian.com/film/2016/jul/04/abbas-kiarostami-palme-dor-winning-iranian-film-maker-dies.

10. See "Ali," Wikipedia, updated December 31, 2019, https://en.wikipedia.org/wiki/Ali; "Ali in the Quran," Wikipedia, updated January 1, 2020, https://en.wikipedia.org/wiki/Ali_in_the_Quran; "Military Career of Ali," Wikipedia, updated December 5, 2019, https://en.wikipedia.org/wiki/Military_career_of_Ali.

11. Abu Ahmad, "The Battle of Khyber," TheTruthMag.com, https://www.thetruthmag.com/index.php/features/story-of-islam/149-the-battle-of-khyber; "Battle of Khaybar," Wikipedia, updated December 29, 2019, https://en.wikipedia.org/wiki/Battle_of_Khaybar.

12. See John Harney, "How Do Sunni and Shia Islam Differ?" *New York Times*, January 3, 2016, https://www.nytimes.com/2016/01/04/world/middleeast/q-and-a-how-do-sunni-and-shia-islam-differ.html?_r=0; Andrew J. Newman, "Shi'i Islam," *Encyclopædia Britannica*, updated September 5, 2019, https://www.britannica.com/topic/Shiite; "Shia Islam," Wikipedia, updated December 26, 2019, https://en.wikipedia.org/wiki/Shia_Islam; "The Sunni-Shia Divide," Council for Foreign Relations, February 2016, http://www.cfr.org/peace-conflict-and-human-rights/sunni-shia-divide/p33176#!/?cid=otr-marketing_url-sunni_shia_infoguide.

13. "National Anthem of the Islamic Republic of Iran," Wikipedia, updated January 2, 2020, https://en.wikipedia.org/wiki/National_Anthem_of_the_Islamic_Republic_of_Iran.

14. Quoted in Mike Gallagher, "The 'Beauty' and the Horror of the Iran-Iraq War," *BBC News Magazine*, September 26, 2015, http://www.bbc.com/news/magazine-34353349.

15. See Deborah Young, "Critic's Notebook: Abbas Kiarostami, the Iranian Artist Who Led the Way for Young Filmmakers," *Hollywood Reporter*, July 5, 2016, https://www.hollywoodreporter.com/news/critics-notebook-abbas-kiarostami-iranian-908350.

16. See "Iranian Revolution," Wikipedia, updated January 3, 2020, https://en.wikipedia.org/wiki/Iranian_Revolution.

17. Abbas Kiarostami, "With the Wind," in *In the Shadow of Trees: The Collected Poetry of Abbas Kiarostami*, trans. Iman Tavassoly and Paul Cronin (New York: Sticking Place Books, 2016), 52.

18. Abbas Kiarostami, "Wind and Leaf," in *In the Shadow of Trees: The Collected Poetry of Abbas Kiarostami*, trans. Iman Tavassoly and Paul Cronin (New York: Sticking Place Books, 2016), 98.

19. Kiarostami, "Wind and Leaf," 99.

20. Quoted in Stuart Jeffries, "Landscapes of the Mind," *Guardian*, April 16, 2005, https://www.theguardian.com/film/2005/apr/16/art.

21. Quoted in Clarence Tsui, "Iranian Director Abbas Kiarostami: 'The Situation in Iran Has Never Been This Dark,'" *Hollywood Reporter*, May 29, 2013, https://www.hollywoodreporter.com/news/iranian-director-abbas-kiarostami-situation-559514.

22. Emile Durkheim, *Suicide: A Study in Sociology*, ed. John A. Spaulding and George Simpson (1897; New York: Free Press, 1951), http://www.bahaistudies.net/asma/suicide-durkheim.pdf.

23. See Ali Shariati, *Fatemeh Is Fatemeh* (Tehran: Shariati Foundation, 1971), www.Shariati.org; "Bibi Fatima: The Rose Garden," Rose Sufi Crescent, August 20, 2006, http://rose-sufi-crescent.blogspot.com/2006/08/bibi-fatima-rose-garden.html.

24. Quoted in Jeffries, "Landscapes of the Mind."

Chapter Two

Kiarostami and Religion

In the words of Oscar-winning Iranian director Asghar Farhadi, Kiarostami "wasn't just a filmmaker, he was a modern mystic, both in his cinema and his private life,"[1] and according to Ahmad Karimi Hakkak and Michael Beard, translators of *Walking with the Wind*, his volume of poetry published in 2002, Kiarostami "places the human inside the natural, often pointing to hints of a grand design just outside the human reach, [sharing] the heritage of Persian mysticism [where] Nature is not only animate but animating."[2] For Kiarostami, nature is the paramount object of meditation, and even in an answer to a practical question, such as why he chose to stay in Iran when other directors had left or, as in his case, had their films domestically banned, his choice of a metaphor eschewed patriotism while expressing love for his nation's land and culture: "When you take a tree that is rooted in the ground and transfer it from one place to another the tree will no longer bear fruit. And if it does the fruit will not be as good as it was in its original place. This is a rule of nature. I think if I had left my country I would be the same as the tree."[3]

Though Kiarostami generally limited spiritual expression to his work, he responded courteously to a *New York Times* interviewer who tautologically asked, "As a Shiite Muslim, are you religious?" Kiarostami adroitly replied, "It's a very private question but if you insist I will answer it. I am not politically religious, but I have some beliefs."[4] Six years later, however, in an extended interview with Geoff Andrew, a critic he personally knew and trusted, Kiarostami made a rather startling statement in reply to being asked if the treatment of sex in *Certified Copy* was "embarking on new territory" in comparison to the films made and set in Iran: "Yes and no. This is nothing to do with censorship or Iran being a Muslim country, because I'm not Muslim." He went on to explain that he didn't disapprove of couples kissing in public, though he thought that private activities were inappropriate for cinema, but the prefatory statement was surprisingly frank.[5]

At the end of *Homework*, Kiarostami highlights the "Oh Lord" prayer to the Creator of the "moon and the sun, all the mountains, hills, and oceans, the beautiful and colorful trees, beautiful wings for the butterfly, nests for the birds . . . snow and rain, heat and cold." In his films and especially in his poetry, Kiarostami follows the Sufi preference for discovering God directly through His "art," the evidence of Creation rather than through ritual or doctrine: "In the shrine / I thought one thousand thoughts. / When I left / snow lay everywhere."[6] In a longer poem, he praises the Creator's work in terms of its loving result, but at the same time, he questions the simultaneous injustice of the world. Each verse begins "The more I think about it / the less I understand," followed by four benevolent completions, two harsh ones, and two mysteries: "why snow is so white," "the discipline / and splendor of spiders," "why mothers / so love their children," "why dogs are so loyal," "why the hands of the poor are rich with calluses," "why truth is bitter," "why the galaxy / is so big," and " why we should be so afraid of / death."[7]

In his 1992 film *And Life Goes On* (alternately titled *Life and Nothing More*), Kiarostami poses these questions in several key scenes. The film is a poetic re-creation of a trip Kiarostami and his young son undertook to northern Iran after a 1990 earthquake killed fifty thousand people, among whom he feared might be the two now-twelve-year-old boys from the village of Koker featured in *Where Is the Friend's House?* which he had shot there four years earlier. In a traffic jam of vehicles bringing relief supplies, the Kiarostami proxy, an unnamed film director driving with his ten-year-old son Puya, is advised to turn off the metaphysically symbolic "main road" by a truck driver who remarks, "I don't know what crime this country has committed to be punished by God like this." The theme is taken up when the director stops on a mountain upgrade to pick up an elderly man carrying a heavy toilet tank back to his village. He turns out to be the man who played the wise old door maker in the previous film, and though he is clearly different from the character he played, he represents a variation on the same stoic wisdom.

In an interplay of language and image, the initial view of the ascending road is rocky and gray as the man explains that he doesn't know what happened to the boys because the road from his town to Koker has been blocked, though the news may be bad because where he lives many have died and most have "lost everything." But the car passes through an area of green trees as the conversation turns simultaneously comic and profound. After the director asks why the man would buy a toilet tank in the near absence of water, the man replies, "For me, it's indispensable. The ones that are living still need this valuable piece of porcelain." A shot of his hand out the passenger window holding the toilet tank in place on the car top punctuates the director congratulating his humble courage, just before the man begins a series of thoughtful reflections.

After they pass the parallel image of a black-robed woman walking with a heavy bundle on her head, the following exchange is a fairly explicit statement of belief in a God who confers life, virtue, and beauty generally but does not reward, punish, or even regard individuals: "Sometimes I think that if so many innocent people lost their lives and I am still alive, the Lord is with me."—"You must be a pious man."—"Pious? Don't misunderstand me. What has occurred is that this disaster has been like a hungry wolf that attacks and goes devouring the people he passes and letting the others live. This is not the work of God. He wants his servants. That's how I see Him."

But if the old man does not question God's justice, then the film raises the question indirectly when he complains that the director not only made him look older in the film, but he also had to wear a hump on his back: "I didn't like it. It pinched me, and it wasn't fair. What kind of art [or God] makes people look older and uglier? Art means beautiful and happy things that touch you. Art should rejuvenate people, not make them decrepit. To continue, being alive is also an art. I suppose it's the most sublime art of all, don't you think so?" The beautiful scenery along the road in conjunction with the words constitutes the film's central message. People are not truly alive until they learn what to love and value. And the progression from a serene acceptance of mortality in the previous film to an indomitable will to live in the character's next incarnation creates the simultaneous sense of wholeness and holiness that *And Life Goes On* conveys.

After they agree that people don't know how to value their peaceful moments before a disaster or until they become old, the old man concludes, "If they gave us the opportunity to live our lives over again after we died, surely we would know how to take better profit of it all." But as the director emptily says, "That's true," the truism is qualified by the simultaneous image of two children about the age of the boys in *Where Is the Friend's House?* While one climbs a tree, the other is busy pounding something as if imitating the relief effort. Achieved wisdom is only a stage in an endlessly repeated cycle that includes the terrible and the beautiful, inexplicable injustice and persistent love. In Kiarostami's *The Wind Will Carry Us*, an elderly country doctor quoting Omar Khayyam to a chastened journalist says that he prefers the pleasures of this world to promises of the next, but unlike Khayyam, who emphasizes religious futility and carnal pleasure, the doctor attributes the nature he praises to the "generosity of God."

That generosity is not diminished for Kiarostami by natural disasters, and Puya (having absorbed the old man's hungry-wolf comparison) tells a woman who laments that it was "God's will" that one of her children died, "God does not kill his children; the earthquake killed them. The earthquake is like a mad dog who attacks whoever is nearest." During his son's conversations and explorations, the director is shown sitting on the steps of the house where they are staying, looking around as if he were taking in the serene beauty of the place rather than the results of the devastation.

As he looks upward toward the right, the camera reveals Kiarostami's painstaking selection and arrangement of the mise-en-scène. Standing, still untouched, next to a pile of ruins, the house is extraordinarily beautiful, with deep, radiant blue railings and posts supporting the roof. In front of the intricately carved vertical parts of the balcony stands a row of eight flowerpots with living plants on the outside of the ledge, a sign of God's generosity that needs active human nurture to survive, as indicated by an empty bottle in the center. The idea is complemented by a clean white sheet hung out to dry in the wind against a background pile of building debris. These are images of work that serves body and soul with no regard for status or reward.

The fictive director appears to be moved by what he sees. Now he looks the opposite way at a green hillside seen through an opening between unfinished wooden posts. Above this frame-within-a-frame, we see a swath of green grass, while at the bottom we see the tops of green and silver trees. As in much of Kiarostami's work, ineffable spiritual experience is suggested by passing through a frame or leaving an enclosure that is sometimes enhanced by the rare use of music. A largo passage from a horn concerto begins as the camera moves through the frame onto the hillside, where twittering birds accompany the music.

The image conveys a relationship between nature and art, in which human art is as natural and spontaneous as the songs of birds, an idea that recurs in the director's later work. God needs human beings as much as nature needs art, and all things given life by the Creator require human nurture. As the music continues, the camera returns to the woman of the house, who has lost her husband and one of her children, continuing the work of recovery. As she emerges from the doorway and leaves the film frame, the camera holds on a shot of the open door with white and yellow grass beneath it and a bare tree branch to its left sprouting green buds at the top.

The director steps back inside the doorway's frame, and the camera cuts to a popular print of a nineteenth-century painting of an old Iranian peasant with a long pipe, sitting next to a table with a glass of tea, a teapot, and a plate of food. An irregular vertical crack extends through the painting from the wall below it and into the wall above. The crack enhances the painting in the context of harmonizing God and man, nature and art, giving it a resonance it would not otherwise have. The continual cry of a white rooster accompanying the horn concerto aurally integrates nature, while a cutback to a close-up of the director begins a sequence that helps viewers to realize that they can actively alleviate rather than simply sympathize with the suffering they observe.

With the music still playing, the director passes the doorway that the woman had previously entered. At first she is unseen when they begin to converse: "Madam, that carpet weighs a lot and has a lot of dust. You alone will not manage."—"I don't have anyone. My husband stayed under the debris."—"And your neighbors?"—"Each one has his own problems." Then the director goes inside, symbolically passing through the frame-within-a-frame into actively participating in "real life." Holding on the image that has no human actors, the camera moves left to a close-up of the previously seen withered branch with greenery at the top. We hear him say that his back is very bad. Then, through the doorway, we see him trying to drag the rug: "It's impossible. I can't move it."

But the frame in which he speaks is symmetrical and beautiful, bordered with a small green bush on the left and white triangular containers on the right. As he and the woman together manage to drag the carpet, the rooster comes to the center of the doorway—the frame within the frame—and standing in profile begins to flap its wings, crowing loudly, as if to lend courage. Once again, nature and art work together, and whether or not he can move the rug, his impulse to help is what matters. Love, even between strangers, remains possible, and though he does not find the boys he is looking for in the course of the film, he discovers that empathetically observing others evokes the best in himself.

The director's active entrance into the scene reflects an earlier exchange with the elderly man who had explained that he moved into this house when his own was destroyed by the earthquake. When the director observed that at least this house survived, the old man replied, "Yeah, that's right. The movie has become reality." The line ironically rejects cliché happy endings, where the good and innocent are ultimately rewarded in this world or the next. Instead, Kiarostami accepts the inexplicability of tragic events and focuses on the endurance of beauty, love, and the "generosity of God" extolled by the country doctor in *The Wind Will Carry Us*.

In that film, the wise old man rejects the otherworldly emphasis in Christianity and Islam by quoting Omar Khayyam: "They tell me she is as beautiful as a houri from heaven! Yet I say that the juice of the vine is better. Prefer the present to these fine promises. Even a drum sounds melodious from afar." The subtitled translation is less directly subversive than Edward Fitzgerald's generally respected nineteenth-century English version, which instead of turning down the metonymic houri rejects Paradise altogether. The quatrain immediately follows the *Rubaiyat*'s most famous passage:

> A Book of Verses underneath the Bough,
> A Jug of Wine, a Loaf of Bread—and Thou
> Beside me singing in the Wilderness—
> Oh, Wilderness were Paradise enow!

> Some for the Glories of This World; and some
> Sigh for the Prophet's Paradise to come;
> Ah, take the Cash, and let the Credit go,
> Nor heed the rumble of a distant Drum![8]

In interviews following *Taste of Cherry*, Kiarostami extolled Khayyam's quatrains as a "constant eulogy of life in the ever-present face of death."[9] In actuality, Khayyam's eulogy of life stems more from a fear of the alternative than from the immersion in nature that inspired Kiarostami. For Khayyam, nature and other human beings are consolatory pleasures, existing only to muffle his obsession with death.

According to Iranian American scholar Hamid Dabashi, Fitzgerald's "exquisite translations" of the *Rubaiyat* accurately mirror the poet's hedonism but fail to convey the danger of a system of law and rule based on religious revelation:

> Central to Omar Khayyam's philosophical disposition, as best evident in his poetry, is the fragility and tragic pointlessness of being. The moon will shine many nights, and we will not be here anymore; there is no beginning or end to this world, and no one knows what we are doing here—theologians, philosophers, mystics, and scientists all sing their own amusing tunes. The clerical establishment in particular obviously did not like these ideas, nor did he care for them, and there are reports that he in fact would go out of his way to scandalize their hypocrisy.[10]

Actually, Fitzgerald's translations extend well beyond recommending hedonistic indulgence to directly undermining bedrock beliefs. In regard to cosmic justice under "that inverted Bowl they call the Sky, / Whereunder crawling coop'd we live and die, / Lift not your hands to It for help—for It /As impotently moves as you or I." And on the discrepancy between Divine justice and inborn defects, a "vessel of ungainly make" bitterly complains, "They sneer at me for leaning all awry: What! did the Hand then of the Potter shake?" And for those that "after some TO-MORROW stare, / A Muezzin from the Tower of Darkness cries, / 'Fools! your Reward is neither Here nor There.'" And "Of threats of Hell and Hopes of Paradise! / One thing at least is certain—This Life flies; / One thing is certain and the rest is Lies; / The Flower that once has blown for ever dies." And most blasphemous of all, "The Revelations of Devout and Learn'd / Who rose before us, and as Prophets burn'd, / Are all but Stories, which, awoke from Sleep /They told their comrades, and to Sleep return'd."[11]

Most of Khayyam's nature tropes exist solely to lament human mortality: "The Rose that blows about us" delights in tossing the "silken Tassel of [its] Purse" into the garden to produce more roses, but the "Worldly Hope" of human beings, whether it "turns [to] ashes" or "prospers," is as ephemeral as "Snow upon the Desert's dusty face"; "Golden Grain" is joyfully flung "to the Winds like Rain," but "to no such aureate Earth are turn'd / As, buried once, Men want dug up again." In a notable jibe at pantheism, the rose is reddest when it blooms "where some buried Caesar bled," and every "Hyacinth the Garden wears / Dropt in its Lap from some once lovely Head," and so the reader is mockingly urged to lean lightly on the herb-lined "River's Lip [bank], . . . for who knows / From what once lovely Lip" the herbs have "sprung unseen."[12]

In Kiarostami's view, however, elements of negativity in Iranian culture are less likely to stem from skeptical poetry than from its history of religious war and colonial exploitation. During a Q&A after a 1998 screening of *Taste of Cherry* at Ohio State University, a professor observed that Iranian culture is often said to emphasize the "negative aspects of life like death and fatalism." In reply, and thinking perhaps of Shiism in particular, Kiarostami attributed the negativity not to Iranian culture but to "Islamic culture where the crying and grief, in which Muslim people have been historically engaged, are very significant. These elements have carried the religion through time and are part of what keeps Islam alive."[13] He made a similar distinction in 1997 in a *Cahiers du Cinema* interview with Serge Toubiana:

> We have a two-speed religion: one, behind the times, where the search does not exist; another, more developed, where the search does indeed exist. Mystical Iranian poetry appeals precisely to the idea of the journey of initiation as a path to learning, and it is really the Iranian culture in all its richness that contains this idea, not the religious culture. Religion has merely followed in the wake of Iranian thought.[14]

However, Iranian thought in the work of the great national poets is vibrantly diverse. A quatrain in the *Rubaiyat* has the poet sending his soul "through the invisible / Some letter of that After-life to spell," only to discover upon the messenger's return that "I Myself am Heav'n and Hell."[15] While Khayyam located an illusory God in the human imagination, the great Sufi poet Farid ud-Din Attar (1145–1221) found a real God in the human heart. Though their tones and messages are diametrically opposed, both are infidels in the eyes of the kind of conservative Islam that still rules countries like Saudi Arabia and Iran. Sometime after the publication of *The Conference of the Birds* (1177), Attar was stripped of his property and banished on a charge of heresy, and as his English translators Afkham Darbandi and Dick Davis point out, reading the poem makes it "not difficult to see why."[16] Instead of pleasing God through ritual prayer and glorying in His presence after death, the poem is an allegory of a quest by individuals to achieve divine union while they are still alive. The premise is irreverent in that, for all Muslims, Muhammad was the last human being to hear directly from God and was therefore the "seal" of a prophetic history beginning with Abraham and continuing through Moses and Jesus.

Attar's story begins when a thousand birds, each representing a separate species, set out in search of their king, the Simurgh. They must pass through seven valleys to reach Him: the Valley of Quest, the Valley of Love, the Valley of Understanding, the Valley of Independence and Detachment, the Valley of Unity, the Valley of Astonishment and Bewilderment, and the Valley of Deprivation and Death. After an arduous journey, only thirty birds are able to endure the traumatic loss of individual identity necessary to reach the Simurgh. But before they meet their God, who would within the rigorous monotheism of Islam be a distinctly separate entity, their Hoopoe leader tells them that the *Si* (which means "thirty") combined with *murgh* (which means "bird") exists within them.

This kingdom of God within is not easily realized because only thirty of the original thousand birds are able to authentically discover this union in themselves. Those who do must be willing to annihilate both ego and conscious control in the final valley: "The seventh Poverty and Nothingness— / And there you are suspended, motionless, / Till you are drawn— / the impulse is not yours— / A drop absorbed in seas that have no shores." And in contrast to the suicidal Mr. Badii of *Taste of Cherry*, who wants to kill himself because he loves nothing, the fulfilled Sufi seeker is motivated only by love: "True lovers give up everything they own / To steal one moment with the Friend alone."[17]

Attar does not decry group prayers meant to bring believers to God in the next world and strongly recommends them as necessary for the few willing to risk loss of self in the here and now. Early in the quest, he warns against deterrence from both rigid believers and rigor-lacking "ecstatics." These phony gurus may trick the seeker into thinking prayers can be bypassed, but the Hoopoe says the seeker should pray through good times and bad until the soul's transformation spontaneously occurs: "Pray in despair and when your goods increase, / Consume your life with prayer, till Solomon / Bestows his glance, and ignorance is gone." And, the Hoopoe adds, be prepared to defend this pearl of great price once it is attained: Why expose this treasure to "those whose blindness claims it is unreal?" It is better to "die deceived by dreams than give / [your] heart to home and trade and never live."[18]

For Kiarostami (especially in the films that depict nature), a scene that may seem to be just an establishing shot or mere background is most likely to convey the film's deeper vision. By making nature more sacred than religiously revealed truth, Kiarostami affirms the ecumenical message of the Sufi poets. Attar describes how a Sufi saint, "cast down by grief" (possibly brought on by the sectarian zeal of his society), felt relief upon passing a Jewish cemetery, where he was overheard saying, "These souls are pardoned and go free: / But this is not a truth that can be taught." Summoned to explain himself before "angry judges" in a religious court, the saint's explanation might have led to imprisonment or even execution in his time, as well as in a modern-day theocracy: "Your government / Accuses them; their pardon's heaven sent."[19]

In his old age, Attar was visited by an admiring young poet who was to become more widely known for centuries to come, in and far from Iran. Through the free poetic translations of Coleman Barks, Jelaluddin Rumi (1207–1273) has become one of the most widely read poets in the United States.[20] Without discrediting Barks, Omid Safi, director of the Duke University Islamic Center, points out that two of his most quoted lines—"Out beyond ideas of rightdoing and wrongdoing, there is a field. / I will meet you there"—are far more pointed in the original, where *rightdoing* is *religion* and *wrongdoing* is *infidelity*. Safi asks us to imagine the fate of a modern Muslim scholar who dared to say that the "basis of faith lies not in religious code but in an elevated space of compassion and love. What we, and perhaps many Muslim clerics, might consider radical today is an interpretation that Rumi put forward more than seven hundred years ago."[21] It is this concept of a "space" elevated above clerical authority that would most offend Iran's theocratic regime.

In interviews, Kiarostami repeatedly described his function as a director in terms that are analogous to the view of God portrayed in *And Life Goes On*:

> There's a Rumi poem [that] goes something like this: You [the actors] are like the ball subject to my polo stick; I set you in motion, but once you're off and running, I am the one in pursuit. Therefore, when you see the end result, it's difficult to see who's the director, me or them. Ultimately, everything belongs to the actors—we just manage the situation. This kind of directing, I think, is very similar to being a football coach. You prepare your players and place them in the right places, but once the game is on, there's nothing much you can do.[22]

Whether or not viewers believe in God as the "Friend" or the "Beloved," as He is called by Sufi poets like Attar and Rumi, the beauty of the world and the fact of human kindness manifest a pervasive love that yields to destruction when fearful cultures shut them out. Two years after Kiarostami said that all his films were essentially about the same thing, he described the main theme of *The Wind Will Carry Us* as opening the "eyes of the heart as wide or wider than those of the body."[23] The film creates that effect through the unusual device of having its socially driven protagonist pretentiously quote well-known poems to feel superior until he may finally feel them and perhaps become a better man.

Rumi, too, in the words of Coleman Barks, addresses the "mystery of opening the heart, [a thing] you can't say in language."[24] Though Barks writes "versions" of previous translations rather than working directly from the Persian, his work has touched the hearts of millions. Hamid Safi praises him for retaining core Islamic elements, noting that Rumi's poetry ranks second only to the Koran "in shaping the imagination of Muslims." He adds that Rumi was not the only one in his time to express the "push and pull between religious spirituality and institutionalized faith" but that he did so "with a wit that was unmatched."[25]

Certainly, Rumi was not religious in a way Khomeini or Khamenei would approve. Neither was Kiarostami, who boldly stated that he was "not Muslim." However, Kiarostami repeatedly stressed his "deep roots in the heart of Persian culture,"[26] and Ahmad Karimi-Hakkak and Michael Beard, the translators of Kiarostami's poetry volume *Walking with the Wind*, hint at the impetus behind Kiarostami's disavowal: "Like Rumi, the poet of the largest questions in all of Persian poetry, [Kiarostami] reaches out to the world rather than focusing on any local topic. His thinking is cosmopolitan, humane, and global."[27]

Barks offers a corresponding reason for his widespread readership: "Just now, I feel there is a strong global movement, an impulse that wants to dissolve the boundaries that religions have put up and end the sectarian violence. It is said that people of all religions came to Rumi's funeral in 1273. Because, they said, he deepens our faith wherever we are. This is a powerful element in his appeal now."[28] Like Kiarostami, Attar and Rumi lived in a time of devastating wars. Attar died violently when the Tartars swept into his hometown of Nishapur in northeastern Iran, while in 1220, when Rumi was thirteen, he and his father fled Genghis Khan's invasion of their home region of Balkh in present-day Afghanistan and traveled to Konya in Anatolia (modern Turkey), a location dangerously close to major battles of the Crusades.[29] Though Rumi's inward turn is biographically attributed to his all-consuming love for the wandering mystic Shams of Tabriz, the outward clash of beliefs and ethnicities must have intensified his Sufi quest to merge with the ultimate "Beloved Friend."

With similar desires to replace creed with direct experience, Makhmalbaf said (in his 2012 documentary *The Gardener*, shot in Israel) that if religion is the cause of war, it would be better to have no religion at all, and Kiarostami was grateful for life and nothing more in the wake of wars and natural disasters. Both follow Rumi's bold sentiments in "Only Breath," where the poet eschews religions (Christianity, Judaism, Islam, Hinduism, Buddhism, Sufism, and Zen); geographical or metaphysical identities, whether natural or ethereal; and descent from Adam and Eve or any other origin story and asserts that he belongs only "to the beloved," as He reveals himself in the physical breath of life.[30]

In a 2005 interview where he avoided overtly stating the spiritual themes implicit in his films, Kiarostami reiterated Rumi's intent to speak of and for humanity in general:

> All the different nations in the world, despite their differences of appearance and religion and language and way of life, still have one thing in common, and that is what's inside of all of us. If we X-rayed the insides of different human beings, we wouldn't be able to tell from those X-rays what the person's language or background or race is. Our blood circulates exactly the same way, our nervous system and our eyes work the same way, we laugh and cry the same way, we feel pain the same way. The teeth we have in our mouths—no matter what our nationality or background is—ache exactly the same way. If we want to divide cinema and the subjects of cinema, the way to do it is to talk about pain and about happiness. These are common among all countries.[31]

For Kiarostami, absolute value derives from directly communing with nature rather than on communal belief. Rumi, too, found salvation in plant, animal, and human physicality as evidenced by such poems as "Spring Is Christ," where plants are martyrs rising from their shrouds, the holy spirit is the wind, the trees are Mary, and divine love makes itself known through sexual love.[32] Just as Kiarostami suggests through his unprecedented cinematic forms and in such films as *The Traveler*, *Where Is the Friend's House?* and *Through the Olive Trees* that only disobedient children can break free of stunting traditions and social tyranny, Rumi counsels readers to invent their own myths rather than accept the revelations of others.[33] Worshippers should seek God in the immediacy of love rather than the distanced reverence of worship because there is no hierarchy of the spirit. God is not superior to the angels, and the angels are not superior to human beings. To bow to God, Rumi says, is like bowing into a mirror because the only reality is God.[34]

But if the Rumi reader or Kiarostami viewer should listen only to God or commune directly with nature, what good is the mediation of art, as a student pointedly remarked during a 2012 workshop in Spain by quoting a line from Rumi: "When a blind man sees, he doesn't need a walking stick." Kiarostami responded that while Rumi used words as his medium, he uses a camera, and the artist's experience of beauty can't "expand" to others without words and pictures. He added that Rumi was too "exceptional" to be a model and that he "as a small person" continues to look for "this walking stick to go easily on this path."[35]

This exchange about the relation between poetic art and the unsayable reality it can only suggest evokes a distinction made by scholar William Chittick between religious prophets and Sufi saints: "The prophets are those people who have received a message from God for a whole community. The saints are those who follow one of the prophets and attain to the state of human perfection to which the prophet calls mankind." In this sense an artist, especially a cinematic artist, can be more like a prophet, one who, as Kiarostami said in his Spanish workshop, transfers "something from someone who has seen to someone who hasn't."[36]

Chittick elaborates on the initiatory power of the prophet to contain his vision in outward forms that the believer then follows. Sufis seek union with God, but they also rely on respected guides and established rituals, such as the dervish dance, to realize their quest. The Sufi saint reaches the Beloved as an individual following a prescribed form, while Rumi and Kiarostami continually forge new forms to suggest new avenues of attainment. Rumi, Chittick points out, does not presume to be a prophet because for him the "basic truth and preeminence of Muhammad's teachings are largely unquestioned" and therefore "his real emphasis is upon the importance of the saint, for he holds that the prophets and saints are of one substance; [and] almost anything said about the former applies also to the latter."[37] Chittick may be right about the way Rumi felt, but the motivation to practice his art belies a complete reliance on Koranic revelation, and for Kiarostami, a self-professed non-Muslim, the cinematic content was a creative synthesis of traditions, while the forms, for the most part, were experimentally unique.

As Hamid Dabashi has shown in his comprehensive 2012 survey *The World of Persian Literary Humanism*, transcendence of theocratic forms is an essential feature of Iranian culture. Since the seventh-century Muslim conquest, except for the first thirty-nine years of Mongol rule (1256–1295), Islam has been the state religion of Iran. During the entire Mongol dynasty (1256–1353), however, Buddhism and Christianity were equally important, and regardless of ruler over the nation's long history, Persian literary culture has remained a "narrative institution unto itself, irreducible to any metaphysical certainty that is Zoroastrian, Manichean, Jewish, Christian, Hindu, Buddhist, Gnostic, agnostic, or above all Islamic in origin and destination—though all these religious traditions, in one way or another, lend their mores and metaphors to its creative and effervescent making."[38]

Kiarostami admired "movies and art [that] take us away from daily life to another state, even though daily life is where this flight is launched from. This is what gives us comfort and peace."[39] In *Ten on Ten*, he laid out an artistic credo that rejected exciting moments in favor of enticing the viewer to reflect on himself and the surrounding world in a spiritual way: "In this cinema, the most important subject matter is human beings and their souls. Man and his complex inner problems are paramount, whereas in presently fashionable cinema, technique, special effects, and exciting storytelling are more important."[40] And though he admitted in another interview that "every movie should have some kind of story," he preferred movies that "didn't attract me or make a lot of sense while I was looking at them, but [included] moments that opened a window for me and inspired my imagination."[41]

His own practice long predated this advice, especially in *Where Is the Friend's House?* where the images of windows and doors comprise a symbolic frame that opens only for "children" brave enough to be disobedient. This fictional film was shot after but released before *Homework*, the documentary that severed ties between Kiarostami and the Center for the Intellectual Development of Children and Young Adults, but it is more subversive than *Homework* in ways that the authorities were too dense to grasp. While the children in *Homework* have been effectively bullied into lying and submission, unanimously saying they prefer homework to cartoons, the eight-year-old protagonist of *Where Is the Friend's House?* learns to disrespect the values of most of the adults in his society. By rejecting the power and wisdom of adults over children, Ahmad Ahmadpur symbolically rejects the theocratic structure of modern Iran, ultimately at the end of the film taking his inspiration directly from God rather than through the self-serving mediation of human authority.

The opening scene where a teacher tries to dutifully condition his second-grade students into knee-jerk submission recalls Kiarostami's antiwar haiku: "One hundred obedient soldiers / entering the barracks. Moonlit night. / Disobedient dreams."[42] This revolution of the mind and heart can best be achieved in adult viewers by returning them to the time when social demands began to replace the creative impulses that make most artists imperfectly adapted to dictated thought and routine work. Kiarostami hoped his films would unlock creative potential by helping viewers to rinse their culturally clouded eyes:

> My aim is to give the chance to create as much as possible in our minds, through creativity and imagination. I want to tap the hidden information that's within yourself and that you probably didn't even know existed inside you. We have a saying in Persian, when somebody is looking at something with real intensity: "He had two eyes and he borrowed two more." Those two borrowed eyes are what I want to capture—the eyes that will be borrowed by the viewer to see what's outside the scene he's looking at. To see what is there and also what is not there.[43]

Symbolism is the tried and true method of awakening the interpretive imagination, and as Elena points out, Kiarostami crafted *Where Is the Friend's House?* into a "parable with deep philosophic meaning," in which the streets, houses, and outdoor locations of small mountain towns were carefully reconstructed to create an inner rather than an externally "real" setting.[44]

Doors, the film's most prominent symbol, illustrate a technique used to stimulate the imagination. They represent a means of conception that can either trap viewers within the frame or awaken their curiosity to escape by sensing what is outside or, correspondingly, what lies beneath the social surface in the human soul. Alfred Hitchcock famously used a closed door to heighten suspense because the spectator would fear an unimaginable horror more than a depicted one. Kiarostami opens *Where Is the Friend's House?* with a closed door to make viewers imagine what Ahmad feels and is beginning to think because cinema typically falls short of literature's ability to enter the mind of an adult, much less a child. Though the film ostensibly concerns a child's anxiety over a homework assignment, homework itself becomes a metaphor for what children learn outside of school and what adults may learn to see once their social blinders have been removed. *Where Is the Friend's House?* is the first film where Kiarostami makes extensive use of the zigzag road to suggest that the most valuable parts of life, signified in general by the film frame, lie outside the straight-ahead field of vision.

The film's opening image illustrates what Kiarostami meant when he said that we can always sense more than we can conceive. He uses a closed blue-gray metal door to represent the limits of our conditioned perceptions and a din of childish voices to represent the authentic feeling thoroughly socialized adults have repressed. Normally, Kiarostami said, "people [who] come to the theater [have] been trained to stop being curious and imaginative and simply take what's given to them." Instead, the viewer should be given an opportunity to imagine "what's outside the field of vision," and because showing a concrete image is inherently limiting, "the only way out of this dilemma is sound."[45]

Thus, the inner life of an eight-year-old child, which is normally ignored, immediately becomes the thematic subtext by having children's voices precede their appearance. Sound is used to convey essence throughout the film, and therefore the first of a collage of adult authority figures who loom over the film is introduced by the sound of the teacher's loud footsteps cutting into the joyful chaos before he enters the door and is actually seen. The initial placement of the camera outside the closed door puts the adult viewer in the place of the initially unseen teacher, in the conventional world outside the still-sensitive vision of the children, which the rest of the film helps to recover.

Although the teacher is a handsome young man in his early thirties, his first words are comically authoritarian: "Who has told you to sit down? Sit down!" Then he walks from the blackboard to close a hinged mullioned window with vertical bars, a key symbol of confinement. His next statement is also unintentionally comic—"As soon as I am late, you show me you don't know how to behave."—because he spends the rest of the scene berating the students for being tardy or not turning their homework in on time. But he tears up the on-time sheets of one boy because they were not in the workbook, which would allow him to trace week-to-week progress. Then he holds up the workbook of Ahmad Ahmadpur, the film's hero, as the proper example. The sequence is important because it subtly predicts that Ahmad has the discipline to persist and ultimately make a rebellious decision based on cumulative knowledge of the adult world he encounters, a type of homework the teacher did not intend.

The lateness motif is a metaphor for Ahmad's development as an individual who initially persists in following the rules until he realizes before it is too late how to circumvent them. By the end of the film, Ahmad has learned to use rather than follow rules. The teacher, however, is unwittingly raising a generation of slaves, a social imperative in most societies, even the often-idealized rural one depicted in the film. As in any society, children are fed and nurtured, but they are also trained to follow rules that benefit the society as a whole, even when those rules stifle individual feeling.

When Mohammad Reza Nematzadeh, Ahmad's friend, falls in the schoolyard, Ahmad reveals an instinct to nurture by taking him to the pump and pouring water on his skinned knee, and as soon as he returns home, his mother sends him to get the baby's bottle and diaper. Ahmad's home is a microcosm of a society where everyone is so busy that their whole identity has become a function of their work. In one shot of the mother hanging out sheets to dry, all we see are hands over the top of the sheet, and later in the film we see a man so completely covered by the load of hay he carries that he looks like a walking haystack, a shot repeated in *The Wind Will Carry Us*.

As Ahmad rushes about to complete his chores, the camera briefly cuts to a shot of his grandmother watering beautiful flowering plants in a row of vases on the balcony railing. Ahmad has absorbed a strong instinct to nurture from his teacher and his family, but he will not remain statically docile like the plants. Throughout the scene, a rooster crows as if to foreshadow Ahmad's awakening, and the baby cries as a sign of the need for help that Ahmad will desperately try to give Mohammad when he discovers that he had accidentally brought home his friend's workbook after he fell in the schoolyard.

Mohammad had forgotten to bring his homework to school on two previous occasions, and he faces expulsion if he fails a third time. But when Ahmad repeatedly tells his mother he must go to the nearby town of Poshteh to return the book, she ignores him at first, then angrily tells him to do his homework and go play. When he still persists, she forcefully orders him to his assigned corner in a small alcove, where he is repeatedly pictured between two confining posts next to a tall samovar as if he had become the usefully productive item society wants individual workers to be: "Don't move from there! Otherwise I will smack you so hard! Do you hear me?"

But Ahmad's empathy for his friend gives him courage. When his mother exasperatedly asks where Mohammad lives and Ahmad says "Poshteh," she says that's too far from their town of Koker and accuses him of lying. As children are expected to be predictable at school and at home, so adults are expected to mindlessly carry on work that benefits the society as a whole and that has little to do with "human beings and their souls," the subject Kiarostami wanted his films to address. Until Ahmad meets the equivalent of a Sufi guide midway through the film, his only adult role models at home are versions of society's average Joes: a father who fills his leisure time with media distraction (a radio that mostly receives static) and a grandfather who apes the societal leaders who bully everyone below them. When Ahmad sneaks out of his house at dusk, carrying the notebook and the pen that become his weapons of liberation, he runs past the grandfather sitting on a bench with a crony. The grandfather, wearing thick glasses to signify his socialized limitations, asks, "Is that our Ahmad? What is he going to do in Poshteh?"

But Ahmad has now embarked on the zigzag road that signifies a spiritual quest, where the wisdom gained is not from achieving the goal but from absorbing unexpected experience along the way. While the unhelpful adults Ahmad encounters are mostly impediments to further growth, Kiarostami uses sound to convey the inner essence of the boy's character. The sound of a steady, slow drumbeat begins just as Ahmad leaves his house. It continues as he runs back past the cradle to get the pen, and the cradle that he is leaving is visually noted when he passes it again on the way out.

Once outside, the film's only musical theme begins as Ahmad's continual running is accompanied by a steady up-tempo drum, intermittently punctuated nonmelodically by a plucked stringed instrument. The use of only two instruments expresses a child's simplicity, while its steady pace connotes the strength of his soul. There is a subtle, repeated, up-and-down phrase that puts the sound in harmony with the up-and-down rolling hills, and its pleasing sound also matches the beautiful scenery of the barren country dotted by trees, with a small piece of blue sky still visible in the lengthening shadows. Ahmad is on the right track.

But that frequently does not seem to be the case because he passes through a series of setbacks that become daunting through their sheer accumulation. The first shot in Poshteh is a closed wooden door on the right and a stairway leading through an archway on the left. At the top of the stairs, Ahmad comes out onto another street, where he asks a "walking haystack" if he knows where Mohammad lives. The voice in the haystack says he doesn't know, leaving Ahmad to inquire at the next house. Kiarostami makes his point about dehumanizing work by having the camera stay on the man who emerges and sits down as if his load had been exhaustingly heavy.

This is the life most of Ahmad's schoolmates will inherit regardless of the kind of work they are suited to do. Their role as domestic animals who serve the powers that be is indicated after Ahmad ascends to the next level, where a cow emerges from a dark passage, which he then runs through. Suddenly a sheet drops down in front of him, and the woman on the balcony above asks him to throw it up to her. But he can't throw it high enough, and he is already learning that one place is like another place. As an adult, her placement on the balcony exaggerates her power over Ahmad and her indifference to his concerns, and after reaching down to take the sheet to give to the neighbor who dropped it, she has no similar help to offer a lesser person who is not her peer.

Here, as at home, adults have made work their priority. The woman's indifference to the child's plea does not match the beauty of the flowers she waters and the beautiful split-level door next to where she stands. It foreshadows the only creative person Ahmad will meet. Unlike the many closed doors he passes, the sides of the top half are swung open and the bottom half has an intricate geometric design of holes that can admit and emit light. And while the woman may take the door maker's craft for granted, like the cinemagoer who ignores these carefully selected details as mere background, Kiarostami's camera wants us to look for the beauty that surrounds us on his film's zigzag path as well as on our own.

Ahmad repeatedly encounters people who can't really see him because they are blinded by hardship, necessity, or their own concerns. A boy he recognizes as a classmate walks up carrying a heavy metal can that he can barely manage. He knows where Mohammad lives but can't take Ahmad there because he has to deliver the milk. In the first scene, the same boy had told the teacher he was sitting on the floor because his back hurt. Now again, the obstacles facing Ahmad's attempt to make friendship more important than work are symbolized when the boy says that Mohammad lives on a steep street with a staircase in front but that there are many streets and houses like that. They are inhabited largely by people who have lost their souls.

The motif of laundry representing the deceptively cleansed surface recurs when Ahmad enters a white stone courtyard where a child's pair of trousers hanging on a line looks like Mohammad's. As he touches the pants and calls his name, the loud cry of a cat recalls the crying baby at home and the maturity of his intent to prevent his friend's pain as he had by rolling up his friend's trouser leg to soothe his wound in the schoolyard. No one answers when he calls up toward the balcony, "Nematzadeh! I have your book!" And the silence is meant to ask the viewers, too, What have you learned from your education? What have you learned from your life?

When he touches the empty pants again, the cat cries in seeming sympathy with the pain Ahmad fears his friend will suffer. When Ahmad knocks on the neighbor's blue-gray door, the same cold color as the one to his classroom in the opening shot, an elderly lady with a cloth covering her face opens the door part way. She says she is sick and that he should go away, but her sickness and her "mask" represent those of societies at large, both the rural one of Koker and the urban ones of Kiarostami's viewers. First, she says no one lives next door. Then she says the pants belong to the grandson of the lady who lives there. The cat cries again when she curtly tells Ahmad to just go away.

But everywhere Ahmad goes in the adult world begins to look the same to the viewer, if not yet consciously to him. Status based on occupation rather than kinship, actual or metaphorical, rules these people's lives. Because Ahmad is eight years old and almost everyone he meets towers over him, low-angle shots of the adults exaggerate their indifference to his intense effort to prevent another person's pain. A contrasting conversation that he overhears on another street makes the point. It begins with a woman saying angrily, "And he comes yesterday evening to ask my husband to help him." When the other woman asks, "What is his profession?" the first answers, "Waiter. He was working three years, but then his boss sold the shop and told him that he had to go away. But since he is my husband's cousin, he told him that he had to help him."

At this point Ahmad ascends a stairway toward the sound of the same self-elevated voice, which now sneers, "He barely has money to eat." Receiving no answer to his knock, Ahmad enters the ironically bright royal blue door where the lady who was speaking is shown running water into a basin: "Who are you looking for, kid?" So far, he has made no direct progress toward his goal, but he has been learning far more than he bargained for. Wherever he turns, he is met by adult figures who can only do the laundry—that is, endlessly attend to the social façade—so it is no real surprise to us that the woman tells him that Mohammad and his father have gone to Koker.

Actually, "Who are you looking for, kid?" is one of the film's most resonant lines because Ahmad is on an unwitting quest to discover the house of the Sufi Friend in himself and through someone else he had not hoped to meet. That person is the antithesis of his grandfather, the first person he encounters when he returns to Koker. And in order to live with people like that (as Kiarostami had to live with the Iranian censors), the first thing to learn is to invent self-preserving fictions. Ahmad is also learning that kinship is where you find it, not in blood relations (or, for that matter, in shared ties of religion, nationality, or social class).

The grandfather has automatic cultural authority over Ahmad, and the interaction that ensues is solely to bolster that authority, which is the way of the world in most structured human groups. First, he asks Ahmad where he is going. Ahmad lies, "To buy bread." Then he asks what the boy was doing in Poshteh, and when Ahmad explains he was trying to help a friend, the grandfather is not only as indifferent as his mother had been, but he also bypasses this concern for human solidarity to assert personal power, much as the leaders of many countries have betrayed their religious and revolutionary ideals.

The grandfather's expressionless face and thick glasses are a visual sign of conditioned surrender to those who presume to play God. All the grandfather knows are variations of omnipotence versus submission, a religious imperative in conservative Islam. First, he demands that Ahmad get his cigarettes, and when the boy, who is in a hurry to help Mohammad, replies, "They may run out of bread," the grandfather assumes a threatening tone: "I do not want to have to repeat it!" The contrast between bread, which supplies communal nourishment, and cigarettes, which are a self-gratifying addiction, parallels the antithetical values that different kinds of people instinctively embrace.

The kinship connection to which the grandfather is oblivious is suggested when his sensitive-faced companion offers him a cigarette. The grandfather refuses it because he has only learned to respect self-esteem based on the little power he can muster:

> I have my own. That was not my point. I want the kid to be educated so that he grows up to be a good man. When I was little, my father would give me one cent a week and beat me every fortnight. And sometimes he would forget to give me the money on purpose, but he would never forget to give me a smack so that he would make me a strong man. And you saw how my grandson behaved. I had to repeat my words to him three times. And we want him to be educated properly, to be a good citizen, because if he is lazy, he will not be useful to society.

The grandfather's companion exposes the practice of using morality and injustice as an excuse to exercise power: "If he listened to you, would you still hit him?"

The grandfather's response reveals how the social order crushes independent thought and expels empathy for peers in favor of identifying with the absolute power that has crushed them, a power frighteningly projected into a punishing, judgmental God. The pattern is passed down from generation to generation. Those who hold power and those who submit to it all signify an omnipotence that can destroy natural kinship. Ahmad retains an instinct to nurture that has died in the socially conditioned grandfather:

> Find a good excuse to beat him every fortnight so that he won't forget. I used to work with an Iranian engineer building roads. After a while, two foreign engineers arrived. They looked at the road and said that it was improperly built. The Iranian engineer said it could be fixed with sand and gravel. The foreigner said we had to completely redo it to make it five centimeters higher so that it would match the contract. When he was leaving, I asked the Iranian engineer, "Why is my salary 6,000 tomans, and they receive 12,000?" He said the other workers would carry out orders immediately but that I had to be asked twice.

The use of *foreign* in the reminiscence is a way of universalizing the situation, and the next sequence shows that the pernicious drive to replace interhuman connection with status is not confined to a particular social system. A door salesman riding a donkey arrives from Poshteh to collect money from the grandfather's friend. The door salesman is ruthless and exploitive, the polar opposite of the door maker Ahmad eventually meets, and the two together comprise concepts of the egocentric God of fear versus the generous God of creation. Like the diversionary salesmen of religion or cinema, the door salesman promises relief from vulnerability and death. After he collects from the previous sale, he turns to another elderly man and pushes his product as a way to "keep out the cold."

The man reveals himself to be an independent soul who is not easily conned: "I like being cold. I already have doors." The ensuing sequence is metaphorically metaphysical: "Come on, grandfather. With these doors your name will be remembered forever. Everyone will say those doors belonged to a great man."—"After I die, what do I need them for?"—"Do you only think about death?" The subtext reminds the viewer that people acquire status symbols so that they can forget about death. The failure of these illusions of immortality is suggested by the salesman's mode of transportation: a donkey that carries him from small village to small village as a comic variant of the monotonous urban journeys of freeway drivers in modern cities. The practice is ancient and spiritually fruitless; only the products and their mode of distribution have changed.

The addiction to security symbols is reinforced when Ahmad returns without the cigarettes. The grandfather is furious because the child's apparent disobedience reminds him of the social impotence he felt after he had been accused of disobedience decades earlier. Again, Kiarostami advises, the only way to deal with people obsessed with power is to fool them. Once again, Ahmad tries to escape one boss's wrath by saying he is dutifully serving another: "But I won't have time to go to the bakery." The salesman interrupts to beg and then simply takes a sheet from the notebook that represents Ahmad's dedication to his friend: "But it's Mohammad's. I have to return it." The grandfather intervenes—"Give it to him!"—unconsciously supporting the structure of a state in which power, seminally wielded by an enforcer God, is then filtered down to the inhabitants of each social level in the highest available form, from supreme leader to abusive parent.

The salesman then forcibly takes the book away, teaching Ahmad and the viewer how culture and education are routinely co-opted and moral ideals are discarded when they are not useful: "I'll only take one leaf. The teacher won't find out." Culture's practical use is underscored when the salesman grabs the book again after giving it back so that he can use it as a prop to write up his order. When Ahmad overhears that the salesman is from Poshteh, he excitedly asks if he is Mr. Nematzadeh and if Mohammad is his son, but the salesman's single mission excludes noncommercial connections, and without a word he jumps on the donkey, which he accelerates with a whip as he returns home from a another day at the office. The drum and stringed instrument that accompany Ahmad's two journeys to and from Poshteh resume as Ahmad intrepidly pursues the mounted man, and although we know he will never catch him, that failure may over time be the hero's salvation. Out on the rolling hills dotted with small trees, Ahmad moves beyond the social trap where, in a brief intercut, his grandfather sits hopelessly rooted.

Back on the multileveled streets of Poshteh, the salesman urges the donkey up a flight of stone stairs, past a beautiful light brown wooden door unlike the mass-produced metal ones he sells. Then, at the end of a second street, he ascends more stairs to a third level, signifying the compelled social ascent that societies whip their children to attain but that Ahmad and the film avoid and reject. The fate of those who are not so lucky is seen when Ahmad descends two levels to discover the donkey tied outside a building. The salesman emerges carrying half of a heavy door, followed by a child carrying the other half. The child is the same age as Ahmad, but he has already been reduced to a beast of burden, the mindless role that he as laborer or salesman will be forced to play.

As a person transformed to a function of his work, the boy is only a variation on a social type. He tells Ahmad that his last name is also Nematzadeh but that there are lots of people in Poshteh with that last name and that he doesn't know Mohammad Reza. In the larger sense, this child and many others need help, but as the unnamed director in *And Life Goes On* discovers, you can't save everyone or even selected individuals. You can only help or be helped by the people you are given the opportunity to reach, when and if they are ready.

The work motif culminates when the boy, holding his wrist as if sore from lifting, tells Ahmad to ask for Mohammad's house at the blacksmith factory, a second beast of burden reference to subtly indicate the role of laborers in societies that ruling elites falsely promote as classless with impartial justice under civil or religious law but with equality in name only. The friend who can spring him from this trap is not the little boy he seeks but the version of the spiritual Friend he soon meets. The sequence begins in a dark street, where Ahmad hears the simultaneous sounds of blacksmith tools and sheep bleating, the docile herd at their unrewarding work. But he also hears the sound of a saw behind a wooden window cover, topped with a pattern of rectangular holes. It is the door maker, busy at his solitary task. Ahmad knocks on the door, and raising the window cover, an old man answers him in the first kind adult voice he has heard since the film began: "What is it, son?" The kinship term is important. His grandfather had only called him Ahmad. The door maker tells him he knows where his friend lives and will show him the way.

Without realizing it, Ahmad has just met the best friend he will ever have. *Friend* capitalized is one of the names for God in the Persian poetic tradition. It occurs, for example, in the Rumi poem "Departure," in which the traveler is reminded by the poet as "friend" not to be diverted from seeking the "Friend" at the end of his life's journey: "O heart, toward thy heart's love wend, and O friend, fly toward the Friend, / Be wakeful, watchman, to the end."[46] As in Attar's *Conference of the Birds*, the goal is not to find a kingly Friend outside of oneself but to actualize that creative love in one's own heart. As Kiarostami put it in an interview, "The journey forms part of our culture, and it is linked with mysticism; for us what is really important is not the goal we wish to attain but the path we must travel."[47] He added that the zigzag path represents desire, and the fulfilment of desire is never at the end of the path but always present along the way after one's eyes are opened. Thus, the tree on the hill that Ahmad repeatedly passes and that he and the untutored audience are unlikely to notice while they are still spiritual children is a "symbol of friendship."[48]

As Elena points out, Kiarostami "created" the tree and the hill on a previously bare promontory, and they are two of the key "words" to his cinematic poem inspired by an actual poem by Sohrab Sepehri, one of Iran's most respected modern poets. "Address," in Elena's words, "openly subscribes [to a] tradition of mysticism, of remote Sufi inspiration."[49] It begins with a rider searching "through the false dawn twilight" for "the House of the Friend." A passerby "with a branch of light in his mouth" points to an aspen at the end of a "garden lane more green than God's dream." At the end of "that lane which appears behind adolescence," the rider should turn first to "the flower of solitude" and then stop at the "foot of the mountain of eternal myths," where a "transparent fear will envelop" him. But then, "in the intimacy" of that "flowing space," the rider will see a "child who has climbed a pine tree to pluck a chick from the nest of light, and from the child [he] will ask: 'Where is the House of the Friend?'"[50]

The poem tells its readers, as Kiarostami tells his viewers, to escape the "false dawn" of socially conditioned experience and to recover their souls by entering a spiritual place that is "more green than God's dream" and beyond the established eternal myths. "More green than God's dream" implies that there is a transcendent spiritual experience in the natural world more authentic than the "eternal myths" of a supernatural God that in Attar's *Conference of the Birds* lead straight to the final valley of Poverty and Nothingness. This place exists only in the human heart, but to find it, Sepehri and Kiarostami say, one must recover the sensibility of childhood, "the land which appears behind adolescence," and abandon the bleating sheep, as Ahmad does when he meets the door maker, whose creative power is inseparable from the "flower of solitude," which he will bequeath to Ahmad. The old man and the boy are in rapport because one is a presocialized child and the other is a postadult child, like Sepehri's guide who plucks another child "from the nest of light" before that light has dissipated into the darkness, where most of the adults in Koker, Poshteh, and everywhere else live.

The old man is not the Friend, but he is one who directs others to the Friend, the traditional function of the Sufi saint. Speaking about the wisdom of Puya, the fictional director's young son in *And Life Goes On*, Kiarostami said, "In Eastern philosophy we believe that you need a guide before you set foot in unknown territory," and even though his father "has the steering wheel," Puya is the "real guide" because instead of talking about the tragedy, he talks about "what interests him." He accepts the "illogic and instability of the earthquake" and "just moves on."[51] Ahmad's guide is more advanced than Puya because he not only retains an active appreciation for what he encounters but he also is able to transmit love and appreciation through his highly refined art. And in order to acquire that art, he has long cultivated the "flower of solitude" that he passes on, eventually in the symbolic form of an actual flower, to a boy whose persistent love promises recognition.

Because he is the maker of many uniquely varied doors and windows, the door maker symbolically perceives existence from a Godlike point of view. As an agent of God's creative power and in this sense merged with God like a Sufi saint, he is a maker of all frames outside any particular one. In "Doors without Keys," Kiarostami's photography exhibit of doors from different times and places, he had intended to take his viewers outside their cultural frames so that they could sense and feel a transcendent message. He reminded them of conscious limits at the end of the exhibit with the placard that read, "We are not able to look at what we have in front of us, unless it is inside a frame,"[52] but on another occasion, he told interviewer David Sterritt that he wanted his viewers to "borrow" eyes that he himself had borrowed (from poets like Rumi or Sepehri) so that they might see "what's outside the scene [they're] looking at. To see what is there and also what is not there."[53]

Some hostile Iranian journalists, thoroughly immersed in their social roles, sensed that Kiarostami was rejecting the limitations of vision that constituted the only world they knew. One said the director didn't look at human beings as equals "but from high above them with dark glasses . . . arrogant, emotionless and calculating." Another said the film "lacked any real audience."[54] They may have been angry because they sensed that their own seemingly real worlds were being discarded as the film necessarily discards those of the teacher, the grandfather, and the door salesman, and so on.

When the old man first appears, he is leaning out his window, emerging from a frame, to help Ahmad make new connections. Just after he and the boy begin to walk down the street, they meet a woman aggressively selling apples. Their exchange echoes that of the door salesman's failure with a prospective customer, supplemented by the biblical connotation of generalized temptation: "Buy some apples."—"I don't have teeth to bite apples."—"Then for your son."—"He's not my son."—"For your grandchildren."—"I don't have grandchildren." The brief sequence contrasts relationships based on the cash nexus to those based on empathy and between obligations based on gene pool ties versus those based on intuitive rapport with an unexpected stranger. This was the legendary connection between Rumi and his Sufi companion Shams of Tabriz, who mysteriously disappeared because (some speculate) Rumi's jealous son ordered his death. Thereafter, Rumi spent years searching for Shams, until he realized that the love he imagined in one person or even one external God had been and always would be within himself.[55]

As the door maker and Ahmad walk toward Mohammad's house, he shows the boy the best examples of his work, just as Kiarostami takes the viewers away from their anxious goals to show them what's worthwhile in the course of the journey rather than at its imagined end. Though the door maker is not God, he sees the world as Kiarostami imagines God views his creation. The door maker knows Ahmad's father and everyone else in Koker and Poshteh because he has made their doors and windows. That is, there is a single source for all cultural beliefs, though power-hungry "salesmen" (like the biblical Satan) are always striving to divide them. The Sufi quest of Kiarostami and other spiritual artists takes children beyond their social fathers (supreme leaders, presidents, etc.) and merge them with the creative source. The deviation of hierarchical societies from an original loving purpose begins to be suggested when the door maker says they are changing the doors and windows he had made, and nobody asks why.

He walks very slowly, as Kiarostami paces his films, to advance the inquiry and to try to calm the caught-in-time rush his immature audience habitually feels: "They have heard that iron doors will last a lifetime, but how long is a life?" and then to relativize even the longest physical life span, he asks eight-year-old Ahmad his age. Life is fully lived and metaphorically extended when it is lived in a fully realized present, the state a craftsman achieves when he is intent on his work. This is the immortality the old man intuitively tries to transmit because Ahmad is approaching the "fall," when the existential joy of being alive is about to be replaced by the gnawing drive to be safely better, to be as gods who are invulnerable but who create nothing.

Cain's "city" is the biblical consequence of the poisoned apple: "My nephew also was exactly eight when his father took him to the city." In films like *Close-Up*, *Ten*, *Crimson Gold* (the script he wrote for Jafar Panahi), and *Like Someone in Love*, Kiarostami elaborates on the urban trap where people are isolated from a spiritual source. Even if they visit a museum or go to a film, most people are too focused on some immediate goal to appreciate what the old man shows Ahmad.

Just before they begin walking together, we see a close-up of the old man's front door, an object so beautiful that it suggests more than aesthetic skill. The upper section, which comprises more than half the door, is carved in a pattern, with spokes radiating from a circle in the center to the borders of a tilted square. This suggestion of creative power emanating from a single source has been replaced by the mass-produced metal doors that represent the work of the city. The door maker says that he and his brother made this particular door forty-five years ago, but the brother had a wife and children and needed more money, so he moved to Tehran. The door maker himself has been to Tehran twice and wants no part of it.

As they pass a striking stained-glass window with a white, orange, and blue-gray oval pattern, the door maker speaks as if he were God lamenting human indifference to His loving work. People striving to enhance their material security forget to enjoy what has been freely given. It is a kind of Cain-and-Abel division. Cain built the first cities as places where envy and competition have replaced kinship: "It saddens me when I see them leaving these windows and doors which I built with so much effort to go to the city," and the idea of recovering kinship connections is implied when he adds, "I'd like to know where they take the old doors when they replace them."

Although Ahmad impatiently wants to reach Mohammad before nightfall, the old man stops at a public basin, reflecting the film's cleansing purpose: "Wait, I want to wash my face, and after we'll continue." The cleansing precedes the introduction of Sepehri's "flower of solitude," which the old man now offers and which is the film's final image. For Kiarostami, art is not an end in itself but a means of referring the viewer back to the source of all creative power. For him, nature is always more beautiful than art, but art is the best way of helping people to see it: "Come wash your face."—"I'm in a hurry."—"We're almost there. Your friend's house is right there. What good water! Spring water! Here take this flower, and put it in the book. Don't lose it. You must watch over it."

Ahmad urges the old man to hurry because "it's getting really late," but as a metaphor of growth, it is already too late for some spectators and never too late for others. The boy worries about the immediate future as he puts the flower in the book, suggesting that viewers who do not get the message now may receive its benefit later. But for the time being, the boy must become accustomed to the fears and adversities that threaten every human life. When they reach Mohammad's house, the audience might be expected to breathe a sigh of relief. Night has now fallen, and Ahmad hesitates to enter the pitch-black entrance to a stairway: "You go through here; it's the first door to the left."

Thunder begins to growl, the wind blows a small piece of paper in circles, and a tethered donkey paws the earth. Ahmad enters the passage and runs back out. The old man asks, "Don't you want to give him the book?" and assures him that he will wait so that they can return together. Ahmad tries again and runs back down, still holding the book, indicating that he is not ready to overcome his fears and reflecting the failures of humanity in general to accomplish a higher purpose until they are ready to stop fearing the unknown.

As a culture-transcending artist, all Kiarostami can do is to continue to quell the divisive fears of an immature humanity by directing their attention to ongoing love. The frames now balance images of black shadows and light from the streetlamps, as the two walk back together: "Let's go through here. I can show you the doors and windows I have made." But again, the artist's adversary is always the demands of the powers that be. Ahmad won't pause to look because he is afraid his mother will scold him for being late. Continually passing through the balanced frames of light and darkness, the viewer who is ready to forget about being late may briefly admire the stained-glass windows with their patterned ovals of color and the light-emitting designs on the carved doorways, but Ahmad, like other immature viewers, can't help but complain that the pace is too slow. The sounds cease after they ascend a lighted stairway, where Ahmad impatiently stops: "Why are you standing there?"—"You are very slow."—"When I was your age I used to run from place to place."

The old man offers comfort, a cover for the cold, which Ahmad refuses because his fear of "being late" again prevents him from accepting the gifts that life has to offer. Guiding the unready requires more than words, and the old man says he can go a little faster if he stops talking, which is fine with Ahmad, as it is with viewers waiting to see where an "inscrutable" filmmaker is "going with this." So the boy runs ahead into the darkness but quickly reappears when a frightening sound sends him running back: "What's the matter Ahmad?"—"The dog is barking."—"That's why we have to walk together." Once again, the exchange resonates with the need for human kinship and spiritual guidance that people feel rather than outwardly profess, but the old man knows there is no way of directly transmitting this feeling: "You go on your own. I'll watch you." The line echoes the many expressions of Kiarostami's belief in hands-off directing that he has stated in interviews, such as the previously quoted reference to Rumi's polo ball, and that he reflexively portrays at the end of *Through the Olive Trees* (see chapter 9).

They part when they reach the brightly lit stairway of the door maker's house. Ahmad gathers his courage and runs off in the darkness, and ascending the steps, the old man casts a huge shadow on the lighted stone wall as he approaches his door. The camera cuts to the woodgrain of a very old wall, which turns out to be inside his apartment, part of an outer layer that has worn away. The rest of the interior has the effect of a sanctuary, one simultaneously human and divine, while outside the dog still barks his warning. The camera suggests that what he represents is partly hidden. His body is seen only up to his shoulders as he enters the door and while he slips out of his street shoes and into a pair of slippers.

On the wall, there is a photograph of a woman dressed in black, someone he has loved and lost, and when he looks out the window and turns his head to each side as if looking for Ahmad, the image shows that though he lacks an omnipotent power to protect, his love remains constant. The dog's barking, too, is constant, but its continuity makes it less alarming, something to be taken for granted in every human frame. Outside all frames, the artist can only plant seeds and hope that they will flower.

An abrupt cut to Ahmad shows him physically safe at home but still in mental turmoil. In place of the old man's voice offering help, we hear the sound of his father's radio, and a cut to the father shows him fiddling with the dial, trying to resume the soccer broadcast that has just cut out, a primitive version of adults depending on television or the internet to fill the void during respites from routine work. He wears a gray shirt and gray pants, but he sits next to a chest of brown wood with an elaborate, studded-metal pattern, something interesting and beautiful that someone else took time to make and that is the antithesis of the blank distraction the father embodies. Outside, however, the wind whistles, blocking the radio signal and foreshadowing the spiritual force in Ahmad rising to destroy the conditioning that binds him to social rules that have kept him from helping Mohammad by finding himself.

As the sound of the wind increases, he refuses to eat the food his mother brings, again signaling the inner revolution he is about to launch and that is not explicit until the following scene. But here, the sounds of the outer storm express the fearful last stage of social departure, experienced by most people at a later age. The mother questioning his rejection of the food—"What is it? You don't like what you got?"—applies to everything his journey has taught him about the adult world, and now, without the old man, he has no one to advise him. The mother repeatedly demands, "Come eat; do you hear me?" but Ahmad quietly refuses, "I don't want to," because he is learning to know what he can no longer swallow. Then she orders him to go to bed, a variation on the shutting down of consciousness that authority demands, but Ahmad protests that he has to do his homework, which by now becomes a symbol of how some children learn to go beyond their assigned tasks and thoughts.

And so his mother says he should do it on the other side of the house because the adults want to sleep, to remain in darkness, while Ahmad, like the old man, remains in the light. He kneels to pick up his notebooks as his father puts the radio on the shelf and passes without looking at his son and his grandfather sits on the sofa, looking down in a stupor. The mother, wearing gray like the father and looming up over the boy, unlocks the door from a lock too high for Ahmad to reach so that he can go through a doorway into another room, where the steady mechanical whistle of the radio has been replaced by the mysterious respiration of the wind.

The camera enhances Ahmad's impulse to heed an inspiration from a spiritual rather than a social source by staying on the family briefly after the boy leaves the room. The mother's shadow remains visible near the door as we hear only the sound of her carrying dishes, the entire identity of one who is no longer a full person because her life has been consumed by work, while the grandfather, the most unattractive figure in Ahmad's world, still sits immobile to the right of the frame, unable to extend his mind or feelings beyond the traumatic intimidation that defines him. Kiarostami uses this technique throughout the film, keeping the camera on a person or symbolic object to leave a cumulative impression on Ahmad and the viewers.

Then the camera cuts to Ahmad, kneeling down in his room. Upon a second viewing, we know what the film does not immediately disclose: that he is copying his own homework into Mohammad's notebook. The sounds of the storm signify the broken barriers, even though his mother returns with the tray of food and in an uncharacteristically gentle voice uses the kinship term for the first time: "Have your dinner, my son. And when you finish, turn off the light and go to bed." But by this time, Ahmad cannot be stopped by cajolery any more than he could be by threats. He will not ingest the world to which his family has been assigned.

The storm blows through the open doors of his window, a sign of the breakthrough that liberates him to act independently. The wind becomes very loud, and a shot out the window shows the washed sheets that the women have been working on so hard whipping around on the line. All the work of society can be destroyed in a war or natural catastrophe, but the inculcation of rigid, soul-freezing ideas can also be destroyed by a natural process in the creative child. While the wind turns the pages of the notebook next to the one he writes in, Ahmad is moved to copy the homework on his own. Another shot out the window shows one of the sheets fluttering on the ground, a visual image of unquestioning obedience torn from Ahmad's soul.

Outside, the mother quickly and efficiently removes sheets from the line, saving them from the storm as Ahmad moves to save his friend from expulsion, the small child's ultimate fear of social wrath. As on the Poshteh street, the sound of a dog, now howling instead of just barking, conveys the fear of a similar fate for Ahmad if his crime is discovered. He looks up with an alarmed expression before another cut to the flailing sheets outside. At the limits of his fear, he has reached a point of transformation, where thought and action come from a mysterious source, whether we want to call it God or the unconscious mind. Just before Attar's thirty chosen birds can reach the Simurgh, the God within themselves, their Hoopoe leader tells them they will be suspended in the valley of Poverty and Nothingness until, "with an impulse that is not theirs," they are "absorbed in seas that have no shores." For this moment of fearful transformation, eight-year-old Ahmad must allow himself to be possessed by a mind beyond the one society admits.

The sequence moves from Ahmad's alarmed expression to a close-up of a white sheet, which his mother picks up, followed by an abrupt cut to the backs of boys in the classroom facing a white wall that matches the sheet. On the proverbial blank page of their being, children are drilled into perpetuating their nation's narrative. Here, in a culture premised on religious obedience, the submission to authority is extreme. When the teacher enters, everyone quickly rises. He tells them to sit without looking at them and opens a vertical window on the left so that half of it swings out, a visual cue of what Ahmad has done. After the storm, light and fresh air stream in. At first, the teacher seems to be in an amiable mood, but tension rises when one boy arrives late and another rises to announce, "Ahmadpur is not here." Thematically, the line applies to more than Ahmad's physical absence. The risk is heightened when the teacher snaps, "I told you not to speak unless you are spoken to," and a disaster appears imminent, when the camera cuts to Mohammad putting his head down on his desk as we hear the other boys getting out their notebooks.

When the teacher begins to check the homework, his words emphasize that if even minor rules are broken, the rulers will notice: "Ghassem Hoiat! Why did you write *pedestrian* with two *s*'s. The word *pedestrian* is written with only one *s*. Is that clear?" The particular word refers back to Ahmad's repeated circular journey, in which he defied his parents and now defies the teacher. The ensuing dialogue indicates the unrelenting obligations these children will increasingly face, some of them in conflict with each other. The teacher asks one boy why there is a stain on his notebook, and the boy explains that his hands were sweating after working with his father on the farm, but instead of sympathy, the boy receives a rebuke: "You need to remember your first obligation is education. And afterward you can help your father on the farm and your mother at home."

The sweating hands also connote fear. What will happen to Mohammad, and where is Ahmad? The tension rises when the teacher reaches a boy who has not done the assignment and again, when he comes to the boy we had seen carrying the heavy door in Poshteh, who says his back hurt too much to do his homework. As before, the teacher says he can let it go only twice, and we know that for Mohammad it will be the third and final time.

The teacher now turns toward a knock on the door, and Ahmad enters. The teacher says, "You didn't come from Poshteh," referring back to the first scene, where boys from Poshteh were given a few extra minutes not to be marked tardy because their town was further from the school than Koker. But the line is nicely ironic because Ahmad has actually been to Poshteh twice the day and night before. So when Ahmad sits down next to Mohammad, he already has one strike against him. He puts the notebook in front of Mohammad just before the teacher arrives at their desk. The tension is at its peak when the teacher demands Ahmad's notebook and Ahmad hands him Mohammad's instead: "This is Nematzadeh's."

For a moment it looks like all is lost, but after the teacher quickly glances at Ahmad's notebook, the camera cuts to a close-up of his pen passing over a page of Mohammad's, and we realize that he hadn't looked at Ahmad's long enough to notice anything identical. Then, flipping through Ahmad's pages, he appears not to see the film's key symbol. At the very moment the old man's flower is briefly exposed, the musical theme that accompanied Ahmad's circular journey softly begins. The film's final words—"Very good. Well done, boy."—redefine virtue by transferring it from obedience to rebellion and from the law to the heart. The journey music during the closing credits is a final tribute to the persistent love that eludes a demanding God to find the Friend.

NOTES

1. Quoted in Andrew Pulver and Saeed Kamali Dehgha, "Abbas Kiarostami, Palme d'Or-Winning Iranian Film-Maker, Dies Aged 76," *Guardian*, July 4, 2016, https://www.theguardian.com/film/2016/jul/04/abbas-kiarostami-palme-dor-winning-iranian-film-maker-dies.
2. Ahmad Karimi Hakkak and Michael Beard, introduction to Abbas Kiarostami, *Walking with the Wind*, bilingual ed., trans. Ahmad Karimi Hakkak and Michael Beard (Cambridge, MA: Harvard University Film Archive, 2001), para. 15.
3. Quoted in Stuart Jeffries, "Landscapes of the Mind," *Guardian*, April 16, 2005, https://www.theguardian.com/film/2005/apr/16/art.
4. Quoted in Deborah Solomon, "Tales from Teheran," *New York Times Magazine*, March 11, 2007.
5. Quoted in Geoff Andrew, "Unspoken Truths," *Sight & Sound* (July 2013): 40–43.
6. Abbas Kiarostami, "With the Wind," in *In the Shadow of Trees: The Collected Poetry of Abbas Kiarostami*, trans. Iman Tavassoly and Paul Cronin (New York: Sticking Place Books, 2016), 62.
7. Kiarostami, "With the Wind," 69–70.
8. Omar Khayyam, *Rubaiyat of Omar Khayyam*, trans. Edward Fitzgerald (1859, 1889), Project Gutenberg, July 10, 2008, http://www.gutenberg.org/cache/epub/246/pg246.txt.
9. Quoted by Alberto Elena, *The Cinema of Abbas Kiarostami*, trans. Belinda Coombes (London: SAQI Iran Heritage Foundation, 2005), 130.
10. Hamid Dabashi, *The World of Persian Literary Humanism* (Cambridge, MA: Harvard University Press, 2012), 120.
11. Khayyam, *Rubaiyat*.
12. Khayyam, *Rubaiyat*.
13. Abbas Kiarostami, "In Dialogue with Kiarostami," interview by Ali Akbar Mahdi, *Iranian*, August 25, 1998, https://asianart.fandom.com/wiki/Interviews_with_Abbas_Kiarostami.
14. Quoted in Elena, *Cinema of Abbas Kiarostamii*, 78.
15. Khayyam, *Rubaiyat*.
16. Farid Ud-Din Attar, *The Conference of the Birds*, trans. Afkham Darbandi and Dick Davis (London: Penguin, 1984); "not difficult to see why" in online introduction only, http://thekingdomwithin.net/wpcontent/uploads/2015/03/The_Conference_of_the_Birds_Fardiuddin_Attar.pdf.
17. Attar, *Conference of the Birds*, 181, 186.
18. Attar, *Conference of the Birds*, 94.
19. Attar, *Conference of the Birds*, 157.
20. Jelaluddin Rumi, *The Essential Rumi*, trans. Coleman Barks, with John Moyne, A. J. Arberry, and Keynold Nicholson (San Francisco: HarperCollins, 1995).
21. Quoted in Rozina Ali, "The Erasure of Islam from the Poetry of Rumi," *New Yorker*, January 5, 2017, http://www.newyorker.com/books/page-turner/the-erasure-of-islam-from-the-poetry-of-rumi.
22. Kiarostami, "In Dialogue"; see also *Ten on Ten*, special feature on *Ten*, directed by Abbas Kiarostami (2002; New York: Zeitgeist Films, 2004), DVD.
23. Paraphrased by Elena, *Cinema of Abbas Kiarostamii*, 158.
24. Quoted in Ali, "Erasure of Islam."

25. Quoted in Ali, "Erasure of Islam."
26. Quoted in Elena, *Cinema of Abbas Kiarostami*, 186.
27. Hakkak and Beard, introduction, para. 12.
28. Quoted in Jane Ciabattari, "Why Is Rumi the Best-Selling Poet in the US?" BBC Culture, October 21, 2014, http://www.bbc.com/culture/story/20140414-americas-best-selling-poet.
29. "Rumi," Wikipedia, updated January 2, 2020, https://en.wikipedia.org/wiki/Rumi.
30. Rumi, *Essential Rumi*, 32.
31. Abbas Kiarostami, "With Borrowed Eyes: An Interview with Abbas Kiarostami," interview by David Sterritt, *Film Comment*, July–August 2000, http://www.filmcomment.com/article/with-borrowed-eyes-an-interview-with-abbas-kiarostami/.
32. Rumi, *Essential Rumi*, 37.
33. Rumi, *Essential Rumi*, 41.
34. Rumi, *Essential Rumi*, 96.
35. See Mahmoud Reza Sani, *Men at Work: Cinematic Lessons from Abbas Kiarostami*, trans. Alireza Lalehfar (Los Angeles: Mhughes Press, 2013), 99–100.
36. On the difference between a prophet and a saint, see William C. Chittick, *The Sufi Path of Love: The Spiritual Teachings of Rumi* (Albany: State University of New York Press, 1983), 119.
37. Chittick, *Sufi Path*, 120.
38. Dabashi, *Persian Literary Humanism*, 10.
39. Kiarostami, "With Borrowed Eyes."
40. *Ten on Ten*.
41. Kiarostami, "With Borrowed Eyes."
42. Kiarostami, "With the Wind," 52.
43. Kiarostami, "With Borrowed Eyes."
44. Elena, *Cinema of Abbas Kiarostami*, 72.
45. Kiarostami, interview, in Mehrnaz Saeed-Vafa and Jonathan Rosenbaum, *Abbas Kiarostami* (Urbana: University of Illinois Press, 2003), 114.
46. Jalal ad-Din Muhammad Rumi, "Departure," trans. R. A. Nicholson in *Persian Poems: Anthology of Verse Translations*, ed. A. J. Arberry (London: Everyman's Library, 1972), http://www.khamush.com/poems.html.
47. Kiarostami quoted by Alberto Elena, *The Cinema of Abbas Kiarostami*, trans. Belinda Coombes (London: SAQI Iran Heritage Foundation, 2005), 75.
48. Quoted in Elena, *Cinema of Abbas Kiarostami*, 75.
49. Elena, *Cinema of Abbas Kiarostami*, 73.
50. Quoted in Elena, *Cinema of Abbas Kiarostami*, 73–74.
51. Quoted in Elena, *Cinema of Abbas Kiarostami*, 96.
52. See "Abbas Kiarostami: Doors without Keys," Curious Creature, 2019, https://www.thecuriouscreature.com/2015/11/20/doors-without-keys/; and Amanda DelaCruz, "Doors without Keys by Abbas Kiarostami at Toronto's Aga Khan Museum @AgaKhan Museum," Culture Toronto, November 22, 2015, http://www.culturetoronto.com/spotlight/doors-without-keys-by-abbas-kiarostami#.WFQeRWPu1jo.
53. Kiarostami, "With Borrowed Eyes."
54. See Elena, *Cinema of Abbas Kiarostami*, 104–5.
55. See Arthur J. Arberry, introduction to *Discourses of Rumi*, by Jalal al Din Rumi, trans. Arthur J. Arberry (1947; Richard, UK: Curzon Press, 1993), para. 11–14.

Chapter Three

Saving the World

Kiarostami's work often reflects Sufic pantheism, but at times it evinces a dualism that has its roots in the pre-Islamic religion of Iran. Founded by the prophet Zarathustra in about 1500 BCE, Zoroastrianism was the official religion of Iran at the time of the Arab conquest in 651 CE. Unlike Christianity and Islam, it was not aggressively conversionary, and during the time it was the state religion, the Persian king Cyrus the Great (630–530 BCE) allowed the people in his subject territories to retain their own religions, most notably the Jews, whom he allowed to return to Israel after a half-century in Babylonian exile. Perhaps tolerance is an attribute of Zoroastrianism because, unlike Judaism, Christianity, or Islam, its primary deity is not omnipotent. Ahura Mazda represents the creative force of the universe, and he is assisted by thousands of spirits called fravashis against his destructive adversary, Angra Mainyu, also called Ahriman.

Good in general means protecting the physical world against Ahriman's work of war, pestilence, and natural disaster, and each human being assisted by a fravashi as his or her guardian spirit is sent into the world as a kind of undercover agent to report vital information for the ongoing battle after he or she dies. In the Persian rather than the Islamic tradition, the good Kiarostami sought to further was more in line with *asha*, the Zoroastrian way of good thoughts, good words, and good deeds, rather than in absolute obedience to a salvific faith and its theocratic agents.[1] There is a Cain-and-Abel distinction in *Where Is the Friend's House?* but there and in subsequent Kiarostami films (as well as those of Makhmalbaf and Panahi), obeying the laws of the state is usually the just-following-orders way of Ahriman. Ahmad's grandfather is on a continuum with Nazis and terrorists, people whose problems are solved by not having to think, or as one Al Qaeda recruit put it, "Jihad is the cure for depression."[2]

Hamid Dabashi writes that Iran's "autonomous literary imagination" stemmed from Zoroastrian roots. After the seventh-century Arab conquest, "Arabic became the paternal language of the hegemonic theology, jurisprudence, philosophy, and science," while Persian remained the language of "mothers' lullabies and wandering singers, songwriters, storytellers, and poets, [constituting] the subversive literary imagination of a poetic conception of being."[3] In the first two centuries after the conquest, the Arab rulers sensed this undercurrent as an existential threat, and the later proponents of the folk tradition who preferred this world to the next, like Omar Khayyam and the doctor in *The Wind Will Carry Us*, were considered "licentious, dissolute, profligate, wicked, shameless, and just plain morally corrupt."[4]

The Islamic word for these perceived degenerates is *Zanadiqa*, a term derived from Zend, the language of the Avesta, the Zoroastrian holy book and its commentaries. Near the end of the eighth century, a chief inquisitor burned these books and crucified their unrepentant devotees.[5] But despite periodic suppression, holidays with Zoroastrian roots are still alive in Iran, the most notable being Nowruz, the Iranian national New Year celebrated on the first day of spring. The most significant Zoroastrian vestige, however, is an item of jewelry, the *faravahar* pendant. Perhaps because it is exclusively Iranian, predating the Muslim conquest, it is a symbol of national pride, the most-worn pendant in Iran. It depicts a bearded human figure in left profile rising from a central disc flanked by the spread wings, legs, and tail feathers of a powerful bird resembling that of a Native American thunderbird. The man's right hand points upward, and his left hand holds a large ring.[6]

The *faravahar* is commonly thought to be the image of a winged fravashi. Although the Islamic revolution of 1979 removed some Persian symbols that the shah had elevated to strengthen Persian nationalism, the *faravahar* was not banned, even though it was not religiously rooted in Islam. In fact, Iranian Islam, for the most part, opposes any religious expression that threatens to substitute an angel or a Sufi saint for Allah. In the Avesta, Ahura Mazda states that he created the physical world in concert with "many hundreds, many thousands, many tens of thousands [of] mighty, victorious fravashis" and that without their help Ahriman would have possessed all of humanity.[7]

Since then, the fravashis continue to guard each human being, as in the doctor's recitation from *The Wind Will Carry Us*: "If my guardian angel is the one I know, he will protect glass from stone." The sentiment is potentially blasphemous in Islam because if a person dies believing that God is associated with or equal to some other entity, he or she will be permanently consigned to hell. While a Muslim (or a Christian or a Jew) seeks to obediently please a paternal God, a Zoroastrian has the cooperative role of a vital helper.

Sufism, too, was targeted by orthodox religious authorities for its presumed equalizing of human beings with God. In 922, the Sufi philosopher Mansur Al-Hallaj was executed in Baghdad for pantheistically saying, "I am the Creative Truth," which was interpreted to mean "I am God."[8] Other Sufis, in the orthodox view, presumptuously say they are close "friends" of God. In twenty-first-century Iran, Sufi devotion to the revelations of their saints and their emphasis on personal religious experience has been attacked as undermining the Islamic republic's "governance of the jurist," which strictly adheres to the Koranic laws as interpreted and sanctioned by state theologians. As a result, Sufis have been banned from government jobs, and some of their religious structures have been bulldozed. In 2006, a Sufi who publicly protested mistreatment by a government official was flogged seventy-four times.[9]

But while the Sufi sentiment that most offends the inquisitorial mind could be so harshly punished in a low-ranking, anonymous person, it had already been enshrined in the country's culture by one of the nation's most honored poets. In "The Creed of Love," Rumi wrote of a seeker who was refused entrance at the "door of the Beloved" because he made a distinction between himself and the One he sought: "A voice asked, 'Who is there?' / He answered, 'It is I.' / The voice said, 'There is no room for Me and Thee.' / The door was shut. / After a year of solitude and deprivation he returned and / Knocked, / A voice from within asked, 'Who is there?' / The man said, 'It is Thee.' / The door was opened for him."[10]

All Muslims hope for this closeness in Paradise, but Sufis strive to achieve it in their earthly lives through visions that include colors and sounds. In this sense Kiarostami's cinema may be considered Sufic, but his philosophy of filmmaking expressed in the self-made documentary *Ten on Ten* stresses the equivalent of Zoroastrian partnership. Until the last chapter, the film places us in the passenger seat of a car Kiarostami is driving on the outskirts of Tehran over the same winding roads driven by Mr. Badii, his suicidal protagonist in *Taste of Cherry*. He explains that some viewers of *Ten*, shot entirely in a car passing through Tehran traffic, said they missed the landscape settings of his previous films, and so in sympathy with people stuck in the mental gridlock of their busy lives, he has brought them to a place he loves, especially because rapid urban development may soon make it impossible to return.

But he also says that the present journey is not about specific social problems but about a "relationship" that he does not specify. In the course of the film, this relationship proves to be a cooperative one between members of a group and their lack of subjection to a central authority. For Kiarostami, absolute directorial control creates unnatural cinema. He breaks the fourth wall in the coda to *Taste of Cherry* because he wants to show people acting naturally, and over the course of his career, he stopped using the clapper board and saying, "Sound, camera, action" (a routine satirized in *Through the Olive Trees*), because it would make his nonactors stiffen up and overact.

Experience taught him that a "master-servant relationship does not work in cinema," and instead of using his DV camera "like a God" to dictate his actor's every move, Kiarostami made them beings of independent will, a relationship he paraphrased after quoting the previously cited lines by Rumi: "He says, you are my polo ball, and you run before my mallet, and I run after you, although I made you up, [which] means that I pushed you forward, but now I need to follow you. Eventually I will take it to the end, but you're the one who determines how to get there. I just determine the direction."

Kiarostami further limits the director's role by explaining that both of the French terms for *auteur*—*metteur en scène* and *réalisateur* (one who gives order to the scene and one who realizes something)—are too pretentious to describe what he does: "In the end credits, I list the names of those who worked on the film without mentioning their functions. I have never realized anything. Never been a *réalisateur*. Reality was constantly being played in front of me. I was merely there to record it." At the same time, even "God-given" realities may be imaginatively altered: "If one pictures a green sky, you can see the sky in a new way." This directorial style has metaphysical implications regarding the improvisatory roles of God and man, Ahura Mazda and human beings. Working together they can create something unpredictably beautiful, but human beings are likely to become destructive if they lack an overview of their connection and remain locked inside themselves.

Kiarostami explains that he uses the frequent device of placing his camera inside a car to reveal an intimacy that is more apparent than real:

> A moving car creates a sense of security for me personally. I imagine my voice getting lost among the noise of other cars. And these iron cells give me a sense of security [that] facilitates my inner dialogue. I insist on hearing my own voice in this dialogue. A person sitting next to someone else might not even pay attention to the other's presence. Each of them narrates his or her own inner world, . . . and this we owe to the confining cell that is the car.

The other confinement that Kiarostami hopes to break is the Hollywood formula for commercial success that preoccupies the brain so that spectators cannot think: These films try to "move them, reduce them to tears, laughter, and fear, [to] use every instrument at [their] disposal to captivate the audience. This is the secret behind the success of American cinema."

Then, paraphrasing the advice of an unnamed friend, he ironically adds, "American cinema has not become successful without good reason, and neither has America. If you want to be a successful filmmaker, I suggest that you never forget the formula of American cinema." At this point he stops the car and yanks the parking brake with a decisive sound, as if he were putting an abrupt end to abstract caution. It is time to escape the iron cells of urban distraction, addictive cinema, and the cult of the ego that confuses celebrity with creation.

After telling the viewers they can now stop looking at his "ugly yap," Kiarostami turns his back to the camera and says, "Now, take a look at some scenery, while I turn on the camera on the other side." Then he gets out and emphatically slams the door. In place of Kiarostami's profile, the film's predominant image, the view out the driver's window from the passenger side shows only trees rippling in the breeze, and in place of his voice, we hear only the wind and sea. After a moment we hear him say, "I'd like to show you something which reminds me of a Japanese haiku."

The camera now moves across the dashboard and out the open passenger door, as if the viewer were getting out. Then, below the passenger windows, it moves toward the back of the car, until it leaves the car altogether. The car's shadow remains to the right of a frame showing a sunlit dirt road with a grass border on the bottom and a tree on a hillside at the top. Finally, as the sound of Kiarostami's footsteps crunch on small stones, even the car's shadow disappears, giving way to a tall pine on a hill with a vista of land and sea behind it. Then the camera shifts to the right, keeping the tree but showing a jutting hill with two small trees, each subtle but significant camera shift comprehending more beauty. The camera returns to the road as Kiarostami begins to speak for the last time in the film: "The cedar tree atop the hill / On whom does it pride itself." The words suggest that the spirit of Creation makes no distinction between great and small.

Even in a world dominated by those confined to their iron cells, other human beings can foster a spirit of generous cooperation. The camera comes closer to the ground, where a small strip of dirt road lies just below the gray shadow of the car, which again covers most of the frame above. Kiarostami continues, "And something else: Light the fire, and I'll show you something." The camera moves down again, until an anthill appears in the center of the frame, just as Kiarostami says that the "something" that he will show will be "invisible if you don't wish to see it" and unheard "if you don't wish to listen to its breath." Now the camera moves to a close-up of the anthill opening, where ants are seen moving all around. But then a corncob carried by a single large ant enters the frame from the left. When it is almost at the hole, another ant emerges from inside and tries to help, but the big ant backs into the hole and pulls the corncob after it. A third ant on the outside gives it a final push.[11]

That is the story Kiarostami wished to tell by a fire that only the attuned spectator can light. The screen goes black with the white lettered words "Abbas Kiarostami," followed by cards (rather than rolling credits), each containing the name of a *Ten on Ten* crew member without naming their separate jobs. If we are to further the spirit of Creation in our collective life, everyone's contribution must count, and no God, leader, or celebrity can do it for us. This is especially true of our responsibility for the earth's environment, and the Zoroastrian legacy most evident in Kiarostami is the religion's emphasis on the supreme value of the physical world.

For the two thousand years of its ascendancy, Zoroastrian Persia framed this vision in a walled garden, a practice that has survived the Arabization of Iran's culture. A Persian proverb reads, "Whoever creates a garden becomes an ally of Light; no garden having ever emerged from the shadows."[12] The garden represents the unity of Creation that Ahriman seeks to divide. Human beings were created as the last and seventh creation to maintain the purity of the first six: sky, water, earth, plant, animal, and fire.

The rigor of this responsibility, microcosmically expressed in making the garden, was no easy task in the desertlike conditions present in most of Iran's interior. But it was worth the cooperative effort of many hands to instill the serene strength needed to resist the anxiety and anger Ahriman depends on. The garden's wall corresponds to Kiarostami's understanding that "we are not able to look at what we have in front of us unless it is inside a frame," and paradoxically, we need a frame to experience a spiritual essence that cannot be contained by sight and sound. And so the garden was a way of creating an enclosure that transcended all enclosures, a fairly clear analogy to a Kiarostami film. Inside the garden's "frame," sunlight, shade, and water nurture all kinds of shrubs, flowers, and trees, especially such evergreens as cedar and cypress, because they affirm the continuity of creation, while the garden as a whole represents the purpose of all human effort.

The other Zoroastrian frame derived from and coequal with the garden is that of the bijar (tree of life) carpet, which violates the Islamic ban on the graven image and which Kiarostami lovingly explores in a six-minute film originally called *Is There a Place to Approach* but retitled *Rug* on the 2010 *Shirin* DVD. The original title approximates the words on the black-and-white title card: "Where is the place to reach / And spread a rug to settle?" by Sohrab Sepehri, whose poem "Address" had inspired *Where Is the Friend's House?* Unlike that film, which depicts the Zoroastrian adversary through the grandfather and the window dealer, *Rug* is a vision of Sufi unity, but the primary image it uses to express its vision is rooted in a Zoroastrian reverence for nature. The film begins with the camera moving up over a green-and-gold rug with a tree in the center containing pale blue birds. Their chirping harmonizes with the voice of a woman reciting Sepehri's words: "Open your eyes to see the lover's beauty glowing everywhere. / Observing this vision makes you think / There is no other than He, the Creator."

Then the camera begins to move right to left along the top border, which has a stylized row of upright cone-shaped canopies in gray, gold, and blue, alternating with small, triangular green trees shaped like candle flames with open centers above an upright candlestick. Fire and trees are especially sacred in the Zoroastrian tradition, and each small tree has an identical one above it, resembling, perhaps the fravashi guardianship of each human person. When the camera reaches the left edge, it moves down to the bottom border, then right, and up again, completing a counterclockwise circuit.

As the camera moves, we see elaborate images of imaginatively shaped and fantastically colored birds and trees, while a male and female voice alternately read a love poem, first to each other and finally to all of Creation. Romantic love becomes spiritual love as we move from the female voice recalling how she and her lover "sat by a stream in absolute silence" and the male voice recalling how they sang "love songs by heart" to all the human and nonhuman beings that surrounded them: "The tree blossomed and the nightingales delighted. / The world got young and fresh / and lovers gathered with joy."

These lovers include the couple in the poem as well as the poet, the rug's weaver, and the filmmaker who love the source of their inspiration and the means they have found to express it. The poem's metaphysical theme comes through as the male voice describes a festival, where "The green grass was trampled / under joyous steps / when all Gnostics and illiterates started dancing together." The choice of Gnostics stems from their theologically elaborate separation of matter as evil from spirit as good, a dualism adopted in the third century CE by the Persian prophet Mani. His doctrine, often blurred in modern English by the commonplace "Manichean" to mean any form of dualism, altered the Zoroastrian fight to preserve the physical world, which is considered an absolute good, to the primordial struggle of ethereal spirits to free themselves from physical bodies, which are considered primarily bad.[13]

In opposition to any religious tradition that strives for "upward" purification, Kiarostami concludes *Rug* by moving the camera down into a celebration of physical nature and then back up, not to transcend it, but to convey the mystery of its source. After completing his overview by circling its borders, the camera descends to a tall tree at the center of the rug. It focuses for a moment on a large blue-and-gold bird and then moves to a fanciful green one with an eight-pronged crest and large tail stylized into nine gold circles. The images suggest the presence of spirit in matter by being simultaneously strange and familiar. Then the camera slowly moves down the surface of the rug and then back up, relishing each abstract pattern of green and gold and each embodied image of a branch, flower, or bird. As it does, a solo violin signals the approaching end with a melody that is both lyrical and piercing, an effect softly intensified by a drum that sounds like a heartbeat.

During the upward movement, the male voice repeats the verse spoken at the beginning by the female voice, where the romantic expands to the spiritual: "How good was that day / under the willow tree?" The woman continues, "Next to a stream, I was sitting with my heart. / We were singing love songs by heart. / We were singing love songs by heart, / and we were sitting in absolute silence." When the camera reaches the golden tree at the center, it pulls upward into space, exposing misty green branches outside the rug's borders. Some of them begin to sway in the breeze, implying in typical Kiarostami fashion that translating nature into art exists to return us to nature with a renewed sense of appreciation and love.

The camera rises until the rug appears suspended in space, but the swaying trees remain around and behind it. They are not transcended, and they do not disappear. White swirls around them lend a magical effect, as if winter snow were swirling above green summer grass. While the camera holds on this image, the music is replaced by the woman's voice: "Be happy and delightful, always." The screen slowly fades to black, and as if to praise universal rather than specific creation, there are no closing credits.

Rug progressively illuminates Sepehri's two lines on its title card—"Where is the place to reach / And spread a rug to settle?" By the end, the rug's weaver and Kiarostami's camera have shown that the place to settle is the natural world in the present life. Elena says that Sepehri's poem "Address," which ends with the line "Where is the house of the friend?" "subscribes [to] a tradition of mysticism, of remote Sufi inspiration."[14] *Rug* and *Roads of Kiarostami*, another short film that Kiarostami made about the same time, are both strongly influenced by Sepehri, Sufism, Taoism, and Buddhism.

Referring to Puya, the young son of the director in *And Life Goes On*, as the film's figure of wisdom, Kiarostami said, "In Eastern philosophy we believe that you need a guide before you set foot in unknown territory," and he repeatedly identified Sepehri as one of his own guides by quoting him in interviews and in his films. He also spoke of the need to see the world with "borrowed eyes," to take his viewers "outside the scene [they're] looking at, to see what is there and also what is not there."[15]

Using one of his prominent metaphors for getting "outside," Kiarostami gets out of his car at the end of *Ten on Ten* to train his camera on an anthill, which he says reminds him of a "Japanese haiku." What is "not there" in that scene is the authoritative voice. What is there is the merged movement of spirit in some of the earth's smallest creatures. Sepehri, who was also a major Iranian painter, anticipated Kiarostami in striving to express a spiritual presence, and while his poetry derives much of this presence from Sufism, much of his painting looks further east. He translated Japanese poetry in the mid-1950s, and in his introduction to a collection of these poems, as described by Houman Sarshar, Sepehri praises the Eastern perspective for its "connection with the organic laws of the cosmos [that were] overtly cultivated by the values and nuances of their ancient myths and pervading philosophies."[16]

In 1960 Sepehri learned woodblock printing in Tokyo from the renowned Unichi Hiratsuka (1895–1997), and for the next fifteen years, he produced a series of landscapes known in Iran as his Far Eastern phase. These paintings, in Sarshar's view, express the "primal unity of the cosmos" by abstracting natural phenomena: "That which is not painted thus reflects the imperceptible, indiscernible mystery of a unified universe; that which is painted, reflects the boundaries of our perception."[17] In one notable series, the "paintings depict clusters of tree trunks in tight closeups that leave branches and foliage out of the frame."[18]

Sarshar's summation applies as much to Kiarostami as it does to Sepehri: "In his vision of the world and of mankind's place within it, Sepehri believed above all in the importance of people's direct relationship with nature, [and he was] unwavering in his belief in a delicate yet essential unity between mankind, nature, and a greater cosmic order."[19] From Taoism he learned

> to believe in an essential oneness between mankind and nature, . . . to see nature as an undifferentiated consubstantial whole in which each constitutive part reflects the organic laws of the great cosmic order . . . [and] in Zen Buddhism he found the value of a constant and consistent meditative self-contemplation; of living in the here and now; of extracting simplicity from complex paradigms and expressing complex thoughts in the simplest, most economic fashion possible.[20]

These worldviews, in conjunction with Persian Sufism, which finds the "contemplation of subtle beauties of the natural world [to be an] ideal venue for arriving at a first-hand experience of the divine," contributed to Sepehri's mature belief "that while a higher unifying truth was innate in all of creation and the knowledge of it intuitively available to all mankind, a conclusive understanding of it was impossible in an individual's lifetime and the search for it a lifelong journey for all."[21]

The search in *Roads of Kiarostami* may not be spiritually conclusive, but undertaking it has become urgent in a way that Sepehri did not foresee. The film's slow, peaceful ascent on mountain roads ends with a shock that could be the end of the road for everything the camera lovingly shows. In an interview, Kiarostami distinguished his cinema from his photographs, which were exclusively "focused on the environment and nature," except for the previously described "walls and doors that show the effect and the impact of nature on human beings." He also spoke indirectly of the Eastern relationship between artist and subject: "In my photography I have tried to remove myself as a barrier between the audience and the subject" and to instill an empathy that would help to preserve the natural world he loved. Although it was difficult to think about, he feared "what will happen to nature when I leave this life." A friend tried to reassure him by reminding him of the coda to *Taste of Cherry*, which projects a "time [to] come when soldiers will have flowers in their hands as opposed to guns."[22]

Although Eastern philosophy and Sufism seek to merge the individual with the all, Kiarostami realized that to be a guide for others whose cultures do not encourage such union, he would need to alter their reality because art exists to break up existing realities and create new ones.[23] *Roads of Kiarostami* was produced by a South Korean environmental group for the Green Film Festival in Seoul, and it expresses a wisdom accumulated from Persian and Japanese poetry to address the nuclear threat in a way similar to that of Pope Francis in *Laudato Si*, his 2015 encyclical on global warming. Kiarostami's photographic and cinematic treatments of nature show that he shared the pope's view of art's purpose:

> The relationship between a good aesthetic education and the maintenance of a healthy environment cannot be overlooked. By learning to see and appreciate beauty, we learn to reject self-interested pragmatism. If someone has not learned to stop and admire something beautiful, we should not be surprised if he or she treats everything as an object to be used and abused without scruple. If we want to bring about deep change, we need to realize that certain mindsets really do influence our behavior. Our efforts at education will be inadequate and ineffectual unless we strive to promote a new way of thinking about human beings, life, society and our relationship with nature. Otherwise, the paradigm of consumerism will continue to advance, with the help of the media and the highly effective workings of the market.[24]

The mind-set that Kiarostami most hoped to change is how cultures envision God. His God is an artist rather than a king or a judge. Nature is seen as God's weaving in *Rug* and as God's poetry in *Roads*. The film includes poetic passages by Kiarostami and Sepehri that correspond to visual and musical elements working together in a synesthesia that transcends any single voice. Kiarostami takes his viewers on a trip to the mountains, where (as in *Ten on Ten*) getting out of the car at the end signifies escaping the viewer's cultural frame. The film moves from the aesthetic elaborations of Sepehri to a visual version of the haiku-like images that Kiarostami verbally employs in poetry.

At the lower levels, Kiarostami travels a well-paved road in the flat land, leaving people engaged in everyday work, a man with a herd of sheep and another with a bale of hay loaded on a donkey. The vistas are wide, and the andante movement of a classical horn concerto creates a contemplative mood, immersing the viewer in the scenery and the moment. After the first five minutes, he begins to speak, recalling how he initially turned to nature just to be peacefully alone, but "every so often I saw a view in exceptional light, and it was so beautiful that I couldn't bear to watch it alone. With a simple camera I recorded some of those moments so as to share an image of nature, as a sort of souvenir with friends who had no opportunity to experience it."

But as he recalls his past impulse to escape and the desire to help others do the same, the image changes from the stills of majestic fields and mountains in the distance to a brief video of a car winding up and down a dusty, zigzag road during the dry season, resembling the time and location of *Taste of Cherry*. In that film, the driver sees no escape but death, but here, the plural word *Roads* suggests a way out. In voiceover, Kiarostami speaks of the compelling power of the road to foster continual growth. He says that the "road has always been a favorite subject for poets and writers [and that it] appears frequently in classical Persian literature, contemporary poetry, and Japanese haiku. He says that for Sepehri, the road is "exile, wind, song, travel, and restlessness," and when he quotes one of Sepehri's poems, the image shifts back to a wide road heading toward the mountains. The poem yearns for origins, but its path begins without a destination: "I hesitate, standing at a fork in the road. / The only way I know is the way of return. / There is no one with me on this road."[25]

At this point the visual road becomes wide and white as it ascends and descends through dark surroundings. The music is still orchestral, but the solo horn takes the lead, corresponding to each seeker's solo search. Once again, we sense the need for departure when the image changes to an aerial shot of a summer landscape, where the details of trees and hills are too far below to be carefully observed. The immobility of the shot and the cessation of the music precede the narrator recalling a state of depression more explicit than that of Mr. Badii in *Taste of Cherry*: "From the first he had borne within him a great sorrow which made him flee the company of others and kept him shut away indoors. It had been so ever since a mourner had asked him, 'Which beautiful face does not end up buried in dust?'"

The "mourner" resembles Omar Khayyam, lamenting human insignificance in the face of death, and Kiarostami's narrator (perhaps personal, perhaps not) is left with a heart "cold at this world" that "neither books nor degrees" can comfort. Using words, the narrator searches for the right personal, road but all he initially finds are "crisscrossed lines on a page of dust like the lines of a child's game drawn on paper." These may be the prosaic markings of science and philosophy that cannot offer the emotional strength that varied forms of poetry might supply.

The video of the car ascending and descending the barren hills returns, but the horn concerto also softly begins as the narrator repeats Sepehri's search for origins in a unique synthesis of pictures, words, and music:

> And at last, when he beheld the path, he saw the tale of man: that man has one road in life, running from the end to the beginning, down which he is endlessly searching for meaning, and in this boundless existence, each has his own road, sometimes endless, winding, sometimes leading nowhere, sometimes a straight line, a path leading to a garden, the shade of a tree, a spring in rocky ground.

Kiarostami then verbally concludes the film's writing metaphor: "And man's road, however small, flows on the page of existence, sometimes without conclusion, sometimes victorious." In this film, the visual road to enlightenment leads up the mountain, not to a "higher" place in the sense of transcending the material body but to a place where the Creator's writing appears on a page of pure, white snow.

After the camera cuts from the video of the car traversing the dry, zigzag road to the film's narrative present, the ascending black road is surrounded by heavy snow. At a point where the road has narrowed to twin tire tracks, Kiarostami stops the car next to a lone dog sitting just outside the car window. The music stops, and the camera stays on the dog as we hear Kiarostami yank the brake and prepare his camera. The dog sits still just long enough for the picture. Then, having established rapport with a nonhuman form of life that many Muslims do not respect, Kiarostami emerges from the "iron cell" of his car onto a blank page of unmarred snow.

In the previously cited interview on his photography, he spoke of the way new-fallen snow produces a "uniquely pristine environment where you see no interference by human beings." Cinematic interference also ceases as the concerto yields to the sound of wind and the cawing of crows. But the camera is careful to include Kiarostami passing a narrow, barred gate just after he gets out of the car and starts to make his way uphill through the deep drifts.

He is dressed warmly, connoting the rigor of achieving this vision that begins with a large flock of crows cawing and circling before they land on the branching filaments of a small, black tree. For a moment they are indistinguishable from the tree, but as Kiarostami approaches, they leave in a cloud of motion only to immediately return as if they were a single being. The synchronized movement of the crows and their blending with the tree confers a Taoist sense of union, but successive shots of a lone crow standing on the snow and a very young colt moving away from the camera provide the metonymy of separate lives that characterizes haiku. Similar shots include a lone horse opposite a small, dense tree; a man on horseback leading another horse; and a small black-and-white dog sitting on the snow.

Just after the crow appears, a Japanese flute begins, providing a minimalist contrast to the concerto and the elaborate language of the preceding voice-over. Meaning is created by the shaping of distinctive forms on a unified ground, and when the marks are minimal, their absolute existence can be more clearly perceived as part of the ground rather than as isolated entities. In this penultimate scene, Kiarostami translates the verbal minimalism of poetry into visual lines of small trees on snow. The horizontal lines are like Persian or Western script, while the vertical lines resemble haiku or other forms of Chinese, Japanese, and Korean writing.

Some shots convey a spiritual presence by deliberately hiding part of the visible object, recalling Sepehri's paintings of tree trunks that leave branches and trees out of the frame to simultaneously show, as Houman Sarshar puts it, the "mystery of a unified universe" and the "boundaries of our perception."²⁶ Kiarostami achieves the effect with a shot of only the bottom of a small tree trunk centered in the frame and another shot of the stump of a huge tree jutting out of the ground, also centered in the frame. But the Ahriman that threatens this cosmic concert has developed an unprecedented power to destroy.

The final sequence begins with a shot of a lone dog on a ridge, with a row of gray trees at a distance behind him, followed by a closer shot of a different breed of dog trotting toward the left. Then a sudden close-up of one of the dogs freezes into a still photograph, abruptly changing the serene tone. The dog has an alert, possibly alarmed look, and he embodies all life on earth just before a sudden blast of color rocks the frame.

The nuclear explosion lasts for twenty seconds. The dog continues to look at us as an orange flame, moving from right to left, begins to consume the screen. A thin, white, vertical line flanked by orange stripes leads the encroaching darkness on the right while greenish smoke in what remains visible erases the last of the saplings growing in the snow. As the light on the left shrinks, a prayer appears on the expanding black screen at the right: "Dear Lord, / Give us the rain from tame, / Obedient clouds / And not from dense and fiery clouds / Which summon death." The prayer is concluded with an "Amen" and attributed to the *Nahjolbalagha*, a collection of sermons, letters, and narratives by Imam Ali, the son-in-law of Muhammad, a figure highly respected in all of Islam and particularly revered by Shias as second only to the prophet (see chapter 1).

But here, God may lack the omnipotence that would prevent humans from destroying his precious work. The screen continues to burn, erasing the verse, until ashes fall from the narrow edge of the photograph, now reduced to a few specks of white light. The last vestige of the collective art of God and man is the sound of crinkling paper, which lasts through the credits, until the whole screen goes black.²⁷

NOTES

1. On Zoroastrianism in general, see Jacques Duchesne-Guillemin, "Zoroastrianism," *Encyclopædia Britannica*, July 10, 2019, https://www.britannica.com/topic/Zoroastrianism; "Zoroastrianism," BBC, 2014, http://www.bbc.co.uk/religion/religions/zoroastrian/; and "Zoroastrianism," Wikipedia, updated January 6, 2020, https://en.wikipedia.org/wiki/Zoroastrianism. On Angra Mainyu, see "Angra Mainyu," Wikipedia, updated January 4, 2020, https://en.wikipedia.org/wiki/Angra_Mainyu.

2. Cahal Milmo, "Iraq Crisis: ISIS Video Calls on British Muslims to Join in Jihad as 'Cure for Depression,'" *Independent*, June 29, 2014, http://www.independent.co.uk/news/world/middle-east/iraq-crisis-isis-video-calls-on-british-muslims-to-join-in-jihad-as-cure-for-depression-9552937.html.

3. Hamid Dabashi, *The World of Persian Literary Humanism* (Cambridge, MA: Harvard University Press, 2012), 58.

4. Dabashi, *Persian Literary Humanism*, 83.

5. See L. H. Mills, trans., *Avesta: Yasna: Sacred Liturgy and Gathas/Hymns of Zarathushtra*, from *Sacred Books of the East*, ed. Max Muller, American ed. (1898; Oxford: Oxford University Press, 1879–1910), http://avesta.org/yasna/yasna.htm.

6. See "Faravahar," Wikipedia, updated January 5, 2020, https://en.wikipedia.org/wiki/Faravahar.

7. See "Fravashi," Wikipedia, updated December 24, 2019, https://en.wikipedia.org/wiki/Fravashi.

8. See A. J. Arberry, *Sufism: An Account of the Mystics of Islam* (1950; Abingdon, UK: Routledge, 2013), 60; Annemarie Schimmel, "Sufism," *Encyclopædia Britannica*, November 20, 2019, https://www.britannica.com/topic/Sufism/History; Idries Shah, *The Sufis* (Garden City, NY: Doubleday, 1964), 424–25, http://www.spiritual-teaching.org/rishi-sufi-teachings/ewExternalFiles/Idries%20Shah%20-%20The%20Sufis.pdf; and "Mansur Al-Hallaj," Wikipedia, updated January 8, 2020, https://en.wikipedia.org/wiki/Mansur_Al-Hallaj.

9. See Megan Specia, "Who Are Sufi Muslims and Why Do Some Extremists Hate Them?" *New York Times*, November 24, 2017, https://www.nytimes.com/2017/11/24/world/middleeast/sufi-muslim-explainer.html; and "Persecution of Sufis," Wikipedia, updated December 25, 2019, https://en.wikipedia.org/wiki/Persecution_of_Sufis.

10. Quoted in Shah, *Sufis*, 357.

11. *Ten on Ten*, special feature on *Ten*, directed by Abbas Kiarostami (2002; New York: Zeitgeist Films, 2004), DVD.

12. Quoted in Shahin Bekhradnia, "Zoroastrianism and the Environment," World Zoroastrian Organisation, http://www.rsesymposia.org/themedia/File/1151633341-Zoroastrianism.pdf.

13. See "Gnosticism," Wikipedia, updated January 1, 2020, https://en.wikipedia.org/wiki/Gnosticism; "Mani (prophet)," Wikipedia, updated December 26, 2019, https://en.wikipedia.org/wiki/Mani_(prophet); and "Manichaeism," Wikipedia, updated January 3, 2020, https://en.wikipedia.org/wiki/Manichaeism.

14. Kiarostami quoted by Alberto Elena, *The Cinema of Abbas Kiarostami*, trans. Belinda Coombes (London: SAQI Iran Heritage Foundation, 2005), 73.

15. Quoted in Alberto Elena, *The Cinema of Abbas Kiarostami*, trans. Belinda Coombes (London: SAQI Iran Heritage Foundation, 2005), 96.

16. Houman Sharsar, "Sepehri, Sohrab," *Encyclopaedia Iranica*, August 15, 2009, http://www.iranicaonline.org/articles/sepehri-sohrab.

17. Sharsar, "Sepehri, Sohrab."

18. Sharsar, "Sepehri, Sohrab."

19. Sharsar, "Sepehri, Sohrab."

20. Sharsar, "Sepehri, Sohrab."

21. Sharsar, "Sepehri, Sohrab."

22. Abbas Kiarostami, "Deep Focus: The Photography of Abbas Kiarostami," interview by H. G. Masters, 2013, *ArtAsiaPacific*, July 8, 2016, http://artasiapacific.com/Blog/DeepFocusThePhotographyOfAbbasKiarostami.

23. Mahmoud Reza Sani, *Men at Work: Cinematic Lessons from Abbas Kiarostami*, trans. Alireza Lalehfar, foreword by Jean-Claude Carrière (Los Angeles: Mhughes Press, 2013), 13.

24. Pope Francis, *Laudato Si*, May 24, 2015, http://w2.vatican.va/content/francesco/en/encyclicals/documents/papa-francesco_20150524_enciclicalaudato-si.html.

25. *Roads of Kiarostami* (2005), bonus feature on *Shirin*, directed by Abbas Kiarostami (2008; New York: Cinema Guild, 2010), DVD.

26. Sharsar, "Sepehri, Sohrab."

27. *Roads of Kiarostami* (2005), bonus feature on *Shirin*.

Chapter Four

War as Suicide

The explosion that ends *Roads of Kiarostami* is suicidal from a human perspective, but because it affects all life on earth, it is also terracidal. In *Taste of Cherry*, Kiarostami uses suicide as a metaphor of killing in any form, even the killing that occurs when people are insensible to benevolent aspects of nature long before this insensibility manifests itself in physical murder. Even if Mr. Badii, the film's protagonist, were not overtly bent on suicide, he would be this kind of killer. He spends most of the film driving through construction sites on the outskirts of Tehran, searching for someone to confirm his death by throwing stones into his self-dug grave and then filling it with earth if he fails to respond after having dispatched himself with an overdose of sleeping pills.

All these prospective accomplices try to talk him out of it, and no one, including the viewer, ever discovers why Badii wants to do himself in. He is an elegant, handsome man, wealthier and more privileged than anyone he sees, but at the same time, he gradually reveals himself to be a lugubrious, neurotic fool. His social elevation reflects on all societal leaders, and the implication after the inconclusive eight-year Iran-Iraq War is that most people who support such leaders would never do so if they could see how crazy they are.

The insanity of the situation and the metaphorical meaning of suicide as killing in general is especially evident in the film's longest conversations: the first with a young soldier who consents to killing opposing soldiers because he needs the money to send back to his family and the second with an old taxidermist who kills and stuffs birds because he needs the money to care for a sick child. The soldier is horrified by Badii's request and runs away, and the taxidermist agrees (perhaps just to put Badii off) after making a long, sincere attempt to dissuade him. It is the taxidermist who tells Badii how he tasted some mulberries on the tree he was about to hang himself from and their sweetness changed his mind. This is the overt meaning of the title, *Taste of Cherry*, but Badii's sarcastic response, meant to reflect that of many viewers, suggests that Kiarostami wants to make his whole film bear out the meaning of the title by being an experience rather than a platitude.

Even the wisest of contextual critics, such as Alberto Elena and Godfrey Cheshire, speculate that Kiarostami made a film about suicide out of personal despair. Others think that he seriously wanted to consider the religious objection to suicide as a sin, but few have considered suicide as a metaphor of humanity's murder of its own experience through war (a major presence in the film) or insensibility to what the doctor in *The Wind Will Carry Us* calls the "generosity of God." Elena thinks the film evinces "profound despair" despite Kiarostami's "enigmatic statement that *Taste of Cherry* is 'a hymn in praise of life.'"[1] A similar hymn concludes *Homework*, but to read *Taste of Cherry* as a cinematic hymn, the viewer has to look past the main character and the rudimentary plot to the myriad details observed in passing—the children, the cheerful workmen, the light, the trees, the birds—in the same way that one savors the language of a poem rather than rushing to find out how it ends.

Roger Ebert in an oft-cited review thought *Taste of Cherry* did not deserve the 1997 Palme d'Or because it has no real story, only a cliché moral propounded by an old man who tries to talk the protagonist out of suicide: "He makes a speech on Mother Earth and her provisions, and asks Badii, 'Can you do without the taste of cherries?' That, is essentially, the story [that] Kiarostami tells in a monotone."[2] Looked at as a poem, *Taste of Cherry* does not express its meaning in a single line. Rather, the "taste of cherry" is present throughout the film, if the viewer reads it in the tradition of the mystical poetry that Kiarostami found "at the heart of Persian culture."[3]

Death is the absence of everything the "man of life" (as Makhmalbaf called him) celebrates throughout his oeuvre. He hinted obliquely that suicide was not to be taken literally when he said, "We could have just talked about death and left out the idea of suicide." And when asked why he included a long blackout after Mr. Badii lies in his self-dug grave, just before the controversial coda that shows the actor who played him and Kiarostami with his crew relaxing in the sun along with soldiers who have stopped drilling for war, the director explained, "I didn't want to show the person actually experiencing the tortures of the process although that would have been the easiest for me to show, with the actor tormenting himself in preparation for death, so I took out the voice and the light as that is the deeper way of thinking about nothingness and death."[4] To overstate the point, if one does not read life as slowly and lovingly as one reads a poem, one might as well be dead.

Badii is already dead in this sense when the film begins. His method of death—sleep and then burial—corresponds to the state of his soul long before he stops breathing. This would be bad enough if it only affected a frustrated individual, but Badii also insists on recruiting others to help him kill, and these others have become inured to forms of legitimized killing through cultural conditioning rather than natural inclination. There is a scene about three-quarters of the way through the film that illuminates this idea and that helps us to see how the film builds to this point from the beginning.

Badii has rushed back to the museum to find the taxidermist because he has second thoughts about wanting Bagheri to make doubly sure he is really dead before he buries him. When he asks the ticket taker where to find him, his description makes it sound as if the name, Bagheri, were an English pun (as the name *Badii* may also be): "He had a bag full of quails for the students. To stuff them." The camera then cuts to the laboratory, where bird sounds, heard at key points throughout the film, mingle with the voices of children who, like the soldiers, are there to learn to kill.

Badii is then shown desperately pacing back and forth outside the window. He is a dark figure, almost a silhouette, against a sepia background, where the colors of the buildings and foliage outside have vanished. Removing the "voice and the light" as the "deeper way to think about nothingness and death" parallels the voiceover of a gruff, old man teaching little girls how not to revere life. First, the teacher voices a distinction as irrelevant as that between Iranian and Iraqi young men: "More partridges! We were supposed to study quails!" Bagheri's response refers us back to Badii's eagle-eyed search for an accomplice at the beginning: "Birds don't fall into the net to make you happy." And the clue is reinforced by a shot of Badii, a black figure of death, motioning comically for Bagheri, a fellow purveyor of death, to come outside.

Then, in an oblique allusion to earlier shots of soldiers doing double-time marches, Bagheri desensitizes children in a gruesomely explicit way. Just as Badii has explained his technique of covering up a murder, Bagheri explains his technique of scientifically excusing one: "First, you have to lay them on their backs and wet the thorax feathers with a sponge. Then slit them open with a scalpel along the whole length of the body. Don't cut too deeply, or the innards will spill out." Earlier, Bagheri qualified his agreement to help Badii kill by saying, "If it wasn't for my child, I wouldn't."

Here, he is teaching other children that it is acceptable to kill the nonhuman life around them, and he voices a perfunctory remorse in an ironically comic exchange when, wearing his lab coat as the equivalent of a military uniform, he joins Badii outside: "That white coat suits you."—"Thank you."—"What were you doing? What birds have you handed out?"—"Quails."—"Did you kill them?"—"Yes, for work."—"You're well then." The idea that is it is "well" to kill and to teach children to kill (a lesson

Homework exposes) is ironically underlined because the object of killing can be anything or anybody: The taxidermist says he killed quails when the teacher made an issue of wanting partridges.

The film means to portray the essence of "bad" people, especially those who devastate living things to gratify their egos by recruiting children with the currency of money or martyrdom. Before the pretitle sequence, a single card appears with the subtitled words "In the Name of God." To a non-Muslim, these words may appear to be ironic: Terrible things are done in the name of God. But they are also a clue to why Kiarostami called *Taste of Cherry* a "hymn in praise of life." Each surah (chapter) but one of the Koran begins with the phrase "In the Name of God, the merciful, the compassionate," and the second line of the first surah praises Allah as the "Cherisher and Sustainer of the worlds."[5]

In this sense the opening line may be an appeal to preserve the world from the terracidal death that ends *Roads of Kiarostami*. An additional perspective may be gained from the Rumi poem "Bismillah," which means "In the name of God" and which is the word spoken just before the ceremonial sacrifice of an animal. The poet urges readers to "bismillah" their old selves to discover their "real name."[6] Kiarostami essentially said the same thing in an interview at the 2000 San Francisco Film Festival: "In my opinion, cinema and all the other arts ought to be able to destroy the mind of their audience in order to reject the old values and make it susceptible to new values. We need to rinse our eyes and view everything in a different light."[7]

In the same interview, he distinguished his own Sufi perspective from that of orthodox Islam: "Religion points to another world, whereas art points to a better existence. One is an invitation, an offering to a faraway place, the other to a place that is close."[8] Though the destination differs, Kiarostami shares the protective impulse that religious leaders attribute to God and assume for themselves. In *Ten on Ten* (2004), he rejects the use of mood-heightening music and surround sound because they tend to make the director omnipotent and the viewers helpless: "In a dark theater, the viewer becomes an innocent child. Light and darkness are magical. Captivating the viewer robs him of his reason, which is worse than emptying his pockets. Sometimes directors try to make up for boring parts with music or say about music, 'We're going to kill them here.'"[9] In *Taste of Cherry*, he uses music only in the coda to alert viewers that the film is about to end and to comfort rather than overwhelm their feelings, which would have been a way of stifling their souls.

The metaphor of suicide as killing in general comes across in spoken dialogue when Badii tries to persuade an Afghan seminarian to further his plan: His arguments have a special resonance in light of the contradiction between "Thou shalt not kill" and the clerical sophistry that sanctions war: "I'm lucky that those hands belong to a true believer. With the patience, endurance, and perseverance that you learn, you're the best person to carry out this job. . . . I follow the Koran when it says that this work will bring you not only Heaven's reward but also a material reward, so you won't need to work [as a laborer] this summer." But the young man who is a gentle soul replies, "Since the Hadiths [commentaries on the Koran], our twelve imams refer to suicide and say that man mustn't kill himself. God entrusts man's body to him. Man must not torment that body The Koran says, 'You shall not kill yourself.' What's the difference between killing someone and killing yourself? Killing yourself is killing."

A similar point about war is made when Badii asks the seminarian's Afghan friend, a construction site watchman, why the one million Afghan war refugees didn't return to their own country when Iran entered its own devastating war: "With the war here, why didn't they go back?"—"The war against Iraq only concerned the Iranians. But the war at home concerned us."—"And our war didn't concern you?"—"You could say your war troubled us, but the Afghanistan War was harder, more painful for us." It's an honest answer, but though Kiarostami does not convey the pain of war directly as Makhmalbaf does in *Marriage of the Blessed* (1989), he does express a sense of its major cause. He knows that religious injunctions have never worked. Practical killers like Badii run governments, and they always find a reason to respond as he does to the seminarian or as men of the world respond to calls for disarmament or environmental protection: "If I had wanted a lecture, I'd have turned to someone with more experience."

Practical minds are not deterred by abstractions, and Kiarostami uses all the resources of cinema to reverse the acceptance of killing that many cultures still sanction. The only form of killing he approves is the Nietzschean destruction of old values through the medium of art. But in *Ten on Ten*, his allusion to Nietzsche indicates that this mental violence must be perpetrated gently and with a subtlety that will enable viewers to think and grow: "Nietzsche said that which is truly deep needs a mask." In various interviews Kiarostami hinted that he chose suicide as a subject for a spiritual purpose. Even though suicide is forbidden in Islam, the scene at the end "opened the door to heaven" and showed that Badii had made a "heavenly transition."[10] That transition would implicitly involve moving beyond egotistic obsession to a heartfelt appreciation of the beauty life offers: "This film tries to express that if you don't have the time for living, the exit is always there. And God created man to have two options, one of them is suicide, the other one I'm not going to explain."[11]

The religious belief that Kiarostami refuses to explain appears at the end of *Homework*, where the boy who is generally afraid of his religion class flawlessly recites a paean of gratitude to the Creator: "Thou who created the moon and the sun, all the mountains, hills, and oceans, the beautiful and colorful trees, beautiful wings for the butterfly, nests for the birds, happiness, games, strength, eyes for us to see, snow and rain, heat and cold. We're all created by you, oh Lord. You granted all I wished for. Fill our hearts with happiness and joy" (see chapter 1). This is a freely given blessing, Kiarostami said, which people have the option to ignore: *Taste of Cherry* is "about the possibility of living, and how we have the choice to live. Life isn't forced on us. That's the main theme of the movie."[12]

Verse 22 of the second surah of the Koran reserves supreme respect for the Creator rather than those who presume to speak for Him: "He who made the earth a habitat for you, and the sky a structure, and sends water down from the sky, and brings out fruits thereby, as a sustenance for you. Therefore, do not assign rivals to God while you know." And though blasphemy in Islam is generally considered to be disbelief in God, doomsday, and the infallibility of Muhammad, Kiarostami would seem to be in particular agreement with a meaning cited in an article by two professors at Central Tehran University: "The word blasphemy [alludes to] ignoring the blessings received by humans [in the sense of] 'ingratitude' and 'non-thankfulness.'"[13]

In one of the taxidermist's dissuasions, Kiarostami links physical martyrdom on a personal or national scale to ingratitude: "No mother can do as much for her children as God does for His creatures. You want to refuse all that? You want to give it all up? You want to give up the taste of cherries?" And the song he sings before he gets out at the museum alludes to the constant love of the Sufi Friend: "My love, I'm flying off, come to me. I'm hounded from my friend's garden, come to me. From happy days before I've fallen on hard times, come to me. Tell me, we barely know each other. You go, I'm your friend. You stay, I'm your friend. In any case, I'm your friend." But these are still just words. People who love poetry can justify killing, and when Badii insists on reassurance, the taxidermist's answer poses the problem: "In any case, you'll do it?"—"If it wasn't for my child, I wouldn't."

What, then, can an artist do to unequivocally reject killing? People have not proved able to "change [their] outlook," as the taxidermist urges, by hearing wisdom pronounced in direct advice or even eloquent poetry. Perhaps cinema, with its wide sensorium, can probe more deeply. As Kiarostami told his students in the 2012 Spanish seminar, "Art and philosophy are not there so you can prove existence. They are here to break up reality and express newer ones which are not forms but norms," and even though story is "essential in times like these," the viewer must be coaxed into reading a film as he would a poem rather than passively waiting for dramatic events.[14]

Through encouraging full attention, Kiarostami may have hoped to create an identification with the whole of existence rather than a particular person, faith, or country: "The very last episode [of *Taste of Cherry*] reminds me of the continuation of life, that life goes on . . . even without Mr. Badii." People who commit suicide might think they are revenging themselves on society, nature, or the powers that be, but they "don't realize that after a suicide [or a war] life still goes on and things stay the way they are."[15]

Figure 4.1. Mr. Bagheri is an assuring and disturbing "friend." Like the soldier who kills to support his family, the taxidermist agrees to bury Badii as efficiently as he bags birds. Zeitgeist Films/Photofest.

Some viewers think the ending of *Taste of Cherry* radically departs from what precedes, but looked at carefully, it bears out Kiarostami's belief that films should begin and end with an image that tells the story.[16] *Taste of Cherry*'s eleven-minute precredit sequence opens with a passenger-seat view of Mr. Badii as he prowls a gathering spot for day laborers soliciting work. The work he wants to offer is not the type they seek, but if the film's last scene depicts war's cessation, then the opening depicts the economic incentive leaders offer humble people ostensibly to prevent but actually to hasten their common mortality. These workers just want to live, while Badii, for a deliberately unspecified reason, just wants to die. Set apart from the desperate people who surround him, the elegant man in his automobile is the archetypal aristocrat on horseback. The workers entreat him as if he were royalty, and what sets him apart from them is that while everywhere in the construction area people are busy preparing for the physical future, Badii scorns mere physicality in an insane quest for transcendence.

Badii is oblivious to the gifts Kiarostami offers the attentive viewer. Though the scene does not show the lush, green countryside of *And Life Goes On* or *Through the Olive Trees*, the golden hills outside the window are tinged with violet light, and the soundtrack carefully includes the calls of birds and the shouts of children. After passing unlaid sewer pipes, connoting discarded life, he passes the hollowed shell of a junked car, where two delighted children of about six or seven tell him they are "playing cars." They smile at him, but he doesn't smile back, and he derives no joy from the journey they eagerly imitate. They are too young to offer practical assistance, but snippets of a phone booth conversation in which a man complains of money problems bring an intent look to Badii's eyes, as if he were a hawk spotting a rabbit.

He summons the man to his car window, but after he offers money, the man thinks he is making a sexual advance and threatens to slug him. The irony here is that while homosexuality may be feared in Iran and the right-wing West, the real danger that Badii represents is the power of the nation-state to advance perverse ideals by offering minimal pay to its poorest people, as in the United States, where a large number of combat soldiers are drawn from the urban and rural poor.

When Badii asks the next man he encounters what he is doing, the man replies, "I pick up plastic bags and liquidate them near the factory," an interesting choice of words because Badii is also engaged in liquidation, which is shown to be more than an Iranian problem when the man's bright

Figure 4.2. Like a nation needing soldiers to fight its wars, Mr. Badii seeks recruits penurious enough to kill for money and sufficiently devoted to family, nation, or religion to capably follow orders. Zeitgeist Films/Photofest.

orange sweatshirt reveals the blue-and-white letters *UCLA*. Badii calls attention to the shirt by asking the man where he got it and if he knows what the letters mean, and the man, who is probably illiterate, answers the first question by saying he found it "near the factory" and the second with silence. He is shy, young, and handsome, with light-colored hair, and when Badii asks where he is from, he smiles and answers, "Lorestan. Are you from Lorestan, too?" Badii replies, "You could say that," overtly because it might persuade the man to collaborate and symbolically because Badii is from everywhere.

The shirt's surprising letters may be a way of universalizing the social condition that having Louis Armstrong play "St. James Infirmary" in the coda more obviously suggests. Lorestan is a beautiful region of western Iran, with mountains comparable to the Colorado Rockies and aboriginally inhabited by the Lurs, a nation of tribal herdsman who speak neither an Indo-European nor a Semitic language. Like impoverished Native Americans who temporarily leave their reservations to eke out small sums in urban centers, the man from Lorestan is not susceptible to Badii's first line of seduction—"Don't you want [money] to get married?"—because he only wants money to send home to his family. And the Native American analogy might be enhanced if we consider that the Lurs adhered to the Ahl-e-Haqq faith (which reveres fire, like the Zoroastrians) and that they were forcibly converted to Islam in 1936, when Reza Shah's army conquered them and using bloodshed and starvation forced the survivors to settle in villages under landlords.[17]

The man shows a flash of anger when some children in a passing car shout, "Pissy, pissy, your dick's all sticky," but Badii, in the manner of all military recruitment, attempts to turn phallic rage and social frustration into a useful weapon: "Don't mind them. They're playing." Badii, of course, is not playing, but when he pops the question, "Would you do something for me?" the man is seen shouldering his heavy bag for a moment before he leaves the frame of the driver-side window. After we hear Badii call, "Where are you going?" the camera abruptly cuts to the title, *Taste of Cherry*, in bright-red letters on a black screen.

In sharp contrast to the soft mauve and gold colors of the opening sequence, the red-and-black title card announces Badii's murderous purpose with colors traditionally associated with evil in Christianity and Islam. In the same way that Satan's wounded ego displaced Adam and Eve from Eden, societal "kings" and their religious cronies have displaced civilized people from their common home. The film makes this point in part by having the universally alienated Badii converse with specific displaced people: Besides the man from Lorestan, the seminarian and the watchman are Afghans, the taxidermist sings the "Friend" song in Turkish, and the young soldier with whom Badii spends the most time is from Kurdistan. The soldier is a recent draftee, still in training and typical cannon fodder for the powers that be. Shortly after Badii picks him up, promising to drive him the rest of the way to his barracks, the young man's poverty becomes apparent. He has just walked eleven miles from Darabad, where he stays during off time with an aunt because even though he has two brothers in Tehran, they have children, and their houses are too small. At home he is a farmer, and when Badii asks him why he has not pursued more education, he diffidently declines to answer.

Before Badii gets to the point of directly asking the soldier to wake or bury him, he begins what he takes to be an ingratiating conversation about military service with a thematically resonant line: "We've got an hour to kill before you're due back. How about a drive?" But to drive with Badii at the wheel means to do the bidding of societal leaders who use a superior vocabulary to double-talk young men into becoming their weapons: "You say the barracks aren't much fun? I had fun when I did my military service. It was the best time of my life. I met my closest friends there, especially in the first six months. I remember we used to get up at four in the morning, shine boots, and go out on maneuvers."

The detail that the first months of training were the best hints at the actual killing that followed on a grand scale for trained and untrained soldiers in the recent war, and the young man's face has an "Are you kidding?" look when Badii fondly recalls his major initiating the count and then insists that his passenger join him as he counts "one-two-three-four" in a voice that sounds like hissing. The soldier remains silent when Badii tries to compel compliance, first by saying, "Don't you think of me as a friend?" and then by forcefully ordering him to count as if he were an actual major.

Understandably, the soldier suspects that Badii is crazy and asks what he wants. The reply satirizes social arguments for bowing to authority when it orders war: "For someone like you, it's the pay that matters. A job is a job. Does a laborer ask if the foundations he digs are for a hospital, a lunatic asylum, or a mosque, or a school? No, he just wants his pay." The equation of lunatic asylum, mosque, and school suggests that Badii's malaise is metaphorically general and that soldiers are not the only ones duped into following orders. When the car stops for a moment, the soldier makes a move to leave, but Badii immediately accelerates as if to say that while he is driving, there is no way out.

After berating his passenger for eleven minutes, it is Badii who steps out of the car to show the soldier the hole he has dug for himself and that the soldier is supposed to fill with dirt. Behind him, the golden hills and violet sky epitomize the beauty Badii imperviously wants to black out, and the twittering quail carefully edited into the soundtrack evoke the resemblance between Badii, the taxidermist, and a nationalist ethic that transforms living things into political and economic tools.

Badii thinks that if he finds people who are needy and minimally intelligent enough, they will do whatever he wants as long as he pays them. Large numbers of people in many countries have been made to believe they should sacrifice their lives to causes their leaders deem right. A Kurd in particular, Badii says, should take killing for granted, but then what nation on earth, Kiarostami implies, does not make its wars the major milestones of its history? What Badii says of one particular people is true of all: "A Kurd has to be brave. You people have fought so many wars, known such suffering. . . . Your villages have been decimated. You probably used a gun, right? Know what a gun is? Why, you're given one, so you can kill when you need to."

The irony here is that soldiers everywhere accept guns to kill other soldiers but at the same time do not see the connection between patriotic wars and collective suicide. The soldier in training accepts killing others as a duty but is revolted at the immediate physicality of Badii's request. When Badii stops at the gravesite and gets out to show the soldier what he must do, the soldier refuses to leave the car, saying he is not a gravedigger and could never throw dirt down on top of people. This prompts Badii to try two predicable ploys: "You're like my son," and "It's God's will that I should need you." When he emphatically repeats "You won't bury me alive!" Kiarostami is saying that by hardening people to accept killing and by raising children to be insensible to the natural world, cultures bury people alive, even when they don't shed their blood in war.

One particular argument transparently epitomizes the Zoroastrian clash between creation and destruction. After Badii rhetorically begins, "You're a farmer, right?" there is a long pause with only the sound of quail to emphasize the distinction between stewards and destroyers of the land. A reverse shot to the soldier still sitting in the car sends an urgent message—Get out of there before the pilot of your ship "wastes" you in service to a sterile cause: "Just pretend you're farming and that I'm manure to be spread at the foot of a tree. Is that hard?" The dialogue proceeds: "You can't throw dirt in a hole?"—"Yes, but not on top of someone, not on someone's head." Most of the frame above the window where the soldier sits is black in contrast to the gold earth outside and the gold of his shirt and cap. It is the soldier, not Badii, who is unwittingly threatened with burial, physically in actual war and internally for accepting its necessity.

Listening to Badii's harangue, the soldier is like the children witnessing Bagheri slitting open the birds. And so, on a thematic level, the soldier and some viewers instinctively know what to do when Badii concludes, "Do you understand now?" The sound of the quail Bagheri has not yet caught continues as Badii walks up the embankment to the car, but as soon as he starts the engine, a quick cut shows the soldier bolting out the passenger door. Like Ahmad in *Where Is the Friend's House?* the soldier intuitively recognizes danger's location, though Kiarostami leaves any conscious realization to his viewers. As the previously quoted Kiarostami haiku reads, "One hundred obedient soldiers / entering the barracks. / Moonlit night. / Disobedient dreams" (see chapter 1).

The soldier runs straight down the hill, shortcutting the zigzag path as the viewer might do before it is too late. Frustrated and angry, Badii gets out of the car to call him back, but the bird has flown the coop. He is already far away, a small figure heading toward an isolated green tree, a symbol for Kiarostami of the nature and life that survives communal disasters in *And Life Goes On* and *Where Is the Friend's House?* A shot of Badii looking up at a cawing crow is followed by a vista of golden hills and pink skies evenly distributed in the frame. Then, as the sound of quail resumes, a wide shot out the driver's side glimpses distant soldiers double-timing to the pile-driver count that Badii had fondly recalled. Beyond the hills, cement factories and construction sites dot the landscape, spreading black shadows near the soldiers. In the same shot, the shadows are surrounded by the larger area of pink and gold, foreshadowing the end of the film, when the black shadow seems to triumph just before the epilogue, where nature and art bring back the light.

A few comic instances suggest that Badii's death wish is the result of social experience rather than a killer instinct. When the seminarian invites him to share the watchman's omelet, the man bent on suicide demurs because "eggs are bad for me," and when he climbs down from the watchtower, he complains that the ladder moves and that it should be fixed with tape. After dropping the taxidermist at the museum, Badii returns to make sure no one makes a fatal mistake: "Bring two small stones. Throw them at me. I might still be alive," to which Bagheri wryly replies, "Two stones aren't enough. I'll use three," and when Badii anxiously persists, "Shake my shoulders, too! You promised me," Bagheri seems to be humoring an obsessed person he never really intended to help: "Even if they behead me, I'll keep my word." The allusion to a horrifically actual form of killing isn't funny, and after the annoyed Bagheri returns to work, Badii is shown nervously rubbing his hands together and then looking up at the exhaust trails of two fighter jets streaking above the city.

The camera cuts to a shot of children running in a physical education class far down the hill from where Badii sits, an embryonic form of the regimentation that drives the marching soldiers and that Badii briefly tries to escape when he is shown uncharacteristically running back to the museum. For a brief time, he seems to feel an impulse to live that unspecified social conditioning has repressed. In that sense, Iran induced young men to become mindless martyrs in the Iraq War, and the U.S. military tried to train draftees to be walking weapons in Vietnam. A brief close-up of a huge, metal tower with crisscrossed diagonal bars suggests the mechanical spirit of societies with little regard for the future of their children.

But Kiarostami's last two scenes make *Taste of Cherry* a tale of life-affirming escape. In a night scene on the hills high above the city, lightning illuminates an isolated golden tree next to the steep, winding road. Distant thunder continues, and the light around the tree grows as Badii approaches, carrying a small suitcase. As in *Where Is the Friend's House?* and *ABC Africa*, thunder and lightning signal a dramatic change, but at the same time, the sound of twittering quail represents a continuity that human folly (so far) has not snuffed out. Despite his promise to the soldier and presumably the taxidermist to leave money in his car, Badii has taken a taxi to his grave, and he sits on a hill, watching the sky as we see the taxi's lights diminish until it disappears far down the hill. When he stands up, he is a wearing a short, light-gray jacket democratically common in Iran instead of his elegant, dark shirt, an equalizing sign, perhaps, of the human community he ignores.

The barking of a distant dog symbolizes life's continuity as we see a close-up of Badii's face in the narrow pit surrounded by stony dirt. The panorama of stars and city lights is gone, and Badii can only stare at an earth denying mirror of his own darkness. But after a moment, he can see the moonlight illuminating a small area of clouds that move from left to right while the moon itself remains stationary, a beacon of constancy in the midst of change. Then, the screen goes completely black for a seeming eternity of screen time, but though death prevails in the visual darkness, the sounds of birds and rain unceasingly remain.

After fifty-seven seconds, a military cadence enters the soundtrack as if soldiers are approaching from far away. Seven seconds later, the black screen suddenly becomes a wide shot of the hills and the road, but now, there is bright greenery at the top and bottom of the frame. A sudden cut shows a cameraman carrying a digital camera, walking over to another crew member holding a piece of equipment. We cannot hear what they are saying, but the soldiers' voices are very loud now. The brightness and color spectrum of the scene and the soldiers' voices do not interrupt the poetic continuity that has shifted to a major key.

The actor who plays Badii walks across the screen from right to left, but now he is wearing a light-pink shirt and gold pants, the colors of the landscape he was oblivious to when he was in character. It is as if he fills out human potentiality by embodying its other half. Having played an agent of Ahriman, he has become a fravashi of Ahura Mazda by taking part in a film that means to protect rather than destroy. His character's alienation is replaced by partnership when he reaches three crew members, one of whom takes a puff of his offered cigarette. The nightmare of seeking accomplices is over. Instead, the filmmakers and viewers can share a moment of simply being alive in a beautiful setting.

No life-or-death anxiety remains; no future needs to be feared or sought. A close-up of a blue-clad crew member has him kneeling in grass, covered with silver weeds, next to a yellow flowering bush that almost hides him. Comprehending large and small, the camera then cuts to a wide shot of green trees separated by a blue waterway, with purple mountains under a line of pink sky. The tranquility is balanced by the military cadence, which is now very close and very loud. But because it is Kiarostami's film, his voice halts their suicidal plan: "Can you hear me? Tell your men to stay near the river to rest. The shoot is over."

His next line, "We're here for a sound take," cues the film's only piece of music, the quintessentially American "St. James Infirmary" from the 1928 recording by Louis Armstrong. For its origin alone, it would be considered cultural pollution by ultraconservative imams, and this may be one reason why Kiarostami, an internationalist and fervent opponent of war, placed it movingly at the end. The remaining visual images also illustrate humanity's responsibility to preserve the spiritual gift of the physical world. The camera moves to the right past green and silver foliage swaying in the wind. Soldiers in tan and gray shirts are then shown sitting on bright-green grass.

As the camera continues to move, one soldier turns and smiles. Then, the camera moves back the other way, showing the same soldier still smiling and holding a large, flowering weed. The image continues a Kiarostami motif of using flowers to represent the cosmic gift that viewers should take from a film. Other notable examples are the door maker's flower in Ahmad's book at the end of *Where Is the Friend's House?* and two instances in *Close-Up*: near the beginning, when the fighter-pilot-turned-cab-driver picks flowers from a garbage pile, and at the end, when the real Makhmalbaf has Sabzian present the Ahankhah family with a bouquet of roses as if to say that art should offer something beautiful and have nothing to do with celebrity or rank.

The camera suddenly moves back to two more soldiers sitting further up the slope. Others are shown on their way up to join the group. In a break from preparing to kill, they become like children, free of their social and political function. Identity with the natural world is shown in a brief cut to a lone soldier almost hidden by the tall grass that surrounds him. The color of his shirt matches the silver weeds so that he blends into the landscape, a part of nature rather than a tool of transcending or defeating it. The camera cuts back to the soldier holding the silver weed, now next to another holding a weed that a third soldier playfully tries to take from him. In the next shot, the setting takes precedence. As two soldiers walk up the steep hill toward the camera, the wide shot encompasses green grass in the foreground, green-and-tan fields in the distance under purple mountains, and blue sky at the top of the frame.

Now, the camera cuts back to the film crew sitting as the soldiers were, just resting on the green hill. The shot connects the crew, the soldiers, and the viewers, no longer socially driven and temporarily freed from the traces of their daily drills. In a final shot, green hills are divided by a road, but here, burgeoning summer supplants the autumn landscape that Badii traveled. A car in the center of the frame moves away from us until it disappears around a curve, at which point the screen goes black. Only traffic sounds accompanied the crimson letters on the opening card, but at the end, Armstrong's slow, stately trumpet creates a calm and lovely mood as the pale-green credits roll.

NOTES

1. Alberto Elena, *The Cinema of Abbas Kiarostami*, trans. Belinda Coombes (London: SAQI Iran Heritage Foundation, 2005), 131.
2. Roger Ebert, review of *Taste of Cherry* by Abbas Kiarostami, RogerEbert.com, February 27, 1998, https://www.rogerebert.com/reviews/taste-of-cherry-1998.
3. Quoted in Elena, *Cinema of Abbas Kiarostami*, 186.
4. Abbas Kiarostami, "In Dialogue with Kiarostami," interview by Ali Akbar Mahdi, *Iranian*, August 25, 1998, https://asianart.fandom.com/wiki/Interviews_with_Abbas_Kiarostami.
5. Surah 1, "The Opening," Holy Qur'an, trans. Abdullah Yusuf Ali, Wright House, March 14, 2005, http://www.wright-house.com/religions/islam/Quran/1-opening.php; see also "The Opening Chapter of the Holy Quran," Islam 101, 2006, http://www.islam101.com/dawah/prayer.html.
6. Jelaluddin Rumi, *The Essential Rumi*, trans. Coleman Barks, with John Moyne, A. J. Arberry, and Keynold Nicholson (San Francisco: HarperCollins, 1995), 70.
7. Quoted in Elena, *Cinema of Abbas Kiarostami*, 192.
8. Quoted in Elena, *Cinema of Abbas Kiarostami*, 193.
9. *Ten on Ten*, special feature on *Ten*, directed by Abbas Kiarostami (2002; New York: Zeitgeist Films, 2004), DVD.
10. Kiarostami, "In Dialogue."
11. "Conversación: Abbas Kiarostami," interview by Geoff Andrew, Morelia Film Festival, posted by FICM, November 12, 2012, video, 1:42:30, https://www.youtube.com/watch?v=ZEC0KGULtaE.
12. Kiarostami, "In Dialogue."
13. Seddigheh Nasiroghli Khiaban and Mojgan Ansari Mahabadian, "An Analysis of the Foundations of Blasphemy with a Focus on the 31st Saying of the Nahj al-Balagha," *International Journal of Humanities and Cultural Studies* 2, no. 4 (March 2016): 1706–18, www.ijhcs.com/index.php/ijhcs/article/download/1603/1683.
14. Quoted in Mahmoud Reza Sani, *Men at Work: Cinematic Lessons from Abbas Kiarostami*, trans. Alireza Lalehfar (Los Angeles: Mhughes Press, 2013), 13, 81–82.
15. Kiarostami, "In Dialogue."
16. Sani, *Men at Work*, 87.
17. "Lorestan Province," Wikipedia, updated December 28, 2019, https://en.wikipedia.org/wiki/Lorestan_Province; see also Ali Torkzadeh, with Saeideh Ajilchi, "Three Days in Lorestan: An Unforgettable Exercise in Alternative Touring," Escape from Tehran, July 16, 2016, http://escapefromtehran.com/iran-travel-tour/three-days-lorestan-alternative-touring/.

Chapter Five

Obscuring the Soul

At the end of *Ten on Ten*, Kiarostami says that his cinema's "most important subject matter is human beings and their souls."[1] For Badii, as for other characters in preceding and subsequent films, the trajectory Kiarostami shows and that he hopes his audience will follow leads beyond cultural frames that can stifle their sensibilities by reducing them to the socially useful functions of their work. Individuals for whom there is still hope must learn to outgrow inculcated ambitions and discover that there is more to life than material security or crudely defined success: In *Close-Up* he depicts a man who values life exclusively in terms of rank and social status to the point where he essentially kills himself in order to masquerade as Mohsen Makhmalbaf, not realizing that being an artist is about creating new values rather than reinforcing false ones. Long after the film's release, Kiarostami felt that *Close-Up* had lasting impact "because it affects the soul" and because "it deals with human suffering more than my other films."[2] This statement reveals an ideal purpose that the other films also express, though in some cases, the suffering may not be conscious or may only become conscious beyond the scope of the film. Usually a major character's realization or ultimate fate is less important than the process of growth or regression that the film concerns. He stated in another interview, "The journey forms part of our culture and it is linked with mysticism; for us what is really important is not the goal we wish to attain, but the path we must travel."[3]

But cultural dead-ends can halt the journey by blocking the path. Anticipating the central character's occupation as a journalist in *The Wind Will Carry Us*, *Close-Up* begins with a journalist who wants to create a self-serving narrative about Hossein Sabzian, the main character. Though not factually false, the journalist's narrative blinds his readers to the inner lives—the souls—of the people he simplistically portrays as well as to their own.

Kiarostami said at Cannes in 1997 that his films "talk about the same things" (see chapter 1), and one of those things is the addictive power of journalism to oversimplify existence and stifle personal growth. Kiarostami based *Close-Up* on a 1989 news interview with Sabzian immediately after he was charged and arrested for apparently attempting to extort money from an upper-middle-class family by posing as Makhmalbaf and promising to put them into one of his movies. Hassan Farazmand's article "Bogus Makhmalbaf Arrested" in *Soroush* magazine seems to have intrigued Kiarostami because Sabzian had a sincere belief in the sanctity of art, while the news story about him serves the actual bogus interests of commercial journalism and the ongoing hypocrisy of social narratives in populous countries, both ancient and modern.

Kiarostami was able to turn the actual event into a literary one by interspersing brief segments of actual footage from the trial into a reenactment by real people steered partially by his direction before the scenes were shot and then edited for thematic detail postproduction. Kiarostami's film in relation to the original article is a counternarrative in which he implicitly compares journalism's creation of people and events to that of conventional cinema while contrasting both to the inward explorations of serious literature and film. In a 2009 interview appended to the *Close-Up* DVD, Kiarostami noted that the film "does something to our soul" because it exposes a person's inner reflections to the camera. He added that it is like Dostoyevsky's works because it focuses so intently on inward suffering, and it remains subliminally present in every film he made thereafter.[4]

In the course of the film, we learn that Sabzian knows almost nothing about the technicalities of filmmaking or even the usual celebrity news of Makhmalbaf's life and activities. He has, however, been deeply affected by the films he has seen and has thought long and hard about their impact on his life. Like Antoine Doinel, in François Truffaut's *The 400 Blows*, who does not understand that he plagiarized a passage from a Balzac novel because it had moved him so deeply that he unconsciously committed it to memory, Sabzian imaginatively identifies with the films he loves, even though their literal situations are quite different from his. He is a divorced, intermittently employed printer's helper who has lost custody of his children and who fills the void of his empty life by finding consolation in stories about people whose sufferings assure him that he is not alone.

During his trial he tells the judge he couldn't resist the urge to impersonate Makhmalbaf because he admired him for the films "he had given society" and the suffering he portrays in his films:

> He spoke for me and depicted my suffering, especially in *Marriage of the Blessed*, just as Mr. Kiarostami does, especially in *The Traveler*. You could say I'm exactly like that traveler. I really liked that film. Due to his passion for soccer, that boy takes pictures with a camera that has no film to raise money to go to a soccer match. But he oversleeps and misses the game, as I feel I have done. I know I'm guilty in the eyes of the court, but my love of art should be taken into account.

Ironically, Sabzian garnered so much attention after *Close-Up* that a Tehran film festival, where he was immediately recognized and admitted, denied entrance to Kiarostami until Sabzian was summoned to validate the man who had in a sense created him.[5] As the title of his interview—"Bogus Makhmalbaf Arrested"—indicates, journalist Hassan Farazmand created a different persona, and when in *Close-Up* Sabzian first appears and a soldier tells him to tell the truth, he sadly replies, "To you I'm just a thief and a con man."

Kiarostami told his Spanish workshop students that a film should begin and end with an image that tells the story.[6] In *Close-Up*'s establishing shot, loud traffic rushes by in the foreground, full of engine noise, horns, and sirens. In the longshot background, we see a small, barred door underneath a blue-and-white sign reading "Police Station." Three small figures appear momentarily, walking left to right inside the barred window, before the camera pans right to a medium shot of the journalist emerging from the barred door. Here, as in *The Traveler*, recurrent barred doors, windows, and fences connote the sense of social stratification and of individual feelings subordinated to "useful" functions.

The tiny human figures in relation to the collective traffic let us know that we are about to see the story of a confining society portrayed by a trapped individual rather than an individual story per se. The journalist has two armed soldiers in tow who follow him along a barred parking lot storing police vehicles. They represent mental and physical authority wielded by the military and media, which keep civilians intimidated or distracted enough to be satisfied with material security and unthinking obedience.

Close-Up counters this by magnifying the value of an individual's internal life in predominant close-ups of its protagonist, to the point that the impression of his sensitive face overwhelms the smallness to which, in the opening shot, individual life has been reduced. The film's title is its thematic message. Regard and penetrate the social mask, the film says, in order to realize a fully human existence. *Homework* is about forcing children, who are individualized in close-up interviews, to wear the social mask as a kind of armor and potentially martyr themselves in future wars, like the one adults at that time are fighting against Iraq. Similar forms of patriotism mask individual variation and stifle growth in many countries.

When the journalist announces his identity on the way to arrest Sabzian, the cab driver says, "A journalist? I took you for a cop." Both laugh, though the line seriously implies that the government and the media unconsciously and sometimes consciously conspire to maintain their symbiotic power. But the cab driver is the kind of independent soul who is immune to social shaping previously portrayed by the old door maker in *Where Is the Friend's House?* and subsequently by the country doctor in *The Wind Will Carry Us*. A former fighter pilot, he is not employed full time by the taxi company and works "off the meter." He has never heard of Makhmalbaf, and he never attends the movies because he is "too busy with life."

The pretitle sequence is the only one where he appears, and it is highly symbolic. His large white sedan waits on the street near the police station in front of a barred fence with barbed wire on top, and a small tree directly behind its rear door provides the only greenery in the frame, foreshadowing his appearance at the scene's end, where he picks flowers from a pile of leaves. His cab proves to be an oasis of humor and kindness in a film otherwise filled with recriminations and self-pity. He is a force for good in a world where the journalist thinks a good story is about detecting "something fishy," whereas continual accusation is the real evil and the cause of wars in which the cab driver has bravely and uncomplainingly served.

Like Makhmalbaf, the cab driver no longer works for a power-seeking group and jokes that he is "part of the ground forces now," to which the journalist, always on the self-aggrandizing lookout, quips, "That could make a good story, too. Air forces on the ground, Ground forces in the air." In a Zoroastrian sense, the former fighter pilot enacts the cosmic battle in his earthly life by resisting political and religious anger and practicing kindness, but the symbol most directly associated with him is a Shia religious ornament that hangs from his rearview mirror, which the camera includes throughout the first scene and emphasizes in several key close-ups to reflexively remind the audience of the film's title and purpose.

The ornament depicts the central figures of Muhammad's household: Ali, the first imam; Fatima, his wife and the prophet's daughter; and their infant son Husayn, who would become the hero of Karbala (see chapter 1). It represents an idealized relationship of selfless love among human beings and is therefore the polar opposite of the society that has created social inequities that have reduced Hossein Sabzian's life to self-pitying fantasy and that have marred the male members of the middle-class Ahankhah family with an ugly form of snobbery.

The journalist says he heard about the case and "thought it would make a good story," which is ironic because the society the Ahankhah family mirrors is a bad story in comparison to the Koranic narrative of the ideal family reiterated in the prayer chanted by the boys in *Homework*: "Oh, Allah, bless Muhammad and his household." In that film, the prayer is trenchantly ironic because the boys come from terrible households in the larger household of a nation gripped by a horrific war. Like Kiarostami's other Sufi guides, the cab driver exemplifies the best way to live in such a brutal world, and he reacts as if he well remembers what happened at Lavizan Air Force Base when the journalist directs him to drive past the place where the shah's soldiers fired on comrades who left to join the revolution (see chapter 1).

Just as he is being given direction by the self-interested journalist, those soldiers on both sides followed the dictates of leaders who had no compunction about shedding their blood. As they speak of Lavizan, the view out the windshield shows a blank, white wall. The journalist says he hasn't been back there since the event, which foreshadows the rest of the film that takes us to a place where wars and revolutions have failed to alter the collective scene.

Taking direction from the journalist, "to the right" or "to the left," may be political satire in such an unchanging world, where both sides leave the page of truth blank and, whatever the direction, someone exploits and someone suffers. Most people are as ignorant of their personal and collective direction as the boy who doesn't know the way to the Ahankhah's street and the man who also doesn't know but emulates the journalist's opportunism by thrusting forth two live turkeys that he wants to sell. With little conscience about any form of slaughter, the journalist jokes, "No thanks, we're off to see a turkey of our own," and then resumes his incessant gloating: "Everyone in film and TV will be talking about it."

But the varying glories of anyone who achieves such notoriety ignore the collateral damage, and just as they are about to arrive at what he expects to be his empowering moment, the sound of children's voices are heard from what turns out to be a dead-end street. Once again, the failure of social power to alter people's inner lives through revolution or vicarious victories echoes through his unwitting words: "How strange that my best story should take place at a dead-end," and then, as if to thematically drive home the point about any so-called advanced society, "What a strange place on a dead-end street."

After the journalist leaves the car, the brief exchange between the cab driver and the soldiers expresses the kind of relationship that is not a dead-end. It is keynoted by a shot out the windshield, where the Shia emblem of macrocosmic love swings back and forth in the frame-within-a-frame, until it stops in the exact center. The ideal group is about to be contrasted to the actual one when beyond the ornament we see the journalist going to one of three doors in a large, walled compound, the third barrier we have seen after the barred police station and the blank Lavizan wall.

After the journalist enters the door on the left, the driver initiates a conversation that has nothing to do with the posturing that ceaselessly transpires in a seemingly more elevated space. He begins by asking why the military rather than the police are taking a taxi to arrest a nonviolent criminal: "Don't the police have their own vehicles?" He receives an unexplained "Yes," but the line is important because if more people emulated Sabzian and refused to act out their prescribed roles, then the national order would indeed be threatened, and the rest of the dialogue during the journalist's absence also concerns social coercion.

The driver then distinguishes the soldiers as individuals by separating them from their function. In reply to the driver asking where he is from, the youngest soldier says he is from Isfahan. The driver continues the theme of social coercion by saying, "Funny. I'm from Tehran, and I did my service in Isfahan, and you're doing the opposite." The soldier, resigned to his role as Sabzian is not, responds, "That's fate." But the driver's adaptability is also conveyed when he says, "Isfahan's a nice place." The other soldier is from a village near Yazd. He still has two more years of compulsory military service because he is single. If he was married, then it would only be a year and a half.

The soldier says he is about to be transferred to Kurdistan, a place connoting conflict and the possibility of violence because the Kurds want self-rule. Mr. Badii in *Taste of Cherry* tells the young Kurdish soldier that he must be used to killing, but the Kurdish village in *The Wind Will Carry Us* is peaceful and idyllic. The mention of Kurdistan, like that of Lavizan, evokes a sphere of danger outside this upscale Tehran street, and the fighter-pilot-turned-cab-driver who has seen war firsthand appreciates the plight of the people who fight their leader's wars. "It'll pass quickly. Then you can go home and get married," he says and laughs as if they were intimate friends.

The soldier knows it won't be easy and responds, "I hope, as long as God grants us good health," a line that pointedly reflects the millions whom God did not protect in the Iraq War. The idea of innocent suffering through direct assault or through the death of conscripted fathers is additionally conveyed when the driver asks the other soldier if he has any children. "One boy," he responds, and the driver says, "God bless him." At this point the same soldier, carrying his rifle, exits the car to receive the written complaint and ID papers from Mr. Ahankhah, who has just emerged. Then the second soldier, also carrying his rifle, leaves the car as we hear the first soldier ask absurdly, "Is he armed?" to which Mr. Ahankhah replies even more absurdly, "I don't think so." But in the context of Lavizan, the exchange more seriously evokes the constant menace of an armed government ruling an unarmed populace, recalling Kiarostami's hope that he would never again see blood running in the streets (see chapter 1) and anticipating the brutal suppression of the Green movement in 2009 and continuing popular revolts in 2017 and 2018.[7]

Kiarostami's general response to political passion and violence is to transform the individual soul rather than to advocate violent change or rigid rule. The two-minute scene that follows is an exceptional moment of patient enjoyment and aesthetic beauty in a mostly somber film. It begins as the ex-fighter-pilot smokes with the driver-side window partly down, as if the barriers that divide people from each other and from nature no longer confine him. He has escaped the trap of social values that obsess Sabzian and that erase love for the sensory world that Kiarostami's subsequent cinema poetically restores. He no longer must fight wars dictated by an authority that is about to curb the imagination of the now-physically-trapped Sabzian, a man who had already been trapped by fantasies of importance. Unlike him, the driver has no time for newspapers or films because as he said, he is "too busy with life." In later films Kiarostami consistently uses art to celebrate nature rather than trying to make an ordered improvement on life in the modernist sense.

Outside the iron cell of the car, whose other inhabitants have been programmed to impose physical captivity and cartoonish definition, the senses come back into play. The driver expands the visual space by swinging the car around the cul-de-sac to a large pile of golden leaves mixed with assorted trash. He gets out and takes a deep breath as he stands next to a tall, green tree that hangs over the pile. Then, he looks up into the bright-blue sky, where a passenger plane trails twin plumes of white exhaust. The parallel and contrast to his former profession is palpable, as is the idea of extracting joy from an otherwise grim situation when he turns and begins to gather flowers from the trash.

The driver has been to war. As a fighter pilot, his mission was to hone in on other planes and kill other pilots. Now, his peacetime occupation gives him leisure to observe his surroundings. The people he transports are subjects of interest rather than high-ranking officers or civilian bosses, and unlike the pilot of the passenger plane, he is in a position to contemplate and understand them.

He is also able to appreciate the orange, pink, white, and yellow flowers he carefully selects, a bouquet anticipating the one Makhmalbaf later instructs Sabzian to give the Ahankhahs. It also echoes the door maker's flower in Ahmad's book at the end of *Where Is the Friend's House?* as a reminder of what to value in comparison to the aspirations to conventional achievement that some children are able to outgrow. The capacity to appreciate color, motion, and play is a childhood virtue that Kiarostami wants his viewers to regain. As the driver walks around the pile toward the camera, his foot dislodges a narrow, green aerosol can with a red tip. He kicks it lightly, and it begins to rattle down the silent, empty street. The camera follows it as it turns left out of the bright sun into the square shadow of an adjoining wall, where it finally rests.

In a 2009 interview at the Marrakech Film Festival included on the *Close-Up* DVD, Kiarostami explained that he included kicking the can because it reminded him of a creative impetus in his own art:

> Some part of our childhood remains with us, and filmmaking is a reflection of childhood. I saw a sloping street and a can lying there, and I thought it was a good chance to play a bit. I wanted the can kicked down the street because I might never again find such a nice street and an empty can on such a lovely autumn afternoon. . . . Kicking the can down the street was just playing around.[8]

For forty seconds the camera holds on a downhill view of a broad, empty street lined on both sides by small trees with yellow autumn leaves, their color amplified to celebration by the clear, bright light. As with the pink-and-gold bouquet in *Close-Up*'s final scene, the unexpectedly long hold on the image makes it likely to remain in the mind after a film that until the end is mostly washed out and dark. Watching the can roll as an object of seemingly irrelevant interest displaces the mind and the eye from everyday concerns, especially when the journalist, who has missed the ride to the police station while rounding up a tape recorder from the neighbors, loudly kicks it twice as he clumsily runs down the hill and, with briefcase in one hand and tape recorder in the other, rounds the corner and disappears.

From the start, the journalist, with his dream of making the big time, has been a comic version of Sabzian. He even has to ask Mr. Ahankhah for money to pay the driver, just as Merhdad Ahankhah later recalls in court how Sabzian cadged money to pay for a taxi. Not having thought ahead to bring a tape recorder, especially when he desperately says to the Ahankhahs, "It's pointless if it's not taped," is overtly absurd but that incompetence only points up the absurdity of avidly pursuing an ambition while missing the street's autumn splendor.

The sound of the driver's childlike maturity is emphasized by the rattle of the can, while the camera remains on two large trees lining the left side of the steep street for fifteen seconds as the can continues to roll. We do not hear it stop until the scene abruptly cuts to the opening titles, under which a printing press noisily skews out the social truth. Two stories are in play here: One is the apparent one of the con man; the other is the indictment of a hypocritical narrative that lacks insight and compassion.

Creative and uncreative play impel Sabzian, but the Ahankhah family's fantasies are pretentiously mundane. Kiarostami said he had some difficulty with the reenactment because the family was "always acting, fabricating because they wanted to be viewed positively. Each did his own thing. The family and Sabzian were trying to justify themselves. They were identical because neither was living in reality."[9] The family is vulnerable because its self-esteem has suffered in the aftermath of the revolution. Though they live in a well-appointed home in an affluent neighborhood, the father is no longer working, and the sons, despite their degrees in engineering, are unable to find suitable work. One is unemployed, and the other works in a bakery.

That explains why the family so readily believes Sabzian because being featured in a film by a prominent director would heal the social demotion they feel they have suffered. But when they finally appeared in Kiarostami's film, they were uncooperative about conveying their true feelings because their primary concern was not to appear foolish. As for Sabzian, his unrehearsed performance is at times naïvely comic. During the reenactment, Kiarostami openly places himself in the courtroom, and when he asks Sabzian if it is okay to film, his leading man replies, "Yes. Because you are my audience."

Then, the erstwhile "Makhmalbaf" reveals that he is woefully ignorant of filmmaking basics that even casual film fans would know. Kiarostami tells him that there are two cameras and one has a close-up lens: "Know what that is?" When Sabzian unabashedly says no, Kiarostami patiently explains, "It has a very tight focus." Then he adds that the other camera has a wide-angle lens that will alternately film the courtroom while the close-up lens will stay on Sabzian. Sabzian's ignorance provides an opportunity to elaborate the meaning of the title. Most of the film zeroes in on Sabzian's sensitive face because it conceives of art as an expression of the soul rather than a manipulation of technique.

Kiarostami hints at his attempt to probe the journalistic surface when he concludes his intervention by saying, "In prison you told me you would plead guilty. But some things are more complex than they seem and not at all easy to understand. The camera is here so you can explain things that people might find hard to accept." And he encourages Sabzian to speak unguardedly when he concludes, "Anything that you find questionable, explain it to the camera."

When Kiarostami said that some things about the story were not easy to understand, he may have meant that Sabzian's literal masquerade exposes the unconscious masquerades of social status and legal morality. In his 2009 Marrakech interview, Kiarostami recalled how Sabzian cried when he had to enter the Ahankhah house during the shoot because he felt guilty about deceiving them but that he was consoled when Kiarostami said, "You didn't lie. You told a truth that's beyond reality. You told them you'd bring a crew to film there. Well, we're your crew."[10]

In one of the few scenes outside the courtroom, medium-long shots rather than close-ups are able to show the extent to which the Ahankhah family is caught in a social network of self-deception that unintentionally validates the title of the film Sabzian promised to shoot there. As an unwitting lead in *The House of the Spider*, Mr. Ahankhah thinks he is trapping Sabzian during the visit to his house that immediately precedes the con man's arrest, but instead, the scene ruthlessly parodies his ponderous investigation.

In a flashback from the court to the Ahankhah living room, the father tells his friend Mr. Mohseni, who is apparently present as a witness, that he was too smart to ever believe Sabzian but that he allowed the ruse to persist to teach his family a lesson. Now he exults in having the culprit dead to rights because when on a previous visit, Merhdad held up a news article and congratulated him for winning a festival award for *The Cyclist*, Sabzian knew nothing about it. Once again, however, the thematic thread that says art is not about celebrity or recognition echoes through the scene when Mr. Ahankhah condescendingly thinks he is cleverly mocking Sabzian, while Sabzian himself speaks about art at a depth Mr. Ahankhah cannot fathom.

Sabzian recalls in court that the family held up a magazine with a photo of the real Mahkhmalbaf and sarcastically remarked how much better looking he was when he was young. Playing detective, Merhdad notes in his testimony that Sabzian had salt-and-pepper hair when they met but that he dyed it later. With an embarrassed smile, Sabzian sheepishly tells the judge that he has dyed his hair for several years to look younger. But he also notes that just before the later scene filmed in the living room, he wrote in his journal, "The Tragic Finale," because even though he knew what would happen, he couldn't stop himself from playing the part of a man who "inspired such respect and admiration."

After sleeping on the Ahankhahs' couch, leaving the next morning, and then returning with Merhdad on his motorcycle in the afternoon, he "could sense completely" that the masquerade was over, but he goes anyway. Once he arrives, he receives little respect as he sits on the sofa in white socks, with his feet splayed outward, while Mr. Ahankhah plays prosecutor for the benefit of what he assumes is a sympathetic friend. However, Mr. Mohseni, reflecting the sensitive spectator who has "followed this from the outset," evinces sympathy for Sabzian and says he hopes that he really is Makhmalbaf. The line serves to accentuate the cruel delight Mr. Ahankhah appears to be having at Sabzian's expense.

The improvised exchange begins to become symbolic when Ahankhah asks if Sabzian slept well. Sabzian says he didn't, and Ahankhah maliciously moralizes, "One often sleeps poorly in someone else's house." For apparent losers like Sabzian, the whole of society is someone else's house, and Mr. Ahankhah's heavy-handed irony paired with Sabzian's thoughtful replies indicate that Sabzian is in fact the wiser of the two: "Yet a sage feels at home anywhere."—"But I'm no sage."—"You certainly look like one."—"Appearances can deceive."

Sabzian's line summarizes the thematic point. He may look like a cheap con artist, but his soul, rather than the social persona that circumstances have allowed him to be, really is wise and perceptive, and his imaginative lie about how he spent his morning hiking in the mountains approximates Kiarostami's own love of nature. Though his literal story is false, its inner truth is real, just as the fictional experience of a story is as valid as the so-called life experience a person has actually had: "This morning, looking out the window, I felt so close to nature and the mountains. It seems to me that a man really needs to be close to nature. One must be in touch with the color of nature to remove the rust covering one's heart." Mr. Ahankhah smiles and nods as if he sees through the poseur's deceit, but when Sabzian quotes a poem, he touches on the Sufi nature of reality itself.

His lines reflect ancient views of the material world as an illusion and of separate identities as a woven veil separating human beings from God: "I asked, 'Why is your face hidden from me?' She replied, 'It is you who are hidden.'" Then he comments, "Human beings hide their true selves," before resuming the poem: "You yourself are the veil, for my face is revealed." His concluding comment merges the surface plot with a reflective gloss, as if he is reflecting on a Rumi poem: "That's the issue: to uncover that true face. That's why I needed to go up into the mountains to study myself. Nature is a mirror in which we can study ourselves."

These lines imply that Sabzian is wiser than he knows. He consciously understands only his social degradation, but he intuitively feels that equality can be found in the divine union that comprehends every living thing rather than in a political structure. For a man of the world like Mr. Ahankhah, this is just more double-talk, and he triumphantly counters, "If you're so fond of nature, why not live a more natural life?" Sabzian gets it and replies, "What about me seems unnatural to you?" Mr. Ahankhah tries to cover by asking why he is still working when it's Friday, a day when most people take the day off, a question he would never address to the real Makhmalbaf. But Sabzian is prepared for this because he has thought about the artistic commitment he has never had the opportunity to practice: "When there's work to be done, the day doesn't matter. Who knows what fate will bring tomorrow? We can't even know what lies ten minutes ahead, and we have to use every opportunity. I love my work, so I'll pursue it no matter the day. We spend many days just waiting. Then finally work came along."

This understanding of the artistic process—that creative work can't be done on a time clock—indicates that Sabzian may be lying about what he does but is not really lying about who he is. Mr. Mohseni and Mrs. Ahankhah sense this, and when the soldiers arrive, she begs them, "Let him finish his lunch," and then appeals to her husband, "Don't let them take him," to which Mr. Ahankhah, seeming to forget the difference between the first time and the reenactment, apparent illusion and apparent reality, reassures her, "Don't worry. He'll be back."

The living room scene is especially illustrative of Kiarostami's feeling that *Close-Up* affects the spectator's soul because it delves beneath the persona of its protagonist and exposes the inner reflections that less imaginative people are conditioned to hide. Sabzian has the soul of a nascent artist when he imagines he is Makhmalbaf, but his socialized "real" self is narcissistic and self-pitying, which accounts for his infatuation with *The Cyclist*. Literally, his social condition is far less harsh than that of Makhmalbaf's Nasim, but Kiarostami's film implicitly reflects on international cinema generally, where people in countries that may be more politically free still suffer from a stifling of soul, even if they don't believe in the soul.

Just before Sabzian's arrest, Mr. Ahankhah's black-and-white moral righteousness is undercut by a shot of the journalist and soldiers arriving through the gauze curtains of the side window, in front of which thin, delicate branches bear bright-yellow leaves. The image augments the scene's revelation of Sabzian's aesthetic sensitivity and supports Mrs. Ahankhah's feeling that Sabzian deserves protection. Sabzian exhibits an alarmed look at first but then resignedly sits on the sofa, waiting to be taken, in a long shot that makes him look especially small. The gauze-curtained yellow-leaved frame is repeated as the guarded Sabzian descends the steps, but this time the image is accompanied by cawing crows, a repeated sound effect for unpleasant events throughout Kiarostami's oeuvre. (Police sirens are also used just preceding the shot of the police station in the first scene and when Sabzian forges Makhmalbaf's autograph in the scene with Mrs. Ahankhah on the bus.)

In the courtroom, the contrast between Sabzian's creative soul and his posturing persona also results in a dual view of cinema. The younger Ahankhah son testifies that Sabzian wanted them all to go to see *The Cyclist* together so that they could discuss it as a starting point for their own film. He wanted to go to a particular theater where he claimed they were showing a less-censored version, an interesting detail because *Close-Up* as a whole is about the unconscious censorship that dulls the real aesthetic sensibilities of people like Sabzian by blaring out sensational headlines like "Bogus Makhmalbaf Arrested." But Kiarostami is making the point that when a director speaks to like-minded people, they essentially do share the same soul. For the span of a film at least, viewers *are* Kiarostami or Makhmalbaf, and for a few, the identification lasts much longer, just as Kiarostami integrated Rumi or Sepehri into himself.

The idea of shared response piqued Kiarostami's interest, and he interrupts the reenactment to ask Sabzian to elaborate on why he wanted to see *The Cyclist* with the family:

> I wanted them to be more interested in the film and have more respect for me as a director, a director who understands the suffering of society, who keenly understands the ills and deals with another social class as though it were his own. I wanted to tell them, "Change your mentality. Don't think a director is different from ordinary people. He's one of you." This is the behavior of a director who's humble and close to the people. I wanted to prove it to them by going to the cinema together.

Though Sabzian appears to be thinking primarily of class difference, the speech applies more to the sharing of soul than the distribution of wealth. The director and the spectator share a need to feel and express more than practical priorities allow. Sabzian's role-playing is only an extreme version of the personal role each person becomes trapped into believing is their authentic self. The journalist whose effort is to reinforce those fixed public identities testifies that Sabzian is a serial deceiver, without understanding that he and his victim are more alike than they are different. He reveals that (like himself) Sabzian works in a "print shop" and that (like himself) he yearns to be important. After the article came out, a woman called him and said that an unnamed man (perhaps Sabzian, perhaps a copycat) promised to marry her and give her a lead role in a film. Some coworkers also claimed that Sabzian kept the money from a paper delivery, lines that also apply to the journalist's ambitions to play an "Oriana [Fallaci]" role and to profit from publication.

Sabzian escapes the prison of society at large through the mythology of cinema rather than conventional religion. He testifies that while awaiting trial in an actual prison, he thought of saying, "Speak Allah's name and your heart will be consoled," but he felt no consolation. But while this prayer afforded no solace, the screenplay of *The Cyclist* "brought calm to [his] heart." It said what he wished he could say by showing the "evil faces of those who play with the lives of others, and the rich who pay no attention to simple material needs of the poor." But Kiarostami is more interested in Sabzian's stifled soul than his material deprivation, and he interrupts for a final time to ask, "Now that you've played this part, are you a better actor than [you are a] director?"

Consciously, Sabzian may only be sensing another opportunity, but he emphasizes frustrated expression more than penurious despair when he replies that he now realizes that acting would allow him to express his "deprivation with every fiber of his being." Still, he seems to miss the deeper meaning of *acting* when, after Kiarostami asks if he isn't acting now, he protests, "No I'm speaking of my suffering. I'm not acting."

But then he spontaneously switches from the self-pitying poor man to the kind of self-reflecting artist Kiarostami and Makhmalbaf really are: "I am speaking from my heart. For me, art is the experience you've felt inside. As Tolstoy said, art is the inner experience cultivated by the artist. I think I could convey my inner reality." Kiarostami then gently prompts him to complete his world-as-stage perception: "Then why did you pretend to be a director?" he asks. Sabzian answers, "Playing the part of a director is a performance in itself. To me that is acting." Kiarostami then probes more deeply, "What part would you like to play?" and after Sabzian says, "My own," he asks a final question that Sabzian can't answer: "Haven't you already done that?"

This is the film's central question. If we all have been in most cases cast by circumstance into social roles, to what extent must we limit ourselves to the role we have been assigned to play? The artist, Kiarostami says, may externally play the expedient role, but his soul can find a more expansive existence by expressing itself in a form that will help to liberate the souls of others. In his final plea, Sabzian makes the soul-persona distinction when he asks the Ahankhah family to forgive him "in the eternal sense," the sense to him that matters. Otherwise, "in the legal sense they can forgive or punish me, I ask the court's forgiveness."

In that the authentic artist in a complex society based on political dominance must always be some kind of outlaw, Sabzian can never be forgiven, but Mr. Ahankhah plays his role as collectively written when he agrees to forgive Sabzian "in the hope that he will become a useful member of society," and Merhdad, who like Sabzian is unemployed, withdraws his complaint because he believes "social malaise and especially unemployment are to blame" and that "unemployment leads to corruption." He concludes, following the accrued but flawed wisdom that when Sabzian "finds a proper job, he will lead an honest life." Of course, as the film shows, a proper job is not going to show people where to find the beauty and value that an oblivious culture is structured to conceal. That is the job of the artist, and when the camera leaves the courtroom, Kiarostami finds an ingenious way of not reducing that job to a didactic cliché.

The Wind Will Carry Us overtly combines cinema and poetry, but *Taste of Cherry* and *Close-Up* both conclude with lyrical passages that exemplify Kiarostami's distinctively "poetic cinema." He told David Sterritt that the "cinema that will last longer is the poetic cinema, not the cinema that is just storytelling [and though] every movie should have some kind of story, the important thing is how the story is told—it should be poetic, and it should be possible to see it in different ways."[11] His cinema also adapted the musical rhythm of poetry, where the alternation of sound and silence, meaning and feeling, is more important than sound alone. Sometimes he created this ineffable space by removing one element and sometimes another. Sound, he once said, is "more essential than pictures, [because] a two-dimensional flat image is all you can achieve with your camera.... It's the sound that gives depth as the third dimension to that image. Sound, in fact, makes up for the shortcoming of pictures."[12] He summarized the idea in another interview: "Suppressing the sound and sometimes the image can lead to a new experience in cinema."[13]

By artfully editing the image and suppressing the sound, the last scene of *Close-Up* achieves the poetic "capabilities of a prism." Sabzian didn't know that his release from jail would be filmed, but Makhmalbaf, who met him at the exit, was mic'd up and expected the dialogue to be heard as he ferried Sabzian on a motorbike to the Ahankhah house. Kiarostami was unhappy with the dialogue that transpired because he felt that Makhmalbaf talked too much about his own emotional relationships. After he asked, "Do you prefer being Makhmalbaf or Sabzian?" and then meant to add "Even I'm tired of being Makhmalbaf," Kiarostami decided to cut the sound before he could finish—"Even I'm tired of being Makh—." In the film we hear Kiarostami say that the sound cut out because there's a problem with either the jack or Makhmalbaf's lapel mic: "It's old equipment." He later commented that he realized that he could "get closer to the emotion by omitting the sound [and that that was] the possibility this film showed me, thanks to Makhmalbaf."[14] The cut-off name with which the sound stops also thematically points up the arbitrary nature of social identity.

Instead of verbal dialogue, the sounds of traffic at the end match the same sounds in the opening shot: cars whooshing by, horns and sirens obscuring the subtleties of soul uncovered by the predominant close-ups of Sabzian's face. At the same time, breaking the aural convention of decipherable dialogue and the visual one of following a moving vehicle through city streets helps to break up the social narrative in which Sabzian has been caught. Careful editing views the flow of traffic and individual vehicles from unusual angles to restore the senses in surroundings that usually deaden them, and the continuous motion is a sharp contrast to the static courtroom shots, the entrapped Sabzian sitting awkwardly on the Ahankhah couch, and the tight shots of Sabzian meeting Mrs. Ahankhah on the crowded bus where that entrapment innocuously began.

Similar shots on the opening taxi ride include the wall at Lavizan and the squeezing of the two doomed turkeys into the visual frame of the cab's passenger window. Makhmalbaf's arrival on a motorbike instead of inside a car keynotes the final scene's sense of release, which begins by emphasizing the bars of the jail after the initial long shot from across the street. As Kiarostami and his assistant discuss losing the sound, the camera stays on a barred fence. Then, after Makhmalbaf walks past a barred window, the sound is restored enough to hear Sabzian weeping when he exits the building as he falls into his hero's arms, but it cuts out again as Makhmalbaf steers the motorbike away from the prison just when the audience would expect to hear the words of this climactic encounter.

Rather than resolving the story line, the scene becomes pure poetry, a rhythmic panoply of color, reflection, motion, and sound. Identical gray jackets separate the two Makhmalbafs from the bright abstraction of the scene. Its predominant colors are simultaneously calm and exalting, a color-wheel harmony of blue and orange. After Makhmalbaf pulls away from the building, the blue wall of a large truck or van passes, just before Sabzian emerges and hugs Makhmalbaf, who, as if speaking to a child, says, "Don't cry. There's no need for that. Look at me. Let's go."

Then, after the blue van passes again, we see a bright-orange car parked near the jail entrance, where a little boy holding his mother's hand (mirroring Sabzian and Makhmalbaf) passes in a bright-orange coat. When Makhmalbaf starts the motorbike, orange and blue cars parked in the foreground are temporarily concealed by a spotless, white bus with a royal-blue stripe. Sabzian's potential transformation may be foreshadowed by a color palette that, aided by serendipity, appears to be consistently deliberate.

The motorbike wends its way through traffic onto a broad avenue, a breathing space like the cab driver's leaf pile. A wide shot from the windshield of the camera truck conveys this freedom, and the larger space is amplified by the windshield's multilined crack, which suggests breaking through the inner and outer restrictions that Sabzian calls his "suffering." The wide shot is followed by a shot of the truck's side-view mirror after it passes the bike. The alternation of the open space and the very small frame does not connote renewed entrapment but rather Kiarostami's recurrent idea of using a frame to express immeasurable space beyond it.

This is partly achieved by the frame's small size, surrounded as it is by an unbounded view that keeps changing from the vehicles' motion. The feeling is further reinforced by the color harmony of bright-orange cars on either side of the mirror's white frame, while inside the small frame, a police motorcycle with a large, blue box in front intermittently passes between the camera truck and Makhmalbaf's bike. Then, the passenger-side window of the truck framed by black trapezoidal shadows on either side is completely filled by the bright-blue side of a passing truck.

After a brief long shot of Makhmalbaf stopping at a flower market, the side of the same blue truck passes from right to left, maintaining the sequence of side mirror and blue "wall" seen before. In his edited footage, Kiarostami echoes the scene of the taxi driver finding flowers in the trash by deriving visual beauty from the urban scene. Unlike his nature photography, where the camera mirrors a beauty intrinsically in the subject, Kiarostami abstracts the colors, shapes, and flow of traffic into a visual poetry that he creates and that the eye must learn to see. In so doing, he guides the spectator as an adult guides a child toward selective close-ups that reveal formerly invisible gifts.

Accordingly, at the flower stand, Makhmalbaf reflexively "directs" Sabzian as if he were a child, showing him that art is about giving the world something beautiful rather than receiving adulation. For the first time in the film, we see Sabzian being nurtured and instructed by an empowered adult instead of trying to play the directive grown-up he had never really become. Vocalized sound now returns for the first time since they left the jail, to continue Kiarostami's impression of Sabzian as an unworldly child rather than the slick scammer exposed by Hassan Farazmand in *Soroush* magazine:

"You can get some flowers here. Count your money. Careful with your money. You need money?"

Here, we see assistance freely offered instead of cajoled. But in addition to giving Sabzian an exemplary lesson in generosity, Makhmalbaf is sharpening Sabzian's aesthetic eye, just as Kiarostami is sharpening that of the viewer. While Makhmalbaf stays with the bike, Sabzian quickly selects a bunch of long-stemmed yellow roses. Then, Makhmalbaf's voice cuts into the blurred sounds of traffic: "Not yellow, my friend. Pick a different color. those red ones are better." Simultaneously, Kiarostami creates a visual bouquet with close-ups that pass in front of the long shot of his principal characters. In so doing, he reverses the conventional use of close-up and long shot by directing the eye to the aesthetics of the scene rather than the fictive denouement.

At the point where Makhmalbaf requests red flowers, a red bus passes, followed by a blue truck with slatted sides, but instead of showing the slats as straight bars, the truck's movement creates a blur that makes the slats look like a woven star. And again, as if to educate the eye to value subtlety more than the broad colors of the social narrative, the delicate petals of the "red flowers" that Sabzian brings back are pink at the top and gold on the bottom.

After they leave the flower stand, the rest of the drive to the Ahankhah home is pure poetry. As the motorbike glides down broad, peaceful streets, the ambient sound is replaced by a lyrical Persian melody by Kambiz Roshanravan, the same one first heard in *The Traveler* when Qassem gets off the bus in Tehran. There, it returns only once, played low and soft by a viola after Qassem leaves the gym and lies down with the workmen on the grass, followed by a devastating silence that lasts all the way to the film's nightmarish end. Here, the same melody lyrically sung by a violin and a cello is tender and emotive, affirmative and lovely. The city streets have turned from a place of menace, defined rather than perceived by the media and the military in the film's opening scene, to an abstract painting of light, color, and motion, anticipating the same effect on the streets of Tokyo near the beginning of *Like Someone in Love*.

Once again, the close-up lens discovers unexpected beauty. The pink and gold flowers, with their long, green stems, are prominent to the left as we follow the riders from behind, and when the camera truck passes them, Sabzian's flowers fill the frame of the passenger window. Just before we reach the Ahankhah house, the screen frame becomes a light-blue windshield that contains a shadow design of navy-blue leaves and branches, and when Makhmalbaf stops the motorbike next to a wall fronted by yellow-leaved saplings and a curved green bush, the sound of his parking brake stops the music. Here, for a moment, the pink bouquet highlights the center of the frame, while the rider's gray jackets have acquired a light-blue tint.

Following this visual poem, the final exchange with Mr. Ahankhah is both pointed and comic. After Sabzian rings the bell, a voice says, "Yes?" but when Sabzian says, "It's Hossein Sabzian," the reply is "Who?" followed by silence, followed by a perfectly timed pause, before Sabzian says, "Makhmalbaf," which is funny not only because the Ahankhahs thought he really was but because the real Makhmalbaf is standing behind him. More silence follows, until Makhmalbaf steps up to the speaker and announces himself, "This is Mr. Makhmalbaf," followed by the hurried sound of an inner door opening, as Sabzian childishly weeps and Makhmalbaf paternally consoles, "Dry those tears." Still waiting momentarily for Mr. Ahankhah to appear, Makhmalbaf asks Sabzian how long it has been since he first came to the house. "Forty days ago," he replies.

The number has a mythical ring of transformation, but the ending presents different views of what that transformation should be. One would be for Sabzian to respect the sanctity of social status, as Mr. Ahankhah does when, with a broad smile, he addresses someone deserving of what he considers authentic glory. "Welcome to our home," he tells the "real" Makhmalbaf. The other would be for Sabzian to extend the soul growth he had begun and avoid rather than accept the submissive normality that Mr. Ahankhah extols and that artists like Kiarostami and Makhmalbaf instinctively reject.

Figure 5.1. Rather than the gifted artist and object of acclaim that Hossein Sabzian aspired to be, the film's final image portrays the true artist as one who humbly offers something beautiful. Celluloid Dreams/Photofest.

Individual members of the audience can hope for one outcome or the other according to their values. They are left to ponder Sabzian's future and perhaps their own with the film's final shot, a freeze-frame of Sabzian looking humbly downward but still holding his bouquet. The image is, of course, a close-up, asking us to look for the soul beneath the mask, but its gray, shallow focus; the faded pink of the flowers still lightly visible at the top right; and Sabzian's gray-blue jacket convey a purposeful ambiguity intended to engage our reflections throughout and beyond the final credits, through which the image steadily holds.

NOTES

1. *Ten on Ten*, special feature on *Ten*, directed by Abbas Kiarostami (2002; New York: Zeitgeist Films, 2004), DVD.
2. Abbas Kiarostami, interview by Tarik Benbrahim at Marrakech Film Festival, *Close-Up*, directed by Abbas Kiarostami, disc 2 (1990; Hartsdale, NY: Criterion Collection, 2010), DVD.
3. Quoted in Alberto Elena, *The Cinema of Abbas Kiarostami*, trans. Belinda Coombes (London: SAQI Iran Heritage Foundation, 2005), 75.
4. Kiarostami, interview by Benbrahim.
5. Kiarostami, interview by Benbrahim.
6. Quoted in Mahmoud Reza Sani, *Men at Work: Cinematic Lessons from Abbas Kiarostami*, trans. Alireza Lalehfar (Los Angeles: Mhughes Press, 2013), 87.
7. See "Mahmoud Ahmadinejad," Wikipedia, updated January 9, 2020, https://en.wikipedia.org/wiki/Mahmoud_Ahmadinejad.
8. Kiarostami, interview by Benbrahim.
9. Kiarostami, interview by Benbrahim.
10. Kiarostami, interview by Benbrahim.
11. Abbas Kiarostami, "With Borrowed Eyes: An Interview with Abbas Kiarostami," interview by David Sterritt, *Film Comment*, July–August 2000, http://www.filmcomment.com/article/with-borrowed-eyes-an-interview-with-abbas-kiarostami/.
12. Quoted in Elena, *Cinema of Abbas Kiarostami*, 36.
13. Kiarostami, interview by Benbrahim.
14. Kiarostami, interview by Benbrahim.

Chapter Six

Prefer the Present

In *The Wind Will Carry Us*, Kiarostami plays variations on the films discussed so far. Here, the main character is a Tehrani journalist, and the film deepens the contrast begun in *Close-Up* between a meretricious public narrative and the souls of individuals within any group. The motif of childhood also persists, although Farzad, the boy in *Wind*, is distinctively different from Ahmad in *Where Is the Friend's House?* and Puya in *And Life Goes On*. Ahmad faces a moral dilemma, and ultimately he chooses love for his friend over the moral injunction not to cheat on his homework. Puya, unlike Ahmad and Qassem in *The Traveler*, was raised gently by his cultivated father and does not need to concern himself with right and wrong.

While his father speaks for conventional social authority at the beginning of the film, Puya, in Kiarostami's words, "accepts the illogic and instability of the earthquake" and talks about "what interests him instead" (see chapter 2). When Puya brings a grasshopper back to the car after stopping to pee along the road to Koker, his father scolds him because "they are dirty" and may infect him if he touches his eyes. But touching the eyes is a metaphor for the value Puya is able to see in nature that is no longer visible to the average adult. The boy disagrees, and anticipating the feeling of stewardship that Kiarostami elsewhere expressed toward nature—"What will happen to nature when I leave this life?"[1]—Puya says, "I would like to look after it and raise it."

He goes on to intuitively express the feeling toward children in general that Kiarostami developed at Kanun, the Center for the Development of Children and Young Adults: "I want it to become a big grasshopper and then to migrate." They then go on to discuss the meaning of *migrate*, which his father regards as a factual quiz, while Puya makes *migrate* a metaphor of some people's ability to adapt and grow throughout their lives: "They eat up all the grass in one place and then have to find a place with fresh grass." The father offers a dismissive "Bravo," thinking to have ended the matter, but then becomes angry when Puya momentarily interferes with his driving by thrusting the grasshopper in front of his face: "See what nice red wings it has?"—"Why did you do that? Throw it out!" The sequence suggests that socialized adults survive by limiting their concentration to immediate tasks and future goals. All of Kiarostami's films are dangerous to that habit of mind. The boy lets the grasshopper fly out the window, and the father tells him to go to sleep in the backseat.

The command represents the general social process of discarding childhood interests, which the artist strives to restore. Out of his father's view, Puya becomes a prototype of Kiarostami himself: When no longer allowed to look out the window, he uses his imagination to elude confinement. Lying on his back, he holds up his hand and works his fingers as if he were taking an imaginary picture. Then, he takes both hands and makes a square frame around his eyes, with the index fingers extended to form the top, the second and third fingers folded in to make the space, and the little fingers extended for the bottom. The camera quickly cuts to the rear window to show what Puya can still see, despite his father's order to lose consciousness.

The window temporarily forms another frame with the tops of a cluster of green trees surmounted by a gray stone mountain. The shot expresses cinema's power to catch and store a passing moment that would usually be ignored. Soon after they arrive in Koker, Puya continues to actively explore by looking for useful objects buried in the earthquake, while his father simply sits and stares blankly at his surroundings, reflecting through the contrast a fundamental difference between the average viewer and the alert witness Kiarostami hopes to reach or create.

This process of recovering the treasures hidden by the earthquake of adolescence bypasses most of the characters in Kiarostami's films. What the principal adult characters miss, the camera shows, but within the story, there are a few characters who share the director's vision. In an interview on the *ABC Africa* DVD, Kiarostami recalled that his films for Kanun were affected by how his child characters viewed the world but that, in his later films, this wisdom has been transferred to the "wise old man type."[2] Of course, the wise, old door maker appears in *Where Is the Friend's House?* which was made for Kanun, and in *And Life Goes On*, Puya and an old man played by the actor who played the door maker share the role of Sufi guide.

A passage from the essay on suicide by Emile Durkheim, whom Kiarostami refers to in *Like Someone in Love* (see chapter 12), implicitly expresses the similarity between people at the beginning and end of their lives:

> Suicide is known to be rare among children and to diminish among the aged at the last confines of life; physical man, in both, tends to become the whole of

man. Society is still lacking in the former, for it has not had the time to form him in its image; it begins to retreat from the latter or, what amounts to the same thing, he retreats from it. Thus both are more self-sufficient. Feeling a lesser need for self-completion through something not themselves, they are also less disposed to feel the lack of what is necessary for living.[3]

After *Taste of Cherry*, suicide becomes a major Kiarostami motif, extending from *The Wind Will Carry Us* through such subsequent films as *Shirin* (2008), *Certified Copy* (2010), and *Like Someone in Love* (2012). In an interview attached to the *Wind* DVD, Kiarostami said that he drew ideas for each new film from characters or themes in the previous one.[4] Though Behzad, the protagonist of *Wind*, is not overtly suicidal like Mr. Badii, his accumulated cultural baggage almost buries him. Behzad has led a television crew to film a Kurdish funeral ceremony in southwestern Iran that will follow the imminent death of a hundred-year-old woman.

His story is intended to entertain urban Tehranis by sensationalizing an exotic custom. While the lady clings to life, Behzad explores the village, but after a week goes by, his three-man crew, which is never seen, loses patience and returns to Tehran. With two exceptions, the villagers do not know why Behzad is there and assume he has something to do with a new underground telecommunications cable that is being laid near the cemetery. Thematically, the pressure of Behzad's work is as suicidal and insane as Badii's unexplained self-destructive "drive," and it is no coincidence that both men's names start with *B*.

Kiarostami said that he depicted Badii's grave symbolically: "Every time the soil was being poured down by the truck, Mr. Badii was seeing his own grave. In every down pouring of the soil and gravel, he was imagining himself under their weight."[5] The major instance of this burial lasts for an emphatic six minutes. After leaving the seminarian, Badii gets out of his car at an excavation site, where he watches a conveyor belt moving rocks and dirt down a spillway into a pile on the ground. In the next shot, we see his shadow reflected on the ground next to the shadow of the falling dirt, creating a surreal frame, like an abstract painting. Badii's black shadow is then blacked out by the larger shadow of a huge steam shovel that completely obliterates all signs of light and life. The scene reverts to "real life," as Badii watches rocks landing in a hole beneath a barred grate, symbolizing the egotistic prison cell in which he is already spiritually dead. Dust obscures the foreground where he sits in a visual echo of the landscape-obscuring clouds of dust his car raises on the road.

A similar near-lethal burial occurs in *The Wind Will Carry Us* after Behzad drives his dust-raising Range Rover to the hilltop cemetery, where he repeatedly rushes to answer cell-phone calls from his producer in Tehran because the signal is not strong enough in the village. The hill is next to a hole in the ground, where a local man is digging the new telecommunications line that, for better or worse, will connect the village to the outside world. Behzad converses with the man after each call and on one occasion keeps a human femur that the man tosses up to him. On his last visit, while Behzad watches an ant moving a large ball of mud, paralleling the work that both he and the digger are compelled to do and with the femur prominently visible on his dashboard, he is startled by the sudden sound of brush collapsing to his right.

He runs to the edge of the digger's hole, where a cloud of dust momentarily obscures the screen. Then, we see a gaping hole next to the shadows of Behzad's legs, as if he were about to walk into his grave. Panicked by the digger's apparent burial by a mudslide, he runs to the edge of the hill and shouts at a man passing on a motorcycle, but the man does not hear him. He is suddenly faced with a situation that threatens physical life, in direct parallel to the diminishing of soul that his compelled work threatens to complete. He jumps in his car and races to get help so that he can save a life rather than hoping to end one, not having realized that pseudo-sophistication and urban cynicism have almost destroyed his own.

Overall, the film depicts Behzad's potential escape from the spiritual grave his societal obligations have compelled him to dig. The placard at the end of *Doors without Keys* quotes the Kiarostami maxim that "we are not able to look at what we have in front of us, unless it is inside a frame."[6] Inside the conventional social frame, people answer to a boss or surrogate God. Behzad is often shown literally running to answer calls from his boss, Mrs. Godarzi, whose name, as Godfrey Cheshire puts it, is a riff on the English word *God* and whose commands must be received on a miniature mountain, the hill where the reporter's cell phone's signal works.[7] Ironically, the funeral, which is expected to draw interest for its scarification rite, parallels Behzad's enthrallment by his secular boss as well as the enthrallment of millions by the world's dominant religions.

The progressive village schoolteacher describes for Behzad how the ceremony left two scars on his mother's face: one to show her love for her husband after his sister died and the other to honor her husband's boss at the factory: "One of his cousins had died. So that my father wouldn't lose his job, my mother mourned a great deal. She scratched her face because there was competition at the factory to hold on to their jobs. Need and necessity, you see? Everyone played along. Everyone pushed themselves forward to please the boss, [to show] that he was loyal."

The teacher remembers the ceremony as personally "painful" and feels that its "origins are bound to the economy." That is, Kiarostami seems to say, people include praise of God in mourning their dead to ensure their earthly security as long as possible: "This ceremony has been engraved on their memory now for generations." At one point, Behzad answers his cell phone to tell his parents that he cannot attend a funeral for a relative because he is too busy working for Mrs. Godarzi. At another point, Behzad has to mollify his crew, who are impatiently waiting for the aged lady to die, by explaining that her son did not leave her side because she was improving but because he had to drive forty-five minutes to tell his boss that he couldn't come to work the next day. When the crew complains that he can't tell them how long they will have to stay, Behzad replies that he can't "strangle her" and that if he knew, he would have to be in contact with "God, or the Angel of Death."

This sense of humanity as being continually constrained from expressing their better selves out of fear of retribution from a higher authority stands in clear contrast to Sufism, where God is the "Friend," and Zoroastrianism, where human beings are necessary allies of Ahura Mazda in his eternal battle with Ahriman (see chapter 3). Kiarostami is not isolating the Kurdish village as backward but instead using its difference to subtly (and safely) highlight the infantile basis of advanced social systems, where monotheism augments the dominance of surrogate Gods (politicians and clerics) by omnipotently convincing the majority to accept their servitude. In a particular parallel to mainstream Shiism, the face scratching resembles self-flagellation to commemorate the Battle of Karbala during the Ashura holiday (see chapter 1), but Kiarostami is more interested in the psychological effect of authority and propitiation on civilized people everywhere.

With more leisure than he is used to, Behzad acts out an erotic fantasy by flirting with the fiancée of the line digger in a dark barn where she milks a cow to provide him with fresh milk, the pretext for which he visits her. Thinking to compel her interest by status and sexual innuendo, he tells her he is her fiancé's "boss" (they both work in communications) and then recites suggestive poetry, intending to captivate her in the same way commercial films compel their viewers into giving up their personal experiences to vicariously identify with high-ranking actors. Behzad has committed the poem to memory to impress others with his privileged acculturation, and in this sense, he is as different from the poets he reads as Sabzian is from the real Makhmalbaf.

Still, Behzad's interest in poetry reveals a potentiality for spiritual development, just as Sabzian does at times when his imitation becomes authentic. Behzad tells the girl that the poet whose words he has just read had only gone to school through the fifth grade and that the girl herself could write poetry if she wanted to. He is intuitively speaking of his own spiritual development, which has been retarded by pride in his formal education but which may still carry enough life to move forward.

The "roads of Kiarostami" lead from subservience to freedom (see chapter 3):

> Philosophers tend to advise us directly and to prescribe things. And naturally we tend to resist that kind of instruction coming from above. But our Iranian poets have a much more delicate and indirect way of showing the ways of the world and telling us how to approach life. I'm more attracted to our Iranian poets than our philosophers because in the way they've put together their messages they've managed to establish a better relationship with us.[8]

By titling *Wind* after a poem by the Iranian modernist poet Forough Farrokhzad (1935–1967) and by having Behzad recite her poem in full during the milking scene, Kiarostami alludes to the transformative power of poetry to help people recognize their souls by rejecting their assigned social, national, and religious roles. One way to do this is by recognizing oneself in a previously remote other. The trip to Siah Dareh, the Kurdish village in *Wind*, recalls Kiarostami's previous trips to rural Iran in the Koker trilogy, his return to an unconventional Tehran in *Ten*, his trip to the pre-Islamic past in *Shirin*, and his final trips to Italy and Japan in *Certified Copy* and *Like Someone in Love*.

Forough's "The Wind Will Carry Us," which Behzad recites in full, expresses a blend of frailty, fear, mortality, and love:

> In my night so brief, alas
> The wind is about to meet the leaves.
> My night so brief is filled with devastating anguish.
> Hark! Do you hear the whisper of the shadows?
> This happiness feels foreign to me.
> I am accustomed to despair.
> Hark! Do you hear the whisper of the shadows?
> There, in the night, something is happening
> The moon is red and anxious.
> And, clinging to this roof
> That could collapse at any moment,
> The clouds, like a crowd of mourning women,
> Await the birth of the rain.
> One second, and then nothing.
> Behind this window,
> The night trembles
> And the earth stops spinning.
> Behind this window, a stranger
> Worries about me and you.
> You in your greenery,
> Lay your hands—those burning memories—
> On my loving hands.
> And entrust your lips, replete with life's warmth,
> To the touch of my loving lips.
> The wind will carry us!
> The wind will carry us![9]

While Forough's famed documentary *The House Is Black* (1963) was filmed in a leper colony and reveals hidden beauty beneath an ugly surface, her poem and Kiarostami's film convey the dread of death beneath a beautiful surface. As in *The House Is Black*, Forough uses darkness or "night" to express a sense of transience and the ever-present imminence of death. "Leaves" may be individual human lives that the wind is always on the brink of dislodging and dispersing from their earthly home: "In my night, so brief, alas / The wind is about to meet the leaves. / My night so brief is filled with devastating anguish / Hark! Do you hear the whisper of the shadows?" The beginning emphasizes despair over frailty; the moon is "red and anxious," and the roof to which it "clings . . . could collapse at any moment."

But the despair is counterbalanced by the eternal presence of love and the certainty of renewal: "The clouds, like a crowd of mourning women, / Await the birth of the rain." And out of sight, "Behind this window" of despair, a "stranger worries about me and you." In the Islamic tradition, green is the color generally associated with deity, and the "you" Forough lovingly invokes can transform the fear of the future to a cherished present in which death is the graceful transition verbally mirrored by the poem's end: "You, in your greenery / Lay your hands / On my loving hands / And entrust your lips, replete with warmth, / To the touch of my loving lips. / The wind will carry us! / The wind will carry us!"

Sufi poets commonly used sensual love to symbolize spiritual love, and that parallel may also have accounted for Iranian censors delaying the release of *Wind* in Iran, but anything associated with Forough would have raised red flags. As the creator of poems that celebrate sexuality as well as being an unabashed divorcée and ardent feminist, Forough was bound to incur the scorn of Khomeini, and it is not surprising that her films were domestically banned for more than ten years after the revolution and fifteen years after her death.[10] Behzad displays his knowledge of Forough's poetry to appear emancipated and modern, but Kiarostami uses her eroticism primarily to satirize Behzad's lack of depth and to pay homage to a well-known poet whose deeper vision he shares.

As Mehrnaz Saeed-Vafa puts it, "Poetry for Iranians is a religion, a religion as powerful as Islam," and for Kiarostami, poetry and spirituality were inseparable. For him, as for Rumi, poetry was the only safe way to express a faith that located divinity in nature rather than above it. Saeed-Vafa adds that after the 1979 revolution, "man-centered" culture was rejected as corrupt and the "mysteries of the system and the universe [could only] be conveyed through metaphor."[11]

The Wind Will Carry Us begins with an aerial shot of a tiny car traveling a zigzag road through a valley flanked by pine trees on the slopes and bare stone mountains further out. In this film, close-ups can be deceptive, while the wide shot directs the eye toward treasures that the car's inhabitants have never learned to see. As Kiarostami said in regard to *Where Is the Friend's House?* the journey in Persian culture is "linked with mysticism; for us what is really important is not the goal we wish to attain, but the path we must travel" (see chapter 2), and the zigzag path in particular represents the realization that the goal of existence is not to reach a desired end but to recognize what one can learn to love along the way.

Behzad is frustrated later when the woman whose death he came to exploit refuses to die, so the time he spends waiting becomes a metonym of how large numbers of people spend the time of their lives. In the opening scene, the news crew is immediately surrounded by the dust clouds that their "iron cell" raises on the road, but they can still scan the hillsides for landmarks that neither they nor the spectator can find. Unlike the screen-filling dust that obscures Badii's vision as he despairs of life and the similar dust that floods Behzad when he is shocked by the apparent burial of the line digger, the high, wide shot shrinks the human imprint to that of the trees, even the largest of which look tiny from this distance.

The first spoken line, "Where's the tunnel, then?" recalls Puya asking his father, "Where is the big tunnel?" at the beginning of *And Life Goes On*, but at that point, he and his father have not reached it, whereas here, another passenger says, "Somebody's been sleeping. We passed it back near Biston." The opportunity to be born into a larger vision once missed can never be recovered for some people, while for others it can. Later in the film, Behzad and the digger exchange repartee about Farhad, the Herculean Persian artist who singlehandedly dug a huge canal called Biston through solid rock to win the love of a queen.[12] It is a pre-Islamic myth that Kiarostami takes up at length in *Shirin*, but here, the mythological reference may refer to the wisdom educated people have already encountered but have not learned.

In the course of the film, Behzad explores the village, and the viewers explore Behzad as a potential mirror of themselves, while the rest of the crew never leaves their room. Kiarostami tells us that you can find what you're looking for if you simply open your eyes. And so, when one crew member feeling lost and seeking direction asks, "Where is the winding road?" another answers, "We're already on it."

Many people look for a personal or theological confirmation from a supreme being or a proclaimed spokesman of that being that their lives are on track. The specific landmark the crew seeks is a distinctively large tree, but in this barren landscape, the sparse trees are all distinctive. Kiarostami identified the tree Ahmad repeatedly passes in *Where Is the Friend's House?* as a "symbol of friendship," and in Sufi terms, God as the ultimate Friend manifests Himself plurally in trees and in human friends: Shams for Rumi, the old door maker for Ahmad, the motorcycling Makhmalbaf for Sabzian, and the motorcycling doctor for Behzad.[13] Travel inside a car, as Kiarostami said in

Ten on Ten, means remaining confined by the ego, while escaping it opens a person up to the direct experience they had as children (see chapter 3).

For this to happen, an adult needs to learn from everything he or she sees, as Puya does with the grasshopper. But the TV crew from Tehran is locked into looking up for advancement rather than around for fulfillment. And so, as one says their way leads past a single tree, another says, "There are a lot around here," and when they finally do pass a large tree isolated on a hill that the audience does not see, one passenger mocks another for having missed it: "Jahan, take a look."—"Too late now, you'll have to look up through the roof, but you won't see it."—"It's so big!" The exchange is ironic because from the film spectator's point of view, all the trees are small in the vast, open landscape.

Finding the way also becomes a reference to the last line of the Sohrab Sepehri poem that forms the title of *Where Is the Friend's House?* (just as Forough's "The Wind Will Carry Us" is the title here). The Sepehri parallel begins when one crew member asks, "What's after the tree," another says, "Nothing," a third says, "Nothing? There's a road near the tree," and Behzad quotes Sepehri's "Address" (see chapter 2): "I'll tell you what there is. 'Near the tree is a wooded lane, greener than the dreams of God.'" The phrase connotes the reason Iranian censors may have delayed *Wind*'s release.[14] It potentially means either that conceptions of God's vision are inferior to human experience of the natural world or that the natural world generates greater beauty than dreams of the world to come, an idea the doctor near the end of *Wind* attributes to Omar Khayyam. After laughing at his own joke, Behzad wittily responds to another passenger asking, "What's after the tree?" with "Read the Address."

He alludes to the part of Sepehri's poem (previously quoted; see chapter 2) where the "passerby pointed with his finger to an aspen," which is preceded by a "garden lane more green than God's dream" and which in the film is the unspoiled country they are passing through at that moment. After the aspen, the poem metaphorically suggests the guide Behzad will soon meet. Beyond the conventions of the religion he mocks and the skepticism he espouses, he may or may not eventually recognize Farzad as the child in the poem he thinks he knows:

> You go to the end of that lane / which appears behind adolescence / then you turn / towards the flower of solitude / two steps more to the flower / at the foot of the mountain / of eternal myths you stop and stay / and a transparent fear envelops you. / In the intimacy of flowing space, / you hear a rustling, / you see a child who has climbed up a pine tree / to pick up a chick / from the nest of light / and from the child you ask / "Where is the House of the Friend?"[15]

Behzad meets a version of the Sufi Friend when he rides with the doctor at the end of the film, but before that, he gains and loses another friend because his intellectual advancement has stunted his spiritual growth. His condition is suggested upon arrival at the Kurdish village when a boy of about ten runs up and asks, "Why are you late?" Behzad does not want the villagers to know of their presence because they may take offense at having a sacred ceremony filmed, so he tells the boy, whose uncle has assigned him to be their guide, that they are looking for "lost treasure."

The surface lie is the thematic truth because like Sabzian, he is unconsciously seeking the soul that his obsession with success has almost smothered. The ambiguity at the end about whether he finds it coincides with the unknown effect the film may have on any particular spectator. Through Behzad's forced vacation and the escape from daily life that cinema affords, they have been immersed in a world where people assume they are alive to help each other live and that life itself is valued so much that everyone contributes to helping a hundred-year-old woman live a week, a day, or a few hours longer.

Behzad, on the other hand, is an unwitting killer like Badii, the young soldier, and the old taxidermist in *Taste of Cherry*. Many likely viewers of a Kiarostami film may also be killers of their own souls. The film offers an opportunity to relearn what they have been taught to forget. The boy whose name is Farzad tells Behzad that he has been waiting since school finished for the day. Here, as in Kiarostami films from *Where Is the Friend's House?* to *Like Someone in Love*, the emphasis is on what needs to be learned outside of school. Formal acculturation is in many ways a deception, and when Behzad tells the boy to tell the villagers that the crew has come to look for treasure, he has him repeat it as if it were a formal lesson: "What do you say?" he asks again. "Treasure," the boy replies. Later, he ironically becomes furious at the boy for not lying to the crew about the old lady's condition, and in a world where value is determined by status, relative truth is not the treasure.

Treasure is a Sufi trope for a God manifested in Creation, and it is no surprise that the idea had to be concealed from those who based their authority on an authoritative God. As Nizami Ganjavi (1141–1209), the medieval Persian poet whose epic romance about the Zoroastrian Khosrow and the Christian Shirin became the basis of Kiarostami's *Shirin*, put it, "Under the poet's tongue lies the key to the treasury."[16] But finding the treasure requires what Elena, paraphrasing French critic Alain Bergala, calls a "reeducation of the gaze."[17] This takes some doing because as Rumi wrote, "Everyone has become a gold seeker, but the ordinary do not know it when they see it. If you cannot recognize it, join a wise man."[18] Kiarostami tries to transmit the treasure by hinting at what lies outside the cinematic frame and by presenting wise children or wise, old men like Ahmad's door maker or Behzad's doctor, versions of the Sufi master described by Rumi as a "king beneath a humble cloak [and] a treasure within a ruin."[19]

In Muhammad's vision, God said, "I was a Hidden Treasure, so I wanted to be known. Therefore I created the world that I might be known."[20] And for Rumi, in William Chittick's imaginative paraphrase, the manifestation of that intent was sometimes gentle and sometimes severe, the difference being not between good and bad behavior but between knowing and unknowing: "Therefore all creatures make God manifest, day and night. However, some of them know this and are aware of their making Him manifest, while others are heedless."[21] As in Attar's *Conference of the Birds* (see chapter 2), the lost treasure can only be discovered in oneself: "The universe was created for the sake of manifestation, in order that the Treasure of Wisdom might not remain hidden. He said, 'I was a Hidden Treasure.' Listen! Do not lose touch with your own substance, make yourself manifest!' God tells us, 'Just as I wanted to manifest My Treasure, so I wanted to manifest your ability to recognize that treasure.'"[22]

In *Wind*, Behzad facetiously answers Farzad's assigned questions about good and evil by reversing heaven and hell: "What happens to the good and evil on Judgment Day?"—"That's obvious. The good go to hell, and the evil go to heaven."—"Is that right?"—"Yes. No. The good go to heaven, and the evil go to hell." And later, when he briefly worries about whether he himself is bad, Kiarostami's focus on the larger landscape cinematically reflects Rumi's vision: "In any case, the perfection of the Painter's infinite creativity demands that He paint both beautiful and ugly pictures. So there is no absolute evil in the world, for evil is relative."[23]

Behzad is a good citizen in the social sense, a hard worker focused on an assigned task, and a more-than-occasional reader of poetry in his leisure time. He is patient and friendly with Farzad, confiding with the line digger, and helpful to the woman in whose house he and the crew are staying. But he has ugly moments, later manifested by a corruptive intent when he reads what he considers to be erotic poetry to the digger's fiancée; when he shows outright cruelty toward a turtle and later to Farzad; and in his overall wish that Mrs. Malek, the dying woman, would hurry up and get it over with so that he can shoot his story and return to Tehran.

Farzad's description of an exchange between Mrs. Malek and his younger uncle who feels guilty for having just arrived also applies to Behzad. In a lucid moment she "recognized my uncle and asked for news of the family. My uncle wept." The love they share for Mrs. Malek ends the feud the uncle had been having with Farzad's mother: "'Am I a bad son?'" he asks her. "'No,' [she replies,] 'you're not bad. You're just very busy.'" The breakdown of Behzad's car when they reach the village refers to the spiritual dead end he has reached, and the initial dialogue with Farzad makes Mrs. Malek's physical condition analogous to Behzad's spiritual one.

Here again, Kiarostami recommends that a character or spectator get ready to leave the egoic shell represented by the car when their ingrained habits "stall" their progress, causing them to "struggle on hills," and their previously reliable "gauge no longer works." Behzad explains to Farzad that a "car's mechanical parts can wear out," much like his in-the-know sophistication, and that a car "can give up the ghost." Farzad's question, "Can it be mended?" provides the film's dramatic tension: Can people like Behzad and the typical urban art-film viewer return to the life-enhancing source Kiarostami strives to restore through his art?

The direction he provides, like that of Rumi, Forough, and Sepehri, is not upward toward abstract purity but downward and backward toward animals, trees, and children. Behzad has a culturally conditioned drive to move up, revealed in his social ambition and in his literally upward drive to answer calls from Mrs. Godarzi, but his ambition, like the biblical pride that "goeth before a fall," threatens a heedless plunge into oblivion symbolized by the line digger's burial previously described.

People who begin as harmless snobs can unwittingly become suicidal as their egos systematically shut down their sensibilities. But introspection in the Sufi sense is foreign to modern sophisticates, and so when Farzad asks if the car can be mended, the two are ascending the steep hill to the village, a visual image that darkens Behzad's patronizing quip: "Yes, don't ask so many questions, or I'll give up the ghost, too, at this altitude." Many shots of Behzad walking next to Farzad are visual correlatives of his phony elevation, and he is continually surprised when Farzad and Yossef, the line digger, have cultural knowledge he assumed to be above them. After the car dialogue, his potential entrapment is further symbolized by the idea that while the dying Mrs. Malek obviously cannot leave her house, the other members of his crew choose not to leave their rooms.

Behzad's exploration of the village indicates that for him and for people who are curious enough to alertly follow him through the film, there is still hope. While walking with Farzad soon after their meeting, Behzad airily quotes some lines that the boy surprisingly completes: "Why is [Siah Dareh] called Black Valley? Why not White Valley?"—"That's its name."—"'When you're fated to be black . . .'"—"'Even holy water cannot whiten you.'"—"How do you know that poem?"—"Our teacher recites poems to us from time to time." If he is not to remain in the dark, Behzad needs to step outside of his social elevation and follow rather than lead Farzad. Like Behzad, Farzad is devoted to work, but unlike him, he has no desperation to complete it. He works the fields, runs errands in the village, and conscientiously does his schoolwork. His manner as he guides Behzad around the village is like that of a miniature adult, and though he respects Behzad's wishes, he speaks to him as an equal, patiently explaining customs Behzad does not understand.

Unlike Ahmad, Farzad lives in a community where he has no reason to fear adults, and unlike Puya, he is fully reconciled to the responsibilities life holds in store and has no desire to go beyond them. He does, however, have anxieties about having left his book in the car because he has exams coming up shortly and insists that Behzad have someone get it for him. The exchange serves to highlight the theme of Behzad's education because the book is on the car's dashboard, the same place that Behzad later places the human femur he has asked Yossef to toss up to him from under the cemetery where their dialogue takes place. Behzad and Kiarostami's spectators have been brought to the village, just as they have been placed in the car with Mr. Badii to continually remember their mortality as the best way to love their lives. That is the self-exam the film wants attentive adults to take.

The tension of the story hinges on whether Behzad can pass the test. Its rigor is initially symbolized when Farzad leads him from the stalled car up to the village and Behzad complains about the steepness of the path. Farzad's answer clearly expresses Kiarostami's sense of art's purpose as a way of helping people learn necessary lessons they might otherwise miss in the limited time of their lives. When Behzad asks if people always take this "tough" path, Farzad replies that it isn't the main path that is a "long way off" (from a Kiarostami film) but that this path is shorter, and when Behzad then complains that his guide is moving too fast for him, Farzad simply says, "It was the best way."

On our path through the film, Kiarostami carefully edits in bird and animal sounds to make thematic points at key moments. These sounds are typical ways of reminding us to kick the plotline habit and to appreciate the senses that God's generosity (as the doctor later calls the gift of life) can afford us. Birds, animals, trees, and mountains are as important to our education as learning what we can of humanity generally through observing other cultures. As Farzad leads Behzad through the streets of Siah Dareh, we hear the alerting voice of a rooster constantly crowing, the occasional bleating of goats, or the mooing of cows that graze peacefully on small plots of grass in the middle of the streets.

When the crew first views Siah Dareh from the outside, they agree that it is a "beautiful village," but then, except for Behzad, their admiration is limited to the picturesque that tourists stash in their bucket lists of world travel. Kiarostami wants us to live rather than simply tour our existence and to patiently regard its subtleties as carefully as he hopes spectators will regard his meticulously edited film. To stay strictly within one's own culture or even strictly human concerns is to confine ourselves to a house that is too small, a house in which our souls will die.

The cultural house is a place of darkness when it ignores the soul in Forough's *The House Is Black*, but in *Wind*, death within the house of one state of awareness holds the potential for continued growth. When Farzad's aunt shows Behzad the accommodations she has prepared for them in her home, she says, "This is one of the rooms. If it's too small, there are other rooms." Behzad's initial inability to step outside of his own concerns also reflects the lethal constriction he may suffer. Physical longevity does not correspond to the internal span of experience. A person can breathe for nine or ten decades and not really have lived very long: "Thank you. We'll only be staying a couple of nights," he says, and many people never really do take the opportunity to take the invitation that Kiarostami offers when he has the woman say, "Make yourself at home."

Early on, Behzad wants to know where Mrs. Malek lives so that he can watch the activity to determine her condition. Farzad takes him up a short stairway, where he says, "You can see her house from here." It is the house of mortality Behzad instinctively tries to remember when he places the femur on the dashboard, but at this point, he just says, "You can't see much from here," and Farzad replies, "Let's go up higher. I'll show you."

When Behzad asks Farzad's mother why they are staying with her sister instead of with her, she continues the growth metaphor by replying that her house is too small and that the visitors deserve better. Kiarostami strives to give his viewers the best house he can imagine, but the only way to do that is by making them aware of the small details they have been taught to miss in life and in cinema. Behzad's potential for escape is indicated when he kindly tells Farzad that he doesn't agree with his mother because Farzad is "small but skillful" and "small things have their value, too." And Farzad unknowingly speaks of Behzad as well when his next line implies that sometimes people must leave the confines of their culture in order to survive: "I'm going to grow. The house won't grow, though."

Some cultures, however, provide more space than others. The appearance and communal interaction of Siah Dareh is something like that of a Native American pueblo. In a community with no stand-alone structures, divisions of high and low dissolve. Some women sit on the roofs of buildings, people and animals mingle in the street, there are no neighborhoods divided by wealth, and there is no insistent rush to buy and sell. Life and death, the body and the soul, interpenetrate each other, and when Behzad asks Farzad the location of the cemetery where he expects to film the custom of a strange people, a rooster continues to crow, just as one does in *And Life Goes On* when the film director finally involves himself in the life of the community.

Farzad's example should be a wake-up call for the spectator, as well. When he excuses himself to get his things from the fields and to get the crew's gear, Behzad teasingly asks if he is more worried about the crew or his book. Farzad unapologetically says his book because "I have an exam tomorrow." His priority should be that of the audience, as well. Social and material obligations should not be taken for granted, at least for those who have the luxury of attending the cinema, and the real work of existence should be understanding ourselves: "In this cinema, the most important subject matter is human beings and their souls" (see chapter 2).

From a Sufi perspective, experience supersedes belief. The people in the village identify with each other, just as Kiarostami identified with the valleys, mountains, trees, and birds. The artist becomes what he beholds. The villagers are led to believe that Behzad works with the telecommunications company that is laying a cable underneath the cemetery. They respectfully address him as "Engineer," but the title is thematically apt because while an engineer typically constructs an object meant to control nature, the artist's work is itself a natural event proceeding from his soul. And the hoped-for result of the artist's work, like that of any new birth, is to give another being the power to fully live. Responding to Behzad's question about Mrs. Malek's condition, Farzad expresses Kiarostami's view of absolute death, the sensory deprivation that envelops Badii before the epilogue in *Taste of Cherry*: "She can't recognize anyone," the doctor says. "There's no hope." To be alive is to recognize absolute value in other living things and thereby leave the house of social and religious authority.

When Behzad takes the call from a satirized version of that authority atop his miniature mountain, he not only leaves his "people" behind but also leaves any stand-in for an authoritative God, rejecting the boss to find the Friend. And the people in the village treat a dying woman as a reflection of themselves in a kinship model that Kiarostami in all his films extends to the world: "Who's watching her? My mother, her family, the neighbors, my young uncle."

By contrast, at this point, Behzad wants this abstract person to die, the film's way of showing how modern urban life fragments a community, making indifference to unknown people an unwitting form of murder just, as the Kurdish soldier is trained to do in *Taste of Cherry* and as the taxidermist treats animals in the same film, as the journalist treats Sabzian in *Close-Up*, or as clashing nations treat each other in *Homework*. All during this early exchange concerning Mrs. Malek's health, vigorous birdsongs reflect the villagers' attitude. These birds, it seems, speak to each other to celebrate life rather than for extrinsic meaning. The same goes for a poetic cinema that purposefully avoids a conclusive end.

After Farzad leaves, Behzad begins to explore the village on his own. Radio music from the nearby teahouse indicates that the villagers are not a backward tribe cut off from the outside world, but they are shown to be different in several significant ways. The woman who owns the teahouse is hospitable to Behzad but not at all deferential, nor is she deferential to any of the men she serves. As a symbol of how Behzad and the spectator need to reframe their assumptions, Behzad discovers that his camera is missing from his car before he enters, but the lady restores it, saying, "It's a miracle it's still here," subliminally alluding to the journalist's jaded sensibilities.

Her lines return the film's viewers to valuing curiosity more than possessions when she explains, "Here, even if your car's gold, no one will touch it."

Figure 6.1. While his crew remains locked in their dark rooms, Behzad surveys the village he considers beneath him, but he ignores its loving nature, symbolized by the flowering plant on the railing in the center of the frame. New Yorker Films/Photofest.

But [we are] opposite the school, and the students are curious." Behzad begins to relearn the world immediately when he remarks, "I've never seen a woman serve tea," a custom foreign to the sexually segregated Islamic republic and a question that the woman answers in terms of the universal experience of humanity and nature Kiarostami consistently explores: "Didn't you have parents? Who served you as a child?"

Behzad's thick glasses help to show that he is not prepared to appreciate variation. The woman's bold speech would rarely be heard in public from the repressed Tehrani women indelibly portrayed by Jafar Panahi in *The Circle* (2000): "Don't park there!" she yells to a man on a motorcycle. "When you start up, you pollute the café. We swallow fumes instead of tea." But the reproach is good-humored, and when a man in the café speaks up to argue, she interrupts, "It's my café, my territory," speaking in a sense for Kiarostami, rejecting the social values that have shaped Behzad but that in this cinematic setting are not going to be served as the refreshment commercial filmgoers expect.

Ironically mirroring Behzad's sense of rank, the woman speaks to Behzad as if he were a child, much as Behzad spoke to Farzad. She tells him that women have three functions: "By day they're workers, in the evening they serve, and at night they work." She continues the film's work theme by

Figure 6.2. Overhead shots from the upper levels of the tiered village show groups of people fully engaged in celebrating their collective life, unlike Behzad, who lives in a perpetual rush to reach "higher ground" than the anonymous individuals he competes with. New Yorker Films/Photofest.

engaging in a comic dispute with one of her customers about whether men or women work harder, which Behzad, with his head swiveling back and forth, watches as if he were watching his parents argue. The exchange shows that no human society can be utopic and that some villagers can be as petty and protective of their limited power as city dwellers.

After the woman initially asks Behzad if he is in telecommunications, she wryly reflects, "This place is a world of communication." Gossip and petty one-upmanship occupy the minds of people everywhere, but there are exceptions. The teacher is sensitive and reflective when he expresses his "pain" over the motivations of the mourning ceremony, and the line digger is literate and the equal of Behzad in verbal repartee. (When Behzad naïvely asks if the femur is from a right or left leg, Yossef replies, "They're not shoes!") And Farzad has been impressed enough by poetry to complete Behzad's quote about people who can't be redeemed.

Those people who can may be able to escape the frame, and so when Behzad picks up his camera to photograph the debaters, the woman immediately snaps, "No photos!" surprising Behzad, who silently complies like a reprimanded child. The woman gives no reason for not wanting to be photographed, in contrast to the media-worshipping Ahankhah family of *Close-*

Up. Being the subject of curiosity in a small village or the small mental scope of the urban world is of no benefit to her or anybody else.

The comic argument has a serious undertone in that it conveys the idea that the paramount human activity should be (in one way or another) the perpetuation of life: "I have three jobs, and the third is the hardest and most important." The artist, too, has the hard job of sustaining the life of the soul. The sexual innuendo is so compelling to Behzad that he impulsively grabs his camera, but before he can snap a shot, the woman snaps, "I should have kept the camera!" Behzad is not used to being publicly scolded, especially by a woman, and having been stripped of authority reverts to childish obedience, looking guiltily chastised as he quickly puts the camera away. The male debater continues the creation-as-work metaphor by retorting, "Don't men have a third job? Only women?"

In Siah Dareh, everyone has some kind of job based on common need rather than individual ambition, and every job is about sustaining the community's life. At this point, a little boy walks past the café driving a cow with a stick, but the job Kiarostami wants the audience to pursue includes observation and introspection, and the upshot of this job, finding purpose in mortality, is suggested when a very old man with a cane seated at another table is summoned by a woman's voice.

The camera follows the old man, and then so does Behzad, thinking perhaps that the summons has something to do with Mrs. Malek. At the head of the path leading away from the café, a black-clad woman standing between protective pink walls stands waiting. A TV or radio antenna stands nearby, but instead of being offered an exotic image of backward people, the viewer receives an image of loving comfort. From a distance, Behzad watches the woman give the old man soup. A quick cut to two brightly clothed young women, one of whom holds a baby, is followed by showing the soup woman bringing a second bowl to a woman who sits just outside Mrs. Malek's door.

If Mrs. Malek's house is the house of death in which everyone will eventually rest, then people's primary work should be to share the "generosity of God" while they are still alive. Behzad must travel much further to get that message from the film's Sufi guide, but at this point, like other members of the intelligentsia, he is far from ready. The teahouse lady makes the thematic point, her voice rising over the constant chatter of her customers and the ceaseless background noise of her radio: "The engineer's forgotten his camera again. He's as distracted as me."

At this point, Behzad receives the first cell-phone call, but the signal in the village is not strong enough, and he jumps in his Range Rover in a rush to get to "higher ground." On his way out of town, he passes through a flurry of activity, where people he does not think he resembles are busy tending to physical necessity. The sound is a jumble of his engine roaring, roosters crowing, dogs barking, cows lowing, and his own voice frantically shouting, "Allo!" He passes a woman adding a length of plumbing pipe to a pile, four boys herding sheep, and two goats humping in a comic echo of the café woman's "third job." But while Behzad must work to please Mrs. Godarzi, these people work purely to sustain life. In the long view, however, Behzad's work, like theirs, is so consuming that he has no time to deepen his awareness of the scene he rushes through. As the boys herding sheep enter an opening in the wall just ahead, we see a Kiarostami zigzag road lined by green trees on one side and a steep embankment on the other.

But Behzad, rushing madly ahead and still filling his ears with his own desperate "Allos," is as invisible to himself as he is temporarily to us in a long shot that reduces him to a rolling cloud of white dust. Then the car appears, moving up a rise where an irregular line of bright-green trees stands on the sunlit reddish-brown earth. Kiarostami said that the tree Ahmad repeatedly passes in *Where Is the Friend's House?* is a symbol of friendship. Here, as in Sepehri's "Address," the trees are a manifestation of the Friend, and the earth is the Friend's house, but most people miss human, plant, or animal manifestations of the Friend because they are too busy looking up. Behzad has become so dependent on a higher authority to validate his life that he is rude to his wife, who turns out to be the caller, and irritable about having to assume kinship obligations of his own that correspond to the one he has been sent to cover: "I thought it was Mrs. Godarzi. I told you not to call me here."

As he walks around on the hill saying he can't attend a relative's funeral, we hear the line digger singing underground. Like Behzad, Yossef is compelled and confined by his work, but unlike the journalist, the digger and the other villagers are fortified by love. We never know exactly why Behzad wants the femur and why he places it on his dashboard, but the object and the act reveal a cavalier attitude toward death. Probably he displays the bone to amuse his crew with a macabre joke on the way home. The edited sequence is meant to contrast his indifference to the reverence for life consistently shown by the villagers. The possibility that he may progress to their attitude is suggested in the next scene as he questions Farzad: "How's the invalid?" he asks. The question the film asks is whether Behzad himself can be cured.

So far, he has not been able to pass into a more advanced state of soul, symbolized by Farzad crossing the curve of a stream on a log that "all the children use" simply for fun, while Behzad ignores the detour and continues straight ahead. The difference is that Behzad is always focused on a future goal, while Farzad can live in the moment. And the film sends the message that alleviating the suffering of others is an empathetic way of appreciating every moment when Farzad tells him that if Mrs. Malek eats soup brought by one of the women, that woman's wish will come true. Later, just after the teahouse lady affecting her usual contrarian façade dismisses a man on a motorcycle—"You're a coward if you come back"—Farzad speaks for the community by thanking her: "May your wish come true. The dying lady ate the soup you gave her."

In valuing love above all, Farzad and the villagers are much more advanced than Behzad and his crew. Behzad's infantile egotism is emphasized by a prolonged, unattractive close-up of him shaving in a mirror and afterward by his repeated quest for fresh milk: first from Farzad's mother and later from the digger's fiancée. As he is about to take a second cell-phone call, this time from the impatient Mrs. Godarzi, Behzad sees Yossef's fiancée race away down the golden hills until she is a speck in the distance.

This idea of love as the purpose of transient existence is taken up as Behzad, standing among gravestones, tries to bolster his validity as usual through condescending literary references that he assumes his rural hearers will not get. This time, he refers to the legend of Farhad and Shirin, which the *Encyclopædia Iranica* says "permeates the whole of Persian culture."[24] He is initially confirmed in his superiority by the digger's apparent backwardness: "I think Farhad dug Biston on his own. Do you know him?"—"Yes, he's a local. He lives three miles away."—"A local? Well done."

Figure 6.3. In this iconic shot, Zeynab races through a graveyard past a lone tree, which Kiarostami said is a symbol of friendship in *Where Is the Friend's House?* Here, conjoined with Zeynab's loving nurture, it may symbolize the constant care of the Sufi Friend. New Yorker Films/Photofest.

In a thematic sense, Kiarostami uses the eight-hundred-year-old myth to show that stories apply universally but in infinitely variable ways to people of all social classes in disparate cultures. Yossef exposes the ignorance of Behzad's supercilious remark when he shows that he has been shaped by the story, while Behzad's reception is purely abstract. "But it wasn't Farhad who dug Biston," the digger begins. The rest of the exchange voices the motivation for building a beautiful village or a beautiful film: "Who then?" Behzad asks, as if speaking to a child, and when Yossef replies, "The love of Shirin," Behzad again comments as if he were competitively comparing knowledge: "Bravo. You know love, too." Then the digger adds, "A man without love cannot live."

The line is resonant because Behzad is unconsciously killing himself by serving the transcendent superiority symbolized by Mrs. Godarzi instead of loving the natural world symbolized by the village and the unspoiled area that surrounds it. Nizami's epic version of the love triangle between the queen, Shirin; the king, Khosrow; and the sculptor, Farhad (*Khosrow and Shirin*) in conjunction with the title poem taken from Forough has a sensual aura that the Iranian censors recognized by forbidding the publication of an eighth edition in 2011 because it included the "indecent" act of Shirin "embracing her husband."²⁵

When Behzad later seeks an opportunity to intimately converse with Yossef's betrothed, he does not just act out a fantasy; he exploits what he considers to be his superior education and social standing to betray a newly made friend. Their bond is based on the constraints of their work, and Behzad sees the parallel when Yossef complains, "I've hit a rock." But while the digger is impelled to persist because he anticipates creating more life with the tea-bringing girl, Behzad's rock is his inability to end the life of Mrs. Malek. In the frustration of an unguarded moment, Behzad is learning to recognize himself in another person, which is the essential gift of the literature he knows but which he is narcissistically unable to feel.

He tells Yossef, "You're lucky. You have a pickax. We can't do anything." He is also learning the value of being alone, free of the demands of Mrs. Godarzi and the complaints of his crew, but instead of valuing the observations he has had time to make, he can only fill his leisure with regressive sentiments, and so when he asks Yossef to ease his vexation by providing some tea, the digger does not realize that Behzad will apply his generous "Help yourself" to the bringer of the tea rather than the tea itself: "If you could give me your Juliet's address, she could provide us with some milk."

The literary allusion is consistent with Behzad's shallow erudition, but the Farhad/Shirin story (like *Romeo and Juliet*) has a tragic ending that helps to darken Behzad's intent and highlight the digger's innocence. He tells Behzad to "knock on any door, and they'll give you milk," and when Behzad persists, "Can't I just ask her for some?" Yossef says, "No problem," and gives him directions. There is a problem, of course, with Behzad's soul, which like Yossef's ax has reached a dead end, and once again, the direction motif, so prevalent in *Where Is the Friend's House?* and significant at the beginning of both *Wind* and *Close-Up*, is a reminder to members of the audience to change direction because many resemble Behzad.

Behzad's precarious state of soul is suggested in the next scene, where he mockingly answers Farzad's question by saying that the "bad go to heaven and the good to hell," but the earthly version of this is culturally and personally variable, and Behzad is already essentially in hell. Feeling guilty for mocking the boy's innocence, Behzad quickly gives him the right answer, and while Farzad runs back into the school to write it down, Behzad glances outside the passenger window and sees a man enveloped in a load of green hay enter a nearby building, echoing the walking haystack Ahmad passes on the streets of Poshteh. The reference to that film evokes the moral ambiguity of Ahmad helping his friend by cheating when he writes the correct answer in Mohammad's notebook, and perhaps the haystack's green color in this version suggests that there is still hope for Behzad, who is uncharacteristically acting from the heart rather than the ego or social obligation.

The image also suggests that his work is largely responsible for Behzad being actually bad in the sense that Farzad's mother answers his uncle's feelings of guilt for not being in constant attendance at Mrs. Malek's bedside: "No, you're not bad. You're just very busy." In a later scene, when Behzad, feeling guilty about being harshly impatient with Farzad, asks the boy to answer "frankly" if he thinks he is bad, he gets the answer he wants—"No, you're good."—"How can you be sure?"—"I know, you're good."—only to immediately exploit the sincere trust he has just received: "Well, since I'm good, can you get me a bowl to fetch milk?"—"I'll get one when I go to work in the fields."—"I want it now."—"I have to go. I'm late. The lady will find you one." Behzad's demands are so outrageously infantile and Farzad's responsibilities so maturely assumed that once again, his delight in his own cleverness is shown to be a way to waste his life when an old woman, completely bent over, passes and a man's voice is heard greeting her, "May God give you health."

Sitting immobile as the life of the village swirls around him, Behzad watches a woman in black emerge from Mrs. Malek's door. He looks disgruntled because apparently her health has not taken a turn for the worse. On the level below him, brightly clad women fold laundry while male voices are heard talking vigorously on the sound track. On the street level, a long line of cows, sheep, and goats mixed together file by, each contributing a distinctive voice to a mélange of sound that celebrates physical life. The scene that follows is about appreciating, protecting, and nurturing this existence, a responsibility taken for granted by the villagers but a lesson that so-called advanced cultures have ignored. The villagers provide for the body, while poets like Forough and Kiarostami provide for the soul, and neither can live without the other.

The next cut takes us just below the surface of the street to show a woman kneading a large, flat piece of dough. As a provider of nourishment, she keynotes Behzad's search for milk, a descent into a realization that is far deeper than his adolescent purpose. Mixed sounds of human and animal life reverberate on the sound track as Behzad tells the bread maker he wants milk. A second keynote image appears as the camera passes a beautiful little girl in a white dress, an image of the innocence he seeks to spoil. The woman rises and calls, "Zeynab!" as she opens an inner door above a stairway. Just before Behzad descends, he asks for reassurance that Zeynab is the digger's fiancée, even though Yossef had said anyone would give him milk: "Is this Kakrahman's house?"—"No. Next door."

The detail lends universality to the scene that follows. Behzad wants something personally specific, but the film gives us something general and poetic. The initial image of Behzad bending to enter the adjoining house recalls the dialogue about spaces that have become too small when Farzad says he will grow but his house won't and when his mother says she has other rooms if the ones she has provided are too small. Then a shot of a low, narrow entrance seen from the inside precedes Behzad bending again to enter. Though the space is narrow, the limited light precedes an expansive experience in the darkness of the cellar below.

When Mrs. Kakrahman leads Behzad to a cellar door identical to the one next door, she, too, calls, "Zeynab!" Apparently, the same girl milks cows in an underground barn common to both houses. The doubled name transforms a single person into the general symbol of creative virtue associated with her name. In the Koran, Muhammad arranged a marriage between a high-ranking widow and a freed slave, probably to make a moral point about social inequality. Later, he, too, married Zeynab, establishing her status as a spiritual partner. She did not refrain from disagreeing with the prophet when convinced of the righteousness of her own view. On one occasion, a woman whom she defended against charges of adultery praised her as being the most "God-conscious," truthful, and generous woman she had ever seen.[26] Kiarostami may have emphasized the name as a tribute to Forough, just before the scene where the film's title poem is heard in full.

Behzad's quest for fresh milk also implies a need for spiritual regeneration, but in order to find it, he and the viewers are taken into a literal and figurative darkness, just as Attar's thirty birds are suspended in a "valley of poverty and nothingness" just before they discover that the king they seek is in themselves (see chapter 2). Instead of darkness being the evil with which it is commonly associated, Kiarostami uses a black screen to open possibility, to point beyond any familiar frame that would serve to deaden sensibility.

Like Ahmad being afraid to ascend the dark stairs after he finally reaches Mohammad's house in *Where Is the Friend's House?* Behzad hesitates, even though he has fastened on a specific sexual fantasy that he is about to indulge: "It's so dark in there," he says as he stands at the threshold of the film's pivotal scene.

Carrying a bucket-handled silver bowl, Behzad begins to descend, advancing toward the camera, until his body blackens the screen for eighteen seconds. Kiarostami typically uses total darkness as a womb symbol immediately preceding enlightenment. In *Taste of Cherry*, the fifty-seven seconds of darkness in Badii's grave precedes his symbolic resurrection in the coda. The French critic Alain Bergala reports that Kiarostami told him that he wanted to include seven minutes of darkness in *Wind* but "couldn't sustain it." Finally, in his next film, *ABC Africa*, he was able "to pull it off" by filming five minutes of blackness relieved only by a couple of lightning flashes from the open window of a Ugandan hotel that has no electricity.[27]

In *Taste of Cherry*, Kiarostami takes out the "voice and the light [as] the deeper way of thinking about nothingness and death" (see chapter 4), but in *Wind*, the black screen precedes a descent from a metaphysics stratified by social rank into a womb where a supernatural heaven can be blissfully ignored. And so, even as Behzad encounters visual blackness, the voices of baby calves, kids, and lambs indicate that once again Kiarostami uses the fear of death to celebrate life.

Considering his overt intent, Behzad's path through a narrow opening to a place that shelters nascent life is a sexual entry, and Kiarostami uses the erotic reputation of Forough to fuse the erotic and the spiritual in depicting Zeynab. Still in total darkness, Behzad asks, "Is anyone here?" just before an incarnation of the best in human nature appears to establish him as a temporary foil, darkness preceding light rather than darkness versus light. "Can you milk the cow for me?" Behzad asks, a metaphor of transferring spirit to his undeveloped soul.

Later in the scene, after Behzad recites "The Wind Will Carry Us," Zeynab asks how long the author studied, and Behzad says that Forough's formal education ended in fifth grade and that anyone can be a poet. But the statement is not literally true because verbal poetry requires verbal talent. It is true, however, in the sense that Zeynab radiates a poetic message in her graceful body and lovely voice. She is a walking poem, and so Behzad is right that anyone *might* be a poet but wrong if his line is taken to mean everyone *can* be.

Cynics may wonder how artists can produce enlightenment in an ignorant world, and Kiarostami answers by initially presenting Zeynab as a mythical bearer of light. The frame depicting her entrance shows a large, substantial hurricane lamp on the left that highlights her lower body as she moves from right to left across the screen. She is wearing a vibrant-orange dress patterned by white blossoms that curve like Farsi script, a combined symbol of physical and spiritual fertility that covers the part of the body from which life will come. Behzad's question has metaphysical overtones—"It's so dark. How can you milk in here?"—as does Zeynab's answer: "I'm used to it. I work here. You'll get used to it if you stay." The qualification is important because the only way to live in the dark is to acknowledge it, and so hope may be dimming for people like Behzad when he says, "I'll be gone before I'm used to it." Zeynab's next line suggests that soul survival requires unconventional adaptations of vision and technique, an internal version of the physical adaptation shown by the earthquake and AIDS survivors in *And Life Goes On* and *ABC Africa*. Even though the electricity is off, Zeynab says, "We have a flashlight."

She sits on a stool next to the cow, the right side of her body spotlighted by the lamp. The image is framed by an opening with vertical wooden bars on one side and a ladder to the right. The camera holds the image for almost four minutes, beginning with the loud bleat of a baby goat that keynotes Behzad's seductive attempt to invade her innocence. The first Forough verse he recites corresponds to the visual image: "If you come to my house," he begins. "What?" she interrupts, calling attention to the words because he is in her house, and though he seemingly is more mature, it is she who embodies the poet's illumination: "If you come to my house, oh kind one, bring me the lamp and a window through which I can watch the crowd in the happy street." Prior to the milking scene, we witness the crowd of people and animals in the happy street. Here, the visual image is a deeper, more iconic affirmation than in the poem. The lamp visually illuminates and symbolically informs the frame, reflexively making this image an emblem of the film as a whole.

Next, Behzad asks her age and how long she has been in school. "Sixteen," and "for five years," she replies as the baby animal sounds continue. They stop completely when he asks if she knows Forough, so that the only sound is that of the milk being squeezed into the bowl, an analogy perhaps to the words Forough dispenses for the soul. She says yes, and though her answer to his next question is literally naïve—"Who is she?"—"Gohar's daughter."—it echoes the digger saying Farzad is a local, implying that the truth articulated in poetry is timelessly embodied in new forms.

Her refusal to tell him her name probably stems from a culturally guarded modesty, but it also helps to universalize her identity. She is so consistently reticent that we can never be sure if she really is Yossef's fiancée, after all. Unconsciously expressing a dilettante's attitude toward poetry and film as entertainment and at the same time using his knowledge of both to empower himself, he reads and then explains the beginning of Forough's poem to suit his purpose: "I'll recite a poem to occupy us while you milk. 'In my night, so brief, alas / The wind is about to meet the leaves.'"

The sound of a baby goat loudly crying betrays his corrupting purpose: "Do you understand? The two are meeting." But Behzad and Zeynab are also meeting, and though Behzad knows the words of Forough and Sepehri, he uses them only to feel superior, like a child pretending to be an adult, so that the animal sounds apply as much to him as to the girl. As before, he seizes every opportunity to tell himself how smart he is: "It's like when you went to see Yossef at the well." "At the well?" she asks because her Yossef is digging a ditch for a television cable, while Behzad is referring to the biblical Joseph, whose brothers left him in a well until they could sell him into slavery. "Bravo," he says as he had said to Farzad and the digger when their apparent ignorance seemed to validate his snobbery. After reciting "Hark! Do you hear the whisper of the shadows?" a line repeated twice in the film's translation, he stops again to ask, "Do you understand 'the shadows?'" to which she replies, "It means darkness," a line that might apply to Behzad's own shadow side as well as to his ignorance.

Other lines from the poem are qualified by the visual image, the animal sounds, and previous scenes in the film. Such lines as "This happiness is foreign to me. / I am accustomed to despair" and "The moon is red and anxious" are countered by the image of milking the cow with a lantern in the dark. Death and disaster simultaneously complement love and nurture, while "The clouds, like a crowd of mourning women / Await the birth of the rain" refers forward both to the women who will mourn Mrs. Malek and to the new life that death seeds.

As if to contradict Forough's line "One second and then nothing," a hen loudly clucks to remind us there is never nothing, that death only breaks the shell for new life to emerge, and when the poem says, "Behind this window, the night trembles, and the earth stops spinning," a calf loudly bawls to remind us that the inextricable web of human, animal, and plant life will continue to thrive. The animal sounds stop completely to set off the reassuring intent, perhaps of God and certainly of the artist: "Behind this window, a stranger worries about me and you. / You, in your greenery. / Lay your hands / On my loving hands / And entrust your lips, replete with warmth, / To the touch of my loving lips. / The wind will carry us! / The wind will carry us!"

The "window" or frame within which an artist's vision must live, even if it points beyond the window to something ineffable, is as full as Kiarostami can make it, and Zeynab interrupts just after "the touch of my loving lips" to say the bowl is full, referring simultaneously to her instinct to guard her innocence and to the holistic vision Forough offers. With the silver bowl now visible on her lap, she interrupts again, "It's full," just before Behzad can say the last line, calling attention again to the poem's fullness and connecting her gift of the milk to Forough's poetic gift. In an impatient tone, as if she has spoiled the intimate moment he tried to create, Behzad recites the concluding line, followed by the loud baaing of a sheep, which deflates his seductive pretense as comically as Zeynab's incomplete attention. He demeans himself further when, advancing toward the open stall door to take the milk, he says, "I'm one of Yossef's friends. In fact, I'm his boss," and then asks her to "raise the lamp so I can see your face: I haven't seen Yossef, so at least let me see his taste."

Behzad hasn't really seen Yossef, Zeynab, Farzad, or Forough for that matter. The girl simply ignores his request, and the camera shows only her lower body as she advances through the frame of the stall door, holding the lamp in a close-up that envisions the life force and the wisdom that Forough embodied in words. As Behzad is about to leave, she reintroduces the subject of Forough: "How long did she study?" When Behzad tells her that she only went to the fourth or fifth grade and that "It isn't about studying," he implicitly refers to the failure of the lengthy education he continually flaunts.

Her innocence and grace have exposed his clumsy pedantry, which is chorally enhanced by the loud bleating of a goat as he makes his final request: "You won't tell me your name and let me see your face. At least light the ground so I don't trip." She may have already illuminated his future path, and when he asks how much he owes her, she says, "Don't mention it," and again after he persists, "Then pay my mother," implying that Zeynab herself is the spiritual nourishment he unconsciously seeks, even though he had come to the village to exploit death and to the barn to satanically invade the innocence of Yossef and Zeynab, to take rather than to give.

The corrective lesson continues when he comes out of the cellar's womb into bright sunlight. For a moment, he is seen looking up while his eyes adjust to the light, before the camera cuts to the narrow door in the pink wall where the bread maker is now grinding flour. When he asks her how much he owes, she says three hundred tomans. Immediately after he leaves, with the camera still on the opening, we hear Mrs. Kakrahman remonstrate, "Why did you take the money?" and then tell her to call Behzad back. "You're our honored guest," the woman says as she gives it back. Stooping his head in unconscious humility within the threshold, Behzad is learning how to live, and he feels genuine gratitude for everything that has transpired within the pink walls where his potential rebirth may have begun: "No. Keep it," he says, and when she won't take it, "Thank you very much. Really." As he walks away, she calls after him, "You honor us."

At the beginning of the film, when the crew thanks a woman working in the fields for directions, she, too, says, "I'm honored," and the respect that the people of Siah Dareh extend to strangers exemplifies the gratitude for life exemplified in every Kiarostami film. For several seconds after Behzad leaves, the camera stays on the woman who, surrounded by several clucking hens, has returned to her grinding, leaving a final impression of protection, nurture, and love.

We never find out whether the lessons Behzad has absorbed in the milking scene become conscious enough to change his behavior, but he soon returns to ingrained habits in the next scene. He is shown on the balcony outside his room, shaving in a small mirror with his back to the camera. He presents an image to the outside world, while his coworkers, still confined to their small rooms, argue with him about staying because Mrs. Malek is taking so long to die. The camera holds on the image of the open door filled by darkness next to him, from which one of his colleagues whines, "You said it would happen in three days. We've been here two weeks. Maybe she won't die. Her son left yesterday. He must have thought she was improving." Behzad tries to argue that the son is a security guard and works forty-five minutes away but then has to admit that only God decides matters of life and death. "What if the event never occurs," one crew member asks, to which he can only respond, "And what if it does?" prompting the crew member to quip, "That means you're in contact with God or the Angel of Death."

The contrary impulses that motivate the villagers and the crew are evident in the visual image. While they squabble, the camera stays fixed on the cerulean-blue doors and the beautifully grained wood railing. In the middle of the frame, a potted plant with a large, pink rose is carefully placed on a ledge just below the railing, and Behzad repeatedly turns to water it with the excess water from his shaving while they argue. He is interrupted by Farzad's "Salaam" from the ground below, and the exchange that follows exposes Behzad's worst side.

He is angry because the boy, upon being asked by the crew, told them about the uncle's departure. The camera angle exaggerates the cruelty of Behzad's words because Farzad looks especially small from the balcony. When the boy says, "I've brought you bread," Behzad coldly tells him to set it aside and then launches into a tirade of abuse: "Haven't they taught you at school that you don't answer a question unless it's asked? I don't want any more bread. Don't come back until you have good news." The comic irony of the line is enhanced when a woman's voice from inside cheerfully calls, "Hello, engineer. My mother wants to know if you want the milk hot or cold," to which Behzad, who has just been shockingly cold to Farzad, tonelessly commands, "Warm it up!" followed almost inevitably by the Pavlovian ring of his cell phone.

Once again, he begins his ridiculous journey to reach "higher ground," where Mrs. Godarzi's demands vie with those of God and the Angel of Death. The higher-authority syndrome that has resulted in his personal snobbery connotes the unintended religious bolstering of power on every level when he complains, "It sounds as if we're guilty." As he speaks, he walks past the familiar huge trunk of the big tree and the digger's teapot steaming on a grate, reminders of nature and nurture as eternal values opposed to his frantic task of making immediate events interesting, evoking the similar satire of journalism in *Close-Up*.

Here, the result of being diverted from the creative impulse in nature extends Behzad's meanness to Farzad to an equally innocent victim when he kicks over a brown land turtle and, leaving it upended, returns to his car. A feeling of being helpless leads people on every social level to direct their hostility to the nearest available object, whether it be one's own family or wars between nations, as in *Homework* (see chapter 1). But this lashing out that nations celebrate in futile assertions of nationalistic pride has in the long view little lasting effect.

With Behzad gone, the turtle rights itself and continues its unperturbed journey over two weathered gravestones and back onto the brown earth that matches the color of its shell. The film celebrates the ongoing life that transcends any individual death, and the celebration of collective life versus the effort of a tiny individual to assert dominance forms a general sense of the good and evil mirrored in Behzad's duality. Seeming to realize that his anger against Mrs. Godarzi's demands should not have been taken out on Farzad, he races back to the school to apologize.

On his first visit there, the teacher summons Farzad by his last name, Sohrabi, an allusion perhaps to Sohrab Sepehri (see chapter 2), one of whose poems Behzad quotes in the opening sequence. The final revelation in "Address" comes to the rider from a child who plucks a chick from a "nest of light." But Behzad is a potential source of confusion when he tells Farzad that the good go to hell and the bad to heaven before correcting his semi-accurate response (given the relativity of "good" and "evil") out of consideration for someone less advanced. On the second visit, however, we see how childishly Behzad himself has just acted, and so when Behzad offers to answer any exam question Farzad might have, the boy answers, "No, I know them all."

Just as he has read but not been informed by "Address" or "The Wind Will Carry Us," Behzad's apology is a failed attempt to understand his own confusion: "Do you remember the first day we met, and the car wasn't working, and I said it's given up the ghost? That day when we were driving uphill, the car gave up the ghost. It had worked too hard and gave up the ghost. Remember what I said? A car, like a man, can give up the ghost." As Behzad speaks, he appears behind the wheel from Farzad's point of view at the passenger window. As on the first visit, the walking green haystack now appears behind him as he speaks. As if recognizing a kindred spirit, Behzad quickly greets it, "Salaam," and the haystack enters a barn, just as it does on Behzad's previous visit to the school and as he himself does in the milking scene.

Farzad, thinking he is claiming fatigue, responds, "You haven't worked this morning. You're not tired," but Behzad actually has been going through an internal struggle that he does not understand. He resorts to excusing his meanness by explaining that when people are idle they can go crazy—"Forget it. Shake my hand."—but it is only when people stop working that they have an opportunity to reflect and grow. Some people use their leisure time to regress, as Behzad does with Zeynab. But as in Sepehri's poem, innocents like Farhad and Zeynab have an intuitive wisdom potentially present in everyone but that Behzad may irretrievably lose because immediately after seeming to have patched things up, his cell phone rings. He abruptly dismisses Farzad—"I'll see you later."—and races off to higher ground, where societal obligations trump internal growth.

Behzad's experience with the villagers who innocently "honor" him cannot take effect as long as he is in thrall to Mrs. Godarzi, but he soon meets a "wise old man type" whose wisdom Kiarostami said supplanted that of his child characters in a progression evident in this film. After the digger is temporarily buried and after Farzad refuses to ride with or even speak to him and after his out-of-patience crew has departed for Tehran, the worldly, wise journalist finally meets a spiritual guide who offers a last opportunity for repair before his soul gives up the ghost.

After the digger is buried by the ground collapsing above his ditch, Behzad drives to the fields to summon workers to rescue him. He then goes to look for his crew, who are picking strawberries. When they call for him to "forget the cemetery" and join them, his decision to keep driving indicates that the humanity his work has almost buried is still alive because the next cut shows him arriving at the hill where the men have rescued the digger. Even though he is no longer underground, we still don't see Yossef because the film wants us to empathize with people in general in the same way that the director in *And Life Goes On* helps the earthquake victims he encounters rather than the specific boys he came to find.

The same is true for the doctor that Behzad now meets. After Behzad lends his car to the workers to serve as Yossef's ambulance, he hitches a ride back to town on the back of the doctor's motorcycle, which is the film's spiritual ambulance. In the two scenes that follow where Behzad rides with the doctor, lines referring to both Yossef and Behzad metaphorically represent the kind of spectator the film hopes to cure. During the dialogue of their first trip, the digger's burial parallels Behzad being so obsessed with work that he has almost suffocated his capacity to enjoy the privilege of being alive. The immersion with Zeynab in the milking scene and now with the doctor are metonyms of the film's effort to awaken its viewers. The doctor's white motorcycle, with its white box of medical supplies, is a rolling clinic for the soul. Keeping this perspective, the metaphors that parallel Behzad's condition with that of the digger coincide with the film's therapeutic purpose: "Will he make it doctor?"—"Yes, he just needed oxygen. He'll get a jab and a respirator."

The dialogue is complemented by the image of the motorcycle heading off into a vast, open space as Behzad says, "It's a miracle he survived," and the doctor explains, "He was lucky. The stone got stuck before it struck his head. Then some other stones gave way. If he gets oxygen, he'll be all right. He was trapped as if he was in a tiny cell." Some children whose presence is unexplained in the middle of what appears to be nowhere run across the road just after the motorcycle passes. They, too, will be lucky if their lives allow them to escape soul-killing tasks.

But for people already locked into the narrow adult space of modern urban life, escape requires shrinking the ego to identify with the whole, which appears in a long shot of the motorcycle as a tiny object moving down the familiar zigzag road in a field of golden wheat. The doctor as driver with Behzad onboard echoes the mentoring image of Sabzian on Makhmalbaf's motorcycle, a vehicle open to its surroundings unlike the "iron cell" of a car, as Kiarostami put it in *Ten on Ten* (see chapter 3).

To be open to one's physical surroundings corresponds to escaping the tunnel vision of literal meaning. When Behzad says Yossef was "covered in dirt," the viewers should recognize that he is unconsciously describing himself, if we recall his lack of empathy for the loving care the villagers show Mrs. Malek, his meanness to Farzad and the turtle, and his attempt to misuse a Forough poem to excite the sixteen-year-old fiancée of a man he befriends. When the doctor analogizes with a quote, "If my guardian angel is the one I know, he'll protect glass from stone," Behzad recognizes the line, saying brightly, "Yes, that's a fine poem. So the glass remained intact," and the doctor, echoing Behzad's "bravos" to Yossef, Zeynab, and Farzad, agrees, as if the metaphor is obvious: "Yes, it remained intact. He'll be saved." But the question the film leaves unanswered is, Will Behzad? Will the viewer?

The inability of an artist to determine his work's effect on specific individuals is indicated when Behzad asks, "Do you mind if I smoke?" and the doctor replies, "No, you should mind." At a certain point, the "stranger" in Forough's poem who "worries about me and you" must realize that redemption ultimately lies with the individual. No single teacher can alter the course of a person's path, and no single work of art can change that path unless the traveler is lucky enough to encounter it at the right time.

For art to take any effect, it must be more than a social accoutrement, and even if Behzad learns to read more deeply, the fate of the world rests with larger forces we can join, though Ahura's final victory over Ahriman seems far from assured: "It's no concern of mine if you smoke," the doctor adds because he can only attempt a cure, but as Behzad said to his disgruntled crew, "Only God decides," and though he seems to show some promise—"The air is so pure here"—we have seen him sink back in the dirt shortly after reciting a poem he knows by heart but does not understand.

Given the intensified awareness of climate change that has gripped the world since Kiarostami made *Wind*, the doctor's faith in nature surviving careless people seems more in doubt than his confident assertion: "It will take more than your cigarette to pollute it." But changing perceptions necessarily precedes practical measures, as Pope Francis said when he urged the value of aesthetic education in moving people to want to save the beauty of nature (see chapter 3). The doctor's cure is simply to share his love for nature with anyone who comes his way rather than to crusade for change.

As he speaks, the motorcycle, instead of racing toward higher ground, gently descends a tree-lined slope. When Behzad asks, "What's your specialty?" the doctor and the director merge:

> "I don't have one. That way I look after the whole body."—"You must have a lot of patients then?"—"Almost no one. I have to ride around looking at nature's beauty, calling on people, doing the odd circumcision, giving jabs, piercing ears, etc. If I'm no use to others, at least I make the most of life. I observe nature. Observing nature is better than playing backgammon. Or doing nothing."

Behzad doesn't quite get it. As he dismounts literally at death's (Mrs. Malek's) door, he can only reiterate the cliché he offers Farzad, which is the opposite of what the doctor has just said: "Idleness leads to corruption." The doctor speaks of work that gives him the freedom to love the life he has received, while Behzad's work assumes an unnatural and absurd importance. Seven women in black sit outside Mrs. Malek's door, one of them holding a toddler as a symbol of renewal. The doctor goes inside, and Behzad starts running up the incline to his room, trying to catch his crew before they leave.

In Kiarostami's films, running is associated with children, and an adult running is a sign of immaturity. When Mr. Badii in *Taste of Cherry* has second thoughts about his arrangement with the taxidermist, he runs back to the museum, a semicomic image of desperately trying to assure any future because even in a nonsuicidal person, habitual rushing ultimately leads only to death. When Behzad arrives at the balcony, he finds open doors and empty rooms, making his headlong rush to higher ground as pointless as Qassem awakening to an empty stadium at the end of *The Traveler*.

Having lost the illusion of adult control, Behzad stands next to the railing, stuffing in the strawberries his crew left, using them for the same infantile consolation his cigarettes supply. The sound of a baby fussing sends him running to get help, just as he did for the digger, but the mother isn't downstairs, so he comes back up and rocks the cradle a couple times. The focus of his attention and energy has switched at least temporarily from hastening death to preserving life. The difference between infantile need and adult nurture comes clear when the woman returns and Behzad says, "You left the baby!" She tells him, "I went to fetch you some milk," the film's way of saying that in a fundamental way, bosses like Behzad may remain spiritual babies. A cut to a shot from the balcony of Behzad coming back to Mrs. Malek's puts him in perspective as a part of humanity passing through the life-death process.

Maturity is accepting one's responsibility to maintain life as long as possible, and Behzad's potential transition is indicated after the doctor tells the women he has "prescribed some pills to ease the pain," and Behzad says he will fetch them from the hospital because they have no car. Behzad begins by giving the workers his car to transport Yossef. Now, once again, he actively contributes something to the community that has fed and housed him. Instead of rushing nowhere in the iron cell of his car, he gets back on the back of the doctor's motorcycle to be exposed (as Kiarostami exposes the spectators) to the extraordinary natural beauty that is usually only background scenery for the plotlines of their busy lives.

The catastrophic upshot of socially driven "advancement" is suggested when Behzad remarks, "I'm like a general without an army." He is on the way back to get his car, and the film's central question at the end is whether people can spiritually grow, given the pressing conditions of their workaday lives. When the doctor asks if Behzad is more worried about Yossef or his car, Behzad says "What do you think?" leaving open the possibility of his reaching spiritual advancement and recalling the beginning, when he asks Farzad if he is more worried about helping the crew or getting his book from the car, and Farzad, just entering the adolescence in which most people remain permanently stuck, answers, "My book. I have an exam tomorrow."

Speaking through the doctor, Kiarostami counsels a longer, wider view. The medicine the film offers will not help people who aren't ready. The doctor says not to worry about the digger because before they even reach the druggist, he will be "up and gone." And Mrs. Malek is already so far gone that the medicine he prescribes for her is only a painkiller; "It won't bring her life." The same goes for such pastimes as Qassem's soccer, Sabzian's experience of cinema, or entertainment in general. For Kiarostami, contemplating nature is the truly transformative cure (see chapters 2 and 3).

The end of Mrs. Malek's physical life corresponds to the spiritual dead end Behzad has almost reached. The cure must begin by silencing the demanding voice on one's inner phone. Behzad tries to take a call, but the wind is too loud, giving an aural dimension to Forough's poem and the film's title as the simultaneous sound of vitality and mortality. If the wind on the physical earth does not drown out the demands of theological and secular bosses, then the arts will only succeed in easing our death: "She's suffering, poor thing. We can't do anything. Let her take this and sleep."

To be fully alive, even if one's body is sound, is to be more than a "bag of bones," as Mrs. Malek literally is and as Behzad is about to become. He blankly reflects that old age is a terrible disease, but the doctor tells him that death is worse: "When you close your eyes on this beauty, the wonders of nature, and the generosity of God, it means you'll never be coming back." Still needing to tune out the inculcated demand for submission, Behzad recalls that "they say that the other world is more beautiful." In a striking image of love for God's bounty in the present moment, the wide, sunlit fields extend to a darkening sky in the far distance. "But who has come back from there to tell us if it's beautiful or not?" the doctor counters.

Then, in a declamatory style, as if he relishes each word, the doctor recites the familiar verse from the *Rubaiyat* that made Khayyam so unpopular with the religious authorities of his time: "They tell me she is as beautiful as a houri from heaven! Yet, I say that the juice of the vine is better. Prefer the present to these fine promises" (see chapter 2). Behzad joins him in concluding, "Even a drum sounds melodious from afar."

As the doctor recites Khayyam, his voice is backed by the rushing wind, while the visual image foregrounds the motorcycle moving first toward the camera and then away from it through mauve hills with golden wheat on one side of the road and green grass on the other. Everything is alive and moving, merging the energy of the poetic voice, the singing birds, and the constant wind. The implication is that art is a spontaneous expression of nature rather than a more ordered improvement. Whether cosmic love exists in another world or not, it certainly exists here. As the motorcycle diminishes far ahead

Figure 6.4. Quoting Omar Khayyam, the doctor exhorts Behzad to "Prefer the present!" as his spiritual ambulance rolls through golden fields toward the unavoidable darkness beyond the frame. New Yorker Films/Photofest.

to a speck at the vanishing point (see below), the wind that carries individuals away does not silence the voice that came through Khayyam and now comes through Kiarostami in the final words of the now-invisible doctor—"Prefer the present!"—just before his voice fades in the wind.

A sudden cut from the bright sun to the residual darkness of a dawning day is a variation on similar scenes at the end of *Taste of Cherry* and *ABC Africa*. But unlike the complete blackouts in those films, the simultaneous presence of heaven and hell in Behzad corresponds to points of light in the first frame of this final scene, where filament-like branches wrapped with white lights foreground the night sky. The darkness around them lasts for thirty seconds and then almost imperceptibly lightens, until the birth of a day is followed by an image of the birth of a man. Instead of coming from the bright-blue door we have seen before, Behzad climbs out of a trapdoor in the floor of a stone terrace, echoing his embryonic climb from the darkness of the milking scene. Now, instead of ascending to higher ground, he descends a gradual slope to the communal and earthly life his social rise had skipped.

Just above street level, he stops to light a cigarette as he looks down seriously at Mrs. Malek's door, where the simultaneous sounds of women softly mourning and a rooster crowing once again merge above and below, living and dying. He resumes his descent to the street, where his mud-caked Range Rover awaits his departure. When he gets in, he rolls down the window as if lowering the barrier that has separated him from the village and adjusts the side-view mirror as if to look back on what he and we have learned.

The idea of holding onto an important part of that is suggested when after driving briefly ahead, he suddenly backs up and then stops to photograph a large group of women arriving to mourn. Apparently, every woman in the village is there. The image connotes respect for the individual while affirming the survival of the group in the same way that Mr. Badii's resurrection as another person complements Louis Armstrong's "St. James Infirmary" at the end of *Taste of Cherry*. Instead of filming a strange ceremony as a superior outsider, the journalist retains snapshots of the love that motivates mourning in any culture.

A shot of Behzad's car disappearing down the street is followed by a long shot of an old man with a cane approaching the camera from the direction Behzad goes. The camera stays on him for twenty seconds, until he is greeted by a woman's voice offering comfort to an image of our common mortality. Then, an overhead shot from the balcony shows the gathered women as a complementary image of comfort, preparing food for the mourners in large, open pots. If we are all destined to mourn or be mourned, then we have Khayyam's poems and Kiarostami's films to sustain our remaining journeys.

From the mourning women, the camera cuts to Behzad seen through the windshield, tossing a bucketful of water over the glass, which the moving wipers then clear. The wipers stop as we hear Behzad enter the car. Then we see his right hand reach over to pick up the bone, which disappears from view as we hear the passenger door close. Through the windshield, we see him hurl the bone into the stream below. Everything looks washed out. His pale-blue shirt is almost white, the banks are a dull tan, and the stream is silver-gray.

But the next shot, a close-up of the bone splashing into the stream, returns sunlight to the scene. The stream becomes blue, and green vegetation thickly lines its banks. As the bone starts to float toward us, Peyman Yazdanian's music wells up from the silence, a moving moment because here, as in *Taste of Cherry*, the nondiegetic sound is saved until the end. It begins with the low, deep note of a trombone followed by a horn above it, and its liturgical quality resembles Andrei Tarkovsky's use of Johann Sebastian Bach's "St. Matthew Passion" at the end of *Solaris* and Choral Prelude in F Minor at the end of *Sacrifice*. Kiarostami once said that "Tarkovsky's works separate me completely from physical life and are the most spiritual films I have seen."[28]

Though Kiarostami may not have been right about Tarkovsky separating God from nature, his own cinema immerses us in the spiritual life of the physical earth. The floating bone shot lasts for a full minute to establish it as a significant remembrance of the film. In close-up it appears very large, an image of death offset by the bright-green vegetation on the lower left. Now, shots of first one and then another brown goat eating white flowering weeds on the bank imply taking nourishment from a single source. Then only the bone appears, floating more rapidly, until a sudden cut to a black screen momentarily precedes the final credits.

As Kiarostami said in an interview quoted at the beginning of this book, all his films "talk about the same things [and] every filmmaker basically makes only one film in his lifetime but he cuts it down and offers it in cinematic installments to his audience over a period of time."[29] These words also describe similar themes in separate poets. The same stream that carries individuals to death carries the vision of Khayyam, Sepehri, and Forough forward. They and innumerable unnamed others comprise the infinite variety of a single voice, a message Kiarostami pursues in *Shirin*, *Certified Copy*, and *Like Someone in Love*.

NOTES

1. Abbas Kiarostami, "In Dialogue with Kiarostami," interview by Ali Akbar Mahdi, *Iranian*, August 25, 1998, https://asianart.fandom.com/wiki/Interviews_with_Abbas_Kiarostami.

2. *The Art of Living*, featurette directed by Pat Collins and Fergus Daly, *ABC Africa*, directed by Abbas Kiarostami (2001; New York: New Yorker Video, 2005), DVD.

3. Emile Durkheim, *Suicide: A Study in Sociology*, ed. John A. Spaulding and George Simpson (1897; New York: Free Press, 1951), http://www.bahaistudies.net/asma/suicide-durkheim.pdf; Abbas Kiarostami, "The Poetry of Cinema," interview by Richard Pena, special

feature on *The Wind Will Carry Us*, directed by Abbas Kiarostami (1998; New York: Cohen Media Group, 2014), DVD.

4. Kiarostami, "In Dialogue."

5. See "Abbas Kiarostami: Doors without Keys," Curious Creature, 2019, https://www.thecuriouscreature.com/2015/11/20/doors-without-keys/; and Amanda DelaCruz, "*Doors without Keys* by Abbas Kiarostami at Toronto's Aga Khan Museum @AgaKhan Museum," Culture Toronto, November 22, 2015, http://www.culturetoronto.com/spotlight/doors-without-keys-by-abbas-kiarostami#.WFQeRWPu1jo.

6. Godfrey Cheshire, "How to Read Kiarostami," *Cineaste*, September 2000, 8–15.

7. Kiarostami in *Art of Living*.

8. Forough Farrokhzad, "The Wind Will Carry Us." The source of the translation used in the film is not cited in the credits. A different but similar version may be found in *An Anthology of Modern Persian Poetry*, ed. Ahmad Karimi-Hakkak (Costa Mesa, CA: Mazda, 1978), 141. That version is the one quoted by Alberto Elena, *The Cinema of Abbas Kiarostami*, trans. Belinda Coombes (London: SAQI Iran Heritage Foundation, 2005), 163–64.

9. See "Forough Farrokhzad: The Most Famous Woman in the History of Persian Literature," Iran Chamber Society, 2020, http://www.iranchamber.com/literature/ffarrokhzad/forough_farrokhzad.php; and "Forough Farrokhzad," Wikipedia, updated January 2, 2020, https://en.wikipedia.org/wiki/Forough_Farrokhzad.

10. Mehrnaz Saeed-Vafa, in *Abbas Kiarostami* by Mehrnaz Saeed-Vafa and Jonathan Rosenbaum (Urbana: University of Illinois Press, 2003), 58.

11. See "Farhad (1)," *Encyclopædia Iranica*, updated December 15, 1999, http://www.iranicaonline.org/articles/farhad%20(1); and "Shirin & Farhad—A Persian Love Story," Fhire-Dekha Forum, December 30, 2007, http://www.fhiredekha.com/forum/index.php?topic=6760.

12. Kiarostami, quoted in Elena, *Cinema of Abbas Kiarostami*, 75.

13. Saeed-Vafa and Rosenbaum, *Abbas Kiarostami*, 80. See also the online excerpt of Mehrnaz Saeed-Vafa and Jonathan Rosenbaum, "Abbas Kiarostami: A Dialogue between the Authors (Mehrnaz Saeed-Vafa & Jonathan Rosenbaum)," November 7, 2001, https://www.jonathanrosenbaum.net/2001/11/40847/.

14. Sohrab Sepehri, *The Expanse of Green: Poems of Sohrab Sepehri*, trans. David I. Martin (Los Angeles: Kalimar/UNESCO, 1988), 45–46; quoted in Elena, *Cinema of Abbas Kiarostami*, 73–74.

15. Idries Shah, *The Sufis* (Garden City, NY: Doubleday, 1964), http://www.spiritual-teaching.org/rishi-sufi-teachings/ewExternalFiles/Idries%20Shah%20-%20The%20Sufis.pdf.

16. Alain Bergala, "L'os et le pare-brise: Apropos de Le Vent nous Emportera d'Abbas Kiarostami," *Cahiers du Cinema*, December 1999, 34; quoted in Elena, *Cinema of Abbas Kiarostami*, 153.

17. Shah, *Sufis*, 17.

18. Shah, *Sufis*, 17.

19. William C. Chittick, *The Sufi Path of Love: The Spiritual Teachings of Rumi* (Albany: State University of New York Press, 1983), 47.

20. Chittick, *Sufi Path*, 48.

21. Chittick, *Sufi Path*, 48.

22. Chittick, *Sufi Path*, 53.

23. See "Farhad (1)."

24. See "Khosrow and Shirin," Wikipedia, updated December 14, 2019, https://en.wikipedia.org/wiki/Khosrow_and_Shirin.

25. See "Zaynab bint Jahsh," Wikipedia, updated December 5, 2019, https://en.wikipedia.org/wiki/Zaynab_bint_Jahsh.

26. Alain Bergala in *Art of Living*.

27. Abbas Kiarostami, "With Borrowed Eyes: An Interview with Abbas Kiarostami," interview by David Sterritt, *Film Comment*, July–August 2000, http://www.filmcomment.com/article/with-borrowed-eyes-an-interview-with-abbas-kiarostami/.

28. Kiarostami, "With Borrowed Eyes."

29. Abbas Kiarostami, Full Cannes Interview, YouTube, 1997.

Chapter Seven

Save the Children

Kiarostami's next film, the 2001 documentary *ABC Africa*, directly extends some of *Wind*'s prominent themes. This time it is Kiarostami himself who is the ostensible journalist, having been commissioned by the United Nations to shoot a documentary about the two million Ugandan children orphaned by AIDS and civil war. Once again, he uses the opportunity to celebrate resilience, just as he does in all his films since his visit to the earthquake victims in *And Life Goes On*. He does include a hospital scene of very sick children in a refugee camp near Kampala, including a searing image of a small, sheet-wrapped corpse wheeled away on a bicycle, but most of the film's visual images depict playful, dancing children, while its sound track consists primarily of people singing indigenous songs.

As in *Wind*, Kiarostami depicts the exotic to convey the universal, and at one point, he joins a children's dance, as if to stress the identification he hopes his international audience will feel. But he does not want that audience to arrogantly think they can benefit the orphans by uprooting them from the vibrant, caring community the film depicts, and at the end, an Austrian couple's adoption of a little girl is not sympathetically treated.

The United Nations may have been expecting Kiarostami to give them a call for compassionate action, as Forough Farrokhzad does in *The House Is Black*, which begins by announcing its intent to wipe out the world's ugliness to relieve its victims. For her, the greatest ugliness is not the physical leprosy she shows but the presumed indifference of her spectators to the plight of shunned strangers. Kiarostami does something similar. For him, the real victims are not the AIDS orphans of Uganda but the seemingly fortunate film spectators, whose societies have lost or never had the kind of culture that enables the Africans he films to love their lives.

He brings these spectators to Uganda, as he brings them with Behzad to Siah Dareh, to experience a "backward" way of life that in many ways surpasses their own. Like Zeynab, who is literally and figuratively equipped with a flashlight to work in the dark, the people of Uganda are strong because their tribal cultures and their closeness to nature have enabled them to adapt wisely to physical and emotional adversity. One scene in particular reflects the ignorance of supposedly more advanced people by transposing two elements from *Wind*: the darkness of the milking scene and the inability of the crew to leave the confinement of their rooms.

The scene begins in a dark hotel room, where a small cloud of mosquitos swirls around a dim lantern. The voice of a crew member is heard saying that it's a good thing they took their malaria pills and another saying that malaria is "like mushrooms. You find out if they're poisonous afterwards." In Kiarostami's poetic style, the dialogue consistently uses a physical threat to imply a spiritual one. People do the most destructive things when they think they're right (as in the Ugandan civil war), and given the long-term consequences of war and repression, they are usually wrong. Kiarostami's voice, recognizable from interviews, is then heard saying the opposite of what the film shows: "Anyway, dying from AIDS is a consequence of a choice made in life. But dying from an insect bite has to be the ultimate betrayal." The assertion is questionable: Its assumption of free will in making the wrong choice seems ironic in light of the various plagues people bring down on themselves. Do they really choose to get AIDS or to go to war or to live in unequal societies bolstered by politically tainted religions?

In the film's larger context, Kiarostami's attempt to moralize the situation is not consistent with the retrospective editing that he achieves. In *And Life Goes On*, Puya tells a bereaved woman that God does not kill his children and that the earthquake was like a mad dog whose victims were in the wrong place at the wrong time. Kiarostami said that Puya is that film's Sufi guide, and he edits in his own reference to "betrayal" because it is a seemingly empty assertion in the literal heat of the moment. The rest of the scene is about living in and with darkness as an existential constant. People should be able to navigate the darkness by now, but the crew, like humanity as a whole, remains unprepared and ill equipped. As a crew member says, "The sign said that the lights go out at midnight. We should have a flashlight." At this point, the screen goes completely black, and the men are left to fumble for matches, which then burn down quickly, suggesting the brevity of light and life.

Like Behzad's crew, these bodiless voices do not adapt well to adversity. "It's so humid in here!" one complains. Then, at the beginning of a total darkness that except for split-second interruptions lasts for five minutes, Kiarostami allows his persona to voice reflections that express his larger purpose. To the question, "How can they live in this darkness?" he responds,

> Two hundred meters back, there was no electricity. Here, it's cut off at midnight. Imagine that grandmother living with thirty-five or forty-five kids in a single room. The sun is gone; life is gone. With no candles, no lights, no television, and no internet, I can't think of anywhere in the world where the sun could be more precious and welcome. They live half their lives within these dark walls, like blind people.

The analogy then applies literally to themselves as they try to find their separate rooms without being able to read the numbers, a reference to the motif of looking for directions near the beginnings of *Close-Up* and *Wind*. "My room must be to the right," one voice says, before we hear a series of doors closing and locks sliding, while outside the elements in which all must live remind us of the common danger that should, but rarely does, put personal concerns in perspective.

What does the future hold? Just before retiring to their rooms, a crew member asks Kiarostami what time they would start in the morning. "Depends on the weather," the director replies. Now the weather symbolizes the threat and the promise of an individual's fate in the outer storms of war and disease and the inner ones of cultural contagion. For two and a half minutes, the screen is black while the human voices remain. Then, a dog barks briefly, before the rest of the night is compressed into another two and half minutes of blackness accompanied by sounds human beings cannot control. Distant thunder gets louder until, with a loud crash, lightning illuminates the leafy branch of a large tree just outside the window. Simultaneously beautiful and frightening, it flashes a second, third, fourth, and fifth time, each flash showing the tree that Kiarostami said is a symbol of friendship in *Where Is the Friend's House?* and that prefigures finding the Sufi Friend in Sepehri's "Address."

At first light, the tree branch stands stock still. Then, it begins to move in the wind, very much alive. Behind it we can see a dark-green tree and beyond that the remaining pillar of an old stone wall, images of human and natural creation enduring destruction. In the largest sense, these images exceed any cultural frame, and as Kiarostami often does, he employs a series of visual frames to imply the ineffable love beyond them. In the installation *Doors without Keys*, he wrote, "We are not able to look at what we have in front of us, unless it is inside a frame" (see chapter 2). Here, he uses a Ugandan setting and specific Ugandan people to recognize the best in all of us.

From the wall's remnant, the camera cuts to the empty vertical window of a door next to the rough-edged frame of a glassless window. Soft, repetitive piano notes signal continuity through all kinds of storms to keynote the indoor scene that follows. Kiarostami is shown inside the gutted building, talking to his assistant: "Look at the doors and windows. That's years of destruction and war." The assistant asks, "And war?" as if the repetition included in the editing is meant to connect the suffering here to that suffered by both sides in the inconclusively foolish Iran-Iraq War, the Vietnam War, or any war. Kiarostami answers, "Yes, the civil war," meaning that all wars are civil wars, human beings versus human beings.

Kiarostami and his assistant are both wearing blue jeans and blue shirts, and the color links them to a Ugandan man standing nearby in a striking navy and turquoise sweater, a little boy wearing a blue shirt and blue shorts, and a little girl in a blue and white dress who enters to dance with two other children already in the room. The home's adult occupants represent the qualities in human nature that have sustained life on earth so far. The camera remains on the dancing children as Kiarostami explains, "Each gives 30 percent of their salary to the government to pay for this house that they share with other families and their children. These two kids are his and that one they adopted because the child lost her parents." The assistant asks, "From AIDS?" and Kiarostami answers as if to reject his earlier judgmental reference to the disease as chosen: "AIDS or malaria, I didn't ask." But of course, they could have been killed in war, and whatever form the adversary takes, it is always formidable: "You didn't see the [size of the] mosquitos last night."

The scene ends with the subject of adoption, which Kiarostami clearly thinks should result in the orphans remaining within their own vibrant culture. The Ugandan man with them is educated, an English teacher, and the other couple who occupy the house are also teachers: "The man lost his wife, and the woman lost her husband, both from AIDS. They each have one child. Now, they are getting married. By chance, tonight is their wedding night." The camera then cuts to the bright-orange sleeve of one woman braiding another woman's hair, presumably for the wedding.

The brightness of their clothing is contrasted to the faded blue and white garments of a well-intentioned Austrian couple in the next sequence. They are soon to take a single two-year-old girl whom they have "rescued" from the million-plus orphans under the misguided assumption that the education and care they can provide will be superior to what she could receive at home. They have come to the camp's abundantly stocked market because they want to collect impressions they can pass on to their adopted daughter, as if their brief visit could ever tell her very much about where she came from. When Kiarostami asks them how they selected this particular child, they have no answer, but the film has shown large numbers of children happily dancing before it shows the "lucky" little girl similarly dancing, already in sync with a rich culture that she will lose in northern Europe.

The camera then includes a striking example of courage and resilience in another child who does not need outside help. Five children, two boys and three girls, are shown carrying bundles of long sticks away from the camera on a dirt road outside the camp. Ahead of them, we see an adult man on a bicycle. The next brief cut shows a little girl inside a building moving a bench. Her adult sense of responsibility connects to the man on the bicycle, now seen from the side, toting a large bunch of bright-green bananas.

But then the camera introduces a new challenge. Outside the clearing, where groups of children inexhaustibly laugh and play, a little girl about nine years old in a checked gray and white dress and the only child seen so far not wearing bright colors carries a bundle of sticks toward the camera on a forest path. Suddenly, a much bigger boy comes and knocks the pile off her head. For a moment she looks at the malicious undoing of her hard work. Then she runs after the boy and hits him hard in the back. After she turns and starts to pick up the wood, the boy returns and threateningly touches her face but does not slap her. The next shot shows he has performed his stunt for a group of smiling companions who are gathered around a bicycle.

Now, the camera returns to the little girl, who works alone while the off-camera children continue to play. Their fused voices accompany her struggle to retie her bundle. After accomplishing that, she stuffs loose pieces from the ground back into the pile, working carefully without panic but quickly, in case the boy returns. That possibility remains because after she stands the pile up vertically, the camera cuts to the boys still chattering and smirking for the camera. Then, we return to the little girl, who kneels, balances the pile on her head, and carefully stands up. Next, she stoops over to pick up a large stick to defend herself from another attack.

Then, as a high-pitched whistle punctuates the playful voices, which are moved by a different imperative, the little girl moves away from them and the camera to a break in the path, where after stopping to look back, she breaks into a run up the right fork and vanishes into the forest. Taken as a whole, the two-and-a-half-minute scene is a microcosm of a will manifested by courageous people everywhere to resist regressive "leaders," who, like the bullying boy, threaten the earth with their backward drive toward dominance.

Another way to challenge the worst in human nature is represented when a young female teacher, speaking in English, says that adult mothers who had at first been overwhelmed by the disasters have come to the camp to learn to take care of their children and that they now feel "really good" about their ability to carry on. Their confidence correlates to the large group of adult women who dance and sing together, just as groups of children had done before. They are accompanied by several men playing a rhythmic melody on bundled pieces of hollow wood that resemble a xylophone. Their music echoes the bundled contribution of the little girl in the previous scene, and it speaks to art's power to pleasurably discipline.

Instead of caroming around in chaotic groups, the children now watch spellbound, as if their parents are providing an important lesson by celebrating the light that follows darkness. They move up and down in place to the rhythm but don't break into a wild dance. Some children are heard singing a melody to the beat, but their focus and ours remains on the adult women responsibly taking charge by transmitting nourishment directly to the soul, just as the little girl collects cooking wood for the body. But for Kiarostami, the soul cannot develop unless it loves the physical world, and he seems to make the point by letting the camera dwell on the dynamically moving breasts and buttocks of a large woman in a sky-blue dress, an icon perhaps of fertility and renewal.

This gathering of adults and children musically proclaiming their power to meet the future is the image of resilience Kiarostami wants us to remember. Some women begin to ululate as the beat picks up, moving faster and faster until the camera, now leaving the dance and shooting from a moving car, moves to the right, accompanied for a while by a woman in white running alongside and then beyond to scattered women and children waving good-bye. As the still-faintly-heard drums diminish to silence, the view out the windshield shows a darkening sky ahead.

Then, we see the familiar profile of the middle-aged Ugandan driver, silent now rather than speaking or singing as he often had before. A female voice sings Ugandan music on the car radio as back in Kampala, we again pass the billboard that depicts a romantic couple on the beach advertising Life Guard condoms. But the life Kiarostami wants to guard is spiritual as well as physical, and the film as a whole shows how traditional music, dance, and kinship have accomplished just that.

And so, in light of the film's larger portrayal of a people rejoicing in being alive together, the cut to the Austrian woman and her adopted daughter pressing her hands up against the window connotes regret over what she will lose rather than the assumed redemption her happy parents feel they have bestowed. The next shot out the windshield indicates that the car is abruptly moving back the other way. Instead of the Kampala neighborhood we have just left, there is a clear, paved road ahead surrounded by a huge expanse of flat, green land lined by distant trees. The frame's empty space implies the promise of new frames and a spiritual space with room to grow.

The next cut shows the delighted Austrian woman holding the child on her lap, but we quickly realize she is no longer in the car because the corner of the pink seat back over her left shoulder turns out to be the confining cabin of an outgoing jet. The bright Ugandan colors have faded to the white of the mother's blouse and the pink of the plastic seat that now enfolds them both. The next cut to a small screen on the seat back in front of them implies that this trip toward higher ground threatens a form of suffocation, the kind that endangers people in civilizations that aspire to transcend nature. In the small frame within the frame, an animated cartoon features a black man placing an oxygen mask over his nose and mouth to assure the passengers that technology will protect them should something go wrong on the way to heaven.

The last shot of the little girl is a close-up in which she raises her eyes to look down on unearthly clouds in an indigo sky. Just before the final fade, children's faces appear on the clouds for a subliminal moment. They serve to remind us that the assumed superiority of Iran's urban culture to that of the rustic Kurds, the presumptive reason for Behzad's visit, is no more misguided than the ill-considered belief that for Africans, life in Europe would be heaven on earth. Instead of a journalistic piece purporting to objectively document pitiable suffering, Kiarostami transforms *ABC Africa* into another "installment" of his ongoing paean of praise for the physical earth. Once again, the wisdom of *Wind*'s country doctor reminds us to make the best of what we already have: "They tell me she is as beautiful as a houri from heaven! Yet I say that the juice of the vine is better. Prefer the present to these fine promises."

Chapter Eight

A Mother Grows Up

Like *And Life Goes On*, *ABC Africa* equates learning to "prefer the present" to finding the good in a trying situation instead of straining toward an ideal future. While these films are moving tributes to human endurance after collective disasters, *Ten* translates the challenge to that of an individual person facing a personal crisis. And while *ABC Africa* is about the love of a nation's mothers for their children, *Ten* is about the difficulty one Iranian woman faces in relating to her son following her recent divorce. On the surface, the challenges are quite different. The Ugandan women are recovering from the ravages of disease and war, while the Iranian woman has to re-create a personal identity in a climate of stifling mores.

Whatever the cause of the challenge, people in Kiarostami's films demonstrate an exemplary ability to gain strength and wisdom from loss. Speaking of this in personal terms, Kiarostami described how he had come to accept the painful consequence of his own divorce:

> Every time I leave a relationship or lose a belonging, I have to replace it with something else. It is very unfortunate that we lose a lot of things as we age. We lose friends, relatives, our appetites, our strengths—there were days I thought if I didn't see my son for two days it was the end of the world, then it became two months and nothing happened, now two years and still nothing happens.[1]

He found solace in nature, and except for most of *Close-Up*, the films covered so far illustrate his desire to share that comfort with his viewers. But all of *Ten* is set inside a car where the divorced woman talks to her son, her sister, an elderly woman, a prostitute, a divorced woman, and a friend as she drives around Tehran. In *Ten on Ten*, the documentary Kiarostami made about *Ten* and the overall purpose of his films, the director talks to the viewers as he drives them around the same undeveloped areas he uses for *Taste of Cherry*.

Whereas *Ten* only shows glimpses of traffic and pedestrians outside the car windows, *Ten on Ten* includes many shots of natural scenery, culminating at the end in exiting the car altogether for a wide view of trees and hills contrasted with an extraordinary close-up of cooperating ants (see chapter 3). Although he respected the viewers who complained that *Ten* lacks the landscape settings they had learned to love, Kiarostami explained that he used the "intimate setting" of a car to probe more deeply into the inner nature of human beings. By returning to the site of *Taste of Cherry* seven years after its release, he invites the audience to think about the parallels: While *Ten* is "about women and their problems," *Taste of Cherry* is about the "abstract inner life of a man." Both films, however, express a "relationship which goes beyond that of a man and a woman and even beyond the problems of children and other social and geographical issues."

That relationship, he then adds obliquely, is about accepting loss and preferring the present. Besides highlighting the parallels and contrasts between the drivers in the two films, he drives the same roads because instead of seeking some future closure like Mr. Badii, he wants to savor a landscape he knows will vanish: "But the more important and personal reason [that I have returned is that] I may no longer have a chance to bring a camera to this place which is one of my favorite places."

Kiarostami's favorite places seem to be anywhere he can find inner or outer beauty that can redeem the ugliness of aggression and suffering. *ABC Africa* emphasizes color, movement, and music to celebrate the beauty of Uganda. At the same time, he includes shots of emaciated children in a hospital and of the boy bullying the little girl (a way of referencing the civil war), and although his films consistently express hopeful possibilities, they are never dishonest or maudlin. In an interview on his photography, he said, "I don't want to cover up or hide anything. There are two natures involved. One nature covers another nature, like one mattress covering the other." In the same interview, he added that while his photographs exclude ugliness, his films are an attempt to "find people's true nature."[2] For Kiarostami, beauty is uncovered by unveiling layers of acquired identity to reach a core capacity for love and nurture. In *And Life Goes On*, natural settings are used to emphasize the generosity and courage of the people within them.

As he observed their "enthusiasm for life," he felt the tragedy of fifty thousand deaths growing "paler and paler." Although he did not find the two boys from his previous film, he decided it was more important to help the survivors who "bore no recognizable faces" but were making every effort to start a new life for themselves under difficult conditions and in an environment of natural beauty that continued as it always had: "Such is life it seemed to say, go on, seize the day." Their group effort had a major influence on his individual outlook and effort going forward. He went there just before his fiftieth birthday, and the experience profoundly affected his life and work: "The earthquake happened inside myself."[3] The protagonist of *Ten* is also an artist whose personal life has been profoundly changed in part by the alienation of her child and the inner resources she must summon to meet what at first appears to be a devastating loss. As in other films dealing with loss, Kiarostami uses physical beauty to evoke the spiritual beauty in human nature, but he does so in an entirely new way.

Kiarostami spoke of his love for snow scenes in his nature photography because it can make a "not-very-beautiful object into a beautiful one."[4] In *Ten*, he does the opposite. He exposes an ugly inner side of his conventionally beautiful protagonist to portray her potential growth from childish egotism toward becoming a mature protector. This involves stripping away layers of pretense, externalized by sunglasses, makeup, and clothing, in the course of reaching the qualities Kiarostami celebrates in the survivors of his preceding films.

The process is at first glance paradoxical. Personal growth requires mature diminishment, and the experience of the main character is reflected by the unusual form of the film. *Ten* is divided into ten episodes, each of which portrays the divorced woman (herein called the Driver) behind the wheel of her car as she talks to her passengers, but Kiarostami establishes a meaningful arrangement by preceding each vignette with a film leader graphic of its number, starting with "10" and ending with "1." These brief images are accompanied by the sound of a projector, an intentionally symbolic presence because the film was shot with a digital camera.

The sound of the projector and a bell that precedes each scene connotes the Driver's ongoing journey, while the numbered lead-ins connote its stages. The reverse countdown corresponds thematically to the Driver losing prideful or selfish qualities on the way to establishing an authentic bond with her child. The reverse numbering also corresponds to a minimalist aesthetic that Kiarostami attributed in *Ten on Ten* to Robert Bresson, who "said we create not by adding but by subtraction, and this is the opposite of sorting symbols, allegories, and sound." This implies that the progression of a good life is like that of a good film. It does not mean that the Driver can take a shortcut to enlightenment or that a good film can exist without symbolic images and sound, which are meticulously edited in all of Kiarostami's films.

Just as a good viewer must carefully consider the symbolic progression of a film before feeling its full impact, so the Driver in *Ten* has to go with the flow of traffic in her life, enduring its stops, starts, and irritations that occur in sync with the concerns and limitations that block her progress from within. For Kiarostami, reducing the nonessential is conducive to being grateful for what one has rather than being miserable for what one will discover was either harmful or never really needed.

In the press book for *Ten*'s 2002 Cannes premier, Kiarostami expresses this minimalist ideal by recounting a story by Milan Kundera about how his father's vocabulary diminished with age until he was left with only two words: "How strange." Then, Kiarostami adds, "*Ten* is my own two words. It sums up almost everything I say. I say almost because I'm already thinking about my next film. A one word film, perhaps."[5] As in *Where Is the Friend's House?*, and *Taste of Cherry*, and *The Wind Will Carry Us*, *Ten* includes scenes of literal and symbolic darkness, but in *Ten* they are symmetrically placed: Scene 7 with a prostitute and scene 4 with a woman who has just learned that her husband is leaving her both express types of blind confinement. Two other symmetrical scenes, 6 and 2, between the Driver and her friend show the Driver's potential emergence from darkness, while episodes 10, 5, 3, and 1 with her son have subtle variations on almost-exact parallels that express Kiarostami's sense of shedding darkness before the dawn.

The Driver's transformation of identity is signaled in the first episode (episode 10) by her invisibility. For eighteen minutes, the camera stays on Amin, her seven-year-old son, and as they argue, we hear only her voice because the person who speaks progressively disappears in the course of the film. The first impression the spectator receives is of a selfish woman thoughtlessly imposing her own frustrations on a child who is not ready to accept or understand them. The film begins with Amin entering the car in early-morning shadow. He has been playing in a park, and now, she picks him up to drive him to a soccer match. Though Amin is supposed to be seven, he is portrayed by a ten-year-old who is the real son of the woman playing the Driver. Even at ten, Kiarostami admitted, the boy was directed to speak better than he did in real life, and the scenes involving him took four months to shoot and then were carefully edited. The opening scene appears continuous but was actually composed of thirteen jump-cuts that Kiarostami said were almost but not completely invisible.[6]

These alterations enable Amin to argue with the Driver on an unnaturally sophisticated level so that the mother often appears more childish than the boy. The camera angles enlarge Amin's size, and the tight framing connotes the mental box his mother is trying to force him into as well as his anger in being denied the childhood space he needs to grow. In the film's first shot, therefore, Amin's face is in shadow as he enters the car, and in the film's first words, his mother directs him to "lower the window [and] let some air in." A moment later, he leans out the window to call to a friend and then leans back with a happy smile: "I saw him in the park."

Instead of involving herself in his life and interests, the Driver quotes a line from a poem to preface subjecting Amin to her own rage: "Such strange times, my dear." Then she immediately launches into a subject that seems at first to be unrelated to him at all: "A friend called me last night."—"Who?"—"You don't know her. She called me." Amin immediately senses that he is being used and becomes angry: "What do I care whether she calls or not?" From there the conversation deteriorates, first because the Driver reprimands Amin for being disrespectful, and then because the friend told her that her parents "never divorced and have always lived in the shit with lots of problems."

Amin is furious at her attempt to make him take her side: "You mean it's good that you divorced Dad, that he was the one in the wrong. Say what you like. I don't believe it!" Instead of trying to explain why she wanted the divorce, the Driver accuses Amin of being "like those children full of hate" because he won't accept his stepfather, who is a "good companion" for her. After a series of reciprocal non sequiturs, Amin puts his hands over his ears while his mother waxes philosophical: "You see Amin, if we lived to one hundred, we'd still argue." She accuses him of being like his father, who wanted her "only for himself," which is ironic because she wants Amin only for herself.

Then she misapplies the obsession to Amin: "No one belongs to anyone, not even you. You're my child, but you're not mine. You belong to this world."—"That's true, but you don't let me speak. I'm only a child. I can't belong to myself. I have to grow up to attain an age that will allow me to belong to myself." She passes over this obvious wisdom and proceeds to berate him with psychobabble more applicable to herself than to him: "You're angry, full of rage because you refuse reality. You want me to feel guilty, to pity you." She follows this with another self-pitying quote with no regard for his ability to understand it: "I feel fulfilled now, like a flowing river. I was a stagnant pond. My brain was devastated." He puts his hands over his ears again, and perhaps the spectator feels the same way because the line about her brain being devastated seems to describe her present state more than the restrictive one she feels she has escaped.

Kiarostami assumes that his spectators, most of whom live outside Iran, will take it for granted that Iranian women are dismally restrained. The thematic point is not to argue an obvious situation but to show that there are better ways of adapting to a disaster than childishly complaining about it. Certainly, the Driver is right to defend having to lie to get a divorce, but just as certainly, she is wrong to aggravate the confusion of her son by launching into a self-soothing tirade of social protest. Amin tells her he can't live with her because she's a selfish woman and doesn't know how to speak to him: "I talk calmly. You get carried away. Once my father marries, I'll go to live with him. You don't let me finish. You never know how to talk."

In the key argument between them, the Driver is abstractly right but emotionally wrong, and Amin interrupts her for the tantrum-like tone he correctly recognizes as that of petulant child:

"You accused my father of being a drug addict."—"It was a good way of getting a divorce. The rotten laws in this society give no rights to women to get a divorce. You have to say that she is beaten or that her husband's on drugs."—"Don't shout in the street!"—"A woman has to die so as to be able to live? I'll shout if I want. I'll say what I have to say."—"Say it calmly. Speak quietly!"—"And he accuses me. I ran away."—"Don't shout!"—"I will. I was like a zombie!"—"Don't shout."

Then he covers his ears, makes a crying sound, and bolts from the car, to which she responds sarcastically, "Bravo!" capping a sorry display she cannot admit was of her own making because she does not yet see that her bitterness is as bad as the tyranny she rails against.

During a long section of these repetitive arguments, the view out the passenger window shows a continuous line of barred fences and walls, as if to say that all these words are getting them nowhere, just as the camera stays fixed on the frustrated face of Amin. Sound also supplements the abrasive tone when the car becomes snarled in traffic, as the Driver in concert with a herd of honking horns shouts, "Out of the way!" In this scene and several others, *Ten* shows people entirely locked into frames of their own understanding without the perspective of the zigzag road that Kiarostami uses in *Taste of Cherry* and *The Wind Will Carry Us*.

But the static visual image does change as soon as Amin leaves the car, and we see the Driver for the first time. Until now, she has just been a querulous voice. Suddenly, she is a strikingly beautiful woman wearing stylish sunglasses and brightly clothed in a white headscarf that leaves the front of her hair exposed and a black jacket with small orange and gold flowers. According to Geoff Andrew, "We haven't seen anyone like this in a Kiarostami film before. Indeed, we probably haven't seen anyone like this in any Iranian movie."[7] In the next scene, as the day heats up, she briefly removes the jacket to reveal a bright-orange dress, and this unique display of color is Kiarostami's way of conveying her passion, energy, and immaturity. These qualities bear a promise of continuing development, and as her clothing and makeup are progressively toned down in subsequent scenes, her sympathy and understanding subtly deepen.

Besides the change in the Driver's appearance and that of a sensitive friend near the end, Kiarostami uses visual and verbal metaphors of traffic and driving to reflect both her outer ordeal and inner turmoil. After Amin exits, the Driver is shown looking for a parking space, a way of reiterating that she left the marriage because she needed emotional space, and when she calls out to a driver, "Excuse me, sir, are you leaving?" the line refers back to the split from her husband. Her irritation with the other driver's pulling back before he can swing out into traffic refers again to the process of marital separation as she impatiently waves him back: "There's room!" Finally, she pulls forward into the man's space, a sign of her taking on a different role, before decisively pulling the parking brake and then leaving and locking the car.

But there will be no respite from her search for a larger self, and as she travels and explores, Kiarostami portrays her as an object of interest rather than sympathy. The scenes where she is insensitive toward Amin prevent any complete identification that might result from her physical beauty. She becomes a person to study, ultimately perhaps to recognize in oneself without idealization or flattery. Kiarostami said that he didn't show the Driver for such a long period at the beginning because that would have allowed the spectators to make a judgment too soon: "I don't want viewers to judge my characters, which is why sometimes I don't show them at all. Just hearing them can be enough."[8] He explained his preference for indefinite endings by saying that he would often leave a film in the middle because he didn't want to be forced "to judge who is the good guy, who is the bad guy, and what's going to happen to them [because] I prefer to finish it my own way!"[9]

We do learn, however, that the Driver is a photographer and a painter and that her need to freely travel and practice her profession has led her to leave her possessive and controlling husband. Her unusual clothing also indicates that contrary to the theocratic ideal, she celebrates the physical body and, in that sense resembles, Kiarostami himself. But despite these positive qualities, she will have nothing valuable to say through her art or to her son unless she works through her own anger enough to realize that she can't help Amin until she and he are ready.

The second scene (number 9) begins with the Driver's sister waiting in the passenger seat while the Driver is out getting a present, perhaps for her brother-in-law's birthday. Like the Driver, the sister appears to be in her mid- to late twenties, but the initial impression presents a stark contrast. While the first scene shows the colorfully dressed Driver skillfully threading her way through heavy traffic, the sister in her heavy, black dress sits picking at her face and fanning herself in the afternoon heat. The visual image of being unable to move in a miserable environment connotes the general condition of Iranian women in the current climate, even though her speech in the scene that follows seems to reveal a surface contentment with her lot.

And although she laughs and jokes comfortably with the Driver, the camera angles and the nervous facial picking connote a social condition conducive to internal ugliness. Her subjection to her husband's demands is reflected in a compulsive seizing of control wherever she can find it, in this case insistently directing her sister how and where to drive on the way to dropping her off at home after her working all day as a preschool teacher. Her work and the women's discussion of their own children's development, along with a second stop where the Driver picks up a birthday cake, connote the idea of an ongoing struggle for maturity in adults, as well.

However, while the Driver continues to evolve, the sister appears to be conventionally stagnant. Her simplistic formula for life corresponds to her first driving direction: "Go straight on. You can go downhill later." These metaphors continue to qualify her advice on how to handle Amin. When she disagrees with the Driver's idea that she will leave her son free to develop on his own, she says, "Go that way!" and when she recalls that she said the Driver should wait until Amin grows to understand (actually good advice), the words are qualified by the realistic uncertainty of the Driver's question: "Go this way."—"Is it a dead end?"—"No, go on."

As the Driver continues to look for shortcuts, a reference back to their impossibility in *Taste of Cherry* and *The Wind Will Carry Us*, the sister's conventionality is expressed by "Go this way, and turn on to the main road." And she has certain set ideas about child-rearing that do not take individuality into account, one of them being a justification of putting her child in a day nursery at the age of three because preschools are not healthy at a younger age, a statement that conforms to a one-size-fits-all rule. The idea is accented by the fact that both women are only thinking of their own child as they converse and not really listening to each other's concerns about children of different ages and temperaments.

The sister's job as a teacher of three-year-olds is consistent with the simplistic advice that adults confidently offer each other. The sister's idea that Amin should get to know his father sounds good at first, until we learn later that Amin is aware that his father watches porn movies after he thinks his son is asleep. At the same time, this is a reality of the world Amin will grow into, whether he follows his father's example or whether, like his mother, his internal inclinations and external circumstances direct him to the independent path his mother seeks. The sister is a kind of Sancho Panza to the Driver's Don Quixote, and although the Driver can verbally concede, "I know you're right," her reaction to the traffic shows that resignation is not in her nature: "Look at that guy, he's an idiot!" referring perhaps to the world in general, as she uselessly keeps hitting the horn. She seems not to realize that complaining about immutable realities is useless and that her anger is idiotic because it is self-destructive: "What an idiot. They're holding up traffic. People are crazy these days."

So the question that arises is, Who is crazier? The person who rationalizes a miserable situation or the person who beats their head against the wall, trying to change unchangeable people. As they approach the bakery to pick up the birthday cake, the sister's directions once again connote pragmatic adaptation: "Go on, follow him, quick. Follow him through. Go on. Don't stop. Pull over there. The baker's just there. Park in the shade. Park on a slant." But the consequences of such advice are then pictured for a second time, as the sister, sweltering in her heavy, black dress, fans herself, barraged by car horns and sirens for another two minutes until the Driver, moving comfortably in her bright-orange dress, returns with a large, pink-ribboned box.

The Driver excuses the delay by saying that a guy outside the bakery was selling videotapes and CDs, which she must have stopped to scan as either an indication of her artistic interests or (depending on the titles) a parallel form of junk food. The oblique reference to a society ruled by the profit motive, which is considered more fully in the Driver's subsequent scene with a prostitute, is then followed up by a man coming to the Driver's window to demand money for parking in front of his shop: "In Tehran everything is for sale," the Driver says as she pulls away.

The last part of episode 9 introduces the recurrent Kiarostami theme of how remembering mortality should result in kinder and gentler behavior but rarely does because most adults remain children and societies are set up to keep it that way. When the Driver asks if the sister's son is still at the same school, the sister replies that he is because "it's not good to change schools." The sister's report on Amin's aggressive behavior toward his cousin is on the surface about a disturbed child but, in a larger sense, applies to the behavior of adult nations who engage in childish wars, especially because the cousin's name, Illiade, appears to be an English pun on *Iliad*, just as Mr. Badii's name is a pun on *bad* and Mrs. Godarzi's name is a pun on *God*.

The sister's attempt to curb Amin's nastiness resembles those of various religions to convince adults to heed "Thou shalt not kill." When Amin says, "If he comes near me, I'll hit him," she tells him, "He's a child. He wants to play. He doesn't know. Be gentle with him. Talk to him. He doesn't know. Be gentle with him." But Amin, like humanity at large, is incorrigible: "The more I help him, the less grateful he is." And once again, a driving metaphor points up the uselessness of good, rational advice: "There's a pothole," the sister says a moment before the Driver jolts over it, and for a moment, there is a relaxed wisdom in their exchange as the sister says, "You found it," and the Driver flashes a smile, suggesting mutual acceptance of future bumps in the road.

But in the meantime, some of these bumps can be disastrous when adults are childishly incapable of avoiding major conflicts. When Amin calls her older son an asshole, the sister tells him, "It was funny when you were little, but no one laughs at you anymore. You've grown up. Be reasonable." But in particular families, as in the human family, wise counsel falls on deaf ears, reflecting the folly of adult advisors who seem to worsen rather than ameliorate the situation: "This way?" the Driver asks, to which the sister responds with a seeming non sequitur that reflects her moralizing futility: "Why this way? Look, I've broken my nail."

All these questions of control and direction are then related to the limited human life span when the sister corrects the Driver about the number of candles on her husband's cake. He's a year younger than Morteza, she says, to which the Driver philosophically responds, "Let him age." Trivially, the sister concerns herself with accuracy about the year he was born shortly before she crudely commands, "Mind that old woman. She's on her last legs but all the same," adding "Don't stop!" when the Driver stops to offer a lift. The old woman declines the ride, saying she wants to walk, a remark that suggests "preferring the present" and prompting the Driver to reflect a wisdom that she, unlike her sister, is likely to attain: "I'll be like her one day."

But when at the beginning of the next scene (episode 8) the Driver picks up the same or perhaps another elderly woman, the prophetic line proves to apply only to advanced age. In the symbolically lengthening late-afternoon shadows, the old woman's obsession with formal religion does not represent the wisdom that the Driver or most of Kiarostami's spectators instinctively seek. Kiarostami noted that the woman didn't know she was being filmed and would never see it because "she doesn't need to."[10] She is not shown, except for a glimpse of her back as she exits the car, perhaps because she voices a representative rather than an individual need for religious consolation.

With the heat winding down as darkness approaches, the driver once again wears her black jacket, while the old woman rambles on about how she protects herself from the existential cold. She is on her way to a large mausoleum where she goes to pray several times a day. The initial dialogue applies the ongoing direction metaphor to organized religion: "Is this a dead end?"—"No. May God bless you and protect you. May he save us from all our worries."—"What's your worry?"—"Don't go down here. It leads nowhere."—"Should I turn back?"—"No."—"Where's the shrine?"—"Over there."—"I'll turn back and take the other road."—"Why go there?"

For this woman, there is only one road. Her husband and only son are long dead, and she fills the emptiness with obsessive prayers for the children and elderly people of the world. She has just sold her house to go on a pilgrimage to Syria, and the only material possessions she prizes are two rosaries for different saints that she shows to the Driver, who comments, "They're beautiful." The sister recalled how the Driver once said that people shouldn't have any close bonds, a reflection of her problematic relationships to her son and ex-husband, but the woman takes this form of psychological amputation to an extreme. She swears "on the severed arms of St. Abolfazi, Roqve, and Imam Hossein" that she gave everything else she owned to a woman with twelve daughters.

But then she unwittingly indicates that this act of charity for one family may have shortchanged her own because she jumps to lamenting that her daughter, who has seven children, has a stomach tumor and is afraid of the operation. Then, she tediously enumerates all the household items she gave away and rattles off the names of places where she has gone on pilgrimage. After this random review of unrelieved suffering and supplication, she exhorts, "May God grant your wishes," followed by a prideful statement of the poverty she has attained: "Of all the wishes in the world, apart from God, I own only this."

Wishing (as religious people often do) to confirm the good news of her contentment, she repeatedly urges the Driver to follow her example by offering to watch the car while the Driver goes to pray. But the Driver, like most viewers, has grown impatient because she has not reached the point where she can sever her bonds with other human beings in her physical life: "No, thank you. I have a lot to do. I'll stay here. Go on. May God help everyone." The line foreshadows the later revelation that she does go to pray, but the scene with the woman serves to delineate a masochistic spirituality that conforms to Shiite martyrdom, a form of prayer that Kiarostami reproves (see chapter 1).

During most of the drive with the old woman, we see only walls or buildings with barred windows outside the Driver's window. We never see the old woman, only these symbols of how a narrow-minded religious fanatic has walled herself in for protection from life. Even at the shrine where an imam's prayers are being broadcast on a loudspeaker, we see only the building's wall. As the woman exits the car, we see an image of the abridged existence she retains—the back of her black chador seen from the shoulders down, which fills most of the frame, blocking out the rest of the world except for a white, vertically barred fence. Her faith has reduced her to a stereotype, and her way offers no escape from the car's iron cell, only a smaller frame, another trap.

The camera now cuts from the black chador to the blackness of a night street to begin episode 7. The Driver has stopped to pick up a young prostitute who, thinking the Driver would be a male customer, has gotten into her car by mistake. While the old woman blocks out the light with fanatical religion, the prostitute operates in the darkness of commercial greed. This conventional opposition of saint and sinner is used in *Ten* as a spiritual parallel. Both are destructive ways of blindly rejecting life and love. And both are diametrically opposed to the Driver's intuitive need to love existence by understanding it. For the first time, we see her without sunglasses and with a full smile, looking especially beautiful in contrast to the sentiments of her passenger, who epitomizes ugly aspects of the secular world. The prostitute is another form of the walking haystack seen in *Where Is the Friend's House?* and *The Wind Will Carry Us*. She has no identity apart from her work and no motive other than profit. Like the old woman at the shrine, she is content with the values she has found and lives securely within them.

From the outset, she resists the whole idea of questioning her existence by repeatedly demanding that the Driver let her out of the car, much like a spectator who expecting simple distraction may feel restlessly shaken by a Kiarostami film. The Driver's first line, "I saw you getting out of the Mercedes," pinpoints where the prostitute is coming from, a rockbound conviction that money is the be-all and end-all of life. She provides a form of escape for other work-bound citizens that corresponds to the porn films that the Driver's ex-husband watches, a regressive shrinking of the mind analogous to the all-day cartoon channel he allows Amin to watch or *The Traveler*'s soccer match that adult men stand in line all day to see.

And ironically, this person who provides escapist entertainment is panicked by a situation where she is being asked to think about the life her profession conceals. That life has a simple goal, and like most spectators of commercial films, her prime concern is to know where she is going: "I'm going nowhere. Leave me here," she says at one point, and at another, "Where are you taking me? I'll have to walk back from here," and at still another, "This is the back of beyond. This place is dead."

But the Driver won't let her out of the car until she has satisfied her own need to fully understand the subjection to routine that society expects, much as her sister unthinkingly has. Under the Driver's relentless questioning, the prostitute, like the sister, reveals that she is proud of having an "honest trade" and a "decent job." An analogy to Amin occurs when the Driver asks why a girl of her age would want to do this. Instead of answering, she keeps trying to silence the Driver and, like Amin, threatens to get out of the car because the Driver's questions threaten the small but secure structure of identity she depends on: "Let me out here! Not too far. Where are you taking me?" She craves simplicity, and she responds to the Driver's impertinent questions like anyone who takes the validation of earning money as a validation of life: "What's the reason you do this?"—"Sex, love, sex."—"That's all life is?"—"It's a trade, it's my job." And she becomes as angry as Amin when the Driver tries to probe deeper than the simplistic narrative she lives: "What is this 'interesting'? Who do you think you are, sitting at your wheel, lecturing me, guiding me?" And as the Driver is learning from Amin, no one can guide a person who is not ready unless, like Ahmad in *Where Is the Friend's House?* he or she encounters the right guide at the right moment.

Unlike the soldier in *Taste of Cherry*, who bolts from the car before realizing that Badii's asking him to be complicit in murder is analogous to his country's asking him to be complicit in war, the prostitute cannot escape the forward motion of the Driver's questions, and when she fights back her arguments are as old as the world's oldest profession. She lives her life in a space "where cars pass by," so she will not have to remember the personal disintegration of an ideal love. Her life is the consequence of rejection by her fiancé, and in this sense, she has found a way of coping, just as the old woman found a way of coping with her husband's death and as the Driver and Amin will have to cope with the disintegration of a familial ideal. Like the Driver, who has tried to console herself by saying that people do not need close bonds, the prostitute insists that her life is easy because she doesn't need anyone, and she clings to this comfort just as desperately as the wives she scorns cling to their husbands.

Forced out of her defensive shell, the prostitute now argues aggressively when the Driver asks if she works only for the money: "Don't you need more sentiment?" The prostitute replies, "You're the same. It's a contract with yourself. You have sex. You take the money. It's give and take. It's the same for you." And the soul-imperiling danger of seeing life as only what you get out of it is signaled by the sound of a siren as the Driver interjects, "Life is all trade?" At this point, the car is barely perceptible, moving in a complete darkness where no flashes of light illuminate the Driver's face: "You're the wholesalers. We're the retailers," the prostitute says, and when asked what happens if she gets pregnant, she simply says she aborts, an act that also applies to the expansion of her soul. Now, with the car stopped in total darkness, the Driver is ready to let the prostitute go: "This is good. It's nice and busy. Good-bye," she says as a second siren sounds and she departs. As with the exiting old woman, a shot out the passenger window shows her from behind, facelessly refusing one car and then entering another.

In contrast, the Driver is always on the move, navigating rather than negotiating her way through life. Some time has passed at the beginning of episode 6 (we don't know how much), and the Driver has changed. She looks serene as she drives in the morning light in a black head scarf, with no sunglasses, makeup, or lipstick and wearing a kind of modified chador with short sleeves over her black, patterned jacket. The sound of the imam praying on the loudspeaker indicates that she is outside the mausoleum where after a few seconds, she stops to pick up a similarly dressed friend of about the same age. The friend flashes her a radiant smile that sets the tone for the film's first empathetic conversation. We learn that they have been to the mausoleum, and although both have had prior doubts about the efficacy of prayer, just being there has soothed them. The Driver seeks solace because Amin has gone to live with his father, and the friend hopes the man she is seeing will propose marriage. Neither is confident that their wish will be granted, and yet their shared intimacy is one of the best experiences that life or a film can offer.

The friend is the first passenger not to give the Driver directions about how to drive and where to go. The intimacy of their connection is enhanced by the smeared passenger window, which suggests the harsh realities of the outside world, while the compartment inside has been affectively transformed. Instead of staying exclusively on one character or the other, the camera cuts back and forth, creating a genuine exchange. The Driver calmly explains her situation with Amin, while the friend confides that she is hoping her male friend will commit himself because although there are no practical reasons for his hesitation, he seems "full of contradictions."

The phrase applies to many of Kiarostami's characters and here especially to the Driver, who loves her son but is struggling to resolve the volatility of her own conflicting emotions. Her underlying rage against her personal situation becomes evident when she breaks the mood by stopping to yell at a carful of men: "How can I get by if you just stand there? And you think it's funny? What an idiot!" And even after they apparently move, she shouts, "You don't care how you park." Their reply bears on the general repression of women in Iran—"This is a one-way street!"—leaving her with the impotent parting shot of "I don't believe it!" followed by their dismissive "Go, sister, go!" as they speed off in the opposite direction.

While the Driver's sister tried to coach her into acceptance with advice like "Leave them be. They're truck drivers," the friend leads by example by remaining quiet and calm. Her former skepticism about prayer—"I used to say you pray to force God to give you things"—applies generally to forcing one's will on other people. The Driver used all her verbal skills to bend Amin to her will, while the friend simply waits, hopes, and now even prays that her man will make up his mind. Neither gets exactly what they want, but in the act of praying together for separate things, they establish a human connection, which for Kiarostami is the best thing about religion. It affirms human solidarity rather than superior power.

The Driver says she has come to the shrine to relieve her guilt about Amin, and in connecting with another unfulfilled person, she discovers that she may not be able to control the men in her life any more than she can redirect the prostitute or anyone else on a one-way street. She can, however, come to know compatible souls, which in general is what Kiarostami did by making films for widely divergent spectators. That feeling is evident in the friend, who sits alone for a minute and a half after the Driver exits the car at the end of the scene. In direct contrast to the sister miserably fanning herself in the oppressive heat, the friend sits serenely in the sunlight, watching the flow of traffic with the smeared window now rolled down, recalling the film's first line when the Driver told Amin to "let in some air."

Episode 5 brings Amin back into the car. The film uses formal repetition with slight variations to subtly indicate the Driver's maturation. She wears the same sunglasses, white head scarf, and black jacket that she wore in the opening scene, but the jacket is closed, and we can no longer see the bright-orange dress. She parks, and as Amin gets out of the white SUV across the street, she asks her ex-husband what time she should bring him back. Once Amin is inside, she offers him an ice cream as she did in episode 10, and once again he refuses, as he does when she asks him for a kiss, but their conversation is quiet and mundane. Amin wants to go his grandma's and wants the Driver to bring his Hercules tape there later along with medicine for his cold, which he assures her is not accompanied by a fever.

These details imply that although neither of them is perfectly okay with the situation, things are calming down. This time, the Driver says nothing about the divorce and acts interested when Amin tells her about his computing classes. Both are essentially being reprogrammed to this new relationship. She listens without passing judgment when Amin tells her how his father blocks the satellite TV channels that he watches alone at night because they include scenes that are too sexy for children, and she does not comment on his permitting his son to spend a lot of time watching an all-cartoon channel.

She is also not perturbed when Amin angrily thinks that she is not going to Grandma's because she is taking a different route, and when he starts to have a tantrum about it, she just smiles and says she knows a shortcut. Amin relaxes and asks if cars can be made with a gear that allows them to fly. She says she's never heard of that, and he says they have them abroad because he saw them on TV. Though there are no shortcuts to emotional equilibrium and they both have to negotiate inevitable obstacles in the traffic of their lives, she drives rapidly and smoothly down wide, tree-lined streets throughout the scene. At the end, she once again leaves the car to buy a cake for a treat rather than an occasion, leaving him alone in the car, just as she left the sister and the friend. Seen alone for almost a minute, Amin stretches his arms and arches his back as if he now has room to grow.

The relative calm of episode 5 gives way in episode 4 to the abject complaints of another friend, whose husband has abruptly divorced her after a seven-year marriage and whose self-pity ignites the Driver's residual rage. The scene takes place at night, and as in the other night scene with the prostitute, darkness conveys the blindness of a stagnant state. The prostitute could not see past the demands of her soulless work, and the divorced woman cannot conceive of a life outside the conventional role of the good wife she has conscientiously played. Just as the prostitute scorned women who cling to men, the Driver repeatedly seeks to console herself with the illusion that people don't need close bonds, and she berates the woman for not facing her version of reality.

But even though the Driver's arguments are abstractly right, they are as futile as her arguments with Amin and as rationality generally is with people who are not emotionally prepared to listen. The Driver seems unaware that her advice is self-serving because she uses this woman's plight to work her way out of her own. The result is a comedy of failed persuasion: "You're weak, very weak, you understand? You cling to someone who leaves you like this?"—"But I was so fond of him."—"Life is so vast. Why depend on just one person?"—"Why not?" the woman says through her tears.

The Driver continues to try to console the woman from a position she has struggled to reach but that is far beyond that of the woman, who is still in shock, especially because her husband left her for someone else. The Driver's situation is different because it was she who chose to leave, and she can only speak from within her own "frame." She tells the woman that she must love herself, that there is more than one man in the world, and that women must not be dependent on men. The trainer at her health club told her that women need a "big ass and big tits [because] that's what men like," and so "if men are that shallow, why should we try to please them? When we're little, we cling to our parents, then to a boy, then to our child, then to our work, like idiots."

But in the nighttime dark, the woman just continues to weep, and Kiarostami implies that people need something to cling to, even if they change the object and the frame. The old woman clung to her belief in a prayer-granting God, despite the death of her twelve-year-old son and her daughter's stomach cancer, while the Driver clings to her philosophy of complete independence, despite her continuing need for Amin's love.

In the Iranian earthquake and the Ugandan epidemic, people lose a secure way of life, but they can't lose their need to share their existence with other human beings, so even though the Driver makes errors of judgment, she tries to help herself by helping the passengers she meets on her journey: "You can't live without losing. We come into the world for that. To win and to lose. Win! Lose! You need to learn what losing's like." Through her tears, the woman says, "Experience, more experience," undercutting and recalling the Driver's good but useless advice in the opening scene: "You see, Amin, if we lived to one hundred, we'd still argue. You must have your own experiences to understand life."

In reply, Amin stuck his fingers in his ears, and at this point, the Driver, too, shows that stoic wisdom doesn't work on real-life stress, as she characteristically honks her horn and yells, "Move it!" at the traffic, which will move only when it's ready. Cogency failed with Amin at the end of episode 10, just as it fails here. As the scene ends, they pull up to a restaurant where there is at first no place to park, until she finds an acceptable one further on. Once again, she must temporarily go backward to move forward, taking time to back into the space before she and the divorced woman walk back to resume the necessity of sustaining their bodies while spiritually moving on.

Parallels with variations convey progress in episode 3, the third scene with Amin. The opening image of Amin in shadow entering the passenger door is the same as in the first scene, but the first time he had a querulous look, and this time he is smiling. For the first minute, the camera stays on him while the Driver speaks, but then it cuts back to the Driver, establishing back-and-forth cuts that indicate they are finally listening to each other. The Driver is wearing the white head scarf and sunglasses, but now she is not wearing the black jacket over the orange dress, which appears darker and more subdued on an overcast morning. The toned-down orange indicates that she retains the vitality of her rebellion, but it also foreshadows her more maternal behavior in the dialogue that follows.

Once again, Amin waves to a friend at the same place he called out "Omid!" (the name means "hope") in the first scene, before settling back and hearing his mother tell him exactly what he wants to hear. She has been to a psychologist who told her, "Amin's a man. He has to grow up with a man. You must let him grow up with his father. Allow him to live with his father because he's calmer and more easygoing." But the Driver has become easygoing, too, a change keyed by the fast, smooth progress of the car as it breezes along a freeway on the way to Grandma's.

The driving metaphors further contribute to the motif of maturation. Amin asks about the gears: "Can we slip it into second?" She quickly says no. She cannot suddenly slow down to his level, but she can attempt to explain the idea of progression from first, which "is for starting," to fifth, for cruising. The necessity of keeping an ordered sequence to keep the car moving recalls Amin asking about a gear to make the car fly in episode 5 and leads into a repeat argument about the way to Grandma's, in which the Driver, without raising her voice, says she knows a shortcut, despite Amin's rising temper, and in fact she has a discovered an efficient way to quell their mutual anger. This has resulted from the unconscious accumulation of patience she has gained from every preceding episode. As the car leaves the freeway, she stops at a light, and when Amin again asks about the gear, she says it is in neutral. Then, she asks him for a kiss, which he refuses because neutral at this point is as far as he is prepared to go. Then, as they resume driving, she offers to cook for him at Grandma's, which he also refuses, another potential provocation.

But this time, the Driver defuses the situation with a humorous fantasy that makes Amin smile: "Tell your father to marry a woman with a daughter, one for each of you. You will look after each other as long as he doesn't lay hands on your wife." She uses the scenario to sublimate her prior resentment at her husband's jealousy and less successfully to compare herself to this future wife, which makes Amin angry. When she says the new wife won't be prettier, Amin names a woman he says is prettier, and when she says, "Okay, but she won't be better," Amin says she will be, and when she asks why, he says there are a thousand reasons. Unable to shrug this off, the Driver creates a satirical sketch of what the ideal Iranian wife should be: She will say her prayers, not wear makeup or miniskirts, stay home all day, do the dishes, cook good meals, and keep a perfect house. Amin retorts, "In any case, she'll be better than you," still smiling because he thinks she is joking.

But he becomes angry when he senses that she is again defending herself and condemning his father. She cannot control her words as smoothly as she controls the car, and she is unable to immediately put the brakes on her sarcasm: "She'll always smell of cooking, and she'll always agree with her husband." Amin's pent-up anger now boils over: "At least she won't be gone all the time. You've talked so much, and not one word convinced me." But we can immediately see the difference in the Driver, who regains control while making one more effort to defend herself: "All right, I surrender. It's good that all life can be summed up in the stomach. If you have money, you can manage without a maid. I have to take photos, paint, or travel. I have more important things to do than wash dishes or vacuum the carpets."

Amin counters, "But the other will never have as much work as you do. You think everyone's like you. You don't know what a mother is." Amin is still contained by the security of society's definition, a frame he is not ready to leave and that the Driver now realizes she should not break. She lets Amin rattle off a series of accusations about how she was late to pick him up from school one day and that she was lying when she said she had to stop for gas. Then, struggling to retain his sense of good and bad behavior, Amin starts giving directions again, even though he has no idea of where he is.

When the Driver tries to smooth things over and offers to cook for him at Grandma's, he angrily shouts, "I don't want you to," and when she tells him not to shout, she reverses their dialogue from the first scene, where when Amin told her not to shout, she furiously retorted, "I will. I was like a zombie!" This time it is Amin's turn, but he unconsciously only repeats a pattern he learned from her: "Don't judge. Stop shouting," she says before he echoes her example. "I like shouting!" After accusing her again of lying about the gas—"Just tell the truth."—she shows that she understands that his feelings supersede her truth: "Okay," she says, "I needed water for the battery," and just before he bolts from the car, she gives it one more try: "Okay, I'm a selfish liar, and the conversation's over." The concession doesn't work yet with Amin, but it does show that the Driver realizes he has made up his mind and that only time will modify or change it.

Patience and recovery are the summarizing themes of episode 2. The Driver is shown with a melancholy look in the gray of an early morning, wearing her white-patterned, black jacket, with the orange dress no longer visible. Before we see the friend from the shrine, she says, "You said he was full of contradictions," a line that also refers back to the volatility of Amin's moods in the previous scene. Then, we hear the friend's voice say, "Yes, but I was wrong. They aren't contradictions. He won't marry me." The camera stays on the Driver because she, too, has just experienced rejection. The friend's voice continues, "He says it wouldn't work."

Then, the camera cuts to the friend, who has a somber expression and a dark-black jacket with a tightly pulled white head scarf, in stark contrast to the radiant smile and white-speckled, black dress she wore before. She says that when she asked her fiancé if he was sure, he said he was, and she told him he would regret it one day. The camera moves back to the Driver as the woman says the thing that hurts her is that he's thinking of someone else, just as Amin has shown a clear preference for his father. The camera then moves back and forth between them in quicker cuts than in any of the previous scenes, as if confirming rapport and identification between the women.

But there is a difference between them, as well. The Driver, with a touch of her usual anger, echoes the tone she took with the divorced woman in episode 4: "He thinks that easily of someone else?" The friend is not comforted by this he-isn't-worth-it defiance and instead sadly says she doesn't know if it's easy for him, but she does know he's thinking of someone else. The Driver is affected by the way the friend accepts sadness without trying to deny it and looks sad herself as she says, "That's hard, isn't it?"

At first, the friend agrees but then says it's not that hard: "The hardest part is admitting that it's hard." This shows a different kind of courage than the fight-back attitude that has confined the Driver to useless anger. The friend has moved beyond blame to introspection: "I'm ashamed of saying that it's hard because I thought everything I liked would happen. I never imagined it would be impossible." This time, the Driver, now driving slowly

Figure 8.1. The Driver looks sad when her friend tells her that her fiancé won't marry her because he is thinking of someone else, just as Amin has chosen to live with his father rather than with her. Zeitgeist Films/Photofest.

and steadily, simply agrees. "I understand," she says with a calm, sad expression on her face.

As the Driver keeps moving ahead, the friend moves ahead, as well: "Sometimes I think that everything I like has to come true." With the car moving past nondescript, gray walls, the friend adds that she thinks she'll "soon be over it," with a resolved optimism that makes the Driver smile and feel relaxed enough to playfully ask if she is being modest because her veil is so tight: "It doesn't suit you." As the light brightens outside the passenger window, the friend slowly undoes the veil under her chin and, with the car now at a full stop, pulls it back from her forehead to reveal hair cropped so short it looks almost shaved. The Driver asks if she has cut her hair, and for the first time in the scene, the smile that illumined her distinct beauty in episode 6 returns: "Am I hideous?" she asks, and the Driver, without a trace of surprise in her voice, responds, "It suits you."

The car remains stopped, as if to signal a transition before a new beginning, and accordingly, the friend keeps smiling as the Driver asks why she did it and repeats that it suits her. Then, the decisiveness of the friend's resolve is shown as, continuing to smile, she pulls the veil back completely, a dramatic uncovering for an Iranian film but one that shows that she, too, like the earthquake and AIDS victims, is ready not just to move on but to face the future with hope and courage. It is just as important that she shares her experience with the Driver and the spectators. Still smiling, she dries her tears as the Driver, speaking from her own experience, says she knows it's hard to lose. Then, using the same words she had directed in a defiant, impatient tone to the divorced woman, she gently says, "I know it's hard to lose. You lose at times, unfortunately," indicating that her feelings are finally in sync with her understanding. When the friend who never stops smiling picks up her purse to get a tissue to dry her eyes, we see the Driver's right hand reach across the frame to brush away a tear.

This is an extraordinary moment because, as Geoff Andrew points out, all the characters up to this point "have been locked in compositional boxes." Kiarostami explained the departure: "At first I didn't like this [disruption of the frame] because I prefer not to show big emotional moments. So I asked them to do the scene again and not do that. But little by little I changed my mind and finally decided it was okay."[11] "Don't cry," the Driver says, as her hand reaches across a second time, and a true Kiarostami moment occurs when the friend once again flashes her extraordinary smile and says, "I'm laughing and crying at the same time."

The gesture of reaching across the frame is the key poetic moment, a reflection of what Kiarostami's cinema hopes to achieve. The Driver asks how she felt when she cut her hair, and the friend says she felt great, but it's clear that she feels even better now that she has shared her experience with a sympathetic friend: "This is the first time I've cried since then." As the friend replaces the veil, the Driver again compliments her new look and tells her not to hurry: "Let your head breathe." Then, she asks if she feels she has changed now that her fiancé is gone. Still drying her eyes, the friend is not afraid to deny the complexity of her feelings: "Yes, much better. But I'd like him to be here." The Driver ends the scene with two words, "I understand," summing up perhaps what Kiarostami meant when he said *Ten* was a two-word film.

The Driver and her friend epitomize in a relation of two the absolute value of human interdependence. They do not need validation or assurance from a single grantor as the elderly woman at the shrine needed from God, the divorced woman needed from her husband, and the Driver needed from Amin. In identifying with each other, they approximate the Sufi feeling that identification with the Creative Source is not an abstraction but a connection between physical beings living imperfect but evolving lives.

The car had been stopped at the end of episode 2. Now, at the beginning of episode 1, the Driver is shown moving forward on an overcast morning, wearing her sunglasses, black jacket, and white head scarf as at the beginning but this time with a serene expression on her face. She stops to pick up Amin across the street from her ex-husband's white SUV, just as she had at the start of episode 5, and once again, Kiarostami uses subtle variations on exact repetition to suggest slow rather than dramatic progress. Both scenes begin with her repeated question, "When do I bring him back?" followed by the husband seeming to think she means "Should I bring him back?" because both times he responds, "You have to." In both scenes, Amin starts to cross the street but then is called back to get his bag, and in both scenes, the Driver asks, "Can he stay the night?" But while the husband says, "No, bring him back," in episode 5, he must invisibly nod affirmatively here because this time they set a time to return the next morning: "What time will you be here?" she asks. "10:30. Is that okay?" he calls back, and she responds as if these exchanges are now routine: "I'll bring him at 10:30."

Following the exchange, the Driver's first words in episode 5 were "Hello, are you well?" to which Amin replied, "Take me to Grandma's." In episode 1, the Driver dispenses with "Are you well?" and simply says, "Hello," allowing Amin to set the tone, with no attempt to set an upbeat mood. During the exchange, the camera shows Amin, still wearing the white T-shirt bearing his blue-lettered name, watching his mother warily. Now, as if relaxing into a familiar reality, he again says, "Take me to Grandma's," as the car moves quickly and smoothly forward. After buckling his seat belt, he looks up with a slight smile into a shadow that fades to the black screen of the final credits.

As in the films that preceded and followed, *Ten* is, in Kiarostami's words, "like a journey, but also a circle. . . . The final moment is like a dawn coming after the darkness: you finally find that it's maybe not quite so difficult after all."[12] The message is borne out by the music, which here, as in other Kiarostami films, is saved until the end. It is Howard Blake's "Walking in the Air" from *The Snowman*, an animated cartoon popular at Christmastime on British and Finnish television.[13] It tells of how a little boy who lives in a traditional home with two loving parents builds a snowman that comes to life and takes him to the North Pole, where he meets Father Christmas and witnesses a celebration of world harmony, in which snowmen and -women from around the world dance in their native garb. "Walking in the Air," sung by St. Paul's Cathedral choirboy Peter Auty, plays as the snowman and the boy fly over landmarks of the entire earth on their back-and-forth journey, and its ethereal melody has been recorded by such varied artists as Cliff Richard, Elaine Paige, and Kenny Loggins.

But *The Snowman* has a bittersweet ending because after returning safely to his parents' home, the boy wakes up to discover that the snowman has melted, leaving only the black hat and scarf that the boy had supplied. But then, the boy reaches into his pocket and discovers the blue scarf that Father Christmas gave him, a sign of the "real presence" of soul and spirit that a story can offer.[14] In *Ten* Kiarostami leaves us "laughing and crying at the same time." The music played by a piano may be bland and continuous—life goes on—but at the same time, it is played in a minor key, as if to say that our sadness can result in something as clear-eyed and beautiful as the film we have just seen.

NOTES

1. Abbas Kiarostami, "In Dialogue with Kiarostami," interview by Ali Akbar Mahdi, *Iranian*, August 25, 1998, https://asianart.fandom.com/wiki/Interviews_with_Abbas_Kiarostami.
2. Abbas Kiarostami, "Deep Focus: The Photography of Abbas Kiarostami," interview by H. G. Masters, *ArtAsiaPacific*, July 8, 2016, http://artasiapacific.com/Blog/DeepFocusThePhotographyOfAbbasKiarostami.
3. Quoted in Alberto Elena, *The Cinema of Abbas Kiarostami*, trans. Belinda Coombes (London: SAQI Iran Heritage Foundation, 2005), 92–93.
4. Kiarostami, "Deep Focus."
5. Quoted in Elena, *Cinema of Abbas Kiarostami*, 179.
6. See Geoff Andrew, *10* (London: British Film Institute, 2005), 43.
7. Andrew, *10*, 43–44.
8. Andrew, *10*, 43–44.
9. Abbas Kiarostami, "With Borrowed Eyes: An Interview with Abbas Kiarostami," interview by David Sterritt, *Film Comment*, July–August 2000, http://www.filmcomment.com/article/with-borrowed-eyes-an-interview-with-abbas-kiarostami/.
10. Quoted in Andrew, *10*, 62.
11. Quoted in Andrew, *10*, 59.
12. Quoted in Andrew, *10*, 69.
13. "Walking in the Air," Wikipedia, updated December 8, 2019, https://en.wikipedia.org/wiki/Walking_in_the_Air.
14. "The Snowman (David Bowie Intro)," directed by Dianne Jackson and Jimmy T. Murakami, 1982, British Channel 4, posted by Foxfire_11, November 30, 2011, https://www.youtube.com/watch?v=rXEoqb0_mrg.

Chapter Nine

Dream a Little

The hero of *Through the Olive Trees* is in love with a girl of a higher social class, and the class structure of the society oppressing him is as old as civilization itself. Kiarostami's comments on the film suggest the enormous weight of the clerically buttressed oppression Hossein escapes: "Now people tell me that I've made a love story, but at first this wasn't very clear to me. Hossein finds himself in a dead-end street, and his thoughts turn to God, who shows," it seems to Hossein, "his solidarity by destroying houses."[1] The end of the film, with some ambivalence, suggests that Hossein has prevailed against the odds and that, in some versions of the story, the idealistic hero might not have to wait for Paradise to receive his reward:

> At first I thought of having the couple walk slowly away into the distance until they could no longer be seen. I thought that there would always be an insuperable class barrier between them, and that there was therefore no reason why the girl would consent. Even less so given that her parents had said so before they died: In a country like mine the dead have a lot of power. . . . [Later,] I said to myself, though, that I could leave tradition to one side and dream a little in this sequence, wishing and hoping that she finally gives him a positive answer. If I only could intervene in a problem of social class. . . . Filmmaking gives me the opportunity to forget about reality sometimes, to break away from it and dream from time to time. And in my opinion the audience has the same feelings at that moment because they share the same desire to change reality.[2]

Through the Olive Trees is an extension on the literal level of *And Life Goes On*, but it is also an elaboration and partial reversal of the earlier film's message. After a massive earthquake in 1990 killed fifty thousand people in the area of northern Iran (that includes Koker, the setting of *Where Is the Friend's House?*), Kiarostami returned with his son and three friends to see if the boys who played Ahmad and Mohammad had survived. Though they could not find them, Kiarostami reported that they returned feeling "joyful and optimistic, and that was a mystery." They had gone there "with a feeling of anguish and come back with a feeling of hope." Because he continued to feel this mystery a year later, he decided to return to Koker to try to "discover the signs and sources of joy and life. And that's how the second film took shape."[3]

While *And Life Goes On* celebrates the general resilience of humanity, even when cherished individuals are lost, *Through the Olive Trees* implies that general survival is not enough. The third Koker film refocuses attention on a single character, who, like Ahmad in *Where Is the Friend's House?*, obediently follows rules until a sudden inspiration gives him the courage to follow his heart. Ostensibly, the film is the story of a film crew from Tehran who wants to extend the story of a young couple who married immediately after the earthquake because the relatives who may or may not have approved had all died. During the filming of *And Life Goes On*, Kiarostami discovered that Hossein Rezai, the young actor who plays the husband, had for a long time been unsuccessfully courting Tahereh Ladanian, the young woman who plays his wife. In the second postearthquake film, the real-life tension between them caused numerous problems on the set that constitute much of the film's thematic substance.

While the film crew's script calls for the lead actor to portray a decisive but insensitive male figure who takes resourceful action in an emergency to ensure the couple's survival, the "real" Hossein, who eloquently courts Tahereh between takes, is a visionary and a poet even though he is illiterate. His illiteracy is an issue; this and the fact that he does not own a house are the major reasons Tahereh's grandmother refuses his persistent proposals. But Hossein's illiteracy also motivates him to want to marry Tahereh because she is a student, and he feels that their complementary skills could shape a perfect union.

He extends this ideal of social harmony in off-screen conversations with the film's director, and devotion to this impractical vision links him to such illiterate "lovers" as Muhammad, Jesus, and most of the Hebrew prophets. Though Kiarostami stated that he was not a Muslim (see chapter 2) and though he clearly prefers Omar Khayyam's love for the present over "fine promises" of Paradise, he also admired the emphasis on social justice and spiritual inspiration that permeates early Judaism, Christianity, and Islam.

Kiarostami uses the real-life name of the actor who plays the film-within-a-film's production manager, Zarifeh Shiva, to make this point and to transform a version of François Truffaut's comic *Day for Night* into a serious comment on religion. Iranians and Indians are descended from an Indo-Iranian prototype that moved southward from the Eurasian steppes about four thousand years ago. One branch moved southward to the Indian subcontinent, while the other settled on the Iranian plateau. Their ancient religion remained largely intact as it evolved into Hinduism in India, while in Iran it was replaced by Zoroastrianism at the beginning of the tenth century BCE.[4]

Kiarostami uses the core Hindu belief in cosmic cycles of destruction and renewal measured against the insignificance of human individuals as an intellectual contrast to the emotional desire of his audience to unite two particular children. For Hindus, human fulfillment comes through abandoning the tiny personal ego and identifying with the vast cosmic all. This fundamental purpose of a socially enabled human life is not easily achieved. It is made difficult by the purposeful web of illusion spun by Maya-Shakti, the female consort or aspect of Shiva, who, as destroyer and deliverer, is one of the three great Hindu gods, along with Brahma, the Creator, and Vishnu, the preserver.

From the Hindu point of view, the fifty thousand lives lost in the Koker earthquake should be accepted as part of the continued destruction and renewal of the world effected by Shiva. Individuals should not presume to question their inconsequential fates in light of these grand cosmic cycles. Shiva is often depicted as half-man and half-woman, and his duality is portrayed in the film by the coldly directive Madame Shiva, the film's "production manager," who, like Maya Shakti, is responsible for supervising a deceptively compelling cinematic world. She is a semicomic version of the Hindu ideal described by Heinrich Zimmer: "[Maya] is the supreme power that generates and animates the display," causing us to be "enthralled by ourselves and the effects of our environment, regarding the bafflements of Maya as utterly real, . . . whereas, from a standpoint just beyond our ken the world, the life, the ego, to which we cling is as fugitive and evanescent as cloud and mist." Within our delusional concerns and surroundings,

> we people and color the indifferent, neutral screen with the movie-figures and dramas of the inward dream of our soul, and fall prey then to its dramatic events, delights, and calamities. . . . Thus we are the captives of our own Maya-Shakti and of the motion picture that it incessantly produces. Whenever we are entangled and enmeshed in vital, passionate issues, we are dealing with the projections of our own substance. That is the spell of Maya. . . . That is the spell of nescience, "not knowing better."[5]

For Zimmer, creation (Brahma), duration (Vishnu), and dissolution (Shiva) constitute the "one divine substance or energy of life." Identifying with this energy "constitutes the victory and solace of this religion [and] accepts the doom and forms of death as the dark-tones of a cosmic symphony, this tremendous music being the utterance, paradoxically, of the supreme quietude and silence of the Absolute." The gainer of such difficult enlightenment should therefore be able to "rejoice at the sight of even the most harrowing of its manifestations," including wars, earthquakes, and social injustice. Thus, the centuries-long persistence of the Indian caste system may be inextricably entangled with the Hindu acceptance of "serfdom and bondage to the life-supporting, life-rushing spell of Maya-Shakti," so that the highest aspiration is not to challenge an oppressive social system but to merge with the serene silence of the Absolute; "What it seeks is to change the serf of Maya into a lord of Maya, comparable to the Highest Being."[6]

At the same time, large numbers of people are condemned by the karma of imperfect past lives to live as virtual slaves. Caste is inherent in Hindu mythology, and each caste stems from a different part of Brahma's body: Brahmins (teachers, scholars, and ascetics) from his head; Kshatriyas (warriors and rulers) from his arms; Vaishyas (traders) from his thighs; and Shudras (laborers) from his feet. Over thousands of years, these rankings have been subdivided into about three thousand castes and twenty-five thousand subcastes, each based on a specific occupation. But outside the hierarchy entirely, there still remain the Dalits, or "untouchables," who carry out despised but necessary tasks, such as cleaning toilets and sewers.

Intermarriage between members of any caste was formerly prohibited and is still uncommon, while in rural communities, food and water sources are not shared. There is no way for people to work out of or marry above their caste because intermarriage continues to be shunned. Although caste-based discrimination was forbidden by India's constitution in 1950, it survives in general practice and is often exploited by politicians, who inflame caste issues to consolidate voting blocs.[7]

Islam in general and Shia Islam in particular are predicated on an ideal equality that anathematizes rigid class distinctions, although (as Kiarostami and Makhmalbaf emphasize) Islamic societies often fall far short of this ideal. Hindu class discrimination is based on the relative unimportance of personal merits. *Through the Olive Trees* conveys an aspect of this limitation by humorously using symbols of the male-female polarity prominent in Shiva worship. The androgynous Mrs. Shiva is part of the male God in the sense that Chinese yin and yang contain the potentialities of each other. But seen in this light, the sexual urge of individual human beings is only the anonymous expression of an impersonal drive that does not involve union with a loving God.

As a fertility god, Shiva is usually symbolized by the lingam, a graphically phallic object of worship. Correspondingly, the yoni, an image of the vulva, vagina, or uterus, is frequently represented as a spouted dish from which the lingam rises. Zimmer describes the combination of these symbols as a "representation of the creative union that procreates and sustains the life of the universe. Lingam and yoni, Shiva and his goddess, symbolize the antagonistic yet cooperating forces of the sexes."[8]

In *Through the Olive Trees*, lingam and yoni symbols are consistently associated with Hossein, who is repeatedly seen carrying a closed cylindrical canteen and an open blue bucket. Even before he appears but immediately after he is initially mentioned, Kiarostami, with pointed plot irrelevance, visually emphasizes a lingam. When Azim, the first actor playing Hossein in the film-within-a-film, is dismissed because he stutters when he tries to talk to girls, the director sends Mrs. Shiva to fetch Hossein, whom the director has to identify for her as the custodian at the crew's camp. Even after she turns to leave, the script emphasizes her name by having the director repeat it: "Madame Shiva, return with Hossein in the car, and make it quick. We have little time."

But then, instead of returning to the director or showing Mrs. Shiva at the wheel, the camera focuses on the side rear of the tan truck pulling away. When it clears the frame, we see a capped, bright-blue cylindrical object about a foot tall standing upright on a ledge in the V-shaped opening between a veined rock face slanting to the left and a thick tree trunk slanting to the right, with a white, flowering bush directly behind it. While the image holds for fifteen seconds, a small bull (another Shiva symbol) enters the frame from the right and slowly circles the lingam.

The lingam's color corresponds to the sky-blue jacket of cinematographer Hossein Jafarian and the blue shirts and jeans of most of the crew, which connotes a dynamic male energy in comparison to Azim, who wears a neutral tan shirt, and the director, a contemplative but spiritually undeveloped urbanite who also wears a tan shirt and who will learn a great deal from his young actor. Though blue is often the color of Shiva's face in traditional depictions, Hossein wears a white shirt and a green jacket, the other colors associated with the male fertility god. Tahereh, though, wears an old-fashioned burgundy dress, which is verbally highlighted when she unsuccessfully insists on wearing a modern one instead. As Hossein's potential Shakti, she resembles depictions of Maya, where red is the "active color of creation, the primordial energy, planning and producing the evolution of the universe."[9] Tahereh has so few lines that she comes close to being a purely symbolic character, especially in the last scene, while Hossein's verbal profusion marks him as a unique, imaginatively gifted individual.

Kiarostami used the artifice of his camera to conjure his spectators into loving the ineffable source of both nature and art. Though social identity may be evanescent, natural beauty is evident, and in general, the purpose of Kiarostami's art is to direct spectators back to that beauty rather than to advocate art for art's sake. But, as with Rumi, only a meticulously crafted art can achieve that end. In *Day for Night*, Truffaut famously had his self-representing director say that, for him, the experience of cinema was more important than that of life. For Rumi and Kiarostami, art is only valuable as it expresses love, and for both, the love of an individual, such as that of Rumi for Shams and Hossein for Tahereh, becomes the hidden treasure that Behzad and Badii fail to feel. Discovering this treasure depends on the mysterious feeling of joy that Kiarostami experienced upon returning to Koker, a feeling of God's munificence even in the face of human evil and natural destruction. And although professed love or prayer may fail to achieve their objects, it is the feeling and the expression that count, not the response.

For Rumi the gift of his talent was never more important than the use he made of it, and ultimately, his love for Shams transcended the personal when he discovered the source of that love through nature and in himself. In the view of Hamid Dabashi, "Rumi gave full expression to a mystical narrative that posited an all-loving God presiding over the worldly manifestation of his omnipresence. Man (degendered) in Rumi's narrative became a Man-God potentially endowed with the realization of all divine attributes. Rumi's journey became a passionate quest inward, toward the realization of God within."[10] While Hinduism supports state and religious authority, Sufism implicitly rejects it by encouraging unmediated union with God.

There is an additional motif in Islam generally that implies that God's original plan includes equality between members of a single religious culture as well as respect for other religious communities: "O people! Be mindful of God who created you from a single soul, and from it created its mate and from the two spread a multitude of men and women."[11] For Iranians the greatest upholders of the prophet's egalitarian ideal were his son-in-law Ali and his grandson Husayn. When Ali became the fourth caliph after Muhammad's death, succeeding Abu Bakr, Uthman, and Umar, a civil war disputing Ali's succession led to an eventual treaty between Ali's sons Hassan and Husayn and the Umayyad tribe, following Ali's assassination by a group of terrorist fanatics called the Kharijites. The terms of the treaty forbade the Umayyad ruler Muawiyah from naming an unelected successor, and when his son Yazid assumed the caliphate at his father's behest, Husayn rebelled. After his army's expected reinforcements treacherously sided with Yazid, Husayn was killed at the Battle of Karbala, which is commemorated by Ashura, Iran's major national holiday (see chapter 1).

The elevation of Husayn to this status (and the resonance of his name in Kiarostami's film) is based as much on his social idealism as his military bravery. The Umayyad dynasty had arisen from a powerful merchant family who initially resisted Islam, and for Shiites they represent the material wealth and class inequities that Husayn considered violations of everything his grandfather stood for. In the view of Ali Shariati (1933–1977), the "ideologue of the Iranian revolution," Husayn rebelled because the "corrupt caliphs" and the "court elites" had betrayed the spiritual ideal of the *umma* (Muslim community), which, as the Hebrew prophet Samuel told the Israelites, should have been united under God rather than a materialist dynasty.

Shariati, a hugely popular sociology professor opposed equally by the government and the clergy, inspired the youth of Kiarostami's generation to overthrow the shah. He believed that Marxism might be appropriate for other countries but, in Iran, Islam, especially Shia Islam, provides a deeper intellectual and emotional basis for lasting change. Islam's energizing motivation stems from the "prophet's intention," which, as paraphrased by Ervand Abrahamian, was "to establish not just a monotheistic religion but a *nezam-e tawhid* (unitary society) that would be bound together by public virtue, by the common struggle for 'justice,' 'equality,' 'human brotherhood,' and 'public ownership of the means of production,' and, most significant of all, by the burning desire to create in this world a 'classless society.'" For Shariati, the Moharram passion plays depicting Husayn's martyrdom at Karbala put forth a single message: "All Shiites, irrespective of time and place, had the sacred duty to oppose, resist and rebel against contemporary ills, [including] . . . multinational corporations and cultural imperialism, racism, class exploitation, class oppression, [and] class inequality."[12]

Shariati anticipated Makhmalbaf and Kiarostami by arguing that intellectuals and artists should take precedence over the clergy in leading the way back to authentic Islam. And he seems to have directly anticipated Kiarostami's ironic use of Hindu symbols in *Through the Olive Trees* by asserting that the roots of the national soul were not to be found in ancient Aryan (Indo-Iranian) mythology (which resembled Hinduism) but rather in the defiant idealism of the Shiite movement. Shariati also distinguished himself in a way that seems particularly relevant to Kiarostami by leavening righteousness with love. The Koranic Husayn loved the way of life his grandfather had established, and that love for a communal ideal was connected to the personal love he had known. Muhammad is reported to have said, "Husayn is of me and I am of him. Allah loves those who love Husayn. Husayn is a grandson among grandsons."[13]

By creatively combining Sufi love with Marxist materialism, Shariati motivated social change through personal transformation, much as Kiarostami does through Ahmad in *Where Is the Friend's House?* and Hossein in *Through the Olive Trees*: "It is love which beyond rationality and logic invites us to negate and rebel against ourselves in order to work . . . for the sake of others."[14] Unlike the Aryan mythology that "left the masses unmoved" and Hinduistically resigned to the status quo, the poetry and human empathy of the Persian poetic tradition could transform society by transforming individuals.

Shariati used the same Sufi metaphors that we observe in such Kiarostami's films as *And Life Goes On, Taste of Cherry, The Wind Will Carry Us, Roads of Kiarostami, Where Is the Friend's House?*, and *Ten*, including the path, the pilgrimage, and the journey. As Abrahamian writes, these symbols are essential to Islam: "Man is on an inward pilgrimage, returning . . . to God who is his original home and friend, and the *haj* to Mecca is its symbol."[15] Humanity itself, in Shariati's words, is "the way, the wayfarer, and wayfaring. Engaged in constant migration from his clay self to his divine self."[16]

Kiarostami's love for the physical world, like that of Rumi and Khayyam, does not align perfectly with Shariati's Gnostic split between body and soul, but his conception of God as the Friend rather than an impersonal destroyer and creator resembles the yearning unconsciously expressed by Ahmad toward Mohammad Reza and Hossein Rezai toward Tahereh Ladanian: "Only Him and you are together . . . you are privately with Allah. . . . Leave this mean world and ignore your limitations. . . . Let your heart be enlightened by love!"[17]

No god concept could be more antithetical to Shiva than the Sufi Friend, and Kiarostami, who said he was not a Muslim, is likely to have agreed with Shariati's benevolent view of God: "In Islam man is not subjugated by God, since he is the Lord's associate, friend, trustee and kinsman on earth."[18] When Ahmad in the storm resolves to help his friend by breaking the rules and Hossein decides to drop the conventional rhetoric of respect and speak his heart directly to Tahereh, Kiarostami celebrates the spiritual intuition Shariati praised: "A 'consciousness' born of 'knowledge' and pregnant with 'love' exists. . . . Intuition needs no light; it is illuminated by thought and able to solve any problems of 'love.'"[19]

Note, however, that intuition needs to be completed by the intellect, the mature reflection Kiarostami hoped his spectators would experience following repeated viewings of his films. Kiarostami, like much of the intelligentsia of his generation, infused his work with spiritually pregnant symbols likely to have stemmed in part from Shariati's opposition to literalist readings of the Koran. For Shariati "symbolic literature is the highest form of literature," and the Koran has "multiple levels of meaning containing all truth for all time."[20]

As a complement to the independence and courage associated with the name Hossein, Kiarostami gives the object of Hossein's affection an equally admirable though decidedly more controversial name. Tahirih (1814–1852; Tahereh is a variant spelling) anticipated Forough Farrokhzad by more than one hundred years as a groundbreaking poet and feminist. She was an adherent of the Babi religion, a forerunner of Baha'i, which then as now stirred persecutory anger in the Shia clergy. Their intolerance may have been based in the faith's putting other prophets on the same level as Muhammad, a point Mohsen Makhmalbaf makes in *The Gardener* (2012), for which he "illegally" traveled to the Baha'i garden in Haifa to shoot.

Tahereh's name connotes one of the few specific qualities Kiarostami chooses to give the object of Hossein's devotion—the decisive independence she shows at the end. In addition to her spiritually infused poetry, the historic Tahirih is remembered for dramatically unveiling herself at a Baha'i religious conference that precipitated her death at the hands of the Persian authorities.[21] She was the uncompromising voice of a scorned religion and a victim of the instated misogyny that Panahi portrays in *The Circle* (2000) and that Kiarostami portrays in *Ten*.

The opening scene of *Through the Olive Trees* underscores the name by highlighting two girls named Tahereh. The scene is set up as being outside the film proper, which in turn contains part of the film-within-a-film that the Tehran crew has come to the earthquake-ravaged area to shoot. The outer frame of the three frames, and therefore the one closest to the audience, begins with the character meant to reflect many of Kiarostami's target viewers. With a group of anonymous girls behind him, whose black chadors match the trunks of the straight row of young olive trees behind them, the director (Mohammad Ali Keshavarz) introduces himself as the professional "actor who plays the director" of the film in which he is now casting the female lead.

Introducing himself as an actor rather than the actual director initiates the theme extended in later films that individual people are variations on eternally recurring human types. In a 2016 interview, Kiarostami elaborated the previously quoted reminder from the Koran that all human beings derive from a single soul when he commented on artistic originality as being analogous to individual human difference:

> The issue of the relation between the original and the copy is not at stake in *Certified Copy*. . . . The idea current in our lives is that we seek the illusion of originality, [but] the actual original is necessarily out of our reach. We should leave the question of originality elsewhere and stick to what we have in our own lives, to what we might consider as fate, [and] we should just be happy with what we have.

And to the question of why he shows the process of filmmaking in his films (a process shown in the epilogue of *Taste of Cherry* and most directly in *Through the Olive Trees*), Kiarostami only said that he doesn't know why he characteristically meets the "challenge of filmmaking through experimentation."[22]

In light of what happens to major characters in the films, the statement amounts to a recommendation on how to live one's life. In the previously quoted analogy to the director as a polo player striking a ball that then goes in an unforeseen direction, Kiarostami expressed a credo that is more than aesthetic. The metaphysical implications are apparent when he explained why *Close-Up* was his favorite film: "If the definition of cinema is a place where the director is God, here you have an example of a powerless God, of the division of the responsibility and the power of the film among the people there, and it is this division of power that makes the film truly powerful, so if there is one film in my filmography that will remain it is *Close-Up*" because the actor-characters insisted on "defending themselves and their position [so that] the director's only job [was] to capture the situation and hold the film together. At the end what had started as a lie turned to truth."²³

For Kiarostami the most important human variation is the greater ability in some (rather than all) people to learn and grow. The gentle, rumpled, middle-aged actor who opens *Through the Olive Trees* explains that he is standing near a "rebuilt school" where he has arrived to single out a girl to play a key role from the identically appearing group and then, after all the girls applaud, he apologizes for being late. The singling out of an individual and the motif of being tied to a time scheme link him to Ahmad of *Where Is the Friend's House?* at the same time that it foreshadows such older sophisticates as Behzad literally running to serve Mrs. Godarzi and James in *Certified Copy*, who is so obsessed with making a train that will carry him to more applause-garnering lectures that he cannot appreciate the love that a woman and a place are offering him at the moment.

In light of the vast cosmic cycles that *Through the Olive Trees* emphasizes in the next scene, the lateness motif illuminates how slow people are to adopt the philosophy of the doctor in *The Wind Will Carry Us.* People who on the surface ought to be more spiritually advanced are as innocent as Ahmad until they learn to love and receive what they are given rather than attempting to micromanage existence on their own. As subsequent scenes during the fictive filming show, the director is needlessly obsessed with accuracy. Almost immediately, he corrects himself in establishing the location as 400 kilometers—no, 350 kilometers—north of Tehran. The point of the detail is to reveal the mind-set of a person officially considered an artist but who lacks the faith in spontaneous inspiration that Kiarostami considers the primary spiritual and creative trait.

He approaches this realization late in his life, although he is otherwise highly developed socially, culturally, and intellectually. He does seem to have caught on by the end of the film because he has learned much from Hossein, an intellectually simple person, just as Kiarostami hoped his viewers would learn from eight-year-old Ahmad in *Where Is the Friend's House?* and as a "rider" learned from a child who picked a chick from a "nest of light" in Sohrab Sepehri's "Address" (see chapters 2 and 6). In subsequent films the potential enlightenment of Behzad, and even more so of James, is far more problematic.

Even at the beginning, the "director" has a sense of the qualities he wants in the girl he chooses, qualities he is still discovering in himself. The theme of differentiation is visually highlighted by the initial appearance of the large, identically clad group and the twin-rowed stand of olive trees behind them. The girls and the trees are equally anonymous. Mrs. Shiva's colors match the trees, an olive-green dress and a black hijab, and her concern matches the resonance of her name. She is in a hurry to facilitate the process, telling the director that the girls are hungry and have exams and that the crew still has a long way to travel. In later scenes she regards the actors as interchangeable. Her get-this-show-on-the-road presence as "production manager" reflects cinematic and general life values that Kiarostami consistently opposed. In Ahmad he portrays the persistent resistance to convention that makes inspiration possible. In this film, both Hossein and Tahereh possess that same quality.

To have the fictional director present himself as the actor playing the director implies that Kiarostami himself relied more on intuitive promptings than on preconceived choice and that any person viewed by others as an artistic authority is (if he has genuine talent) only a medium for a higher authority. As at the end of *Ten on Ten*, where Kiarostami replaces himself with a shot of cooperating ants, the film-within-a-film's director is only playing a part that the cosmic powers that be have cast him to play. Kiarostami or the creative source within him wants the young female lead to have a bold but not overly defiant spirit. Unlike the first two girls who give their names, Tahereh Ladanian looks straight at the camera as she clearly speaks her name and then repeats it for Mrs. Shiva, adding that she lives beside the Lakeh bazaar and has no precise address, suggesting that her home had been destroyed in the earthquake, though that is not the case with her character in the film.

The second girl to interact with the director is also named Tahereh, and though she is bold and confident, her values are not consistent with the kind of rebellion Kiarostami wanted to project. She teases the director by saying that they won't be able to see whoever is chosen for the film because his films aren't popular enough to be shown on television. The director, looking for support, asks the group if they should film anyway, and they all good humoredly chant, "Film it! Film it!" But not to be so easily subdued, the second Tahereh retorts, "Yes, but you must show it!"

Both Taherehs promise the independence the role requires, but the second Tahereh is more like the typical adolescent, whose rebellion is limited to the changing fashions of her time and place. The poet Tahirih had this rebellious courage but applied it in a more intelligent way. Tahereh Ladanian becomes especially important in compelling audience attention because through most of the film, she is shown with her face concealed, looking down at a book as she and we listen to Hossein's heartfelt pleas between takes of the film-within-a-film. If, as Kiarostami assumed, Hossein is winning us over, the dramatic tension lies in whether he will win her over. Her unresponsive silence required by social norms becomes a mirror of a sympathetic spectator's inability to interfere.

As the focal point of Hossein's gaze and our own, Tahereh is meant to compel the same feeling in us that Kiarostami said he himself felt in regarding the characters and the situation: "If I only could intervene in a problem of social class, [I would give Hossein what he wanted,] and in [my] opinion the audience has the same feelings . . . because they share the same desire to change reality."²⁴ And so it turns out to be the first Tahereh who is chosen because her affect is right and because her unexpressed opinion is not tied to a popular conception of what a film or a life should be. But we do not discover this until her first appearance a little later, where she expresses a mild form of teenage rebellion in a voice that closely resembles that of Ahmad in *Where Is the Friend's House?*

The opening credits that follow the casting scene roll over the upbeat horn music of a wedding march accompanied by a barking dog, signaling a comedy but one that has serious overtones. The credits conclude with the words, "Written, produced and carried out" (rather than directed) by Abbas Kiarostami. Then we see Mrs. Shiva driving her tan truck past a solid wall into the misty, green countryside. In accordance with the control associated with her name, she is frequently seen driving with a male passenger. Ahead of her, the windshield shows a herd of sheep and then a man herding two young bulls, the animal conventionally associated with Shiva and later specifically with Hossein. But counterpointing this journey into the greenery of the past, present, and future, a voice on the truck radio refers to individuals who significantly rebelled against the caste systems in which they lived.

The announcer identifies the day's date on two Muslim calendars, the solar hegira used in Iran and Afghanistan and the lunar hegira used elsewhere and "again, as the thirtieth of May, 1993." Islam is considered to have begun in 622 CE with the hegira, when Muhammad journeyed from Mecca to Medina to escape persecution from polytheist authorities, and Christianity began with the birth of Jesus, whose threatened birth and ultimate death came at the hands of imperial authority. Similarly, the deaths of the historical Husayn and Tahirih were also perpetrated by political entities expediently upholding entrenched values.

Such values cannot be sustained by leaders alone but must be perpetuated by unquestioning citizens who stay safe by following rules. The first passenger Mrs. Shiva stops to pick up turns out to be the same man who plays the teacher in *Where Is the Friend's House?* and who in "real life" is an actual teacher, lending a comic note to Mrs. Shiva's compliment, "You were very good in that role." True to his prior part, he begins by apologizing for the chalk she requested by attributing its imperfection to the students he instructed to make it, and though he knows how to make an implement of writing, he does not know how to use language beyond a practically immediate need. When he says she will find better chalk at the school when she gets there, she replies that she is not going to the school but needs it for the clapboard.

The teacher has never heard of a clapboard despite being in the previous film and explains that he does not care for cinema or art in general but needs extra money because of the earthquake and asks for a small role in the film.

Mrs. Shiva immediately agrees to his modest request, and the scene is meant to show the difference between great visionaries, like Jesus and Muhammad, and even small ones, like the film's Hossein versus the mass of people who are content with life and nothing more. As in the previous film, the teacher can only train children within the narrow scope of social rules, and when Mrs. Shiva lets him off, he runs (a sign as in *Wind* of living one's life to please authority) to catch the shoe factory minibus, which will take him most of the way to school.

The connection between *Friend's House* and *Olive Trees* continues to be explicit when Mrs. Shiva stops to talk to the two boys who play Ahmad and Mohammad in the first film. They are seen running in the side-view mirror (referencing the past) to the point where she has stopped. Even though they appear to be only slightly older versions of the boys we remember, their "roles" in this new incarnation have changed. The boy who played Mohammad Reza in *Friend's House* now identifies himself by his real name. Ahmad Ahmadpur, the name of the earlier film's young hero, now appears as his real-life brother, Babak Ahmadpur. Though they still have the same souls, their roles and significance in this regeneration of reality have changed.

This time they have a harder, more manlike affect, having gone through puberty and assumed a somewhat macho manner. And this time they function primarily as an audience rather than as actors when they appear later at the filming, which Mrs. Shiva (ever assigning roles) invites them to attend. Both boys carry potted plants that Mrs. Shiva has requested to decorate the set, and potted plants (as in *Friend's House*) become a significant symbol of children in general who are lovingly nurtured but expected to be essentially set decoration by the parental powers of the societies where they live.

That is why Kiarostami makes Hossein a version of the great heroes of religious and artistic history, both despite and because of the fact that he is poor and illiterate. It is he rather than the director (an image of refined culture) who personifies qualities that by the end of the film can transform sophistication to wisdom, technique to inspiration, and cynicism to love. And he may also have the power to free young people from the social compulsions that are about to entrap Tahereh when Mrs. Shiva arrives at her home.

In the opening scene, the girls are no more distinguishable from each other than the stand of olive trees behind them. But the film gives us an opportunity to look *through* generic humanity, as if locating a particular tree (which occupies the TV crew at the beginning of *Wind*), to see that, contrary to Mrs. Shiva's Hindu attitude, individual human beings do matter. Based on his work at Kanun, the Center for the Intellectual Development of Children and Young Adults, Kiarostami developed an admiration for exceptional children who resisted authority (see chapters 1 and 2).

Tahereh's parents have died in the earthquake, and she and her grandmother now occupy their home, which she now owns. Mrs. Shiva is miffed that Tahereh is not there when she arrives. Always in a hurry to facilitate the general production and uninterested in individual people, she refuses to sit with the grandmother, who complains that Tahereh is recalcitrant and asks that Mrs. Shiva pour her some water because her legs hurt and she cannot come downstairs to get it. The grandmother's immobility is an important detail because it echoes that of the rigid grandfather in *Friend's House* and therefore associates Tahereh with Ahmad; also, "not coming down" foreshadows her refusal to listen to a proposal of marriage from someone unworthily poor and irredeemably below her.

The scene also subliminally affects the spectators' later hope that Hossein will succeed because if, as the grandmother laments, Tahereh won't listen to her, then she may listen to Hossein. As they speak in front of a potted red rose, another symbol of the immobility her granddaughter refuses to accept, the girl arrives with a friend who has lent her a modern dress that she wants to wear in the film. The friend runs off, echoing the shyer children in *Homework*, while Tahereh defies the formidable Mrs. Shiva, who insists that she wear an old-fashioned country dress, because the modern dress "suits her," and she won't wear another.

Tahereh goes upstairs to change into the dress to prove her point, and Mrs. Shiva's patience is at its limits. Roosters crow loudly, and chickens cluck, sounds that continually recur during the similar scene of the film-within-a-film, where the voices of Hossein and Tahereh are heard from behind a closed balcony while they remain invisible to the crew. As in *And Life Goes On*, these natural yin-yang sounds connote a process of renewal that elevates nature over art. Even so, Mrs. Shiva wins this battle: she tells Tahereh that she can't be in the film if she doesn't follow the rules. Before they leave together, Mrs. Shiva selects a flowering plant to borrow from the grandmother, just as she is borrowing Tahereh, whom she expects to be equally docile. The extended bickering over the dress also foreshadows the scripted Hossein's male-empowered bickering with Tahereh while she is upstairs during the film-within-a-film: Tahereh cannot argue back as she does with Mrs. Shiva, a privilege that natural rather than social reality allows her.

In the "real" scenes between Hossein and Tahereh during breaks on the set, she sits still listening silently as she ostensibly reads her schoolbook, while Hossein speaks insistently of love and social justice in a manner that Kiarostami apparently hopes will "destroy the mind" of his viewers "in order to reject the old values and make them susceptible to new values."[25] When human beings presume to do this, they are, from the Hindu point of view, usurping the prerogative of Shiva, while in the Shiite culture of Iran (culturally but not actually), they are following in the footsteps of Muhammad and the historical Husayn. After the hero's male persistence is comically foreshadowed by the prominent lingam symbol following Azim's dismissal, we see Hossein for the first time in Mrs. Shiva's truck wearing his green (fertility) jacket and a facial expression that habitually suggests repressed resentment.

When Mrs. Shiva asks him to recite his few opening lines, he says, "But I know them," and then angrily complies. But there are other important things in this initial journey for him to learn. When the road is blocked by a construction crew doing earthquake repair, Mrs. Shiva and the foreman argue about dispatching men to clear the road. She insists she is in a hurry, and the foreman says he and his men have traveled a long distance to make money to feed their families and can't immediately stop just for her. When the foreman says she should send Hossein to help the crew, she replies, "That's your job, not his." So Hossein is learning something about social head-butting by watching two self-important people argue. Both represent assumptions of authority based on rank, and both consider themselves more important than the people below them.

But he also learns something about decisiveness and circumventing rules when Mrs. Shiva suddenly backs up and drives through the dirt and around the roadblock. Hossein thanks her for not sending him to clear the road, which he explains he could not do because he has decided to stop working in construction, a first indication that he aspires to more in life than just feeding a family. When she stops to ask directions from a group of workers sitting by the road, one of them calls, "Hey Hossein! Aren't you important?" He is mocked again for presumption by Mrs. Shiva after he asks her why she asked someone else for directions when he is from the area: "I thought since you wouldn't tell me your lines, you wouldn't give directions either," she says condescendingly, as if to remind him to be promptly obedient in response to whatever he is asked to say or do. In relation to the "production manager," Hossein is expected to submit to whatever life or the god Shiva in the Hindu system grants him. Unlike Mrs. Shiva, the film's director in off-set conversations is sympathetic to Hossein and interested in the details of his life, more like the Sufi Friend in relation to a single mortal than a Shakti spinner of group enthrallment.

In his scenes alone with Hossein, however, the director assumes at some points a superior worldly knowledge as if he were God-like in comparison to Hossein's humble innocence, but he, too, is only a work in progress. After Mrs. Shiva leaves the set to retrieve Hossein, the director has a scene with the children in attendance, which places him halfway between the role of the rule-bound teacher of *Friend's House* and the potentially transformed observer of the drama in which he plays an unplanned part. He begins the scene by playfully putting himself on the level of the children while not realizing that he, too, has much still to learn.

Just as he circulated through the group of high school girls in the opening scene, he begins by asking the boys if they will permit him to cross the rope barrier between them. Enjoying the pretense of play with an empowered adult, some shout "yes," and some shout "no." Then, seated among them on a stool, he plays the role of a traditional teacher, asking them the name of their Gilan Province capital (Rasht) and what product the district is known for (olives).

But after the children enthusiastically display their knowledge in the non-classroom setting of a game, the director asks a more pointed question: "What is cooperation?" There is a pause before one child tentatively replies, "To work with others," and another adds, "To be kind to others." These answers foreshadow the constant complaints Hossein directs toward Tahereh in the film-within-a-film, as well as the bickering among the adult crew, who should know better, versus the ideal of social harmony intuitively propounded by Hossein between takes when he begs Tahereh to join him in an ideal society of two. This, however, seems quite unlikely after Hossein arrives at the set, and though as promised he recites his lines perfectly, Tahereh refuses to reply. Her silence forces the end of the day's shoot and frustrates the director at the same time as it piques his curiosity. Driving the truck back to the camp alone with Hossein, he says, "We had to stop because of you. What has happened between you and that girl?"

Hossein explains that, contrary to his country upbringing and the class distinction between them, he simply fell in love while engaged in his usual backbreaking labor as a bricklayer's helper. The feeling of love was sudden and immediate, and there had been no prior social contact of any kind between him and the girl or her family. Without counseling or an intermediary, Hossein's revelation of love is not unlike the unsought vision of a prophet: "It was in Eynollah's house, God bless him, where I worked. This girl lived in the house just opposite. She was sitting on the stairs studying. She was there in front of me and appeared so gentle to my eyes, a girl so nice that I could see myself getting married. The idea of marrying her occurred to me."

But romantic desire in the mundane world is not so simply gratified, and when Hossein asks Tahereh's mother for her hand at the end of the workday, not only does she refuse, but she also gets him fired from his job. When Tahereh's parents are killed in the earthquake, Hossein tells the director that he thought God punished them for rejecting him: "I told myself that it was my heart's moan that had destroyed their homes." Underlying these lines is the kind of frustrated rage that fuels religiously justified wars and revolutions or acts of personal destruction.

When Hossein asks Tahereh's relatives how they can reject him for not owning a home when so many homes were destroyed by the earthquake, their answer—"Can't you see that everything is being rebuilt?"—and therefore that nothing has changed still "burns in [his] heart." The failure of people in general to change or learn from wars or natural disasters, as well as the failure of violent revolutions to create lasting change, is reflected in the director seeming to be so moved by Hossein's frustration that he asks him not to continue, as if he and we have too often witnessed the unjust return of the repressed.

Then we see a poetic version of irredeemable injustice in a flashback to Hossein importuning the grandmother at the cemetery, where a large number of quake victims are being mourned by their families, most of whom, like the survivors of a war, have learned little from their loss. Here, once again, the message is symbolically expressed in what we see through the olive trees and beneath the pastoral surface of a community supposedly far from the corruption of Tehran but permeated with the worst and most regressive qualities in human nature.

The scene begins in bright sunlight on a close-up of a light-blue flag fully extended by a bracing breeze, accompanied by the sound of funereal prayer. Then, the camera moves into deep shade, where we see only black tree trunks below their invisible green canopies. Hossein, however, wears his green jacket, as he seems to represent the claims of earth against the presumptive claims of ordained authority represented by the grandmother, who walks with a cane ahead of him wearing a sky-blue dress. Her color matches the sky-blue flag and asserts far-from-dead claims to transcendent authority.

Arguing with her is like beating his head against one of the brick walls social necessity forced him to build, and their dialogue pits an instinct to grow and change against the death grip of the past, the same conflict that Kiarostami sets up between Ahmad and his grandfather in *Friend's House*:

> "Give me at least two reasons [for refusing my request]."—"You are illiterate and you have no home."—"But what matters is intelligence, kindness, understanding."—"You may be nice and understanding, but you need to have a home."—"She chose me, and you prevent us from living together."—"The answer is no. You are illiterate and you have no home. You have a hollow head. Stop thinking about her. If not, I will make your life hell."—"If her parents were still alive, at least I would have some hope, but with you, nothing."—"If they were alive, they would not give her to you. Not even them!"

And as crows begin to caw, he calls after her as she turns up a wooded, fairy-tale-like path: "Are you sure that your granddaughter also feels this way?"—"The answer is no!"

Then, as we watch Hossein walking dejectedly back the way he had come, we hear a voice telling him to walk faster, and we realize that we have been watching a scene from the outermost film that the actor-playing-the-director had come to cast in *Through the Olive Trees*'s first scene. A cut to the camera crew shows Hossein sadly taking a seat on the ground, while a baby cries loudly for a full minute, as if to vocalize both what Hossein feels now and to potentially promise what he may happily hear at some time after the film ends, and the viewers can imagine what eventually transpires between its young leads. The seeming trickery of this scene plays into the world-as-stage motif, the idea that every culture and every individual is subject to the maya of their particular time and place, but at the same time, a select few will strive to change that reality because their innate individual imaginations demand it.

After we return to Hossein and the director in the truck, Mrs. Shiva, going the opposite way in the other truck, pulls up with Tahereh in the passenger seat. With both vehicles stopped, Mrs. Shiva walks around to the driver-side window of the director's truck to whisper that they "must get rid of one or the other" because Tahereh will not speak to Hossein and to request permission to bring in the girl who was their second choice. As they speak, Hossein's eyes are glued to Tahereh, who turns for a moment and gives him a brief, ambiguous look, conveying the sense, regardless of what she literally means, that they are both trapped in the passenger seat, ceding control over their lives to the drivers of whatever group they are forced to serve.

The director, having heard Hossein's backstory (as has the audience), cannot so easily dismiss individual emotions and refuses without giving a reason: "No, Tahereh is more suited to the role." This is the first direct

Figure 9.1. Hossein looks crushed after the grandmother rejects his plea to marry Tahereh, but the angled clapboard over one shoulder balanced by the tree trunk over the other suggests that nature may have an even chance against ingrained illusions of social rank. Miramax Films/Photofest.

disagreement between Mrs. Shiva as the enforcer of collective order and the director, who unconsciously emulates the care of a personal God whose sympathy does not translate to control. He becomes a proxy for the "powerless God" Kiarostami imagined himself to be and perhaps for an empathetic Creator who cannot fix the fate of the souls he especially loves. In several sequent scenes, the film makes a clear distinction between people who accept that fate and those who don't. Those who don't accept it possess a greater proportion of the youthful drive to perpetuate and renew the world, regardless of their chronological age.

The scene at the camp to which the director and Hossein then return expresses a dimension of tradition that is more complex and benevolent than the grandmother's hidebound snobbery. The elderly camp cook is a culinary artist, somewhat reminiscent of the old door maker in *Friend*. But though he retains his skill at creating beautiful specimens of traditional cuisine, for which he is complimented by the director, he does not act as a guide for Hossein, with whom he shares a tent, only complaining to the director that he had to sleep outside because Hossein kept him up reciting lines about socks. Although his wife of fifty years died in the earthquake and his children, who now live elsewhere, do not visit him, he says he has no desire to remarry when the director wonders if he would not like a companion in his declining years.

As he sits with the director, the camera includes various cooking implements, including a tall, orange container probably used for fuel. It is a variation on the lingam, and its color is autumnal, as opposed to the colors associated with Hossein, who is then shown watering various flowering plants to be used in the film. These opening details show how anxious Hossein is to keep his job because he wants to stay close to Tahereh and why he argues with Mrs. Shiva when she accuses him of not performing tasks due to oversleeping.

The campsite is on a hill overlooking a vista of olive trees, where early the next morning the director tells Farhad, the actor who plays the director in the film-within-a-film and who plays the actual director in *And Life Goes On*, that if he calls "Hello!" with sincerity in a loud voice, the dead will answer him. Farhad tries and only hears an echo, but then after the director leaves and he begins to walk away, he is startled by a loud bang like a gunshot. The reverse shot to the trees shows them swaying in a strong wind, as if to say that the souls of the dead are now comprehended in the single soul of nature. While the dead, who in local tradition haunt the valley, can only say "hello" and "good-bye," the valley itself has its own message of natural benevolence.

Always consistent with the advice of Khayyam to love the moment and that of Rumi, who finds God in the beauty of this world rather than the next, Kiarostami continually elevates an ongoing present. With the sound track suffused by the vitality of a strong wind, the camera slowly moves right over a stand of trees, most with dark-green leaves but some glinting silver, until it passes a lone pink tree in the middle of the frame. Then, through a sunlit opening, the God's-eye view reveals two women with small children far below on bright-green grass.

After Kiarostami spoke of Tahereh's parents rejecting Hossein before they died, he added, "In a country like mine, the dead have a lot of power."[26] He may have been referring to the ongoing empowerment of deadly social assumptions, while in the larger frame of the natural world, the dead, like the old cook, cede the future to descendants some of whom may change by adapting to changing conditions. Among the human beings of most societies, however, each present generation tends to seek partial immortality by believing that their own societies have reached perfection and that the values they have lived by should last forever. When, in the next scene, Hossein, riding in the back of the truck with the director, complains that the dead are nicer than Tahereh because at least they answer him when he calls out over the valley each morning, he does not realize that the dead have actually answered him through Tahereh's grandmother, while Tahereh herself has been promisingly silent.

The audience gets a new sense of how unusual Hossein is after the director has Mrs. Shiva, who is driving, stop to pick up a group of women and girls who are walking along the road. They are returning from the bazaar at the roadside, where many other victims of the earthquake have chosen to temporarily stay because they do not want to leave the comfort of the familiar surroundings where their families have lived for generations, even though they must travel a long way on foot to obtain the necessities of life. Although the director and Farhad marveled at the purity of the country air, this scene does not idealize the people who live there.

The director wants to know the name of the sixteen-year-old daughter of a woman who keeps her head scarf constantly over her mouth because, as we soon see, she has no front teeth. The girl herself is so shy she hides her face behind her mother's shoulder because, as Hossein explains, girls in this region are not permitted to speak to strangers. The director tells Mrs. Shiva to get their address, which the woman will not give him, and when Mrs. Shiva asks him why he wants it, he replies that he wants the daughter for a shot of women washing clothes in a stream. For the director, people like this are just anonymous types that he can use to paint a pretty picture. We have also seen that these people are so resistant to change that they will not speak to strangers and continue to reside in mostly ruined houses regardless of the hardship because they cannot adapt.

Initially, Hossein, too, is just a bucolic type to the director. He is just as low on the social scale as these women, but his sense of himself and the world has not been determined by his family, education, or economic position. When the director, trying to be helpful, asks Hossein why he does not court a girl like the one they have just seen because they are both of the same social class and would have more in common, Hossein replies that, yes, she is "handsome," but she is illiterate. Then, he voices a utopian vision that has the quality of revelation because he cannot read: The literate should marry the illiterate, the rich should marry the poor, and people with houses should marry those with none in order to help each other. If the rich only married the rich and the educated the educated, he continues, "nothing would work."

But, of course, that has been the way of the world for centuries, and that is why most societies are in fact dysfunctional. Because Tahereh already owns a house, he wonders why the grandmother would reject him for being houseless because you can't rest your head in one house and your feet in another. The director gently scoffs at his innocence by informing him of something he has never thought of: "Of course you can own two houses: one to live in and one to rent."

Hossein's social naïveté is counterpointed by the greenery the truck drives through that matches his green jacket and his indomitable will to perpetuate his best possible self rather than the caste entrapment to which he has been forever assigned. When Mrs. Shiva stops to pick up Tahereh, she emerges from the green door on her balcony wearing the country dress she has been ordered to wear, but her appearance does not foreshadow her decisive refusal to continue to be driven by Mrs. Shiva and hopefully by any domineering authority just before the film ends. The roles both characters are forced to assume in the film-within-a-film are seemingly emancipated, but as their real selves, Hossein and Tahereh are more cautious and thoughtful than the impulsive adolescents they are asked to stereotypically portray.

All the scenes, except the one in the cemetery, from the film-within-a-film take place in front of the two-story home, which the newly married couple have taken over. These scenes consist of multiply repeated takes of dialogue primarily between Farhad, the actor who plays the director in *And Life Goes On*, and Hossein, who plays an earlier version of himself that Kiarostami now portrays as misperceived in the earlier film. Here, the scenes are implicitly an extension and revision of the idea that simply being alive is enough in a society where, as Hossein had been told, everything including and especially the old class distinctions were being "rebuilt." Much of his plea to Tahereh between takes concerns the new house he will build for them as well as the relationship of equality and mutual respect they will enjoy. Immediately after the earthquake, the fictive couple slept under a plastic sheet and ate roasted tomatoes, the only food left from a relief truck by the time Hossein got there. They married immediately because no relatives had survived, and Farhad comments condescendingly that the plastic sheet was their nuptial bed and the tomatoes the wedding feast.

The scene we observe being shot takes place five days after the earthquake, but Hossein and Tahereh unrealistically act as if they have been married much longer. Visually we only see Farhad and Hossein at the bottom of the stairs, and aurally we hear Farhad question Hossein briefly about the earthquake's aftermath, while most of the dialogue is comprised of trivial complaints that Hossein directs toward Tahereh, who remains invisible upstairs. Not only has nothing changed among social classes after a tragedy from which people should have gained some wisdom, but also nothing has changed among ordinary men and women who should cherish each other respectfully because they are lucky to be alive.

The theoretically wise director of the "actual" film reflects mundane reality by absurdly insisting on irrelevant details, which necessitate four takes of Hossein heard asking Tahereh the whereabouts of his white socks; Tahereh answering, they must be in his shoes; Hossein replying that he's sure they're not, but he will check; Hossein going downstairs, finding the socks in his shoes, and calling to Tahereh that he found them; and Hossein answering Farhad about the number of relatives he lost in the quake. Everything goes as planned, except that Hossein keeps saying he lost twenty-five rather than sixty-five relatives. When the director calls, "Cut!" and corrects him, Hossein says, ignoring the distinction between reality and the fiction he is supposed to represent, "But sir, I only lost twenty-five!"

But the director is more concerned with precisely following his script than the profound tragedy of its subject because, like the social structure of the community, the process of his art is built on tried-and-true formulas rather than on common sense and the obvious fact that losing twenty-five relatives is bad enough. When Hossein finally says sixty-five on the fourth take, a crow caws loudly, just as one had in the cemetery, as if to suggest that the director's rigidity here is as bad as the grandmother's. In another scene after Hossein tells Farhad (echoing the earlier film) that the earthquake proves that it is the duty of people to repopulate the earth, Tahereh, watering the plants upstairs, spills water on Farhad, and Hossein berates her for being careless. Sticking to the script, which portrays the director as wise, Farhad tells him not to shout at her for something so trivial in the light of what has happened, a line that comically reflects the actual director's obsession with technique—"Cut! Hold your head up when you speak!"—and Mrs. Shiva's abusive sarcasm toward Hossein and later toward Tahereh.

The traditional attitude of male mastery that the script calls for Hossein to display and his fictive opportunism after the earthquake may help to inspire bold courage in the real Hossein near the end, but his own sensibility is imaginatively poetic. Between takes, while the crew fusses and argues about technical details of collective necessity, Hossein is instinctively concerned with the love-enabled growth that he and Tahereh will accomplish together. While the upper echelons of this minisociety are, in Hossein's words, "busy directing," he tells Tahereh a tale of how their life will be.

He would have "more tact" than to yell at her about socks as he must do in the sitcom lines the societal cliché requires, and he would not marry her to have her cook for him or do household chores. Instead of the societal imperatives of male dominance and breadwinning, he proposes building a house and a relationship where they will live and "laugh together" in comfortable affection and mutual respect: "Sometimes I will serve the tea, and sometimes you will," he says after being tasked with serving tea to the crew, even though, as a lover and dreamer, he is actually the lead actor in Kiarostami's world.

As birds continually sing and a rooster crows, Hossein describes the nest he will build. When Mrs. Shiva is heard issuing an order to get rid of the heavy bag of plaster Hossein has had to carry up the stairs through repeated takes, he tells Tahereh he will save the plaster and buy more to refurbish the abandoned home they are in, where a window opening on a view of the mountains will "cheer your heart." And the wealth of flowers that have been brought to decorate the set, he says, is a foreshadowing of those that will be at their wedding. In addition to the aesthetic details that he imagines without having derived them from books or conversations with educated people, Hossein has thought long and hard about practical survival.

He tells her exactly how much money they will need to live on and how he will earn it while she studies. He will do whatever is necessary to support them, even working again as a bricklayer, an occupation he had sworn never to resume. Ultimately, he says she will assume a profession in which she will "earn more than a doctor," a revolutionary condition of female independence, especially in their rural society where Hossein has never been exposed to feminist rhetoric of any kind.

And although he has never read a book and probably never seen a film, he has an intuitive sense of how to create a dramatic situation that neither Tahereh nor the audience want to end. We never see her face, so we do not know what she is thinking when Hossein takes a gamble by telling her to turn the page of her book if her answer is no. She picks up the page but does not turn it, as if she does not want to go beyond the experience of Hossein's dream, mirroring the audience, who, Kiarostami gambles, has also been charmed and is not anxious to turn the page to pursue a more compelling plot. The metaphor of dwelling on the page rather than being constantly jolted by narrative action is the essence of Kiarostami's "poetic cinema," as he describes it in *Ten on Ten* and various interviews (see chapter 3).

Hossein has intuitively beguiled Tahereh into wanting to hear more. If she turns the page, it would be the equivalent of a bored spectator leaving the theater, even though she could continue to perform the part she had been hired for. Staying suspended in a theoretically less important moment of her prescribed role, the break time that is theoretically less important than the work time is an essential Kiarostami theme, the seemingly less important inward feeling that makes life worth living.

And so, Hossein's improvised personal story is the more interesting one of an individual who transcends his surroundings than the one of collective resilience that inspires the scripted extension of *And Life Goes On*. After the director irritably calls "Cut!" five times because Tahereh calls out "Hossein" instead of "Mr. Hossein" as she drops a small package down to him while he is leaving for work, Hossein comes forward and explains that many young women in the area no longer use the honorific when addressing their husbands. The director gives in and calls an end to the shoot, but the detail suggests that perhaps everything may not be rebuilt the way it was, and if women unite to resist demeaning customs, then there may be a chance that Tahereh will similarly regard Hossein for who he really is rather than the unworthy peasant her grandmother insists he should admit he is.

But if he is not the expendable person society and Mrs. Shiva have consigned him to be, then the fluidity he displays also suggests the possibility of hopeful change in individuals, regardless of their environment. Hossein has the male persistence that favors mating throughout the natural world. That part of him is suggested by the constant birdsong and rooster crowing edited in the soundtrack in front of Tahereh's house when she first appears and in front of their fictional house (which Hossein wants to make their real house) during the shoot. As he moves around on the second floor and next to the stairway where he performs with Farhad, lingam and yoni symbols in pairs of tall and short glasses, cylindrical pitchers and round bowls, are frequently seen.

And when several minutes after serving tea to the entire crew after the shoot ends, one crew member asks for tea, he flat out refuses, saying, "I've already done that," to which the crew member, representing the childishly spoiled members of any pampered class, responds, "Yes, but Reza drank mine." Because the filming is over and he does not need the job any more to be close to Tahereh, Hossein can stand up for himself, and he is unresponsive when someone asks him to come down and move a heavy piece of equipment.

In contrast to Mrs. Shiva, who sarcastically comments, "He doesn't want to get his hands dirty," and a crew member, who cluelessly adds, "We are all equal," the director, whose sympathies have deepened from hearing Hossein's heartfelt sentiments in the truck and heeding his advice about old and new customs among the rural women, says, "Guys, Hossein is tired. Leave him in peace." Mrs. Shiva, true to her name, is indifferent to peace, focused as intently now on erasing the production as efficiently as she set out its scenes with the chalk she commandeered for the clapboard. Still angry at Tahereh for refusing to say "Mr. Hossein," she treats her principal player like an incompetent child, sharply ordering her to take her book and her plant: "You're not going to say your lines correctly. You're finished."

Her tone is as unfeeling and uncalled for as the earthquake that demolished thousands of "illusory" lives, and by then ordering Babak and Ahmad to take their plants, as well, she recalls the unbending rules Babak as Ahmad in *Friend's House* must circumvent. Now Hossein must find a way to circumvent the rules after the pretext for his being close to Tahereh has ended, and as he stows away the last props in the house, the sound of a helicopter bringing more recovery supplies is interrupted by the horn of Mrs. Shiva's truck, which sounds the exact note that began the wedding march under the opening credits when she first appeared.

On that hopeful note, the film's last section begins with Hossein holding a cylindrical silver canteen and a blue bucket and Babak and Ahmad holding their plants, sitting in the bed of the tan truck, while Tahereh sits in the passenger seat. As we hear the crew continuing to wrangle about how to transport equipment, Tahereh abruptly gets out; takes her tall, red-flowering plant from the truck; and starts to walk down a dirt path away from the camera. Hossein, looking very alarmed, alerts Mrs. Shiva, who calls out, "Wait, we're leaving soon. It's a long way to your house." But Tahereh responds with a familiar Kiarostami line: "I know a shortcut!"

In the life journey he repeatedly depicts, characters usually discover shortcuts when they can no longer continue on the long, difficult path they have been following. Ahmad cannot copy the homework in *Friend* until an internal storm symbolized by an outer one suddenly makes it the inevitably right move to make, and the Driver in *Ten* uses the term to persuade Amin that she knows a better route only after she has adapted to the changes in her life. On the other hand, the shortcut in *Taste of Cherry* that Badii wants to take proceeds from failures of perception, a point made when the old taxidermist tells him the long way to the museum is more beautiful, and Behzad may or may not realize the value of the prolonged journey that the doctor tries to teach him at the end of *The Wind Will Carry Us*.

In the second scene of *Olive Trees*, the teacher directs Mrs. Shiva to take a shortcut after he runs to catch the shoe factory minibus, which is ironic because for him there is neither a long journey nor a shortcut, only an unchanging routine of identical days, and for her, as for Behzad, every move is about finding a shortcut, with little appreciation of what is along the way. The director, now seeming to have learned the lesson of Rumi's polo ball, then gives Hossein the opportunity to write his own story rather than the social one his prior life has written or the cosmic one Mrs. Shiva's symbolic name represents: "Do you not see we are discussing the transportation? You are young. You can walk."

With this final granting of permission to direct himself, Hossein quickly sets off down the path, dutifully carrying the canteen and bucket, which symbolize the apparent necessity that still burdens him. After passing a stand of dark-trunked trees, he comes close enough to Tahereh to begin his last urgent appeal while remaining a respectful distance behind her. As she moves ahead at a brisk pace, her burgundy dress harmonizes with the breathtaking beauty of the scene, open mountain vistas overlooking pink and silver trees swaying in a sunlit breeze. This is the essence of Kiarostami's poetic art, putting the emphasis on the process of their journey rather than its outcome. Near the beginning of the scene, Tahereh ascends a zigzag path, the symbol of the life journey on which no shortcut appears until the traveler is ready to leave it. Like the reader of a poem, a spectator's experience of the feelings and sensations of the moment take precedence over expectantly following a plotline.

Speaking of life as a journey in relation to *Where Is the Friend's House?*, Kiarostami said that in his culture the journey was linked with mysticism and that "for us what is really important is not the goal we wish to attain but the path we must travel"[27] (see chapter 2). In *Olive*, as in *Friend*, the zigzag path represents "desire," which the seeker does not realize is fulfilled by persisting in the quest rather than achieving its goal. And while a single tree on the hill that Ahmad repeatedly passes on his journeys to and from Poshteh is, according to Kiarostami, a symbol of friendship, the groves of trees through

Figure 9.2. Carrying her book and a flowering plant as she advances through the olive trees, Tahereh blends culture and nature in Kiarostami's dream. Miramax Films/Photofest.

which Hossein and Tahereh pass seem to symbolize the ongoing love of the Sufi Friend.

While the camera presents images of abstract beauty, Hossein's appeal calls attention to the generative potential of language when he protests Tahereh's persistent silence near the end of his long monologue: "No one would suppose that you do not have language." His own language is resourcefully heartfelt, especially because he cannot read, and its substance is based on freedom from authority. While "lots of young couples live with their parents at first," he will work steadily so that "little by little we will have a house." And as with the situation he set up on the balcony, symbolizing dramatic tension by asking her to turn the page of her book, he gambles on a make-or-break response: "The filming is over. If you don't answer now, I won't ask again," which is a thematic way for the film to say that the seemingly fateful cycle of history can end and that now human societies can write a better story, more profoundly spiritual and dissident than any that political revolution has managed to achieve.

His plea combines social justice with love, just as Shariati's did, and it is refreshingly free of political platitudes. He tells her not to listen to her grandmother because the "old think only of rich men with houses and factories," whereas "intelligence and understanding" are what really count, and that she needs a "good husband, not some old nut." He tells her that he does not want to possess her for her beauty or anything else, wanting only for them to "have a place in life" where free from worry they will live together "elbow to elbow." And begging her to respond in kind, he reminds her. "God gave you a language to respond to someone like me."

And as he continues, he makes a case for language as a medium of personal and collective love: "Explain that look you gave me in the cemetery. That look dragged me and made me follow you all this time. I want your answer, not your grandmother's [because] I am not worse than anyone, [and] we are as good as anyone." Their union he promises will be his absolute priority beyond any supposedly higher loyalty that might divide them as personal beings devoted to each other: "There are girls more beautiful than you, better than you. I could marry anyone, but I will not do it. I want to marry you. You who has neither father nor mother. What do you think? You don't speak. At least let me carry your flowerpot. If I knew that it was yours, I would water it. I would not allow Muhammad to touch it."

This minor but revealing bit of blasphemy associates Hossein with the spiritual independence of Kiarostami himself, who said he was "not Muslim" but who was eulogized by filmmaker Asghar Farhadi as a "modern mystic"[28] (see chapter 2). Like Ahmad, Hossein takes inspiration directly from the Friend rather than another human guide and even, as his line suggests, from the most respected religious authority. When he resorts to authority in appealing to Tahereh, he does so only to reject the edict of her dead parents, who were not as wise as the director who told him to "work hard and be brave." The words are ironic because no human "director" ever encouraged Hossein to persist, and in fact, the film director told him he would have more in common with the girl they picked up in the truck because she, too, was illiterate: "The dead, they knew? He must know. He studied in the city. Tehran, the great city. He studied. He knows what he says."

Midway through Hossein's long plea, the director emerges through a stand of olive trees to watch. What then unfolds is what the spectators may feel by looking through rather than at the film's beautiful surface—the guiding presence of the Friend inexplicably choosing those he can help because they are situated at just the right time and place to unconsciously hear and speak for Him. Like the kind of film director Kiarostami professed himself to be, the Friend does not control or predict what the characters he has created will do. He gives them potentiality, but he does not direct their lives. He may send a message to a select few, some of whom may be great prophets while others may be innocents like Ahmad and Hossein who will be able to hear and convey His hopes for humanity at large.

While Hossein observes some verbal conventions of religion by saying, "God bless them," when referring to Eynollah, his former boss and Tahereh's parents, and though he says that he *felt* in the past tense that the earthquake was a response to his "heart's moan," his continually expressed deprivation makes it clear that he no longer believes that. He never prays, except perhaps to Tahereh, whom he believes to be the godlike grantor of all he desires, but she is not the source of his love, and at the point he feels he is about to lose her forever, he arrives at the shortcut his heart reveals.

Following a brief shot of the watching director, who mirrors the audience, the camera shows Hossein hurrying up a zigzag path to the crest of a steep hill, where he calls out hopelessly, "You have a heart of stone!" Then he puts down the canteen and the bucket, comic symbols of the sexual drive, and when their clinking stops, Hossein ceases to be burdened by biological and social necessity. After a brief shot of Tahereh emerging into the open and disappearing over the crest of a hill, the effortful sound of his implements is replaced by a powerful wind that comes up suddenly, just as it did before Ahmad abruptly realizes what he must do to save Mohammad.

Standing stymied for a moment with his hands clasped behind his head and depleted finally of the language he accused Tahereh of lacking, Hossein virtually leaps into silence by scrambling down the steep slope in a zigzag pattern to keep from falling, before he makes a beeline into a stand of feathery, pink trees, which Kiarostami's camera seems to love as much as Hossein loves Tahereh. Then, we see him far below, racing onto a green plain with the pink trees still prominent in the right foreground, their color evoking the burgundy radiance of Tahereh's dress.

At the end, both Hossein and Tahereh, specific human beings whose story has involved us in our own limited time and place, have been reduced to white dots moving inexorably away from our view, even as the distance between them closes. With the spectators placed far above and away from the dots, the stationary camera conveys a timeless stillness in relation to one human being who, obsessed by the diminishing time within his tiny scope, rushes to achieve a personal purpose to which nature in all its splendor seems indifferent. But as Kiarostami said, he wanted to "dream a little" in this sequence, and he believed that the audience felt the same because they have the "same desire to change reality."

The frame holds for an extraordinary three minutes, until at the point that the Hossein dot is about reach the Tahereh dot, and designed art interferes with the randomness of nature in the form of the sprightly fourth movement of the Concerto for Trumpet in C Major by Dominic Cimarosa (1749–1801), a contemporary of Mozart. In addition to the idea of interfering with nature through music from the Enlightenment or age of reason, Cimarosa is an appropriate choice because he died after a harsh imprisonment imposed for resisting the return of the Bourbon monarchy to his native Naples. But while he lived, the operas he was best known for are "remarkable for their apt characterizations and abundant comic life."[29]

The music builds, slows, and pauses just before Hossein reaches Tahereh. Then, an instant after the two dots merge, it launches into a joyously fast *Allegro Giusto*, as one of them flies back toward the camera, until the small but fully visible Hossein emerges onto the green plain from the silver-leaved trees far below. For a few moments, he continues to run toward us without slackening his pace. Then, just after he reenters the stand of pink trees, the color associated with Tahereh, the horn concerto is replaced by the same wedding march heard under the opening credits. With nature now fully supplanting art, its blaring joy begins at the moment the screen goes black and the closing credits start.

NOTES

1. Abbas Kiarostami, quoted in Alberto Elena, *The Cinema of Abbas Kiarostami*, trans. Belinda Coombes (London: SAQI Iran Heritage Foundation, 2005), 110–11.

2. Kiarostami, quoted in Elena, *Cinema of Abbas Kiarostami*, 112–13.

3. Abbas Kiarostami, "Abbas Kiarostami: In Conversation With . . . : TIFF Bell Lightbox 2016," interview by Piers Hanley, posted by TIFF originals, July 5, 2016, video, 1:58:26, https://www.youtube.com/watch?v=-1CCPg5UY-E.

4. See "Ancient Iranian Religion," Wikipedia, updated December 26, 2019, https://en.wikipedia.org/wiki/Ancient_Iranian_religion.

5. Heinrich Zimmer, *Myths and Symbols in Indian Art and Civilization*, ed. Joseph Campbell (Princeton, NJ: Princeton University Press, 1972), https://archive.org/stream/HeinrichRobertZimmerMythsAndSymbolsInIndianArtAndCivilization/Heinrich+Robert+Zimmer+Myths+and+Symbols+in+Indian+Art+and+Civilization_djvu.txt.

6. Zimmer, *Myths and Symbols*.

7. See Hari Bapuji and Snehanjali Chrispal, "How Twitter Got Blindsided by India's Still-Toxic Caste System," Conversation, December 4, 2018, http://theconversation.com/how-twitter-got-blindsided-by-indias-still-toxic-caste-system-107792; and Rajesh Sampath, "Racial and Caste Oppression Have Many Similarities," Conversation, June 19, 2015, https://theconversation.com/racial-and-caste-oppression-have-many-similarities-37710.

8. Zimmer, *Myths and Symbols*.

9. See Zimmer, *Myths and Symbols*; see also "Which Is Lord Shiva's Favourite Colour?" Quora, updated April 8, 2018, https://www.quora.com/Which-is-Lord-Shiva-s-favourite-colour.

10. Hamid Dabashi, *The World of Persian Literary Humanism* (Cambridge, MA: Harvard University Press, 2012), 122.

11. Koran 4:1.

12. Ervand Abrahamian, "Ali Shariati: Ideologue of the Iranian Revolution," *Middle East Research and Information Project* 102 (January–February 1982), http://www.merip.org/mer/mer102/ali-shariati-ideologue-iranian-revolution.

13. "Husayn Ibn Ali," Wikipedia, updated January 9, 2020, https://en.wikipedia.org/wiki/Husayn_ibn_Ali.

14. Ali Shariati, quoted in Mohammad Omar Farooq, "Humanity and the People Power: A Tribute to Dr. Ali Shariati," September 2000, https://web.archive.org/web/20060314034911/http://globalwebpost.com/farooqm/writings/islamic/ali_shariati.html; and "Ali Shariati: Islamic Fundamentalist, Marxist Ideologist, and Sufi Mystic," accessed January 15, 2020, https://web.archive.org/web/20141223143901/http://www.angelfire.com/az/rescon/ALSHAR.html. See also Morteza Hashemi, "Shariati, Ali," Global Social Theory, accessed January 15, 2020, https://globalsocialtheory.org/thinkers/shariati-ali/; Nathan Coombs, review of *Ali Shariati: Between Marx and the Infinite An Islamic Utopian* by Ali Rahnema (IB Tauris), Culture Wars, May 11, 2008, http://www.culturewars.org.uk/2008-05/rahnema.htm; Muhammad Sahimi, "Shariati on Religious Government," PBS Frontline, August 31, 2009, https://www.pbs.org/wgbh/pages/frontline/tehranbureau/2009/08/shariati-on-religious-government.html; "A Brief Biography of Dr. Ali Shariati," Dr. Ali Shariati, 2017, http://www.shariati.com/bio.html; and Editors of Encyclopædia Britannica, "Ali Shariati: Iranian Intellectual," *Encyclopædia Britannica*, updated January 1, 2020, https://www.britannica.com/biography/Ali-Shariati.

15. Koran 4:1

16. Koran 4:1

17. Abrahamian, "Ali Shariati."

18. Shariati, quoted in "Humanity and the People Power: A Tribute to Dr. Ali Shariati" and "Ali Shariati: Islamic Fundamentalist, Marxist Ideologist, and Sufi Mystic." See also Hashemi, "Shariati, Ali"; Coombs, review of *Ali Shariati: Between Marx and the Infinite An Islamic Utopian*; Sahimi, "Shariati on Religious Government"; "A Brief Biography of Dr. Ali Shariati," Dr. Ali Shariati; and Editors of Encyclopædia Britannica, "Ali Shariati: Iranian Intellectual."

19. Abrahamian, "Ali Shariati."

20. Shariati, quoted in "Ali Shariati: Islamic Fundamentalist."

21. "Tahirih," Wikipedia, updated December 18, 2019, https://en.wikipedia.org/wiki/T%C3%A1hirih.

22. Kiarostami, "Abbas Kiarostami: In Conversation With."

23. Kiarostami, "Abbas Kiarostami: In Conversation With."

24. Kiarostami, quoted by Elena, 112–13.

25. Quoted in Elena, *Cinema of Abbas Kiarostami*, 192.

26. Kiarostami, quoted in Elena, *Cinema of Abbas Kiarostami*, 112–13.

27. Kiarostami quoted by Alberto Elena, *The Cinema of Abbas Kiarostami*, trans. Belinda Coombes (London: SAQI Iran Heritage Foundation, 2005), 75.

28. "Not Muslim," Kiarostami quoted in Geoff Andrew, "Unspoken Truths," *Sight & Sound*, July 2013, 40–43; "a modern mystic," Farhadi quoted in Andrew Pulver and Saeed Kamali Dehgha, "Abbas Kiarostami, Palm d'Or-winning Iranian film-maker dies, aged 76,"

The Guardian, July 4, 2016, https://www.theguardian.com/film/2016/jul/04/abbas-kiarostami-palme-dor-winning-iranian-film-maker-dies.

29. Editors of Encyclopædia Britannica, "Domenico Cimarosa," *Encyclopædia Britannica*, January 7, 2019, https://www.britannica.com/biography/Domenico-Cimarosa. The entire fourth movement of the Trumpet Concerto in C Major, *Allegro Giusto*, from which a passage is taken for the film, may be heard at "Domenico Cimarosa: Concerto for Trumpet (4/4): Allegro Giusto," posted by Ayden434, September 27, 2011, video, 2:31, https://www.youtube.com/watch?v=sHGm9wb146M.

Chapter Ten

The Manly Game

In a 1995 interview given a year after the release of *Through the Olive Trees*, Kiarostami revealed his rather shocking plan for a sequel entitled *Tahereh's Dreams*, in which Hossein kills Tahereh after a second earthquake ten years later. As he once said of a profound personal change after his first visit to Koker—"the earthquake happened inside myself"—the earthquake inside Hossein was in all likelihood compensation for a failed ideal, like the violence that results from the driven dreams of revolution, terrorism, and war. As in *Taste of Cherry* and *The Wind Will Carry Us*, mental collapse would have been shown through a metaphor of its aftermath, the mounded dirt and rubble through which Hossein drags Tahereh's body before he pulls a wall down on top of it in the opening scene.

The role of the on-screen spectator used in *And Life Goes On* and even more prominently in *Through the Olive Trees* and *Shirin* was to be played by a child who, like the audience, envisions death as an erasure of identity—"all we can see is a pair of feet"—and the impotence that follows its violent perpetration: "Hossein turns toward the camera with a grimace of worry."[1] By associating the earthquake with the devastation arising from frustrated dreams, Kiarostami implies that acts of personal and collective murder are inevitable diseases that, like the rabidity of a mad dog or a hungry wolf (as Puya calls natural disasters), periodically beset the human soul.

Prior to this, Kiarostami alludes to physical and mental violence by showing the effect of war on the children in *Homework*, mentioning the internecine attack on soldiers deserting the Lavizan Air Force Base in *Close-Up*, and providing the dissecting instructions of the taxidermist in *Taste of Cherry*. He also portrays the mental murders of Behzad wishing Mrs. Malek dead and Behzad's potential self-murder when the line digger is almost buried alive in *The Wind Will Carry Us*, but he does not actually show physical violence until the opening scene of *Crimson Gold*, which he wrote for Jafar Panahi but did not direct.

In his last three films, however, Kiarostami returns to the tragic actions he would undoubtedly have probed in *Tahereh's Dreams*, where the director as a proxy for Kiarostami himself interviews the criminal in jail, just as in *Close-Up*, when he interviews Hossein Sabzian. *Shirin* includes wars, suicide, and a patricide, while *Certified Copy* concerns a man who, like Behzad, vents a verbal cruelty that he does not realize is simultaneously killing him. And in *Like Someone in Love*, which visually and verbally refers to several films by Alfred Hitchcock, a Japanese sociology professor is directly exposed to the kind of physical attack he abstractly considers in his book on the "causes of violence in society" (see chapter 12).

Taste of Cherry poetically professes the idea that all killing, personal or collective, is a form of suicide, and *Like Someone in Love* has a pointed reference to Emile Durkheim, the "father of sociology," whose *Suicide: A Study in Sociology* remains a seminal work on the subject. Durkheim distinguishes three types of suicide: egoistic, anomic, and altruistic. All three stem from humanity's need to be attached to something transcendent because the individual person is so limited spatially and temporally that, without something greater, "we cannot avoid the thought that our efforts will finally end in nothingness, since we ourselves disappear."[2]

Egoistic suicide increases when people no longer identify with the goals and values of their society, while anomic suicide is endemic to societies where traditional curbs on desiring wealth, fame, or pleasure have dissolved: "Without limits set on these desires, the passions are unregulated, and the individual's expectations do not correspond with reality. Consequently, the individual is perpetually unhappy." Both types of suicide result from a "weakness of social solidarity and an inability for society to adequately integrate its individuals."[3]

Durkheim's third category, altruistic suicide, is particularly relevant to Iran's culture of martyrdom. Social "disturbances," such as wars and revolutions, rouse collective sentiment and stimulate a partisan spirit of patriotism, "concentrating activity toward a single end [that] at least temporarily causes a stronger integration of society."[4] Individual soldiers or revolutionaries typically "reflect a courageous indifference to the loss of one's life (albeit to the loss of others' lives as well)."[5] For Ali Shariati, the inspirational "ideologue" of the 1979 revolution, martyrdom is a "true jihad that guarantees honor, faith, and the future of the powerless." It enables all Shiites to become active followers of the Koranic Ali and Husayn in a timeless fight for spiritual truth and social justice: "In the permanent battle of history, everywhere and everyplace, all fields are Karbala, all months are Moharram, all days are Ashura." For Shariati, battlefield death is superior to peaceful survival (life and nothing more), and martyrdom is an "invitation to all ages and generations that if you cannot kill, die."[6]

Dying for a partisan cause or a religious ideal was anathema to Kiarostami (see chapter 1). When asked in 2009 if he considered himself a specifically Iranian filmmaker, he replied that he felt no particular sense of patriotic pride:

> I am a citizen of the world. I never decided to be born here, so there is no honor to be living here. . . . I am not ashamed of being Iranian [but] it wasn't my decision to be Iranian. To stay after the Revolution was my choice, and I did, I was happier here, I had a better life. When I am outside the country, it feels good to be recognized as an Iranian director. I belong somewhere, that is the most important thing. This is the geographical credit, let's say. It's like giving an address, it's just that I come from that part of the world.[7]

This attitude coincides with Durkheim's hope for a universal humanism that would supplant sectarian conflict:

> The moment approaches when the only remaining bond among the members of a single human group will be that they are all men. . . . Since human personality is the only thing that appeals unanimously to all hearts [and] since its enhancement is the only aim that can be collectively pursued, it inevitably acquires exceptional value in the eyes of all. It thus rises far above all human aims, assuming a religious nature.[8]

Preceding the attainment of such an ideal, Durkheim describes an atmosphere in which fashionable philosophy and reformist zeal are opposite sides of the same coin: Socialist revolutionaries, "even if they do not despair of the future," share with pessimistic philosophers like Schopenhauer a "single sentiment of hatred and disgust for the existing order, a single craving to destroy or to escape from reality."[9] This observation anticipated the twenty-first-century concurrence of postmodern materialist pessimism in Europe and America with the epidemic of religiously inspired war in Asia, Africa, and the Middle East.

Kiarostami's films after *Ten* respond to this malaise as both an international and an Iranian problem. During the presidency of Mahmoud Ahmadinejad (2005–2013), dissidents were routinely tortured, while academics and artists were imprisoned, suppressed, or driven into exile. Ahmadinejad exploited Shiite culture at every turn, even using it to excuse economic hardship by associating it with the sacrifice of martyrdom. He attempted to divert domestic discontent into jihad against the usual suspects by convening a Holocaust denial conference in Tehran to delegitimize Israel, and he concluded his 2010 speech to the United Nations by apocalyptically imploring the "mighty Lord [to] hasten the emergence of Imam Mahdi."[10]

The terracidal ending of *Roads of Kiarostami* (see chapter 3) may have been a response to the inconsistency between Ahmadinejad's push to develop nuclear energy for peaceful purposes and his bellicose rhetoric. Certainly, Kiarostami must have felt, as Makhmalbaf openly said, that Ahmadinejad and Khamenei were killing the soul of the nation by silencing its artists.[11] He was uncharacteristically vocal in his support of filmmaker Jafar Panahi, for whom he had written the script of the socially provocative *Crimson Gold* and who was finally arrested in 2010 after years of challenging the government's repression of women and its hypocritical stance on social equality in his films as well as his open support for the aborted Green Revolution of 2009. Although Panahi was released from prison and put under house arrest in 2011, he is no longer able to legally make films in Iran. Even so, he secretly smuggled out three films that were shown at Cannes (*This Is Not a Film* [2011]) and the Berlin International Film Festival (*Closed Curtain* [2013] and *Taxi* [2015]).[12]

When Kiarostami was asked in 2010 if he was concerned that his support for Panahi might affect the planned shooting of his next film in Iran, a film he was never able to make, he replied that for years the government had refused to give him permits to make films and that, when he did so anyway, they prevented their Iranian release.[13] As it turned out, *Shirin* was his last domestically produced feature, and though the story it tells is universal, its cultural basis is Iranian, and even in the subsequent films he made in Italy and Japan, Kiarostami's transmission of Persian Sufi traditions is evident. As he said in a previously quoted passage (see chapter 2), "When you take a tree that is rooted in the ground, and transfer it from one place to another, the tree will no longer bear fruit. And if it does, the fruit will not be as good as it was in its original place. This is a rule of nature. I think if I had left my country, I would be the same as the tree."[14]

Kiarostami often removed key cinematic elements to deepen his spectators' involvement, such as the ruse of having the sound equipment fail at the end of *Close-Up* or "removing the voice and the light" rather than depicting Mr. Badii's death at the end of *Taste of Cherry*, but in *Shirin* he achieves the ultimate subtraction by omitting the visual story altogether. In David Bordwell's succinct description,

> The film severs sound from image [to retell the twelfth-century romantic narrative poem *Khosrow and Shirin* by Nizami Ganjavi], but we don't see it at all. What we see are about 200 shots of female viewers, usually in single closeups, with occasionally some men visible behind or on the screen edge. The women are looking more or less straight at the camera, and we infer that they're reacting to the drama as we hear it.[15]

Deborah Young compares *Shirin* to Kiarostami's theater play *Taize*, in which a "traditional religious drama is performed in costume while screens show films of an Iranian audience's emotional involvement with the story." In *Shirin* "we see only the reactions of a female 'audience' watching a film that only exists in the mind of the viewer."[16]

This is true for what we see because the actresses are not actually watching the story of *Shirin*. Kiarostami gave each actress five minutes to pretend to watch a love story they had personally experienced or imagined: "The more you forget that you are in front of a camera and the more you think of yourself in a dark movie theater, the better. This movie has no director, no organizer. It's you and only you."[17] What we hear, however, is more poetically pointed than a Scheherazadic tale meant only to evoke 1,001 meanings. In 2000 Kiarostami said that he wanted "to provide for film the advantage of literature" by creating a cinema where he could do as much as possible without "actually showing it" in order to engage the spectator's imagination.[18]

But what he could not say was that attuned spectators, especially in the poetry-imbued culture of Iran, might use their imaginations to construe the metaphorically subversive religious message the film contains. Just as Shakespeare used a pre-Christian tale in *King Lear* to express an ironic repudiation of providential justice by substituting *gods* for *God*, Kiarostami used the pre-Islamic myth of the love between a Zoroastrian Persian prince and a Christian Armenian princess to question orthodox monotheism by satirizing the adolescent exaggeration and inevitable failure of romantic love.

In Nizami's original epic and in Farrideh Golbou's *Khosrow and Shirin*, a 1998 prose version adapted for the screen by author and director Mohammad Rahmanian, a major character commits suicide when he hears a false report of his beloved's death, and the narrative as a whole conveys the idea that romantic love is a form of suicide because it shuts everything else out. While the principal actors in the story we hear engage in acts of destruction or make themselves miserable over singular obsessions, the multiplicity of beautiful faces that we see contradicts the notion of any supreme ideal. The 113 spectators, many of whom are recognizable Iranian actresses, act as a kind of silent Greek chorus universalized by the notable presence of the non-Iranian Juliette Binoche.

By using actual actors instead of the nonactors he favors in previous films and by equalizing their public faces with the film's actual onlookers, Kiarostami expresses a democratic vision that is simultaneously social and spiritual. Whereas Panahi is more explicit about showing social and economic problems, Kiarostami probes their underlying cause. In 2000 he told an interviewer that the "religious censors have unfortunately shown they do not pay any attention to economic problems [and are only] sensitive about [detecting] undermining religious ideas."[19]

The religious idea that Kiarostami undermines had to be subtly expressed if he was to elude the clerical retribution that had been meted out to some of his Sufi forebears (see chapter 2). Rumi urges his readers to go beyond a single God above nature and learn to see God in nature, just as on another level, he learned to go beyond the supreme ideal he saw in Shams to see the Friend in every living thing. Instead of striving to achieve union with a cosmic king, Rumi (like Attar in *Conference of the Birds*) advises spiritual seekers to remember that whatever they are seeking is already in themselves. His metaphor of the adoring lover bowing into a mirror because the only reality is God resembles the Sohrab Sepehri poem quoted by Kiarostami in *Rug*: "Open your eyes to see the lover's beauty glowing everywhere / Observing this vision makes you think / There is no other than He, the Creator" (see chapter 3). Kiarostami put this another way when he said that looking at the faces of *Shirin*'s spectators is like looking at the water, ducks, and driftwood that his stationary camera had filmed in *Five Dedicated to Ozu* (2003).

In the first episode of *Five*, which was shot on the shore of the Caspian Sea while Kiarostami was visiting Panahi and planning *Crimson Gold*, we watch the waves buffet a piece of driftwood until part of it breaks off and washes out to sea. Kiarostami's description of the process reveals his sense of natural elements as collaborative partners in the same way he democratizes human beings in his other films. Instead of using an explosive device to break the wood, a barrier to block and release the waves, and an out-of-frame pulley to draw the broken piece away, Kiarostami saw his partners as the wind and water: "You need a tail wind and a good wave. As backgammon players say, 'It's how the dice fall that counts.'"[20]

In the same interview, he went on to illustrate his point about avoiding the illusion of omnipotence by recounting the tale of how an Indian maharajah sent the Iranian emperor the game of chess that one of his philosophers had just invented "as a symbol of Indian intelligence," and the emperor had his vizier invent backgammon as a return gift. The "wise vizier" understood the "logical and warlike thought" behind chess. He wanted to show the maharajah how a game of dice, by taking "full control away from the player," would teach him that "there are other factors contributing to his destiny than skill, intelligence, and experience."

A wise person, he continued, allows for accidents that include hidden factors variously called destiny, fate, or God's will: "I believe in a combination of these things . . . as elements of a hidden pattern." Some artists are chess players who do not respect these "undeniable" powers: "[For them] everything is ruled and controlled by the gods of the scene, the producer and the director."[21] In other interviews, he said that *Close-Up* was his favorite film because it seemed to make itself, and in that film, as in *Five*, he felt more like a spectator than a director.[22] He makes the point in *Shirin* by turning recognizable actors into spectators, so that their collective beauty rather than the glamorizing of any particular person symbolizes the best in existence, while the unseen narrative that many consider a national epic becomes a cautionary tale about childish egos divisively seeking perfection. He put it another way in the opening scene of *The Wind Will Carry Us*, where the Tehrani crew has trouble locating the landmark of a single large tree because, as one says, "there are a lot around here," and again at the end of *Ten on Ten*, when he leaves the driver's seat of his "iron cell" to train his camera on a team of ants moving an object much larger than themselves (see chapter 3).

Two passages in *Shirin* refer directly to the connection between supreme elevation and social destruction. During a battle that Khosrow is about to lose, he asks his magus Shapur why the enemy soldiers who had once been his indolent serfs have become such ferocious fighters: "Were they promised paradise, treasure, or power?" The reply rejects Shiite Iran's ethic of martyrdom, much as Makhmalbaf does in *Marriage of the Blessed*: "Deception is more effective than the promise of paradise." And when Khosrow asks what they should do now that the war is hopeless and they are doomed, an officer advises him to live to fight another day: "We can skip this defeat. The main player of this chess game is deception [and only] the pawns aspire to royalty. The king should retreat to his fort." And later, when Shirin complains to the same magus that she is bored with being queen and her only joy is thinking of Khosrow, the magus tells her that her people feel a similar joy in thinking of her. Revering an idol who they do not realize is of their own making, Shirin's pawns "fall to their knees, they worship you. But you know it's all about their fascination with the throne."

The film's opening titles are printed over a series of fourteen color illustrations from what may be a medieval book. Their selection (credited to Kiarostami's son, Bahman) conveys a sense of collective fascination with rich, royal, and beautiful people. All the pictures center on one or both principal characters, but six include servants and four include large retinues of anonymous soldiers watching Khosrow hunt or fighting and dying in bloody battles. These images are intended to be carefully noted because they are the film's only visual clues to the narrative prior to the film proper, when they are replaced by the nuanced expressions of the on-screen viewers.

The legend of Khosrow and Shirin is considered a national treasure.[23] And because people in general like films about sex, violence, and romantic love, the opening emphasis on still images connotes humanity's unevolved state, and the narrative develops a motif similar to that in Hitchcock's *Vertigo*, which concerns the danger of falling in love with a two-dimensional, static dream. The sequence comprises a remarkable visual poem. The first image of lions with human faces confronting each other on either side of a huge central crown keynotes the ongoing presence of regressive rivalry in contrast to the next four images of formally posed people in decorous groups. But the fifth picture has Khosrow looking down from his horse at a lion devouring a gazelle, the bloody throat of which ironically matches a small, red-flowering bush in the exact center of the frame, and the image after that is of Khosrow disguised as a peasant, viewing the naked Shirin bathing before they have met and before they attach the ideal of perfection to each other's bodies.

Not recognizing the love of his life without the myth attached to the portrait he pursues, Khosrow rides on, just as the audience may move on without recognizing the exposure of romantic and spiritual delusions these images reveal. The next image of Khosrow and Shirin in a blissful romantic embrace, formally flanked by a male and female servant, is followed by a shot of the two on horseback, accompanied by a large group of soldiers anonymously witnessing Khosrow aiming an arrow at a small animal that is already being ravaged by a hunting dog.

The next picture escalates the approach to brutality, with Khosrow standing over two small lions with human heads, which, as in the opening image, face each other over a now-much-smaller central crown, as if to shrink monumental historical events to irrational eruptions rather than heroic triumphs. Behind these figures, two opposed armies in disciplined ranks stand ready to act out the compulsive duel between the two foregrounded lions. Then, after two more scenes, probably picturing the politically arranged marriage of Khosrow with the sister of the Byzantine Caesar, the screen explodes into a scene of carnage overseen by charging cavalry trampling the bodies of mutilated soldiers.

The sense that all wars are familicides is consummated when the final picture shows Khosrow's son with an upright sword, standing over the reclining figures of Shirin and the father he has just slaughtered. Khosrow has a small red spot of blood on his chest in the center of the frame, echoing the red-flowering bush centered in the scene of the lion devouring the gazelle. Throughout the introduction, the film's lovely, romantic music plays steadily without modulating from image to image, as if to blur the disparity between chivalric ferocity and courtly love that the illustrations consecutively expose. Taken as a whole, the opening sequence displays enduring rites of mating and dominance that commercial cinema may reflect and poetic cinema can reveal.

The destructive effect of these instincts is paradoxically aggravated by the exclusively human drive to transcend them. After the credits the story begins with Shirin narrating from beyond the grave, as a chorus of grieving women ritually laments Khosrow's death: "Listen to me, my sisters. It is my turn to recount my story. Right here, by the lifeless body of Khosrow. And here we are, me, Khosrow, and you, my grieving sisters. You look at his dead body, and you cry. You listen to my story, and you cry. Through these tears, I see your eyes. Are you shedding these tears for me? Or for the Shirin that hides in each one of you."

Then, she begins her own version, beginning with a symbolic recollection of playing blindman's buff with a group of girls in the springtime mountains at the age of seventeen. A friend's lines reflect the experience of the film itself when she tells the blindfolded Shirin to "open your ears [and] just follow our voices," and when she adds, "You are surrounded by flowers. Choose one, and enjoy its nectar," the flowers correspond to the women we see in the audience, each of whom might be exclusively loved.

But exclusive love can be a blessing and a curse, a motif initiated when the girls gasp after one finds a piece of wood painted with the face of an impossibly handsome man. When Shirin demands that they remove her blindfold, a swooning companion teases, "If you do that, you will be defeated," and another sighs, "This defeat is worth hundreds of victories. It must be a portrait, engraved by Mani." As Shirin beholds the object of such awe, she comically exclaims, "Never mind the artist. Whose face is it? A prince perhaps. . . . Or an angel!" But then, alarmed by the portrait's mesmerizing power, another warns, "The traits might be of an angel but performed by a demon's hand," and still another agrees, "Portrait of an angel, work of a demon!" From this point on, the dialogue takes on a sinister tone: "Leave the portrait, it is damned!"—"Damned?"—"Its bad omen will be inflicted upon you."—"Let us leave this place. This place is haunted by the portrait!"

But once Shirin's Edenic delight in her valley of waterfalls and wildflowers has been lost, she can no more recover her formerly firm footing than can *Vertigo*'s acrophobic Scottie Ferguson once he has been possessed by a portrait's power. They try to escape, but "where to?" as one says, and as another (metaphorically referring to the life journey) adds, "It is not even noon. The excursion is not over yet." Thinking they are safe, they rest by a stream where, to Shirin's dismay, the current ominously washes the portrait ashore: "This portrait. . . . Here it comes again!"—"Where is it?"—"Near that rock, immersed in the water."—"Damn this beauty! Let us pray, to get rid of this demon."—"Who is he anyway? Robbing my heart and my soul?"—"Oh Shirin, princess of Armenia, why are you so enraptured by him, yourself desired by thousands!"—"Let us go back to the palace! Right now, the demons are after us."

But even in the palace, where the orphaned Shirin lives with her doting aunt, the queen, the portrait haunts her dreams and then, to her waking horror, materializes by her side. In a parallel to *Romeo and Juliet,* she implores her nanny to explain:

> "My nightmares are never ending, but this time they follow me through the day. What is this?"—"The portrait of a handsome man."—"Why is it here?"—"I thought it to be your usual mischievousness."—"I'll be damned if I know anything about this sinister portrait."—"It might be the doing of one your friends."—"Why? To inflame my passion? At first sight, I gave up my heart to

this longing. What a bitter game for sweet Shirin. But who is he, dear nanny?"—"You are feverish, my sweet. You are burning with fever."

The "he" who has inflamed Shirin's passions is not the subject of the portrait but its creator. The prophet, poet, and painter Mani (216–274 CE) had been banished, restored, and finally executed by three Zoroastrian kings who tolerated or despised his radical separation of the spiritual realm from the physical world. The Manichaean King of Light had created the original man as a perfect being who would one day descend to earth as the redeeming Christ, while the Adam commonly thought to be the first human being was created by a demiurge variously known as Ahriman, Satan, or Yahweh, who was the lowest of the great king's emanations.

This demiurge is a blind and foolish trickster who ignores or competes with the true god and who has created the material world as a deception to prevent the divine spark in human beings from attaining the gnosis that would allow it to return to its original union with the King of Light. The demiurge has a crew of demons called archons to assist his concealment of light by seducing human beings into preferring his husk of darkness to the divine spark concealed inside.[24]

It is easy to see why Golbou and Rahmanian would make Mani himself the demon tormenting Shirin's dreams and why Kiarostami found the story so congenial. The story characterizes the removal of value from the natural world as a bizarre distortion. Shirin's aunt tells her to discover the source of the "handsome portrait," the godlike image that "crept even into [her] chamber," by visiting a magus who lives (predictably) on a mountaintop where he has received "all the secrets of the world." In a narrative aside to her attendants as they grieve Khosrow's death, Shirin briefly breaks the story line to reflect on how the portrait had circulated before reaching her through a friend, the film's way of saying that Shirin has been culturally infected but that she now realizes that the answers she seeks have been invented by self-aggrandizing religious authorities who exploit centuries-old obsessions: "It took me a while to realize it was all a game, a grotesque vaudeville. It had changed hands and finally ended up in the hands of my confidante. And that fake magus, the impostor, [used it to pull] the strings of all the puppets."

In fact, all the magus can tell Shirin is that the man in the painting is "Khosrow, prince of Persia, who has fallen in love with you the same way you fell in love with him. He saw your portrait." The magus is given another line of thematic wisdom when he tells Shirin that the mature love waiting to be discovered as a cosmic principle will first appear to be confined to a single object: Khosrow and Shirin have both seen a "beautiful portrait which was not the image of love, but love personified."

This hierarchy of praise is consistently satirized by the superlatives describing the horse bequeathed by the royal aunt to her royal niece. Monotheistic superlatives extended downward into structured societies have long kept kings and holy men in power: "You know all that?"—"And more."—"Your horse, for instance, is your aunt's, Shabdiz, the greatest of all horses." When Shirin hesitates to trust such a glorious steed to take her straight to Khosrow's palace in Persia, the magus urges her to undertake her journey with no more understanding than the simplest onlooker might muster: "Please help me, omniscient man. I don't have the heart to stay nor the courage to go."—"Do as you're told. Ride Shabdiz, and go full gallop to Madaen. Your destiny awaits you."

A series of back-and-forth journeys then follows, as each lover arrives at the other's palace only to find that the one they so strenuously sought is now in the place they have left. That is, both might have found the love of their life at home in the same way Attar's birds discover that the king they seek already lives within them. On one of these crossed journeys, Khosrow, disguised as a peasant, sees the exhausted Shirin bathing naked in a stream but then resumes his journey as blithely as if he had glimpsed a rock or a tree because the nude or "real" Shirin is not the goddess Mani drew. Shirin's line again reflects on the film's visual mirror of its audience, all of whom are as beautiful as the gods they worship: "Who is looking at me? Is it Khosrow?"

And when Khosrow arrives in Armenia, he is announced to Shirin's aunt as an "exhausted horseman [who] says he is a prince in disguise," just as all presumed princes are only peasants in disguise, a perspective Kiarostami personifies through the prismatic Hossein in *Through the Olive Trees*. The idea that these illusions of rank are abetted by religious authority is reiterated when Shirin, now living in Persia but not yet married to Khosrow, receives the magus, bearing a message from her lover: "Here comes a new farce! Once you pretended to be an omniscient magus. Now you are Khosrow's messenger?"—"Back then it was an act. Today, I am being truthful."—"I despise the truth that comes from a charlatan like you."—"Khosrow awaits you in Armenia, in your aunt's palace."—"Khosrow invited me to Tisfun and fled to Armenia himself?"—"For affairs of state, Madame. The state has reasons that even reason ignores."

The magus is indifferent to love and wisdom, and Shirin's union with Khosrow is no more than a feature of the political drama the magus serves to bolster. When Shirin recalls how an idealized love has taken her from the happiness she shared with friends to obtain what now looks like a false promise, the magus can only respond with another shibboleth: "The road to love is always hazardous, Madame. Be courageous. Shabdiz and I look forward to the journey." Shirin immediately senses that the role she has been cast to play benefits the "producer" of the story more than it benefits her: "What if it's a new scam? Another plot against me? What's my part in this play?"

Her part turns out to epitomize the collective one of the chorus on the sound track and the women we see in the film's audience. When Shirin returns, Khosrow has once again departed. He has gone to Persia to reclaim his kingdom after his father was blinded and captured "by one of his generals greedy for his throne." While the blind warriors of the world engage in "this manly game," Shirin's aunt speaks for the families left behind: She asks Shirin not to leave her again, but Shirin knows she can never return to childhood or regard existence as secure: "I must sleep and either dream of Khosrow or have a nightmare of the war."

The narrative now switches to sounds of battle, with swords clashing and men screaming in agony. On the screen, one of the spectators looks down as if she cannot bear to see. At this point the magus tells Khosrow that it is time to retreat because, for them rather than for their soldiers, "deception" is more effective than promises of paradise, treasure, or power. The magus then instructs Khosrow to be indifferent to his army's fate because the important thing is to stay in power. In this "tricky game of destiny," all they need is forty men: "It's never too late to fight." Deception and self-deception continue when Shirin, who is not yet married to Khosrow, urges him to regain his kingdom for the sake of the heirs they do not yet have.

But because he needs the military support of the Byzantine Empire, he cements a political alliance by acceding to a loveless marriage with Maryam, the emperor's sister. This betrayal coincides with the demise of Shirin's loving aunt, whose deathbed advice voices an ideal to which the world's leaders are largely indifferent: Her kingdom (thematically, the world) will, in the aunt's words, be Shirin's to receive, and when the niece promises to "cherish these people as my own children," her aunt voices the unrealized ideal with which the story ends: "Procure them a better life. Free travel and exempt from taxes. A peaceful life so that the prey and the predator, the sheep and the wolf, drink from the same spring."

The aunt's death is sobering enough to induce an embryonic movement in Shirin from infantile longing to mature responsibility: "The hard times are upon us, and the thought of Khosrow is not so vivid." While Khosrow kills soldiers to satisfy a misbegotten obligation, the story shifts from war to another form of suicide: the confusion between love and victory. The idea of being rendered helpless by an idealized sexual attraction was introduced when Shirin's girlhood companion warned her not to remove her blindfold because gazing on the portrait of Khosrow would "defeat" her. But the idea that the victory is not that of the portrait's subject but that of its creator is implied in Shirin's rapturous response: "This defeat is worth hundreds of victories. It must be a portrait engraved by Mani."

With Khosrow engaged in his obligatory social role of waging war, the film introduces Farhad, the third member of the love triangle referred to by Kiarostami as an "architect, a mathematician, [and] a statue maker."[25] Calling Farhad a "statue maker" does not refer to the legendary feat for which Farhad is celebrated, but it does speak directly to the artificiality of the cultural roles satirized by the film's highly stylized sound track. To relieve her feelings of loneliness and boredom in Khosrow's absence, Shirin feels the need for diversionary pleasure, the function of entertainment in general as performed by artists who work to earn rewards granted by the powers that be. The gods of such artists are the social superiors and approving public who validate their efforts and their lives. This in effect produces an art of flattery because its makers and recipients are narcissistically enabled to see themselves as they wish to be rather than as who they are.

Shirin initially yearns for a simple, sensual escape when she summons the renowned architect and mathematician to her palace because she feels a need for "fresh milk," and because the "prairies are too far away and the roads are bumpy," she wants him to build a canal to transport satisfaction for her craving. The sexual innuendoes are inherent in the story, but the film's exaggerated vocal delivery lends them a comic quality consistent with its overall perspective on cultural delusion. The comic tone is confirmed as Shirin expresses her frustration: "Nothing agrees to our palate: neither the sweets made for our pleasure nor the delicacy of the meat." Farhad is so instantly smitten that he can barely hear: "Master, are you listening to me?"—"Yes, Madame. You were talking about meat and sweet Shirin." Then he promptly faints, "his eyes fixating," until Shirin commands the women to pour water on him, and he awakens whispering her name.

Shirin narrates her memory of this meeting over the dead body of Khosrow, where the film began, indicating that the conceptual power of romantic myth trumps that of politics or religion: "How to forget that gaze, virtuous, tender, and soft? I should not be thinking of Farhad at Khosrow's' death but blame it on the world, cruel to lovers, which endowed Farhad with that gaze and not to anyone else, not even to Khosrow." But the gaze Shirin fell in love with misrepresents her. Just as Hossein in *Through the Olive Trees* loves his idea of Tahereh rather than the person he does not know, Farhad loves his idea of Shirin, not Shirin as she is.

Within the larger myth of Khosrow and Shirin, the character of Farhad in particular has a mesmeric appeal that the *Encyclopædia Iranica* describes as "permeating the whole of Persian culture," from folklore, to literature, to the visual arts.[26] Kiarostami elaborates the Farhad side of the love triangle because it speaks so directly to his perspective on the destructiveness of replacing nature with art. He referred to the story as a widely assumed quintessence of love when Yossef in *The Wind Will Carry Us* tells Behzad that the "love of Shirin" rather than Farhad himself "dug Biston," and again, in response to Behzad's supercilious compliment—"Bravo, you know love, too."—Yossef adds, "A man without love cannot live" (see chapter 6).

The line has ironic resonance because Farhad ultimately commits a Romeo-like suicide when Khosrow deceives him into thinking Shirin is dead, but Kiarostami portrays the suicide as psychological, even before Farhad makes it physical.[27] Though Farhad is literally an architect, he digs Biston as a Herculean superhero with only stone cutting tools and his bare hands. As his tools change the natural substance of the rock, he recites a eulogy to romantic love that disproportions the world: "All the sky has to offer is love. The earth would be a desert without the rain of love. . . . The flame of love is the best gift of this world." As in *The Wind Will Carry Us*, where Behzad seeks fresh milk as a sexual surrogate, Shirin arrives bringing milk to cool his "burning heart." She initiates their dialogue as a kind of parody of female attraction to the action hero: "I am here to see you. To see your strong arm fighting rough stone and cold steel," while he experiences her arrival sensually as "perfume coming from the mountains" even before he and the alluring rider, "with hair flowing in the wind," begin to speak.

Shortly after he greets her with "My God! Are my dreams becoming reality?" she notices Farhad's echo of the portrait by Mani that seduced both Khosrow and herself: "Isn't this my portrait looking back at me as if was my reflection in a mirror? How could you remember me in the slightest detail after only one encounter?" Farhad's answer indicates that he has never really seen her at all but has instead endowed the rock with the "face [that was already] engraved in my heart." The engraving etherealizes the sexual passion sensed less delicately by Shabdiz, Shirin's "greatest of all horses," who neighs almost to the point of screaming when Shirin offers the milk. "If only this horse would stay calm," she says, to which Farhad naïvely replies, "Shirin or the milk? For which one of the benedictions should I be grateful?"

But the benediction that is Farhad's rather than Shirin's begins to have a negative effect corresponding to the unhealthy exaggeration it thematically represents, as Shirin asks how Farhad can work so hard in the blazing sun that has made her so dizzy she almost faints. In a Clark Kent transformation, her devotee responds by hoisting Shabdiz with Shirin still astride onto his shoulders and carrying them both back to her distant palace. "I must be dreaming," she says of the feat, to which Farhad offers a starry-eyed rejoinder: "You came to transform a nightmare into a sweet dream."

But for Kiarostami, it's the other way around. Before Shirin meets Farhad, she "dreamt of a knight, who had a branch instead of a head, where a dove had his nest. Was it a dream or a nightmare? I cannot tell." It is a vision like that of Mani, a cultural denaturing of the Creator's work composed of natural elements bizarrely combined. Though the vision may depict one who inspires love, it is the kind of distorted love that is absorbed in its object to the point of suicide, much like the Iranian soldier who "loved Imam Khomeini" so much that he courted death "with joy" and, even with grievous injuries, later reflected, "I think it was beautiful. It was a very elegant moment. I would rather die in that moment than live after the war. It was so nice" (see chapter 1).

Shirin is the culmination of Kiarostami's mission to dispel the cultural demons by showing his spectators that they are intrinsically beautiful and that they do not have to earn the validation of a king who promises paradise only to those who meet his demands. The on-screen spectators may be enthralled by a cultural myth that ends in suicide and murder because they cannot see themselves, but as Kiarostami said in comparing *Shirin* to *Five*, beauty is as inherent in the human face as it is in driftwood, waves, and birds.

While Khosrow competes with alpha generals for control of the material world, Farhad competes with God (whom Mani reduces to a demiurge) to create a world superior to the natural one he has received. In so doing, he not only cancels out and therefore threatens nature, but he also suicidally devalues himself. For Farhad, marrying Shirin would be the equivalent of religious salvation, and his monumental endeavor represents absolute submission to that quest, a reduction to nothingness that he operatically celebrates as he returns to work after delivering his goddess: "I was a spindrift. / I melted in the sea. / I was a shadow at the beginning / laying down on the ground. / As soon as the sun appeared / I disappeared."

When a riding companion praises "this beautiful song," Farhad seems to sense that his poetic need arises from sexual sublimation: "I don't know if it's beautiful, but if this feeling couldn't be turned into a chant, it would have burned me down." The companion responds with the inculcated feeling that nature is in dire need of improvement: "Without these songs, the world would be a living hell!" But for Kiarostami, such songs of self-abasement are themselves hellish. When human beings try to socially or religiously legitimize themselves, they end up transforming the heaven they already have into standing over or lying under their mirrored foes.

Political and intellectual strivers, Khosrow and Farhad are variants of the same archetypal drive, though one plays the role of an established god, and the other, his demiurgic antagonist. Khosrow's loyal counselor Shapur explains that men like Farhad "chose the order of art and science" instead of courting kings: "These kinds of men are inclined toward rebellion." And when Khosrow asks why Farhad would then submit to love, Shapur replies, "Love and rebellion, two sides of the same coin. Disappointed by one, they turn to the other."

In the scene where Khosrow confronts Farhad, the king's threat to cut off the sculptor's hands for presuming to usurp his love has bearing on the plight of artists like Makhmalbaf and Panahi in the Islamic republic. Their renown undermines the illusion of perfect supremacy that political rulers arrogate to themselves because artists divert the devotion of the collective Shirin that the rulers presume to command. But Farhad, unlike Sufi adepts of the past and dissident artists of the present, weakens his integrity by passively sentimentalizing the prize both seek. When Farhad exposes his narcissistic exaltation by saying that his threatened hands obey his heart and his heart obeys Shirin—"My shredded heart is burning for her."—Khosrow skewers his naïve hypocrisy: "Are you talking about love or engraving? Boasting about a shredded heart? Love deserves better."

But in the battle for the devotion of a nation's people represented by the on-screen audience of women, political and clerical leaders are on the whole more vulnerable, envious, and dangerous than artists. Khosrow explains why a man like Farhad would provoke the antipathy of a man like him: "Your name is endangering our glory [because] your voice fills the plains and the mountains." His artistic inspiration earns accolades Khosrow cannot match: "But what is this new prowess? Taking Shirin and her horse on your shoulders, wandering around town and leaving the passers-by astonished? I have to wash away this disgrace." But Khosrow's only means of retaliation are the political tools of physical power and deception. He challenges Farhad to a battle he will lose because his boast of wearing the "tough armor of rancor" and wielding the "bitter sword of vengeance" will only succeed in transmitting these self-consuming powers to a rebellious son who will kill him. Farhad, on the other hand, will destroy himself because he cannot transfer the object of his love from a specific person (or nation) to the world at large.

Because the story of Khosrow and Shirin is so well known, Kiarostami does not include the scene where Khosrow and his counselor plot to induce Farhad's failure to complete Biston by falsely telling him Shirin is dead. By removing the literal cause, Kiarostami poeticizes its result. When the messenger reports Shirin's death, he is actually describing the imminent death of Farhad: "She renounced the throne searching for a hopeless love. But Iran offered a funeral instead of a wedding. Shirin died in her bloom." Then, instead of describing the sculptor's suicide, the script emphasizes the story's metaphor of blindness. Farhad faces his death like a martyr, implying that he has been made as blind by grief as he was by love. He sacrifices the art he might have transmitted to his heirs because he cannot settle for an existence of inherent beauty rather than the limited beauty his obsessed imagination shaped: "Take my stone-carving hand and lead me," he tells the messenger in his exit line.

Shirin resumes her narrative by reiterating its artificiality: "Damn this game of man that we call love." She has already referred to the events and emotions of her tale as a "farce" and a "vaudeville," and while she and Khosrow fell in love with a portrait limned by Mani, Farhad dies for his own "certified copy" of a romantic ideal painted by innumerable others on the basis of an unknown original. The queen laments that, with Farhad, "Shirin was buried, too," and "all the lovers died," which is belied by the tearful audience of lovers we see on-screen. And the monstrous son who ends the story was potentially present in forebears who were both lovers and killers, whether they physically killed others or blindly killed their sensibilities pursuing a personal version of "Shirin."

Even near the end, when Khosrow and Shirin appear to have reached mature fulfillment, Shirin realizes that blissful dreams inevitably become nightmares, an ongoing verbal motif that culminates in the last scene. With Maryam and Farhad now dead, Khosrow feels they have attained perfection: "We waited so long for this embrace, my sweet."—"I am fearful, Khosrow."—"Why are you fearful, on this serene voluptuous night?"—"I fear that this embrace turns out to be a dream. Like all the dreams we had through the years which would turn into horrible nightmares once awake."

The fear is well founded because Shirin sees that Shiroyeh, Khosrow's son by Maryam, has "much ambition" and a "demon in his eyes," the same word used to describe the ambition of Mani, who wanted to replace the Friend's world with the superior one he dreamed. Moreover, Shiroyeh's eyes are filled "with rancor," the very word for festering rage that Khosrow uses to describe his hatred for Farhad. The seeds of the next war are present in every peace, as long as human beings suicidally prefer a dreamed paradise to the present that Khayyam and Kiarostami urge them to love. Khosrow uses the usual flattery to try to soothe her, but calling her "Shirin, queen of all fairy tales" only compounds the problem because in the tale they have lived he himself once played the ogre. His threat of doing to Farhad what kings like himself had done to others is echoed when Shirin tells her fictive attendants and her on-screen audience that Shiroyeh cut off the hands and feet of his brothers and imprisoned his father, familicides that in one way or another continue to happen: "But you, my sisters, you know the story better than I do. Here is another manly game."

But even after the sound track records the invasion of their bedroom, where Khosrow is murdered in a horrific scene of hoarse shouts, clanging steel, and dripping blood, Shirin's final lament sustains a series of self-pitying half-truths: "Are you shedding these tears . . . for the Shirin who through her life neither received any favor nor any attention [or who] was in love, a love that was never returned?" Then, dismissing the whole of her life that unfolded following her girlish delight in games, rain, and sunshine "with a rainbow in her eyes," she resorts to a "small dagger to relieve those many years of exhaustion."

After we hear her emit a sharp cry as she stabs herself, the camera scans the crying on-screen women, many of whom, like Juliette Binoche, have received much favor and attention. Following the heroine's death, the male and female voices continue in a minor key for fifty seconds before the white-on-black credits begin. The names of all the women present roll by for a long time. There are no stars. It is everyone's story, a story Kiarostami accepts but does not respect.

Throughout his oeuvre, Kiarostami encouraged his viewers to recover the rain, sunshine, and rainbows that are continuing joys for people freed from competitive aspiration. When one of his actresses told him that the personal story he instructed her to recall was very sad, he gently demurred, "[Your imagined] movie is not at all sad. It's even a bit happy. There are pleasant scenes, there is nature, music, song, there is a butterfly, a bowl filled with fruit, a vase full of flowers, butterflies are dancing, nightingales are singing. Butterflies are dancing in the moonlight, and stories are like that." When the same woman said that there is nothing happy in her story, Kiarostami replied, "Life is somewhat joyful, though, [and] those who are experienced enough know that all these joys are not everlasting. Buddha says life is a place to suffer. We know that joy does not last forever, so we do not react instantaneously to temporary joy." After the makeup artist touched her up and the woman, now smiling, said, "Under the eyes won't do good anymore. It's been so many years," Kiarostami turned the remark into a further reflection on overcoming the resistance to natural process that his subsequent films depict: "Imagine if years passed, and you had no lines. What would you do? Life would become so terrible if there was no change, inside and out."[28]

In his general instructions to the cast, he praised the framed story he wanted his viewers to understand rather than the deceptive one the story's characters endure: "Think of a love story. It brings a little bit of joy. Some of you are more experienced and know more about love and frustration. It keeps threatening you, so you don't show your happiness much. And then we reach the end of the tragedy like many classic love stories that bring about frustration, but this, however, is sort of a success."[29] The success of the story lies in the poetic language that conveys its ideas rather than its plot as exemplified by recurrent metaphors of sweet and bitter, dream and nightmare, portraits and engraving. Throughout the posturing speeches and tragic events, the camera dwells without condescension on the faces of its on-screen viewers, whose emotional reactions are as beautiful and natural as the scenes of non-human nature that Kiarostami lovingly shares in previous films.

He said that he included the coda in *Taste of Cherry* so as not to leave the audience with a cruel memory of self-destruction, just as a grandmother might by ending a frightening fairy tale with "After all, it's just a story."[30] In *Shirin* he found a way to combine the story and the coda by keeping the survivors' compassionate humanity continually in view. He knew that tragic stories could be cathartic, and he essentially said so as one of his actresses was leaving his living room, where his instructions to draw on personal memories had induced an intense response: "I hope with all these tears we didn't hurt you." When she says he didn't, he continues, "It's like a bath for your eyes. You are, in fact, playing, but your pictures are real. We don't always have the chance to watch such private moments picture by picture."[31]

In the same interview where Kiarostami said, "I'm not Muslim," he also said that, though he did not disapprove of people kissing in public as he had seen couples do in Italy, he preferred not to show private activities in his films: "If people don't normally see something in public, why would I expect or force them to see it in the cinema?"[32] Regardless of the personal religion, which he did not disclose, his reluctance to invade the private emotions of his actors and spectators is consistent with the traditional Islamic ban on the graven image.

He had said that in his cinema the most important subject is "human beings and their souls," and the individual soul in the Sufi tradition is also God, Kiarostami can no more depict the soul than he could depict God.[33] The effort, therefore, was to find a way to communicate spiritual experience without resorting to iconic clichés. Kiarostami accomplished this by not showing key elements that filmgoers have come to expect,[34] such as leaving out the "voice and the light" as a way to experience Badii's death in *Taste of Cherry*, cutting the sound during Makhmalbaf's ferrying of Sabzian to the Ahankhah house at the end of *Close-Up*, and the five minutes of nighttime blackness in *ABC Africa* just before a sunlit transition where the glassless windows of a house show the courage of its occupants by connoting what they have endured: "Look at the [empty] doors and windows. That's years of destruction and war."

This practice of removing elements, showing without showing and speaking without speaking, is not simply a technique of stimulating spectators' imaginations; it is a key part of the aniconic spiritual tradition with which Kiarostami was imbued. In mosques, the empty prayer niche (mihrab) that faces Mecca represents the presence of Allah, and both Kiarostami and Sohrab Sepehri were attracted by the Taoist and Buddhist Absolute, the Sunyata or Void. In Judaism and Islam, the proscribed image was originally intended to combat idolatry, but as the tradition evolved, it became a way of reminding people that the most valuable parts of their lives were subjective and intangible.

And so in *Shirin*, when Kiarostami has the actor voicing Farhad express his devotion to the female ideal he worships, his paeans of praise are absurdly histrionic, while in a more sympathetic portrayal, Hossein in *Through the Olive Trees* loves an idea of Tahereh that in an unfilmed sequel tragically fails because the image and the experience do not match. When Kiarostami referred to Farhad in an interview, he did not praise him as the great Persian lover that the tradition conceived but as an architect and "statue maker," epithets that might also apply to Hossein. Both characters work materially in stone, and both fail to confine the God they seek to a single incarnation.

The Sufi emphasis on experiencing God throughout physical nature helps to explain how Kiarostami could become renowned for the beauty of his images and still be in sympathy with the sentiment underlying the aniconic ban. The Koran itself does not forbid images of living things, but several hadiths (commentaries on the Koran) report Muhammad refusing gifts decorated with animal images, saying, "The angels of mercy do not enter a house in which there are pictures of animals," and condemning graveside pictures of pious Muslims.[35]

Although these proscriptions were not strictly followed in Persian rugs and miniatures or in Shia funereal practice, they seem to say that appreciating Creation means not trying to confine its essence to displays of technique or self-serving concepts of superior biological and social forms. Certainly, Kiarostami would not have found the cult of personality any more attractive in Iranian posters of religious leaders than in the obviously shallow idol worship of politicians, actors, or athletes in the West. Kiarostami portrays this worship of unworthy gods in *The Traveler*, where Qassem's religion is received from sports magazines, which transmit the spiritual desertion that ultimately appears in the rubbish-strewn stadium that he races through and hopefully beyond in the final scene.

Kiarostami purges his work of soul-sapping narratives of heroes and villains, victories and defeats, by using nonactors and omitting the elements those narratives use to drain the energies and wallets of their regressed recipients. There are no embodied supreme beings in his films, and every person portrayed (as in *Shirin*'s audience of women) is a certified copy of an unknown original. While Plato used a similar concept to disparage art as only a crafted imitation of a physical imitation of an abstract "idea," Kiarostami had a Sufi reverence for every aspect of the embodied world as worthy of gratitude and love.

His way of showing that love was to create an art that somehow makes us feel what cannot be shown or said—the mysterious joy he felt after visiting earthquake-ravaged Koker or the similar joy of the AIDS-surviving dancers in *ABC Africa*. He ultimately went beyond the one-word feature he half-seriously proposed after *Ten* by concluding his career with the virtually wordless *24 Frames* (2017), but even in the elaborate dialogue of *Certified Copy*, he shows us how to listen through the words his characters think they mean to sense the souls they don't believe they have.

NOTES

1. Alberto Elena, *The Cinema of Abbas Kiarostami*, trans. Belinda Coombes (London: SAQI Iran Heritage Foundation, 2005), 119.

2. Emile Durkheim, *Suicide: A Study in Sociology*, ed. John A. Spaulding and George Simpson (1897; New York: Free Press, 1951), http://www.bahaistudies.net/asma/suicide-durkheim.pdf.

3. Paul Caris, "Emile Durkheim (1858–1917)," Internet Encyclopedia of Philosophy, accessed January 15, 2020, http://www.iep.utm.edu/durkheim/.

4. Durkheim, quoted in Caris, "Emile Durkheim."

5. Caris, "Emile Durkheim."
6. Ali Shariati, quoted in "Ali Shariati: Islamic Fundamentalist, Marxist Ideologist, and Sufi Mystic," accessed January 15, 2020, https://web.archive.org/web/20141223143901/http://www.angelfire.com/az/rescon/ALSHAR.html.
7. Abbas Kiarostami, "A Conversation with Kiarostami," interview by Arsalan Mohammad, PBS, January 5, 2009, https://www.pbs.org/wgbh/pages/frontline/tehranbureau/2009/01/a-conversation-with-kiarostami.html.
8. Durkheim, *Suicide*.
9. Durkheim, *Suicide*.
10. See "Mahmoud Ahmadinejad," Wikipedia, updated January 14, 2020, https://en.wikipedia.org/wiki/Mahmoud_Ahmadinejad.
11. Mohsen Makhmalbaf, "IFFR 2013—Interview with Filmmakers Mohsen and Maysam Makhmabaf by Ronald Glasbergen," interview by Ronald Glasbergen, posted by grazenNL, January 31, 2013, video, 41:16, https://www.youtube.com/watch?v=7Cfu-6qqOYk.
12. See Ed Gonzalez, review of *Crimson Gold*, *Slant*, October 2, 2003, https://www.slantmagazine.com/film/review/crimson-gold; Jonathan Curiel, review of *Crimson Gold*, SF Gate, March 26, 2004, https://www.sfgate.com/movies/article/FILM-CLIPS-Also-opening-today-2803514.php; Roger Clarke, "Jafar Panahi: Home of the Brave," *Independent*, September 18, 2003, https://www.independent.co.uk/arts-entertainment/films/features/jafar-panahi-home-of-the-brave-87605.html; and "Jafar Panahi," Wikipedia, updated October 21, 2019, https://en.wikipedia.org/wiki/Jafar_Panahi.
13. Abbas Kiarostami, "A Double Bill with Binoche and Kiarostami," interview by Dennis Lim, *New York Times*, May 21, 2010, https://artsbeat.blogs.nytimes.com/2010/05/21/a-double-bill-with-binoche-and-kiarostami/?_r=0.
14. Quoted in Stuart Jeffries, "Landscapes of the Mind," *Guardian*, April 16, 2005, https://www.theguardian.com/film/2005/apr/16/art.
15. David Bordwell, "The Movie Looks Back at Us," David Bordwell's Website on Cinema, April 1, 2009, http://www.davidbordwell.net/blog/2009/04/01/the-movie-looks-back-at-us/
16. Deborah Young, "Iranian Film 'Shirin' a Rewarding Challenge," Reuters, August 29, 2008, https://www.reuters.com/article/us-film-shirin/iranian-film-shirin-a-rewarding-challenge-idUSN2933629320080829.
17. *Taste of Shirin* (2008), directed by Hamideh Razavi, bonus feature on *Shirin*, directed by Abbas Kiarostami (New York: Cinema Guild, 2010), DVD.
18. Abbas Kiarostami, "One of Your Scenes Is Missing," interview by Peter Lennon, *Guardian*, September 14, 2000, https://www.theguardian.com/film/2000/sep/15/culture.features1.
19. Kiarostami, "One of Your Scenes."
20. "Kiarostami on Making of Five," posted by Haridas B, June 17, 2008, video, 8:12 https://www.youtube.com/watch?v=xu9cbCJKLs8.
21. "Kiarostami on Making of Five," posted by Haridas B.
22. Abbas Kiarostami, "Abbas Kiarostami: In Conversation With . . . TIFF Bell Lightbox 2016," interview by Piers Hanley, posted by TIFF originals, July 5, 2016, video, 1:58:26, https://www.youtube.com/watch?v=-1CCPg5UY-E.
23. See "Khosrow and Shirin," Wikipedia, updated December 14, 2019, https://en.wikipedia.org/wiki/Khosrow_and_Shirin; "Nizami Ganjavi," Wikipedia, updated January 10, 2020, https://en.wikipedia.org/wiki/Nizami_Ganjavi; and "Shirin," Wikipedia, updated January 10, 2020, https://en.wikipedia.org/wiki/Shirin.
24. See "Gnosticism," Wikipedia, updated January 13, 2020, https://en.wikipedia.org/wiki/Gnosticism; "Mani (prophet)," Wikipedia, updated January 12, 2020, https://en.wikipedia.org/wiki/Mani_(prophet); and "Manichaeism," Wikipedia, updated January 12, 2020, https://en.wikipedia.org/wiki/Manichaeism.
25. Abbas Kiarostami, "*Shirin* as Described by Kiarostami," interview by Khatereh Khodaci, *Offscreen* 13, no. 1 (January 2009), http://offscreen.com/view/shirin_kiarostami.
26. See Heshmat Moayyad, "Farhad," *Encyclopædia Iranica*, December 15, 1999, http://www.iranicaonline.org/articles/farhad%20(1).
27. In order to show the universality of the story, Kiarostami "did a preliminary three-and-a-half-minute sketch for this film, 'Where Is My Romeo?' made for the Cannes film festival in

2007, using [footage from *Shirin*] but with the soundtrack from . . . Franco Zeffirelli's *Romeo and Juliet* (1968)." Jonathan Rosenbaum, "*Shirin* as Mirror," Cinema Guild Home Video, accessed January 15, 2020, http://cinemaguild.com/homevideo/ess_shirin.htm. See also Bordwell, "Movie Looks Back."

28. *Taste of Shirin.*
29. *Taste of Shirin.*
30. Quoted in Elena, *Cinema of Abbas Kiarostami*, 139.
31. *Taste of Shirin.*
32. Quoted in Geoff Andrew, "Unspoken Truths," *Sight & Sound* (July 2013): 40–43.
33. Abbas Kiarostami, "With Borrowed Eyes: An Interview with Abbas Kiarostami," interview by David Sterritt, *Film Comment*, July/August 2000, http://www.filmcomment.com/article/with-borrowed-eyes-an-interview-with-abbas-kiarostami/.
34. Kiarostami refers to this practice in many interviews. For an especially clear explanation, see "S. F. Said Interviews the Great Iranian Director about Rossellini's *Viaggio in Italia* (1953)," *Daily Telegraph*, September 28, 2002, http://www.telegraph.co.uk/culture/film/3583299/Filmmakers-on-film-Abbas-Kiarostami.html.
35. See "Aniconism in Islam," Wikipedia, updated January 6, 2020, https://en.wikipedia.org/wiki/Aniconism_in_Islam; Editors of Encyclopædia Britannica, "Aniconism," *Encyclopædia Britannica*, updated January 11, 2016, https://www.britannica.com/topic/aniconism; and "Aniconism," Wikipedia, updated December 29, 2019, https://en.wikipedia.org/wiki/Aniconism.

Chapter Eleven

The Soul of Art

Though Kiarostami made physical departures to Tuscany for *Certified Copy* and Tokyo for *Like Someone in Love,* his last two features carry though character types and thematic ideas from his preceding body of work. *Certified Copy* is about the ambiguous relationship between a British art critic named James Miller and a nameless French woman who seems at first to be an admiring fan and later appears to be his estranged or former wife. Their external connection remains mysterious, but their increasingly intense emotional interaction is difficult and deeply felt. The thesis of the critic's book entitled *Certified Copy* asserts that copies lead to the original and therefore certify its value. But Kiarostami believes the opposite. In a previously quoted interview published six years after the film's release, he explained that the relation between the original and the copy is not "at stake" in *Certified Copy* and that originality is always an illusion because any pure origin is "necessarily out of our reach [and therefore] we should just be happy with what we have."[1]

Kiarostami's sense of originality is simultaneously spiritual and aesthetic. No human being or work of art is absolutely unique, and artists are not independent of the general creative force that flows through them, whether they are unconsciously following an archetype or consciously copying other artists. Ultimately, there is only one Creator for Sufi artists like Rumi and Kiarostami, as is true in Islam generally: "O people! Be mindful of God who created you from a single soul, and from it created its mate and from the two spread a multitude of men and women."[2]

That one Creator is the essence of any living or man-made thing that façades of individual difference disguise: "The ordinary man, thinking that he is on the path of enlightenment often sees only a reflection of it. Light may be reflected upon a wall; the wall is the host to the light. Do not attach yourself to the brick of the wall, but seek the eternal original." Stylistic differences in works of art provide new containers to reveal the continuing benevolence of the Friend because, as another Sufi proverb has it, "Water needs an intermediary, a vessel, between it and the fire, if it is to be heated correctly."[3]

In his Iranian films, Kiarostami used nonactors to prevent the vessel from obscuring the life-giving water inside or the "walking stick" (see chapter 2) from becoming so ornate that it impeded the journey's purpose, but in *Certified Copy* he makes the point in reverse by casting Juliette Binoche, the internationally acclaimed superstar, in the leading role. While James, the famous film critic, is played by William Shimell, an opera singer unknown to most filmgoers, Binoche's character (identified only as Elle in the credits) is the anonymous owner of small-town antique shop and his adoring fan. In the opening scene, James receives applause on a stage, while Elle is introduced as a rapt auditor of his packed lecture.

Kiarostami and Binoche became friends in the mid-1990s after Binoche won both the French César and Venice Film Festival best actress awards for her performance in Krzysztof Kieslowski's *Three Colors: Blue* (1993), and possibly through contact with Binoche, Kiarostami may have realized that he and Kieslowski had much in common. As previously noted, Kiarostami said that in his "cinema the most important subject matter is human beings and their souls."[4] He recalled his decision to cast Binoche in *Certified Copy* (for which she won the 2010 best actress at Cannes) as based on a spiritual perception: "The film started to build according to the story that I was telling, but also according to my knowledge of her as a woman with her vulnerability, with her sensitivity, with what I knew about her soul."[5]

In a documentary appended to the *Certified Copy* DVD, Binoche reflects on her answer to Kiarostami's question, "Why do you act?" by saying that what she goes through "as an explorer of the soul gives me so much joy because I'm entering a world I'm discovering, gaining and letting go of knowledge at the same time."[6] In the same documentary, Kiarostami acknowledges that Binoche succeeded in letting go of her movie-star persona so that, as the shoot proceeded, she "had changed into just one of the crew." He adds, "She was showing great interest in her character, and she was giving a highly professional performance in front of the camera. At the same time, it appeared that she had no other contracts or concerns. In front of the camera, she hadn't changed into a star. Instead, she'd become an ordinary person but with all her talents."[7]

Kieslowski, too, realized the extent to which a public image obscured his purpose. An astute interviewer observed that the more concrete and tangible his films became, the "more metaphysical they seem to become," adding that by using "more and more closeups [and moving] ever nearer to the characters and objects," he seemed to be "searching for something beyond the concrete or the physical." When asked directly what he was trying to capture, Kieslowski replied, "Perhaps the soul. In any case, a truth which I myself haven't found." The remark prompted Kieslowski to recall a fifteen-year-old French viewer who, after seeing *The Double Life of Veronique* (1991) three times, realized that "there is such a thing as the soul, that it really exists."[8]

Kiarostami would have concurred when Kieslowski went on to say, "That's something beautiful that [makes it] worth all the money, energy, time, patience, torturing yourself, killing yourself, taking thousands of decisions, so that one young girl in Paris should realize that there is such a thing as a soul. These are the best viewers. There aren't many of them but perhaps there are a few."[9] In *Double Life*, two physically identical young women (played by Irene Jacob) lead parallel but ultimately quite different lives. They are not absolutely the same; they are not absolutely different. Both are variant copies of an unknown original. Kiarostami might have been interested in Kieslowski for practical reasons, as well. Both were sponsored by the same MK2 French production company, and both were expatriate artists who had been subjected to crude political censorship in their home countries. (*Certified Copy* was eventually shown in such limited Iranian venues as film clubs and universities but was banned from general release because Binoche's "attire" was deemed to be too revealing.)

Kiarostami may also have had an interest in the work of Milan Kundera in common with Binoche because her breakout role had been in Philip Kaufman's 1988 film adaptation of Kundera's novel *The Unbearable Lightness of Being*. Kundera, too, was an expatriate artist after departing Communist Czechoslovakia, and Kiarostami quoted him in the press book for the Cannes premier of *Ten* (see chapter 8). In his own work, he parallels Kundera's practice of conceiving his entire oeuvre as continuous, with themes and character types recurring in successive works. James, for example, is a variation of Behzad in *The Wind Will Carry Us*. Both are as spiritually shallow as they are impressively literate and pretentiously verbose.

But Kiarostami's sense of loving life as the Friend's gift especially synchronizes with Kieslowski's luminous vision in *The Double Life of Veronique* and the *Three Colors* trilogy. In *A Taste of Cherry*, *The Wind Will Carry Us*, *Certified Copy*, and *Like Someone in Love*, Kiarostami elaborates the suicide theme Kieslowski develops in *Blue*, *White*, and *Red*. In these films both directors explore suicide in forms of personal loss that metastasize into cynical withdrawals from life in general. While *Blue* is about the resilience that follows personal loss, its theme music composed to celebrate international unity indirectly celebrates the endurance of love in a climate that continually threatens war.

This is the overt point of Roberto Rossellini's *Journey to Italy* (1954), the film that most directly influenced *Certified Copy*. The domestic war between a wealthy British couple traveling in Italy portrays the underlying causes of national wars and social injustice. Kiarostami knew that political assumptions would underlie the experience of watching *Certified Copy* because the audience would think of him as an Iranian director making a film for the first time in a Western country and because of the seemingly irreconcilable cultural difference that separates Iran from the West. Accordingly, James generally insists on speaking only English, though it becomes apparent that he is fluent in French and Italian, and there is one particularly ugly scene where he becomes disproportionately hostile toward the continental custom of tasting wine for approval because he thinks it is hypocritical and meaningless. His intolerance, which is inconsistent with his overall sophistication, is prefigured by the arrogance of the lead British character in *Journey to Italy*, which takes its viewers on a historical tour of a country ravaged by many centuries of war and natural disaster.

In an interview given after *Taste of Cherry*, a film in which war is treated as mass suicide, Kiarostami said that the similarity some critics noticed between his films and Italian neorealists "had to do with Italy after the war and here in Iran, you see a situation which is again, a [country] after a war, an eight-year-old war."[10] As in *Taste of Cherry*, there is a connection between individual ingratitude for life and the venting of compensatory aggression that, on a collective scale, results in wars in which large numbers of people unaware of what motivates them slaughter each other for some unnecessary cause. The major message of *Journey to Italy* is determined by its post–World War II setting, where the most devastating war of that time becomes a metonym of all wars.

Casting against type as Kiarostami did with Binoche, Rossellini cast Ingrid Bergman, his iconic wife, in the unhappy role of Katherine, a woman trapped in a soured marriage to Alex Joyce, her absurdly selfish husband. While Alex arranges to sell a villa he has inherited from his uncle, Katherine finds temporary relief from their mutual torture as a naïve, sensitive viewer of Roman art treasures, most of which are copies of Greek originals, just as she and her husband are variations on eternally infantile conflicts made present in the film through allusions to imperial history, epic poetry, and classical drama. Rossellini ends his film by showing that, in light of human history, it is virtually miraculous that human love has survived.

On the last seemingly hopeless leg of their journey to Italy and through the history of their species, and with Alex coldly planning the details of their divorce, their car is brought to a halt by a huge crowd celebrating the feast of San Genaro, the patron saint of Naples. Outside the car Katherine is swept away by the surging crowd so that Alex, improbably clearing a path to reach her, finally folds her in a passionate embrace: "Oh, I don't want to lose you!" Katherine exclaims, as a man marching between two young priests holds up his crutches and waves them across each other at the tail end of the religious procession, which takes a seeming eternity to pass. Rossellini unapologetically says that, looked at logically, we ought long ago to have destroyed ourselves. Only a miracle, however much we may scoff at such things, can explain our survival.

Their immersion in the crowd also accentuates the comic obverse of realizing common identity in an earlier scene, where Alex upbraids an Italian servant woman at the villa with "How dare you speak to me that way!" when he can't understand a word she says. The creation of *Journey to Italy* makes the point in reverse: an Italian director presenting a film in English, starring a British actor, his Swedish wife, and numerous Italians in supporting roles to portray human interdependence, anticipating Kiarostami as an Iranian director presenting a British opera singer, a French superstar, and a supporting cast speaking alternately in English, French, and Italian.

In addition to elements of *Blue* and *Journey to Italy* in *Certified Copy*, there are also echoes of previous Kiarostami films. Like James, Behzad in *The Wind Will Carry Us* exemplifies the separation of head and heart, while the Driver in *Ten*, though more complex, is similarly compelled by her professional activities, even though she loves her son and is desperate to maintain an emotional bond with him. In *Certified Copy*, Kiarostami divides the Driver's internal conflict between James and Elle. James is driven by his profession and his intellect, while Elle focuses on personal relationships. Binoche explained these divisions in terms of how she and Shimell approached their roles:

> It was hard at first for William to understand that acting is not about memorizing lines. [It is primarily about] emotional and sensational memory, not intellectual memory. His character is more rational and intellectual, [but just as] some writers are more related to the body or the heart, his character stays on the head and ignores what makes the body functional, [while my] character is more related to the hidden side.

She extended this attempt to touch the hidden side (the soul) by saying that serious film "has to transform you without you noticing it," and that this effect "comes with silence, a way of hearing, a tone of voice or gesture, [which is] beyond mental capacity."[11]

Certified Copy opens in the town of Arezzo, where James's lecture centers on the theme of translation, Kiarostami's metaphor of transmission between parents and children, works of art by different artists, and separate works by a single artist: "I am particularly interested in the idea that the word *original* refers to birth, [and] I would take the parallel to its extreme and draw a parallel between reproduction in art and reproduction in the human race [because] it might be said we are only the DNA replicas of our ancestors." While there are similarities between James and Elle as competing egos, there is also a significant difference between a predominance in some people of aggressive rivalry and in others of nurturing protection.

Outside the frame of any particular culture, there is a universal association between varied forms of war as a childish need for personal power and the adult responsibility for the survival of the world's children by preserving their capacity to love rather than fear the life they have been given. In *Wind*, *Ten*, *Certified Copy*, and *Like Someone in Love*, mature adults are people whose souls are advanced enough to protect children because they themselves are no longer childish. Behzad is childishly egotistic and careless in his treatment of Farzad, while the Driver in *Ten* begins as if she were her child's equal and ends as the guide he needs. The same is true for Elle in *Certified Copy*. She begins by squabbling with her teenage son and by looking up to James as if he were her brilliant leader and ends by sensing that James is a child and that it is her responsibility to keep him from the mental suicide Kiarostami portrays in *Taste of Cherry*. The final realization of her gift would be to accept the personal privilege of protecting an individual child and the artistic privilege of protecting the world's children.

In the opening scene, the camera emphasizes the disparity between a tour de force display of intellect and maturity of soul. After a grand entrance in which James with affected indifference says he would rather be out in the sunshine, and after he has condescendingly lavished praise on his Italian translator, who also receives a round of applause, the camera conveys a different kind of translation. With the applause continuing, Elle's midteen son Julien, who may or may not be James's son, enters down the same aisle through which both of his parents have separately entered. Julien as the literal child is, as Elle later says, the "certified copy of his father," and as the film eventually reveals, James, the acclaimed middle-aged adult, is just as childish as Julien.

Elle, James, and Julien are all dressed in navy blue, which connects them as a family, and Julien, whose name alliterates with James's, has long hair and a confident, somewhat hostile look that resembles that of his father. After James mentions that some of his readers may know that the idea for his book came to him while he was in Florence in the Piazza della Signoria, where, as we later discover, he was fascinated by seeing a mother and her small child repeatedly return, we see Julien looking bored and unhappy. The camera stays on Julien as James says that the word *original* derives from a Latin root that means "being born" and that he would like to draw a parallel between reproduction in art and reproduction in the human race, just before a cut to Elle talking to the translator and then looking back to the boy. Literally or not, James is Julien's origin, just as he himself is prefigured by innumerable aspirants to greatness, regardless of their degree of general acclaim.

At one point during James's speech, we hear the faint sound of a church bell tolling outside. It tolls again loudly as Elle and Julien, who has forced her to leave early, emerge into the sunlight. Thereafter, it tolls to celebrate both weddings and (implicitly) funerals, until at the film's culmination it symphonically reminds us of the mortality that James vainly rushes through time to escape. Elle walks ahead of Julien (like the woman who led a child and inspired James's book) toward the fast-food restaurant, where Julien baits her about being romantically rather than intellectually interested in James. She listens calmly as if she is used to his teasing but is provoked when he taunts her for telling James not to include Julien's surname in the book he signed for him. The audience can retrospectively speculate about the literal meaning of Elle's instruction, but the thematic point is that James does not take responsibility for Julien or for anyone else because his readers are also his heirs.

Having learned from Julien that Elle has given James her phone number, we are abruptly taken to a frontal shot of a dark stairway descending between ancient, bricked walls. In the small, arched frame at the top, James is carrying his suitcase (as Julien carried his backpack), which he sets down before he descends to the showroom of Elle's antique shop, as a low-pitched clock tolls the hour, echoing the outdoor bell. The descent to an ancient darkness evokes Behzad's descent to the milking stall in *Wind*, a womb symbol connoting death and potential rebirth.

No one is present, and as James waits for Elle to arrive, he inspects Renaissance statues of women and children. The clock sound hints at inevitable death, and the film suggests that people like James (who are likely to be Kiarostami viewers) should redirect their gaze toward living things rather than artifacts of the past. They should learn to use such artifacts (including the films of Kiarostami) not as ends in themselves but as directives to the beauty one can presently perceive in people and in nature. In the dark antique shop, only dead replicas are visible, and as if he were becoming subliminally alarmed, James calls out, "Hello?" but cannot otherwise dispel the silence.

The camera comes to rest on a bust of Cupid, the child who is the symbolic link between James and Elle as well as between the people of the world who need to love their children more than power or prestige. With James trapped in the womb of his own ego, the camera remains on Cupid for an extraordinary forty-one seconds, while we hear Elle's voice from the front of the store and then her footsteps before she arrives (maternally carrying a cat) to rescue James from his isolation, just as she tries to do in the larger course of the film.

While the sound track has James presciently saying antiques are admirable but dangerous and that they should go out into the sunshine, the camera frames a symbolic source of light by focusing at the beginning and end of the scene on a three-pronged lamp with a torso like that of a slim woman. The "neck" extends up on either side of the curved-up "arms" to a bright-white light emanating from a golden shade. Four small figures from prehistoric civilizations, two on each side, stand facing the lamp, giving it a timeless aura, as if the fertility statue they appear to worship is the generative source of all we are.

Though Kiarostami is a feminist in the sense that he portrays women as intellectually equal to men in *Ten*, *Shirin*, and *Certified Copy*, he is more concerned with the advanced nurturing soul regardless of gender, as exemplified by the old door maker in *Where Is the Friend's House?* and the doctor in *The Wind Will Carry Us* and the friend of the Driver in *Ten* who courageously accepts painful change. In the course of the film, Elle comes to resemble those characters, and as the church bells ring out, their reminder of transience and the "generosity of God" that Badii and Behzad ignore, Elle leads James up into the light, where she takes the wheel of her silver car, driving him as *Ten*'s Driver drives Amin and as Kiarostami drives the viewer to a "place [that he and we will] find interesting."

On the way, James tells a joke about a man walking on the beach who finds a brass lamp, from which a genie appears, who grants him three wishes. The man is hot and tired, so he requests an everlasting bottle of Coca Cola, but the genie says he is in a hurry and demands that he make his other two wishes, to which the man replies, "Okay, two more bottles of Coca Cola." James thinks the joke's moral is that the guy is so simpleminded he doesn't realize what he has been offered. But the joke is on him. He has set the parameters of his time with Elle and Julien (their lives together on earth) by insisting that he must be back by 9:00 p.m. to catch a flight. As he tells the joke, the camera stays on Elle because she and Julien are the freely offered gifts that James is not wise enough to choose.

Before they arrive at the "interesting place," they exchange airy remarks about beauty being in the eye of the beholder, referring to works by Jasper Johns and Andy Warhol's soup can, as they pass vistas of cypress trees on golden hills that evoke scenes from *And Life Goes On* and *The Wind Will Carry Us*, images of natural beauty that transcend and outlast cerebral experiments. When they arrive at the art museum in nearby Lucignano, the parking lot is full, not because people come to see original treasures, but because the sacred aura of its wedding chapel promises happy, long-lasting unions. That is, the copies people seek there are of loving relationships and healthy children rather than access to greatness, and in fact, the museum's most notable work is itself a copy. A bell tolls out this hope as Elle's car descends an embankment to the parking lot in a shot evoking a similar descent to the Natural History Museum in *Taste of Cherry*, an image that connects the literally suicidal Badii to the naïvely suicidal James.

Marriage is briefly an affirming counterpoint in *Taste of Cherry* when an engaged couple asks Badii to take their picture, just as another couple asks the demurring James to pose for a picture with them outside the chapel. In *Close-Up*, marriage symbolizes hope for a more just and secure society when the cab driver tells the young soldier who has come to arrest Sabzian that, when his military service is over, he can go home and get married, and marriage as the essence of a better human future comprises the whole plot of *Through the Olive Trees*. In *ABC Africa*, Kiarostami visits a house in Uganda where two teachers who have lost their spouses to AIDS and who each have one child are about to marry and form a new family.

The idea of forming a new family or reforming one that has been lost is an emphatic motif in *Certified Copy*. Julien repeatedly telephones Elle, much to her annoyance, though there is never any question that she would leave him as James has done if he is literally his father or as he metaphorically does by caring only for his reputation and career rather than the children that his intellect might guide.

While walking from the parking lot, James asks Elle, "Did you get married here?" At that moment her cell phone rings, and by answering it as she customarily does throughout the film by saying "Oui?" Kiarostami establishes a bilingual pun—"Did *we* get married here?"—in light of the subsequent question of whether she and James really are or were married. Identifying as "we" rather than "I" is a thematic thread in a film that makes much of language as a form of division and national pride.

After the phone call, Elle complains that when she tries to protect Julien, he says things like "We're all going to die, so what?" James flippantly replies, "If a philosopher or a writer says this, we think it's wonderful," but Elle feels rather than thinks that life is precious and doesn't want to renounce the possibility of a loving relationship as an essential part of the best life offers. At first, she seems cynical about marriage and children: "If people knew what a hard time they were going to have, they wouldn't have those stupid smiles on their faces on their wedding day. Kids just want to have fun. We have to worry about the consequences. He was standing in the rain. I said, 'You'll get a cold and die.' He said, 'So what?'"

For Kiarostami, whose whole oeuvre is devoted to reminding us of natural beauty and human courage, James's cavalier stoicism is phony and shallow: "The world is full of indispensable men. He's quite right. We're all going to die. Nothing lasts forever." Elle says, "Oh, come on, this is just for books. When you're alone and you're dealing with it, it's fucking hard. I'm sorry." And James is wrong about nothing lasting forever because general qualities in humanity do last, and Kiarostami consciously and Elle instinctively work to keep the best of these alive. It is Elle who identifies with the loving hopes of the young couples as the film proceeds, while James becomes increasingly embittered because his absolute egotism has reached a dead end.

This is shown by his remaining oblivious to the lesson of the particular painting that Elle has brought him to see, even though it epitomizes the thesis of his book. The idea that the museum's most prized painting is an admitted copy satirizes the insensitivity to art that propels thousands of tourists to momentarily glimpse famous originals in Italy and France. For Kiarostami, there is no such thing as an original, and the value of a work of art depends on the feeling it stirs in the viewer rather than its provenance, the reputation of the artist, or its monetary value. A copy can do this just as well as an original, and every work and every person are themselves copies, whether they have been dubbed originals or not.

Elle takes James to see a painting of a woman in a gold dress, a "*Mona Lisa* type," that she calls an "original copy." A guide then tells an arriving group,

> This is the famous *Musa Polimnia*, the portrait of a woman whose dramatic story is told on the cartel next to the painting. For years, the painting was believed to be Roman art. It wasn't until the twentieth century, about fifty years ago, that it was revealed to be the work of a skilled forger from Naples. However, the museum decided to conserve this fabulous portrait as an original. It is actually as beautiful as the original. It was made in the eighteenth century, and it was considered as an original for two hundred years. After the Second World War, in-depth research revealed even the name of the forger who made this amazing work. The museum then decided to keep it with great care. In a sense, it's our *Mona Lisa*. The original is in the Herculaneum near Naples. It was discovered as part of a Roman fresco. The excavation director was from Tuscany, and he commissioned the forger to make this perfect copy so as to claim it was found in his region and use its prestige for Tuscany.

James muses that the original painting was only a reproduction of the girl in the picture, and "in that sense, even the *Mona Lisa* was a reproduction," either of the portrait's subject or an ideal image in his mind: "Do you think her smile was original or that Leonardo just cast her smile like that?" He is unable, however, to see the correspondence between his artistic theories and his own life. Elle, on the other hand, attempts a reproduction, a copy of their honeymoon or perhaps just a honeymoon with someone real or imagined. The point, Kiarostami implies in such films as *Close-Up* and *The Wind Will Carry Us*, is to give yourself to the feeling regardless of the facts, to appreciate the emotional moment rather than the factual or journalistic truth. In responding to Elle's question about where he got the idea for his book, James has an intuitive rather than a conscious understanding that his book about originals and copies unconsciously concerns a larger, ongoing creation.

Elle says she didn't hear the part of his lecture where James explained how he got the idea for his book because she was leaving with her son, which is the point of the difference between her active participation in creation as opposed to James's distanced theories. But deep down, James does sense that creation in life and creation in art require love, the source of the essential life force he is imperceptibly losing:

> I was in Florence for a cultural conference, staying in a hotel. Every morning as I got up for my shower, I would see the same woman coming down the street. When she got to the corner in front of the hotel, she would stop and look back until she saw the little boy. And when she'd seen him, she'd turn and walk on. It was the same at the next corner. They just never walked together. The mother would be fifty yards ahead, but the boy made no attempt to catch up. They were only together in the piazza.

When Elle asks why he found them so intriguing, James says he already knew them, a teaser for viewers trying to determine the literal truth of their relationship, but in another sense, he may already know them because he was or still is the little boy trailing behind the more spiritually advanced Elle.

The *David* statue in the piazza that the mother was "telling the kid something about is only a copy. The original's in the Accademia. But the mother hadn't told the boy that, I'm sure. The boy was looking up at the statue as though it was a genuine, original authentic work of art." As James speaks, he looks up as if he were the boy, while Elle tears up, identifying as a cinema spectator might do from empathetic experience.

The particular statue that the mother and child contemplate is also a symbol of male power and aggression. The 1501 Michelangelo original was placed in the Florence public square. Its biblical subject represents the resolve of the small republic of Florence to defend itself from larger city-states, and the statue's resolute eyes warningly faced Rome. In 1873 it was moved to the Accademia Gallery in Florence, and in 1910, the replica was placed in the piazza. The statue was a news item in 2010 (the year *Certified Copy* was released) because of an ownership dispute between the municipality of Florence and the Italian Culture Ministry.[12] The issue played into Kiarostami's satire of people who confuse the value of art with ownership and prestige, a major theme of *Close-Up* (see chapter 5).

When James describes the mother and son in Florence, he is standing because he has just brought the coffee, and he gestures theatrically, while Elle sits and observes like a film spectator. His performance moves her because she identifies with the woman he describes, who may or may not be her. James thrusts his hand out as he says he would see the same woman coming down the street. He looks up and raises his hand with the index finger extended as he describes their progress until they got to the corner, at which point he crosses his arms to imitate the woman's pausing after she spotted the little boy behind her. He resumes gesturing with his index finger in this over-the-top performance to accompany the woman proceeding to the next corner, which he could see because his room was on the corner of a building, where he saw her through one window as she approached and another after she passed. The windows conform to the Kiarostami motif that we are only able to view the world through a preconceived frame, a frame that the auteur tries to exceed through the ambiguous identities of the actors in James's story-within-a-story and then of James, Elle, and Julien themselves.

At the end of his monologue, Elle says, "Your coffee's cold," as he smiles and sits down, satisfied with his performance, which has been technically accomplished but cold. After he exits to take a cell-phone call, the coffee bar lady playing the spectator within her own cultural frame praises Elle for having such an attentive husband: "He looks like he's still courting you." Elle replies that he's never home and he only speaks his own language: "All he cares about is himself, his job, and his friends." Then, when James reenters, the coffee bar lady unwittingly initiates what at first appears to be a charade by commenting, "How strange you don't speak Italian after five years here with your family." Elle whispers that the lady mistook James for her husband—"Obviously, we make a good couple."—and James, immediately catching on, reveals that he understands the lady speaking in Italian just as he later understands and responds to Elle in French: "My family lives their lives, and I live mine. They speak their language, and I speak mine."

The abrupt rudeness of his reply signals a reversal of affect. The thespian grace he displayed in recounting the origin of his book is consistent with his actor's appearance and charm, but for Kiarostami, theatrics obscure the soul. Then, when James seemingly pretends to play the role of the husband the café lady thought he was, he is no longer acting, and the childish egotism that is often masked by a celebrity image is glaringly exposed. In general, the soul James now projects denies and crushes love in others because his adult experience has crushed his own hope of love, as is the case with innumerable cynics like himself.

This loss of hope in the possibility of human connection is first expressed by Elle sarcastically quoting him, saying, "My son and wife live their lives, and I live mine!" and then metaphorically expressed by a call from Julien, who is searching for something he lost, just after they leave the coffee bar. Elle interrupts the call to comment on the same center-of-the-universe mindset that the Driver faces in Amin: "The certified copy of his father! He cannot hear anyone, just does his own thing!" Then, getting back to Julien, she delivers the message that Kiarostami wants to convey to the viewer in the larger course of the film: "Ah, you found it. Now do your homework, and stop calling me."

The corresponding assignment for Elle and James is to discover who they really are by becoming aware of the extent to which they have become trapped in the adult roles circumstance has cast them to play. Now, when the introductory roles of celebrity and admirer have been dropped and it appears initially that they are consciously playing different roles, their before and after "real" selves become ambiguous so that their souls can be revealed. When Elle describes Julien as the "spitting image of his father, stubborn as a mule," she seems to be referring to James in his post-coffee-bar role. But

James breaks through one of the parameters of that role, the one that particularly provokes Elle, by suddenly responding in French, as if speaking Elle's language is an intuitive gesture of kindly intent: "There's always a way with kids."

There may be a way for James, too, as there may be a way for Behzad at the end of *The Wind Will Carry Us*, but the way depends on breaking through their clueless frames of smug superiority. Elle and James are spontaneously trying to break through in the subsequent dialogue, where each speaks in the other's language. Elle says in English that she can't find the "way with kids" because James is never there and that two parents are needed to play "good cop, bad cop." James asks in French, "Am I supposed to play the bad cop?" to which Elle responds in English, "No need to play, darling." Stung by this, James reverts defensively to English, "Sometimes one parent has to be away," to which Elle, now going on the offensive, snaps in English, "But in your case, it's constant." James's linguistic switching as an emotional attempt to lessen hostility applies to relations between nations, as well. The initial post-coffee-bar dialogue between James and Elle suggests that language and culture are acquired roles and that people might begin to free themselves from these roles by witnessing their relativity in a multilingual film.

When Elle complains that having to play both good cop and bad cop is "unbearable," the film shows us that it is also freeing The important thing is to "get real," the thematically resonant phrase she uses to lash out at James for his unhelpful advice about Julien. As they speak at odds about defining roles in the narrative they are trying to form, they walk down a lovely street of ancient stone walls and flower boxes, a setting independent of strenuous striving, just before they descend a stairway to the museum. Elle goes on ahead, leaving James sitting dejectedly on a bench in a dark alcove outside the chapel. Just behind him, the glass of a framed poster reflects his back.

At first, he refuses to leave this frame when Elle returns and asks him to let himself be photographed with a young couple in the chapel who have begged her to get James so that the four of them can be photographed together because Elle told them that they had been married there fifteen years earlier, and it appears to the young couple that the chapel's reputed luck will bless their marriage, too. After refusing Elle and then the groom, James finally accedes when the bride, in her white dress and carrying her bouquet, pulls him by the arm—"Sir, you can't refuse."—and physically overcomes his inertia, foreshadowing Elle's similar attempt in the final scene.

James is trapped in his postmodern pessimism, and when he and Elle leave the chapel, the bells of death and renewal are tolling as she says in French, "What you said was beautiful. But why did you have to sound so ironic?" Maintaining the language difference that sustains emotional separation, James defends himself in English: "It's not cynical. I saw the hopes and dreams in their eyes. I couldn't bring myself to support their illusion. I know it won't last long. They'll get a taste of reality later. You can't expect a tree to keep its blossoms after spring is over." During this voiced consolation for what he considers inevitable disappointment, the couple walks down streets that resemble dark, shadowy corridors, until they emerge into a sunlit patio with many green plantings, where Elle asks what will happen when spring ends and James responds, the "Garden of Leaflessness," quoting the title of a Persian poem, from which he then quotes the additional line: "Who dares say that it isn't beautiful?"

The poem's author is known for a pessimistic vision that is as much at odds with the visual surroundings of nascent greenery as its leafless metaphor is with Kiarostami's hope for renewal in the snow scenes of bare, black trees in *Roads of Kiarostami*. Mehdi Akhavan-Sales, known primarily by his pen name of Akhavan, was a highly regarded mid-twentieth-century poet who felt that Iranian culture had steadily deteriorated from its pre-Islamic glory to a sterile nadir under the shahs. The failure of Mohammad Mosaddeq's 1953 coup aggravated this belief, and his later poetry alludes to Zoroastrianism and implicitly to the ascendance of Ahriman, the Zoroastrian principle of evil in contemporary life.[13] But "The Leafless Garden" contains a seed of hope because, like James, it can choose a different fate than the one it expects. Even though the "depressed orchard / Expects no spring" and its "eye sheds no warm luster / And on his face no leaf or smile grows," the orchard has the choice James must make at the end of the film: "It can grow or not grow, wherever he wants or doesn't want."[14]

For Kiarostami, the choice to grow is impelled by the contemplation of nature, and as he said of the faces of the women in *Shirin* and as he shows in Elle, they are as beautiful as the birds, trees, and waves he celebrates in *Five* and his photography. In 2006, he named an installation shown in London *The Leafless Garden*, not to lament sterility as Akhavan had done, but to direct people's gaze to the unabated glory of creation.[15] In a later interview, he described it as an installation of one hundred realistic prints of trees surrounded by mirrors to give the impression of being in an infinite forest: "I found it quite striking that this museum in London was on a street lined with beautiful trees, and I wondered why people would pay to see my artificial trees rather than just observing and admiring the trees outside. I even shot some footage from outside and inside where you see people rushing in from outside passing real trees to see these paper prints of trees." Kiarostami extended a friend's comment that the purpose of the exhibit was to make people appreciate real trees to a philosophical reflection that underlies the purpose of art in *Certified Copy*: "And this is what our life is about. . . . When things are in their usual background, we take them for granted, we need some context, person, or artist to show to us and tell us [how] to see it."[16]

In Kiarostami's 2010 journey to Italy, the leafless despair of James serves as a foil to Elle's courageous hope. Back in the street, the bell tolls once as Elle sees something that interests her. The camera stays on her as she circles around toward the left, until we see the black lower limbs of two sculpted figures in the middle of a fountain. Though we still don't see the sculpture, the two argue over its artistic merits, but their judgments are clear projections of their own states of mind. Elle likes the way the woman rests her hand on the man's shoulder, while James says he "has nothing to do but protect that woman, [and] you can't be immortalized for that."

The idea that reactions to a work of art, even those of a sophisticated critic, are emotional projections is suggested by the camera not showing the statue until Elle and James stop in front of a wall mirror that reflects it. Their simplistic black-and-white evaluations are indicated because the black statue appears white in the mirror as James says, "All you see is a woman resting her head on the shoulder of that monster," and Elle replies, "It's because he protects her that he's become eternal." Then their argument turns childish: "It's stupid," James says, to which Elle retorts, "Then your book is stupid too, [because you wrote] that the 'personal, the creative, [and] the inventive' were not what mattered," to which James, now furious that his presumed superior opinion has been challenged, blurts out, "What you're saying makes me hate everything. Art, originals, copies, this statue, you, everything."

Elle then tries to win this unwinnable game on the basis of popular taste: "Let's go ask people." She returns with a couple fifteen to twenty years older than they are who have come to Italy for the fifth time because "it's a big open-air art museum." The woman, wanting to present herself as knowledgeable, answers Elle's question about the statue's quality as if she were recalling a paragraph from an art book: "I feel that the statue or the artist, via the statue, has tried to show us the sheer power of a man hewn out of a single block of stone." But that is not what Elle wants to hear because it does not coincide with what she overheard the woman say before, which is closer to her own feeling.

Because the woman now seems to be at a loss for words, her husband interjects his version of what he thought she said: "What touched you in this sculpture was the serenity on the woman's face as she rests on his shoulder. You said she gave the impression of having someone to rely on. Of not being alone." This version suits Elle perfectly, and in conscious triumph but with authentic longing, she smiles warmly at James.

Like the coffee bar lady, the older man now becomes an interpreter of the real-life narrative he observes, which is doubly ironic because the film's viewers are themselves uncertain of the relationship. Taking James aside, he now becomes an actor in a story he has just invented, a copy of a preset narrative absorbed at a prior time:

> You are a knowledgeable man, but you could be my son. That's why I'd like to give you a piece of fatherly advice. I think that all she wants from you is that you walk beside her and lay your hand on her shoulder. That's all she's longing for. But for her it's vital. I don't want to know what happened between you, but all your problems can be solved by a simple gesture. Do it, and set yourself free.

The advice reinforces the subliminal drama by repeating a universal need, and it echoes Elle's affection for the statue because she likes the way the woman rests her hand on the man's shoulder. In the documentary appended to the DVD, we see this image of affection that is never actually shown in the film. While the woman has her hand on the man's left shoulder, a winged Cupid (evoking Julien) rests on his right shoulder, with a stream of water coming out of his mouth. Leaving this concrete image to the imagination in the actual film has the effect of universalizing the emotion, and this is even more apparent when we discover in the documentary that the statue itself is a fiction that was erected in the fountain expressly for the film.

Even more relevant to the idea that we react with equal validity to a work of art whether it is an original, a copy, or a cinematic fake is Binoche's recollection of how in real life she didn't like the idea that her character liked the statue because it represented a "prehistoric protection" that women don't need any more.[17] Her initial reaction was based on a sincerely felt Western feminism, but in the overall context of the film, she may have come to realize that everyone regardless of gender needs to be lovingly reassured. If at a certain point that assurance is not forthcoming, a person in need, like Elle and the Driver's friend at the end of *Ten*, must herself become the rock he or she can depend on.

Consciously or unconsciously taking the man's advice to heart, James puts his hand on Elle's shoulder as they walk to a restaurant. Things start out well, and the motif of language as a marker of harmony or strife is keynoted as both speak French to each other in pleasantries about how hungry they are (a metaphor of emotional need) and how the charming restaurant is empty because "it's too late for lunch and too early dinner" (a metaphor of their stage of life).

Elle smiles happily as James, assuming an in-charge male confidence, snaps his fingers to summon the waiter and orders a bottle of red wine in Italian. Then he asks Elle in French if the wines are good in this restaurant. She responds by joking, "Not as good as ours but better than yours." But the innocent remark irritates James's already-wounded ego, especially because his superior judgment as an art critic has been challenged in the preceding scene, and after Elle returns from glamorizing herself in the bathroom with earrings, a necklace, and fresh lipstick, we see a different James, whose fear-based hostility progresses in the course of the scene from petulance to cruelty.

Kiarostami's original Farsi script probably included careful instructions for Binoche and Shimell to switch languages to express harmony or hostility. The scene in the restaurant implies that maturity of soul involves recognizing the similarities of people in varied cultures while at the same time respecting their differences. Having suffered the exposure of personal weakness after the identity switch in the coffee bar, James tries to recover his self-confidence by lashing out in English, first belittling the waiter, who he thinks is ignoring him, and then ranting about the "stupid" convention of sampling the wine and then having to say it's wonderful even if it's "corky," as he says this one is: "If it's bad, you've got to say so."

Deep down James isn't talking about wine at all but about the lies he has told himself concerning his responsibilities to a wife and child. But in denial, his increasingly vicious attacks, first on the wine and then on Elle, are now expressed exclusively in English: When she jokingly tries in French to restore the happier mood with which they entered the restaurant, James explodes with disproportionate rage: "How could I forget, the French know everything about wine." Then, after pouring her a glass, he spits out the frustration he has apparently harbored for years: "You like it? You drink it!"

Elle's response resonates with Kiarostami's overall philosophy as reflected by Khayyam's "Prefer the present" quoted by the doctor in *The Wind Will Carry Us* (see chapter 6). Remonstrating with controlled anger in French, Elle speaks to James as a viewer might have wished to speak to Badii or Behzad: "Are you out of your mind? Why are you doing this? Can't you just enjoy what you have instead of moaning? Can't you just be here for a change? Look around you. Be here!"

But Elle, too, is not herself quite ready to be realistically where she is. While James has resigned himself to living in the leafless garden, Elle wants to rekindle a honeymoon. She has brought James to Lucignano, just as someone hoping to evoke romantic feelings might take a partner or a hoped-for partner to a romantic movie. Vicariously celebrating with the young couples she sees through the restaurant window as if it were a movie screen, Elle wants to join them, to live their lives as she formerly lived or imagines she lived hers, but instead, she and James are thrown back into their disappointed lives once the movie ends.

James refuses to look when she sees the couple they were photographed with in the chapel, now just outside the window, saying in French, "What a dream place. Look how sweet they are. Two lovebirds." Then, despite his sour expression, she laughs, trying in vain to lighten the mood and make him join the "film" she is trying to create by imitating the characters she sees in the frame of her fantasy. Just before she put on her makeup and "costume," Elle turned to look out at the revelers in the street through the venetian blind in the bathroom, as if she were preparing to join them. Now, she invites James to animate her storyboard: "Look at your wife, who's made herself pretty for you. Look! Open your eyes."

James's reply hits her like shattering glass. He counters the romantic invitation she extends in French with a vicious English slap: "This is just not the moment! It's five o'clock. I'm hungry. I need a drink." With her fantasy in ruins, Elle's face assumes a tragic Pagliacci expression and then an ugly, angry look as she divests herself of the persona she dreamed by removing her earrings. Then, they exchange recriminations, his in English, hers in French, about how he fell asleep before she could join him on their anniversary night. James defends his fatigue by recalling how she told him she once almost fell asleep while driving from Rome to Florence with Julien asleep in the back seat.

James may be right to say, "It's just not reasonable to expect to feel what that newly married couple feels. Not after fifteen years," and the recollection of Elle being asleep while driving at a dangerous speed may symbolically apply to the revival of feeling she is trying to instill during their limited time in Lucignano. But neither is able at this point to accept the unrecognized needs of the other with kindness and understanding. The surface argument becomes increasingly petty—"It was our fifteenth wedding anniversary, and all you do is snore."—"I do not snore!"—but their cumulative skewering of self-worth finally probes so deeply that James cannot take it any more: "I apologize. I apologize for last night. I apologize for five years ago. I apologize for the restaurant, for the waiter, for the wine. I apologize for the last fifteen years, and I apologize for my existence."

Just after James walks out, the young bride they were with in the chapel appears outside. She and the groom motion Elle to come to the window. Elle signals that she is coming and then, unable to open the window, blows kisses and calls out congratulations in Italian. Her inability to open the window signals the end of a regressive fantasy, where the "screen" no longer provides escape. Outside the romantic set of the restaurant, Elle becomes a different kind of director, still leading James but now, like Kiarostami following Rumi's polo ball, willing to let the characters and the story tell itself.

A cut to James has him standing alone next to a beautiful, old, wooden door that he does not see, just as he has not seen Elle. He says he is hungry, and Elle brings him a thick piece of bread. He takes it with a sad look, as if he were a scolded child. Then he follows her down the street like the boy he described in Florence and as Elle led Julien. As they walk past a high stone wall, a church bell begins to toll. Multiple bells chime in when they reach the church door, a general symbol of framing in Kiarostami but in this case an extraordinary one: Layered arches of white and gold surmount a silver inlaid door turned inward to reveal a vertical black rectangle, the entrance to a transformative mystery we cannot see. Elle goes in, followed after a moment by James, and her affect after she emerges suggests a sudden change of heart, a breakthrough to the soul like the one that ends *Journey to Italy* or like the loving acceptance that comes over the Driver's Friend after she leaves the shrine (see chapter 8).

With both inside, momentary darkness fills the screen. Then, we hear the sound of a squeaking door, before the camera cuts to an outdoor shot of an old man with a cane emerging from the church with an old woman. Both are bent over like the man that Behzad sees as he leaves Siah Dareh and the woman repeatedly seen in Kieslowski's *Three Colors* trilogy. The bells continue to peal as James is seen following from the black rectangle of the door. As the old couple advances toward the camera, James leans on a pillar behind them until Elle, too, emerges, and both are seen following their future selves, who are still visible in the foreground.

The bells stop ringing as Elle sits on a brick stairway to take off her shoes, while James, speaking gently (and therefore in French), asks, "Does it hurt?" She responds quietly in French as if they have both stopped acting, "I'm okay. I shouldn't have worn these shoes. Nothing's changed here." But James senses that much has changed and continues the intimate, effortless exchange in French: "But you . . . you've changed. I don't think you used to go to church." In a line that evokes the friend in *Ten* cropping her hair after leaving the shrine, Elle says that she went in to take off her bra and that she just needed to be on her own, but James wants to know why she did that in a church and mentions that he saw her praying. In all the scenes with James, Elle wears a simple gold cross, and though she does not seem particularly religious, she (like the Muslim women in *Ten* who pray at the shrine) is seeking relief from the struggle to conform to a culturally imposed ideal. Kiarostami, following the example of Sufi poets like Rumi, did that by immersing himself in nature and by allowing the creative process to be driven by a force outside of himself.

The honesty of Elle's divestment moves James, who may also yearn to escape the obligations of his socially acquired role: Coming down to her level, he sits next to her on the steps. "I'm sorry," he says. "Really sorry." She intuitively nurtures both of them when she suggests that they should learn to see through social trappings: "You didn't see I removed my lipstick either."—"Yes, I did."—"Not even when I had it on, nor my earrings. The problem is, you don't see me, whereas I noticed immediately you'd changed your perfume," and rubbing her head on his shoulder, "You could have shaved for me today for our anniversary," as she caresses his chin. Now the accusations of disregard have become gentle reminders of a long intimacy. "It's a habit," he says softly. "I only shave every other day." She responds, still caressing his chin and smiling, "I know." As an indication that she has touched his soul, the whole conversation transpires lovingly in French.

The final scene reveals Kiarostami's sense of cinema as a certified copy of life that is as valid as personal experience if it touches the spectator's soul. In fact, a film that moves us enough to think deeply about it may become as firmly etched in our memory and as potentially life changing as anything we have encountered in real life. Kiarostami made this point when he first told Binoche the film's story as if it had actually happened to him and then asked if she believed him. When she said yes, he replied, "It's not true!" Taking his point, Binoche later reflected, "To this day, I'm sure he lived this story. Just as I'm sure he didn't."[18] And in the DVD documentary, she adds that he told the story in detail and in perfect English (a copy in itself of a story conceived in Farsi that transpired in Italy) and that on different occasions the story had different origins, stemming from letters or from someone he met in Tehran or from his imagination. Binoche understood these variants in the same way viewers are invited to understand *Certified Copy*: "It's hard to say [what's true] because everything's true and everything's invented."[19]

For Kiarostami, the ability to tell a lie that touches the soul is the essence of poetic art, and he makes this point especially clear through Ahmad in *Where Is the Friend's House?* and Hossein in *Through the Olive Trees*, two innocent characters who learn how overt lies, if delivered for a loving purpose, are superior to literal truth. In those films the ability to tell such lies is a spiritual gift that comes to Ahmad, sitting with his notebook in the storm, and to Hossein on the rim of a steep ravine just when Tahereh seems to be forever out of reach. Kiarostami depends on this kind of inspiration in his work, and Elle becomes this kind of director after she emerges from the church. At the end she becomes courageously creative, realizing that she cannot control James's response to the love she offers but that she can remain true to herself by giving him the best story she can imagine. The idea of memory in the scene is intentionally ambiguous, not just because we do not know if James really experienced what she asks him to remember, but because cinematic stories in general are more or less moving to the extent that they resonate with the personal memory of each spectator.

Is it just a game or an actual memory when Elle asks James to look around for the hotel where they spent their wedding night? As they proceed down the street, they come to a building with pots of red flowers on both bannisters, a Kiarostami trademark that says there is always something beautiful to see if you open your eyes. But to experience the beauty that has become invisible to adult eyes, a person has to spiritually die and then be reborn, as suggested by Badii's death, followed by the coda in *Taste of Cherry*. The long indoor staircase is dark, perhaps threatening because James is ascending to a kind of death where Elle hopes to make a fundamental change in who he is. Elle has preceded him in this sense and literally into the room. When he turns on the light upon entering, she tells him to turn it off, to remain for a while in a womblike semidarkness just as Behzad does in

Zeynab's barn. Initially, we follow James with our eyes because he is the spectator the film is trying to reach, while Elle, the director, is visually absent but vocally present.

When she tells him to open the window and look to his left, the line is consistent with Kiarostami's attempt to help people escape their personal and cultural frames. But James sees nothing that might evoke love because he lacks imagination. He cannot make a connection between what he has lost and what Elle (and Kiarostami) want him to recover because he is trapped in a world of literal fact: "On your right, look." As he looks out the window, his profile is reflected in the glass of the vertical window that has swung open to his right, as if to say that some people will never be able to see beyond the projection of who they think they are: "Don't you remember anything? I can't believe you've forgotten." In the reflection we see him look down and away. We can't see his actual face as he starts to stand, and he remains dark and faceless as he complains: "You know I have a bad memory. It's not fair to test me like this."

As with Binoche's uncertainty about whether Kiarostami was remembering or imagining the story he told her, Elle now vividly recalls or creates their honeymoon night. It does not matter whether her narrative is factually true; it only matters that it is lovingly delivered to save James from an ill-conceived necessity in the same way Ahmad saved Mohammad. The camera cuts from James in darkness to Elle in partial shadow on the bed as she tries to bring James into the light. Resting her head on her right hand, she says quietly, "Lying here, I remember everything. You slept on this side." And then, pulling the pillow down next to her, "The pillow still smells of you."

When Elle says that she remembers every detail and asks if he wants her to tell him, he says no, and when Elle says that nothing has changed, her words actually imply that James must change before it is too late: "You see nothing has changed. You haven't changed. You're just as you were. Just as gentle, as attractive . . . as cold." Again, as the camera cuts back to James in the darkness, she says, "I know it's to protect yourself but just as cold." The dialogue then becomes increasingly layered because, in trying to coax James out of darkness, Elle says nothing has changed, when in fact she has become kinder and more resourceful, a maternal guide that James may or may not recognize and follow.

When James denies being cold and Elle asks if she has changed, he replies with a cliché: "You're even more beautiful." When she whispers, "And even more stupid," he denies his former arrogance: "I never said that." Elle has grown beyond petty word games, and once again she responds as if she were soothing a child: "You see, if we were a bit more tolerant of each other's weaknesses, we'd be less alone. I know one can live alone, but did you see that couple [who came out of the church]? I envied them. Didn't you?" But James, still afraid of ageing and death, can only mumble, "Not sure," while Kiarostami through Elle urges people to cherish the gifts that surround them: "Stay with me," she whispers in close-up. "Stay. It's better, better for both of us. For you and for me. Give us that chance."

But James, like the viewer who regards cinema as pastime, is compelled by what he considers more pressing matters than finding eternity in the moment. Still in darkness and unmoved by Elle's appeal, he reverts to the safety of work: "I told you. I must be at the station by nine." Drowning in work, Kiarostami shows through Behzad, is a form of suicide. As he told Geoff Andrew, *Taste of Cherry* "tries to express that if you don't have the time for living, the exit is always there. And God created man to have two options, one of them is suicide, the other one I'm not going to explain."[20]

The sentiment comes to cinematic fruition here. James stands and turns to leave. The window is visible as birds fly past, and for a moment, the frame is entirely black and white. Then, with the camera in close-up returning to Elle, still lying on the pillow, the image becomes warmly nuanced. Her expression is somewhat sad, but she has a slight smile, and the set of her mouth suggests persistence, courage, and acceptance, regardless of how he reacts. This is the attitude of the artist, as well, trying to tell the world to accept and love the best they have been given.

James goes to the bathroom, evoking the argument about how he fell asleep while Elle was in the bathroom. But while we do not see her again in the film, we know that she will not fall asleep and that she knows what matters. The camera cuts to James, still in darkness, but after a moment, the bathroom light illuminates the extent to which the ego can deplete the soul. With his joyless eyes now staring into the unseen mirror's small frame, the pre-sunset light reveals his mortality in ways that previous shots have not. The lines in his forehead and the bags under his eyes have become distinctly visible, implying now, in a literally different light, his spiritual enervation.

The sound of water dripping in the sink connotes his life draining away, while the bell in the church just outside the open window tolls eight times, a reminder that the decision he must make with only an hour to get to the station is crucial to how anyone chooses to live the time that remains. But James may never awaken. After a little over a minute, he smooths his hair back with his right hand, perhaps a reminder of the narcissism he can't escape, and exits to the left, leaving us with a beautiful shot of the old church surmounted by a golden dome, which could just as well be a mosque because no cross is visible.

Twin bells that have sustained generations through the night and welcomed them to a new day now peal joyously, proclaiming a message of love for those alert enough to hear. They taper off after eighteen seconds and then stop for four seconds, before resuming as the final credits roll over the open window, suggesting alternate possibilities for James and for us. But while the fate of individuals may vary, the general future remains hopeful. The bells play subtle variations, which slowly soften as the darkness grows. A diminishing area of blue sky remains for two minutes, until finally, with thirty seconds left, the screen goes completely black.

NOTES

1. Abbas Kiarostami, "Abbas Kiarostami: In Conversation With . . . TIFF Bell Lightbox 2016," interview by Piers Hanley, posted by TIFF originals, July 5, 2016, video, 1:58:26,https://www.youtube.com/watch?v=-1CCPg5UY-E.
2. Koran 4:1.
3. Idries Shah, *The Sufis* (Garden City, NY: Doubleday, 1964), 18.
4. Abbas Kiarostami, "With Borrowed Eyes: An Interview with Abbas Kiarostami," interview by David Sterritt, *Film Comment* (July–August 2000), http://www.filmcomment.com/article/with-borrowed-eyes-an-interview-with-abbas-kiarostami/.
5. Abbas Kiarostami, "Q&A: 'Certified' Director Abbas Kiarostami," interview by Nick Vivarelli, *Variety*, May 18, 2010, https://variety.com/2010/film/markets-festivals/q-a-certified-director-abbas-kiarostami-1118019551/.
6. Juliette Binoche, in *Let's See Copia Conforme*, directed by Irene Bufo, 2010, special feature on *Certified Copy*, directed by Abbas Kiarostami, disc 2 (2010; Hartsdale, NY: Criterion Collection, 2012), DVD.
7. Abbas Kiarostami, in *Let's See Copia Conforme*.
8. Krzysztof Kieslowski, "An Interview with Director Krzysztof Kieslowski on the Making of the Three Colors Trilogy," accessed January 16, 2020, http://www.petey.com/kk/docs/intrview.txt.
9. Krzysztof Kieslowski, *Kieslowski on Kieslowski*, ed. Danusia Stok (London: Faber and Faber, 1993), 210–11.
10. Kiarostami, interview by Anthony Kaufman, *IndieWire*, March 19, 1998, http://www.indiewire.com/1998/03/abbas-kiarostami-speaks-about-taste-of-cherry-82999/.
11. Binoche, in *Let's See Copia Conforme*.
12. See "David (Michelangelo)," Wikipedia, updated January 11, 2020, https://en.wikipedia.org/wiki/David_(Michelangelo).
13. On Mehdi Akhavan-e-Saless, see Saeid Rezvani, "Akhavan-e Saless, Mehdi," *Encyclopædia Iranica*, May 19, 2016, http://www.iranicaonline.org/articles/akhavan-e-saless.
14. Mehdi Akhavan Sales, "The Leafless Garden," Mehdi Akhavan Sales, December 31, 2012, https://www.mehdiakhavansales.com/the-leafless-garden/.
15. On the Kiarostami exhibit *The Leafless Garden*, see "Kiarostami Forest at the V&A," artdaily, March 8, 2005, http://artdaily.com/news/12901/Kiarostami-forest-at-the-V-A.
16. Kiarostami, "Abbas Kiarostami."
17. Binoche, in *Let's See Copia Conforme*.
18. Quoted in Godfrey Cheshire, "*Certified Copy*: At Home and Abroad," Criterion Collection, May 23, 2012, https://www.criterion.com/current/posts/2303-certified-copy-at-home-and-abroad.
19. Binoche, in *Let's See Copia Conforme*.
20. Abbas Kiarostami, "Conversación," interview by Geoff Andrew, Morelia Film Festival, November 12, 2012, https://www.youtube.com/watch?v=ZEC0KGULtaE.

Chapter Twelve

It's a Jungle Out There

Kiarostami's last feature film, *Like Someone in Love* (2012), shot in Tokyo, is about the relationship between an eighty-year-old retired sociology professor, a late-teen university student and part-time hooker whom a former student sent him as a gift, and her dangerously jealous auto mechanic fiancé. At first glance, Takashi Watanabe would appear to be a wise old man like the door maker in *Where Is the Friend's House?* or the doctor in *The Wind Will Carry Us* with Akiko, the sweet, childlike student, resembling Ahmad or Farzad. But even though Takashi has written a definitive textbook on the causes of violence in society, he has much to learn about actual violence from which his intellectual immersion and academic prestige have served to shield him.

Like James in *Certified Copy*, this elevation, imaged in the literal elevation of his book-lined apartment, has at some earlier time estranged him from his family, but unlike James, he now seeks a remedy to assuage his loneliness by nurturing someone else, a natural instinct of late maturity. The boyfriend, Higuchi Noriaki, personifies a major obstacle to love between individuals and groups in complex societies, much like the grandfather in *Where Is the Friend's House?*, Mr. Ahankhah in *Close-Up*, and Mr. Badii in *Taste of Cherry*.

As in *Certified Copy*, rigid definitions of what relationships between characters are supposed to be are reversed or left purposely ambiguous. In the scene near the beginning, where Akiko meets Takashi in his apartment, it is not clear whether the two actually have sex, especially considering their age difference. In the "Making of *Like Someone in Love*" featurette on the *Someone* DVD, Kiarostami asked the cinematographer, the art director, the producer, the assistant director, a production assistant, and a makeup assistant what they thought, and all of them said "nothing happened." Rin Takanashi, who played Akiko, thought nothing happened because, if it had, her character wouldn't have trusted Takashi enough later to call him when she was in trouble. Kiarostami was surprised and intrigued by these reactions because "in the script I wrote, she went straight to the bed and slept with him." But having asked his sample audience how they felt, he minimized without entirely eliminating the sexual implications of the scene because he realized that most viewers wouldn't like it, and "even Mr. Okuno [who played Takashi] wouldn't like it."

This ambiguity about what characters do suits his preference for delving instead into what characters feel: "In the intimacy between two people, something can happen that is not visible but that is imaginable." And (paradoxically) cultivating external ambiguity is his way of arriving at the "absolute truth" of the heart: "So I offend the viewer by depriving him of the scene he wants to see, by making him see another reality to which I aspire . . . something of another order, something deeper." And as in his preceding work, he identifies that something by quoting a letter from Vincent Van Gogh to his brother Theo: "When I see these lovely Flemish girls, I am more driven to reach their souls than to grasp their bodies."[1] But in this film, Kiarostami concerns himself more directly with society's perversion of the soul's growth and of children being diverted from benevolent guidance than he had in any film since *Homework*. He achieves this secondarily through visual images of social distraction but primarily through the suppressed rage of Noriaki, who as a type is no more of a time bomb in the modern world than he has always been in hierarchic cultures.

Takashi meets Noriaki while he waits in his car outside the university, where he has driven Akiko to take an exam after their night together. The dialogue reveals that Noriaki is all about domination and rigid control, the same values absorbed by children subject to repressive laws in Iran and by children in the modern West (which now includes Japan) unwittingly addicted to the pernicious rankings of constant competition. As in *Certified Copy*, Takashi pretends to play a role that later becomes real, that of Akiko's grandfather. In an ideal sense, this relationship would connote guidance toward growth and change, but Noriaki lives by rules that he considers fixed, unchanging, and morally correct. He says he is glad to meet Takashi because, even though "nowadays people get married without consent of the family," for him it is necessary and important. Then, he proceeds to explain that he has become solvent by establishing a small auto shop because he values work above useless learning: "I left school when I was sixteen. I know that some people prefer to drift through college. I wanted to work." Despite his relatively low social standing, he is proudly independent, earning enough to help buddies in need and able to do other things when times get tough: "Work, it's something important."

But Takashi has learned the hard way that work is not paramount and, trying to head off disaster because of how he and Akiko met, says that she and Noriaki are too young to marry. Marriage here becomes a symbol of benevolent connection, not only in other familial relationships, but also between the collective members of the body politic. Noriaki takes Takashi to mean sexual experience and says he has been with several girls and that "women don't need experience before marriage." Takashi says their future doesn't look rosy because he has witnessed Noriaki roughly grabbing Akiko on the university steps, and Noriaki admits that though they often disagree and don't talk through their problems, he has taken his grandfather's advice to heart: "When you meet your better half, marry her. Don't let her go." He seems to believe that Akiko validates his life: "If I lose her, I won't find another like her." But Akiko chafes under his control, protesting angrily as he recalls, "Who do you think you are? You're not my husband." Moreover, she irritates Noriaki by turning off her cell phone because, as we know, she has to hide her source of income and because subtextually a growing part of her needs to move beyond the physical security he offers.

The unconscious bargain they have mutually struck resembles the social contract: Don't question authority, and you will be mentally content and physical safe. When Akiko puts Noriaki off about not answering the phone because the battery has been a problem, the lie reveals that she is having a hard time sustaining the relationship, as the film's opening scene pointedly reveals, and her soul's instinct to grow, which has kept her in the university, is driving her away from Noriaki because his primary instinct is to establish dominance by stifling awareness: "She didn't give me a clear answer. Isn't it weird? So you understand. That's why I want to marry her. That way she won't have a choice. She knows nothing about life."

Noriaki's own idea about life is parroted from societal leaders who present the world as so dangerous that only they can provide security: "You should also know we live in a jungle." He understands better than anything she might learn from the "dusty books" that do not reveal what he knows firsthand: "This city is merciless.... So I will marry her. That way I will be able to protect her." And when Takashi cautions that if they marry she still may not answer his questions, Noriaki uses the law as he understands it to undergird the need for dominance as practiced on one level by the controllers of society and on another by workers (as in *Homework*), whose low self-esteem compensates for lack of material possessions by asserting absolute possession of their families: "If we get married, she will be obliged to answer me."

Theories from the dusty books that purport to explain why we live in a jungle enter the conversation when Akiko reenters the car and fears that she made a mistake on the part of her exam about the theory of evolution by identifying its author as Durkheim. Takashi consoles her by explaining that she was partially right because "Durkheim reinterpreted Darwin's theory." Durkheim believed that greed was the predominant value in densely populated societies and that the inability to satisfy that generally held vice by those who lack power would result in higher rates of suicide and, by extension, the projection of that frustration into violence against others. The Darwinian struggle of competing species to obtain the same necessities is mitigated in society when members of different social classes are conditioned to have different goals and needs. Competing species can coevolve if their "niches" are different, and social peace will remain as long as different subgroups can live within the psychological and material parameters that sustain their identities: "The musician no more competes with the carpenter than the moose with the beaver. To each his own niche. When niches don't overlap, their occupants don't compete."[2]

Durkheim's adaptation of Darwin accounts in part for Noriaki's rage at the end of the film. He does not see Takashi as a threat as long as their roles in relation to Akiko are clearly separate. Driving together in Takashi's Volvo, the three look like a peaceful family grouping, but as Kiarostami shows in *Shirin*, the difference between the children has more to do with their souls than their social situation. Social theory doesn't adequately explain the threat of internecine violence in all societies, a threat more comprehensively conceived in the Zoroastrian tradition as an eternal battle between Ahura as Creation and Ahriman as Destruction (see chapter 3).

Sometimes this battle occurs between separate people or groups and sometimes within a single person. It then becomes a question of which trait becomes predominant, a question left open in the cases of Behzad and James. Speaking of Takashi, Kiarostami said that he wanted to show how someone who "isn't very nice [can] become someone familiar, with character traits that are acceptable, even pleasant."[3] When Takashi was younger, he was not ready to become the guide for his own family that he becomes for Akiko. And Akiko, as the intuitive rather than simply the enrolled student, needs what he can give her, not just the primitive protection that Noriaki offers.

In the opening scene, Noriaki represents the soul-stifling certainty Kiarostami detests because it leaves no room for growth. The setting is a lively bar, where we hear Akiko on the phone to Noriaki before we see her, as if she is initially indistinguishable from the buzzing life around her. Her first words, "I'm not lying," are not a lie in the literal sense. She is with her friend Nagisa at the Café Teo, but when she adds, "When did I ever lie to you?" she is lying about their relationship. After Noriaki orders her to go to the bathroom and count the tiles on the floor so that he can come back and count them later, Akiko hangs up on him and exclaims to Nagisa, "What a crazy guy!" The kind of knowledge Noriaki wants is a factual clue to discover what he would consider a crime, so his absurd demand is a parody of the knowledge offered by conventional detective films.

Noriaki is imagining the plot of a story of betrayal, but Kiarostami, who always diminishes plot in favor of character, immediately establishes the innocence he wants Akiko to represent when we first see her sitting with Nagisa. Nagisa's hair is dyed bright red, and her dress is slate blue, an impersonal color that Kiarostami later associates with Noriaki and daylit Tokyo. Contrastingly, Akiko's hair is natural, and she wears a short, light-green dress, the color of spring leaves, under a white cardigan patterned by dark-orange flowers on thin branches that spiral delicately upward.

Her clothing symbolizes a capacity to develop a sensibility attuned to the natural beauty Kiarostami always directs viewers to value, while the atmosphere of the place she presently inhabits threatens to trap her in the with-it vacuity to which Nagisa has already succumbed. This is exposed when she tells Akiko a joke she has just learned and found uproariously funny about how a male millipede tells a female millipede on their wedding night that he is so tired that he needs her to tell him which legs to spread. The joke is a reminder of the primitive sex without feeling in which the girls professionally engage as well as the automaton Akiko would become for her mechanic spouse, who wants to drive her like a well-maintained car. Akiko doesn't find it funny and doesn't pretend to laugh, a sign that there is more hope for her than for Nagisa.

To help young people still alive enough to be saved from such a dismal fate, Kiarostami speaks transparently through Akiko's pimp, Hiroshi, who enters with an assignment that he hopes will change her perspective. Ostensibly, Hiroshi is referring specifically to Akiko's relationship with Noriaki, but through him, Kiarostami speaks to a myriad of viewers less mature than his older guides: "Listen. This is your own life. I do not want to intrude, but continuing with this story, you will only feel pain. You will be destroyed. You must bring it to an end."

Realizing the innate difference between the searching Akiko and the rule-bound Noriaki, Hiroshi tells her that both are "having a hard time" because Noriaki cannot abide lines being crossed, while Akiko, like Ahmad in *Friend's House* and Hossein in *Olive Trees*, is creatively driven to overstep them. No one is at fault here because they can only act at the promptings of their contrary natures, and as the "director" of the story to follow, Hiroshi takes the liberty of subtly advising some people how to live by urging them to take a different path from that of their authoritative leaders: "Ever since you became a couple, you keep on suffering. It's your own business, of course. But it's also mine. Only you can decide whether to break up. I tell you this for your own sake."

Akiko tries to remain regressively safe by begging off: "I can't tonight. I have to study for my exam," a line evoking the important lessons that Ahmad and Farzad learn outside of school, and additionally by needing to meet her grandmother who has traveled from their small town to visit her in Tokyo.

Through Hiroshi, Kiarostami responds that Akiko has already expanded her horizons too far to be helped by an actual grandmother who was only part of her early childhood and will not understand the dilemmas she faces now: "You are worried for her. There is no point, however, in seeing her and leaving after a while. She won't enjoy it. Relax, and let her return to her house."

That house is now too small for Akiko, and it is time for her to learn from someone Hiroshi says he respects, a highly educated person whose ability to help her may or may not turn out as he hopes, but like Kiarostami, he gives Akiko a better chance by directing her to a source of accumulated cultural wisdom, a master of the dusty books Noriaki scorns. Though she makes a final attempt to remain adolescent by virtually screaming that she won't go, Hiroshi is as supremely confident as Kiarostami that she now has no choice but to stay with the film he has written, even though he knows it may take a different direction than the one he planned.

Akiko can remain comfortably unaware for a while, but waking up is the hoped-for fate of a Kiarostami viewer: "You have already refused. Stop with the questions. You will see for yourself. Come on. Finish your drink and go. You will sleep in the taxi." Then, in an unusually expressionistic shot, Hiroshi literally leaves the room while his transparent body is still seen from behind superimposed on Akiko until she, too, leaves the room, only to be enveloped once again as she returns with her purse, as if Hiroshi magically contains her.

The surreal reflection now returns to literal reality when Akiko walks forward through Hiroshi's body with her purse and coat. Then they turn together to the right, where he opens the door through which she obediently passes. Just outside, she puts on her coat under bright-orange English letters reading "Bar Pizza," a sign of the surface glitter she is leaving. Hiroshi follows her down the steps; hails a cab; and, after consigning her to the driver, leaves her and us with the hope that her journey of awakening may be a "safe trip" and that, for now at least, she has time on the way to "take a small nap." Following the initially humorous and lovely scene of her meeting with Takashi, that journey proves to be anything but safe, but the same is true for anyone who risks the adventure of leaving a too-small shelter of unrelieved certainty.

Akiko does not nap as long as the taxi moves through downtown Tokyo. Kiarostami called the scene "pivotal," probably because it shows Akiko leaving her childhood forever and because it also hints at her uncertain fate in the dangerous world she is entering. In the DVD featurette, Kiarostami reflects that he did not know how Rin Takanashi, the actor portraying Akiko, would play the scene, and he seems to feel about her as the viewer might feel about her character: "This is Akiko. She's so childlike. She's going to do this sad scene. I don't know how she'll do it, but I have faith in her."

His way of casting expresses a hope for the character that corresponds to his hope for real children to find their best selves in a challenging life. A film can only point the direction, and it only works with people whose souls are receptive: "In fact, it's a cycle. You choose the person you think is right, you get caught up in her game, and you let her lead you. The poet [Rumi] says, 'Like the ball bounding at the end of my mallet, you make me run, though I sent you flying.' A person you imagined, now you find her in flesh and blood. And now you just have to follow her."[4]

As the journey to Takashi begins, Akiko listens to a series of phone messages from her grandmother, who addresses her lovingly as "dear," "darling," and by the diminutive "Ki." She tells her she has brought the book Akiko requested, a detail pertinent to the granddaughter's exploratory nature, and she says that she has seen a photograph of someone who looks like her and another who looks like Nagisa with a phone number at the train station, a detail that suggests superimposing a work identity over the open, searching child we see when she leaves the taxi. The grandmother repeatedly says she would like to share a meal with her granddaughter, the same hope entertained initially by Takashi, but while Takashi's meal is thoughtfully elaborate, the grandmother's desire for plain soup or noodles is symbolically too simple for the communion Akiko now craves. So Akiko and the driver, another Kiarostami stand-in, look very sad as the taxi passes through an alien scene that offers neither regressive comfort nor opportunities to grow. To portray this alienation here and later in the film, Kiarostami uses reflections on the outside of the cab window glass as a way to differentiate the deceptive outer world from the soul he hopes to reach.

The grandmother says she will wait on a bench under the statue outside the station, and on the way, the camera moves alternately from Akiko inside the cab to what she sees out the window to reflections of the passing scene on the window glass. After a message from the grandmother asking if Akiko misses their small town of Matsuda, the next message is a cold, incomplete call "from the bank," which accompanies signs in English connoting the disappointing allure of international commerce, including (in another food reference) the ubiquitous white-and-green "Subway" over a nebulously beckoning marquee reading "Sweet Paradise." Another prominent sign over a large store reads "Top Shop," a subliminal invitation to purchase an imitation (though not the actual) rank of queen bee in a spiritually backward world.

In addition to its leveled sensations, the urban hive offers the addictive jolts of mass entertainment selectively conveyed by a movie marquee showing a row of sinister faces, including two glaring Caucasian women and two furiously angry men, one Caucasian and one Asian. The appetite for such entertainment proves in the film not to be safely vicarious when Noriaki is possessed by the "manly" rage that (as *Shirin* shows) is not exclusive to modernity.

While *Like Someone in Love* is about children, it is not a film for incorrigibly childish adults, and Akiko bids a permanent farewell to childhood when she asks the driver to make two passes around the square in front of the depot, where she can glimpse her grandmother waiting on the bench. The first pass emphasizes the imposing statue that epitomizes the spirit of the place. The huge figure of a medieval warrior holding a sheathed sword from which a closed bag dangles suggests the false promise of reward for those who identify wealth controlled by the few as the major virtue of a nation. For the powers that be, the tender love of a grandparent is an irrelevant trifle.

The camera shows Akiko viewing this image from inside the window, which, as a Kiarostami trope, connotes the way the modern world frames itself. She can see the grandmother only for a moment because a white van pulls up alongside at the traffic light, blocking the grandmother but leaving the statue fully visible. Corresponding to the blocking traffic, the camera now moves outside the window to show Akiko obscured by the reflections of outer light that threatens to entirely overtake the life of a socialized child.

The second pass repeats the pattern. This time Akiko, now seen from inside the car, can see her grandmother more clearly for a few seconds until once again the social blur inundates her perception. While the camera in the first scene shows Akiko enveloped by the director's vision represented by Hiroshi's transparent body, the camera now cuts to Akiko enveloped by the side window glass, which can only reflect the distracting lights of the urban show. She turns her head, desperately trying keep her grandmother in view as the cab circles the square, but then a large crowd of people waiting to cross the street again blocks her view. Once more the back of the statue is seen looming over the remaining sliver of the grandmother on the bench as the cab turns. A clock begins to toll, suggesting the kind of irreversible moment James faces at the end of *Certified Copy*.

The driver (as both viewer and director) has a melancholy look, perhaps because he has seen Akiko wipe away a tear in the rear-view mirror. Soft, orchestral music begins, seemingly from the car radio, although the radio has not been heard before. It has a nondiegetic effect, as if to help us gain or regain perspective on what Akiko has lost. But then, as if encouraging her to face an unknown future, the music switches to a vocalist performing an upbeat popular song, while Akiko takes out her compact and begins to put on lipstick, assuming the outer role she will have to play in her particular time and place.

Once out of the congested area, an overhead wide shot highlights a symbol of an alternate journey, a commuter train zooming over an overpass above the freeway, suggesting a life of unconscious obligation rather than the alternative potential that Takashi as her next "director" now offers. "She's been asleep since we left Tokyo," the driver says as he drops her off, and sleeping behind glass becomes a metaphor of the illusory safety people need to feel in a world that constantly threatens danger, as the insulated British couple has blithely forgotten in *Journey to Italy*.

When Akiko cautiously enters Takashi's apartment, she is reflected in a small mirror just inside the open door to the bedroom, suggesting the small frame of her experience. Directly to her left, a table lamp with a green-gold shade matching her dress throws a warm light on an orange brick wall, matching the flowers on the cardigan we saw before. But for now, she still wears a gray outercoat as she gingerly circles around, inspecting books and photos as if she has entered a marvelous wonderland. She finds shelter here from the aggressive demands of Noriaki and the regressive guilt associated with her grandmother, but there is a foreshadowing of the fragility of that shelter when she stops for a moment to look out the large black picture window directly behind Takashi, who is talking on the phone at his desk, fending off an insistent client.

The parallel is immediately apparent because Akiko has also been introduced being harassed or implored by a series of calls and messages. As with Akiko, one call is from a relative—"Your sister is worried."—and the next he then takes off call waiting from an aggressive voice that he can't dismiss. Having retired decades ago from his position as a sociology professor at the university Akiko attends, Takashi is now a professional translator, a theme harking back to the opening scene of *Certified Copy*, where the translation of language becomes a metaphor for the translation of specific character traits from parent to child as well as generally human ones from generation to generation (see chapter 11).

The man on the phone wants five lines to promote his son's art exhibit. They begin with a quote about parenthood: "My honorable son, Sekigutsi Masahiro states: 'A parent's work never ends. To be a parent. . . .'" This introduces the theme of transmission, which the man on the phone parenthetically applies to Takashi—"Something you will also know."—an impertinence that Takashi quickly quashes—"Forget the comments."—even though thematically the comments are the point of this introductory scene. The man's idea of parenthood, however, is the opposite of Kiarostami's. He thinks being a good parent is about promoting wealth and reputation, a priority that Kiarostami uses to contrarily define his sense of an art uncorrupted by commercial motives: "I will give you the basic idea and you write the words. 'The exhibition of my honorable son, with support from the cultural organization, Tanaka, will open to the public on 18 December.' About the rest I'm not sure. Just make it sound nice."

While the sound track conveys what art should not be, the camera follows Akiko, acclimating herself to a different inner world when she stops in front of a large print of a girl in a kimono looking up at a white parrot on the branch of a potted plant. This literally framed image, flanked by the two warmly glowing green-gold lamps, is the entrance to a larger frame through which her life can be reconceived. She examines it slowly and lovingly, making it a thematic priority. Takashi yearns for a similar expansion at the very moment he struggles to free himself from the frame forced on him by the phone: "I have things to do. Hurry up."

The thing he has to do is for Kiarostami the most necessary thing one can do in life, pass down one's accumulated wisdom to a child, and so the casual pleasantries, "I've been waiting for you for some time" and "You have a nice place here," refer to years of preparing to fulfill his life and the mental space Akiko needs to grow. And she is the one who first expresses what she most needs when she asks, "Do you like this painting?" Takashi is delighted by her question and explains that *Training a Parrot* (1900, by Chiyoji Yazaki) is 111 years old and is famous because it is the first Japanese painting done in a Western style with a purely Japanese subject.[5]

Because the painting is about teaching, which is occurring at the moment Takashi speaks, and because it is about a synthesis of styles whose only common original is in human experience itself, the dialogue repeats the emphasis in *Certified Copy* on the unity in diversity of human expression throughout the world. The words of Takashi's minilecture here about the history and provenance of the painting are abstract, but the tone is warmly personal, and Akiko's response illustrates Kiarostami's repeated emphasis in interviews on how his films are meant to give each viewer an opportunity to reflect more deeply on their own lives.

And as in *Certified Copy*, the mass-reproduced print is as valuable as the original because it has the same power to extend the viewer: "I got the same one as a gift," Akiko says. "My uncle gave it to me on my fourteenth birthday. He told me that he'd painted it. When I arrived in Tokyo two years ago, I went to the university museum, and I saw it. Then I understood that he was joking." She goes on to recall how her family told her she looked like the girl in the painting and how her grandmother made her an identical kimono. Then, she borrows a pencil to put her hair up in a bun to show him how she looked when she wore the kimono to village festivals, a connection that makes the painting's power immediate rather than just a historical innovation.

When Takashi explains that the girl is teaching the parrot to speak, Akiko recalls that her grandmother told her that the parrot was teaching the girl and that's how she, too, sees it. This exchange reflects the mutual expansion that both characters undergo in the film, and it again echoes *Certified Copy* in that the lessons each teaches the other are transmitted through centuries rather than just between them. In this sense, both parrot experience learned from others who have in turn learned from others, stretching back infinitely in time to a point predating personal or national styles. As Kiarostami says in the "Making Of" documentary, "All stories are clichés, [usually] told in a clichéd manner, [but] telling them in an innovative way allows you to get away from conventions."[6]

The visual images here tell the story in a unique way. After Akiko first enters, Takashi offers to take her coat, which she refuses, saying she is still a "bit cold," but after the exchange about the painting, she learns that Takashi has read all the books that surround them (a feat she considers astounding), and she has asked about the photos of a younger and an older woman, Akiko feels safely intrigued. Assuming that the younger woman is his daughter and the older one his wife, Akiko says she resembles both because she wants to be close to him, even though she is not yet sure which role she wants to play.

The sexual element is introduced when she tells Takashi Nagisa's millipede joke, which she says she doesn't get, and when she asks him to explain it, he tells her to come and have some wine because it's clear that familial rather than sexual companionship is what he had in mind. The ambiguity of the scene that follows is as intentional as the marital connection of James and Elle in *Certified Copy* because the scene is meant to express a meeting of souls rather than bodies, whether that meeting is platonic or not. And so, after Akiko has exposed her personal past, she is ready to make herself at home.

The nature of the relationship is emphasized again when, on the way to the bathroom, she stops under the painting to remove her coat and then goes back the other way to carefully hang it on the corner of a bookshelf. Then, turning back again in her short, green skirt and white cardigan, she smiles more like an elated little girl than a sex-work professional as she walks back the other way to prepare for what may literally only be bed. But once she is in the bedroom, her invitation for Takashi to join her is teasingly sexual, and it forces Takashi to have to be uncertain about the short-term future he had planned and the viewers to assume whatever they will about the carnal connection that is never spelled out.

After Akiko enters the bedroom, the narrow doorway represents the small mental space in which she still lives, as well as the limited scope of erotic expectation that some viewers will have. While she was in the bathroom, Takashi has been putting the finishing touches on the set he has imagined by turning on low dance music and pouring the wine on his tastefully set table. But once in the bedroom, the professional side of Akiko takes over, and she tries to make him act out the smaller sex scene she knows how to play rather than the tender, nuanced one he had prepared. With the black picture window as a recurrent motif, Akiko is not so much drawing Takashi into an erotic fantasy as preparing him to adapt to unexpected events, something he has not done often in his elevated life as a renowned scholar.

Before he enters the bedroom to coax Akiko to come out to share the warmth of the meal, we see her clothes flying across the opening to suggest rather than show her nakedness in the manner of an old Hollywood film. She says she would rather sleep than eat, reviving the metaphor of staying safely unconscious, which a retreat into erotic cliché might also accomplish. Staying in her own space rather than his confers the authority to ask questions in a knowing, suggestive tone, which is the opposite of her awed, little-girl wonder in the previous scene.

Takashi enters the room and sits facing the camera rather than Akiko, whom we now do not see because she is playing someone she is not, the streetwise hooker who knows more that the old scholar (as in the "dusty books" stereotype voiced by Noriaki). She begins by asking if Takashi knows Hiroshi because "he gets you girls" and teases that she smells perfume on the pillow. Then, continuing in a put-on come-hither voice, she asks him which side of the bed he sleeps on, and while Takashi repeatedly asks her to come out and eat, she just as insistently asks him to come to bed. The crude simplicity of her scenario is suggested by the straight, functional, black floor lamp next to Takashi's chair in contrast to the symmetrically glowing green-gold lamps that set off the painting.

Here, the visual image represents Akiko's immaturity, but the language operates on symbolic levels that imply her eventual emergence. She rudely rejects the broth "with little shrimps" that Takashi has obtained because it is a specialty of her region: "I hate it! My grandma used to make it." On a metaphoric level, she is no longer a little shrimp, and she can't go home again. And again, with the subtext referring to her development, she mentions that it is now the season of clementines (an especially sweet orange) in her region and that she has not been home since New Year's because both she and Takashi are entering a new phase.

The phone's ring ends the dialogue, but it stops ringing before Takashi can answer it in the other room, where his movements in the now-familiar space are as pivotal for him as Akiko's were in the taxi. He turns off the answering machine in front of the green-gold lamp, which is doubly reflected in a mirror on the left and through the transparent window curtain on the right. Then, he goes to the window and looks out into the blackness of the night, with its undivulged potential for danger and courage. For a long twenty-six seconds he stands there, watching the tiny lights move on the street below. He hesitates as he turns away but then walks slowly back toward the bedroom, stopping for a moment in front of the painting's keynote revelation before continuing toward the bedroom.

As he walks, the stereo plays Ella Fitzgerald's version of "Like Someone in Love," subtly amplifying the line "Sometimes the things I do astound me," as he proceeds to abandon his plan for the evening and as events will prove for the rest of his life. After bending to turn it off, he decides to let the music continue and proceeds to the table, where, after a long drink of wine, he decisively blows out the candles.

Suddenly the phone rings again, but instead of going to pick it up at his desk, he abruptly returns to the bedroom, where the immediate cut shows the table lamp softly illuminating Akiko peacefully asleep while leaving the wall above darkened to a shade of the now-familiar green-gold associated with her. Now, whether they make love (which seems unlikely) or not, he has made the emotional commitment that James is unable to make to Elle. Takashi unplugs the machine, turns off the lamp, and quietly exits, leaving Akiko lying on her chosen side of the bed, while the near side, his side, remains empty.

The light slowly fades but does not go completely black, before a quick cut abruptly changes the atmosphere, just as the sudden switch to playing hostile spouses changes the tone in *Certified Copy*. In a strikingly expressionistic image, the entire frame is an abstract reflection on Takashi's windshield of blue-and-white daylight, bright and beautiful but cold as ice. As in the taxi scene, window glass is not just a reflexive film screen but also a way of conveying the vulnerability of the passengers to the outside world and the multiple threats that can easily shatter its fragile shield.

Blue and dull gray are the dominant colors of the outside world that Takashi and Akiko now navigate as he drives her to an early-morning exam at the university. Through the windshield, every article of clothing now has a bluish tinge, suggesting their forced acclimation to the cold world they encounter. Everything outside seen from inside the car has the same blue tinge, as Takashi drives down an early-morning single-lane street devoid of trees, cars, or pedestrians. The road presents no obstacles, but the narrow emptiness of its passage also predicts the narrow mind space of the urban jungle in which men like Noriaki can barely contain their pent-up rage.

As groups of students walk up and down the building's steps, Noriaki waits at the top, indistinguishable from the peaceful others until Takashi sees him violently grab Akiko, who struggles to get away. The sense of hidden danger revealing itself is enhanced as students pass in front of them, making it harder for Takashi to follow through the side window of his navy-blue Volvo. This might be a forgettable image of an anonymous tiff if Akiko had not become personally real to Takashi and the viewer, but the danger to someone else has suddenly become our danger, especially because we know a little more about Noriaki than Takashi does: We have heard him harass Akiko on the phone in the first scene. The idea of screen violence intruding into real life continues when Noriaki descends the steps and rests against a wall, still partially hidden by a tree. Then, a bell begins to toll, evoking a major transition for Takashi as it does for James at the end of *Certified Copy*. Now, his life of ideas is about to be invaded by the physical threat that viewers of screens usually convince themselves will always happen to other people when Noriaki, still seen through the windshield, approaches the car and raps on the window.

The conversation begins innocuously enough—"Excuse me, do you have a light?"—and Takashi, still somewhat apprehensive, having seen Noriaki physically shaking Akiko, opens the window just enough to offer him the car lighter. Briefly, the threat seems to abate as Noriaki retreats to smoke against the wall, but then he returns to initiate the previously quoted conversation, which indicates his belief in the forceful control of thought and action, values that intellectuals like Takashi or artists like Kiarostami instinctively oppose. Though their verbal exchange is a polite debate, the physical image now has the violent person safely observed through the window from the shelter of the car.

The old man tries to head off danger by advising unpossessive appreciation of immediate experience: "Love her, but don't marry her," the proffered wisdom in previous Kiarostami films, but just as such wisdom is lost on the majority of people in the larger world, it only makes Noriaki insist more strongly on a life he can control. And so Noriaki becomes a working-class variation on the mind-set of people who rule populous countries around the world. Sticking to his principles, Noriaki sees tolerant acceptance as a cop-out, the surrendering cynicism of old age: "I'm just telling you how things are. You can either accept it or reject it," the old man counsels, to which the zealous believer retorts, "Your only goal is to discourage me."

As a type, Noriaki is a danger to the world, and having gained access to the car, he takes over when Akiko returns. Akiko told Takashi she needed to go to a bookstore, a symbolic priority that is decidedly different from the car's other passenger, whose purpose, like that of a political leader, is dominance justified by protection. This is conveyed by his warning that the Volvo's timing belt sounds shot and that Takashi must pull over immediately for him to see. Here and in the scene to follow, the metaphor of looking under the hood is obvious. Confirming his suspicion that "it could snap at any time," Noriaki's line refers specifically to himself and simultaneously to the ever-present collective threat: "You took the freeway like this?" He then directs them to his shop, where he can prove his worth by fixing it immediately.

After telephoning one of his employees to order the belt, he reveals that he has recently focused his generalized anger on that same person—"What a jerk!"—because the mechanic found one of Akiko's anonymous advertising photos and teased him by saying it looked like her. Infuriated, Noriaki attacked him, and later at the garage, when Takashi sees the hefty mechanic, he wonders how "that shrimp" could punch out such a giant, to which Akiko responds, "He has a third-degree black belt in karate." As they speak, parked in a narrow service aisle, a large, macho motorcyclist pulls up next to them. Takashi asks if she likes the idea of her fiancé's prowess, and because she is beginning to follow a path where Noriaki cannot follow, she responds evenly, "I used to." When Takashi asks what exactly she sees in him, she answers, "I'm not sure."

The narrow space of the reception aisle is indicative of the small world that Noriaki, emulating larger leaders, absolutely controls. He now appears in a blue jump suit, lighter and more luminous than that of anyone else. It is a clear contrast to the dull-blue sweat jacket and loose, gray T-shirt he has worn up to now, and like a military uniform, it signals command. As they wait, with Akiko staying in the backseat looking worried, an expensive silver car pulls up in the adjoining aisle. The middle-aged driver positioned, as is customary in Japan, behind the wheel on the right side addresses Takashi through the open passenger window on the Volvo's left side, saying that thirty years ago he had taken his course at the police academy, and although he has left the police, he was fascinated by the professor's last book about "violence in society." The former student will prove to be a threat to Akiko and Takashi because he may now be a private detective who will return Noriaki's automotive favors by locating Takashi's house at the end, thus making violence in society all too real.

But even if the cause of that violence is not specific on a plot level, it is symbolically visible in Noriaki's behavior in the tight physical space. Motioning another driver forward, he drones the direction as if he were a machine, "A bit further, a little more," followed by a staccato, "Stop!" Then he repeats the process as Takashi backs the Volvo out. During these carefully edited movements, we get a glimpse of the small working space crammed with disabled vehicles that, like many of their drivers, have been run down by the constant pressure of straight-lane lives. At the beginning of *And Life Goes On*, Puya and the director escape the gridlock into a space where the soul can breathe, as do Behzad and his crew in *The Wind Will Carry Us*, although unlike Puya's father, they are so citified that they are indifferent to the breathtaking beauty around them.

Here, Noriaki seems to pose no threat as he leans in the open window, a symbol of the safety he later shatters. He appears polite and kind, refusing the old man's offer to pay as they depart and telling him he can now drive "worry free." He says, "You're good!" when they clear the aisle and wishes him a "safe trip," as Hiroshi wished Akiko, but all these lines on a second viewing have a subtle air of menace because anyone's journey in a world where the possibility of natural disaster enhanced by climate change, epidemics, wars, or terrorism is necessarily precarious.

Knowing Noriaki, as Kiarostami more deeply knows human nature, Akiko is very worried in the car on the way to the bookstore. Takashi, still feeling blissfully happy now that he can be a grandfather to a sensitive child he can teach and comfort, tells Akiko that she needn't worry if Noriaki finds out from the detective that he is a professor when she had said her grandfather was a fisherman: "Never mind. Everyone has two grandfathers. One from the father and one from the mother. One can be a fisherman, and the other, a professor." To sum it up, he says, "What will be, will be," in Japanese and then surprisingly sings "Que Sera, Sera" with the first two words in Spanish and the rest in Japanese: "the future's not ours to see, what will be, will be."

Akiko nods as if she is comforted, and Takashi smiles as if delighted by the unaccustomed spontaneity of breaking into song, but film buffs may remember that when Doris Day sings the song in Alfred Hitchcock's *The Man Who Knew Too Much* (1956), the verse is deeply ironic because she is pounding a piano and singing as loudly as she can to signal her kidnapped son, who is in mortal danger, that he will soon be rescued because she is safely nearby. And so when they arrive at the bookstore, a reminder of the cultivated safety that had charmed Akiko in his apartment, Takashi's assurance—"Don't get anxious. You have nothing to worry about."—seems blithely shallow in light of what follows.

His vulnerability appears almost immediately when he falls asleep while stopped at a traffic light, implying the physical strain for a person of his age of fending off the threat of Noriaki and a metaphorical distancing from reality that echoes Akiko's retreat into sleep during the opening taxi ride and her subsequent escape to familial security when she falls asleep in his bed. After almost a minute, a loud car horn wakes him, and the metonymic transition from sleeping to waking corresponds to the arc of his overall journey, as it does for Elle in *Certified Copy*, who also falls asleep at the wheel. We see him dozing through the windshield glass for almost a minute, reestablishing life's fragility through the thin protection of a pane of glass that shelters him from the physical danger he has not yet had to face.

For the viewer, the glass might also represent the limited frame in which we try to form a conception that will make us feel safe. Just after Takashi parks outside his apartment, the woman across the alleyway, who we later learn has been watching him for years through her own limited frame, complains that parking there blocks her view. Takashi (who Kiarostami said is not a very nice man) rudely dismisses her, even though she offers to wash his windshield in exchange for slightly moving his car, a small additional reference to the limited vision that is as vulnerable to danger as glass is to steel or stone.

The apartment Takashi now enters is a monotonous gray, illuminated only by the gauze-curtained daylight from the big picture window overlooking the street, where the sound of children playing outside is a continual reminder of what he misses inside. The window as the only source of light dominates the frame, but its opaque, white curtain blurs the view as if it were hiding what really matters. To the left of the frame, a tall bookcase with glass doors can be seen reflecting the ambiguous light, while the books inside cannot be seen. Takashi turns on the answering machine and walks over to a light-gray chair, where he picks up a dark-gray blanket, from which a bracelet falls, suggesting that he took it from the bedroom the previous night and used it for a cover while sleeping in the chair.

After he goes to the refrigerator to ladle a lonely bowl of the "special soup," the answering machine picks up a call requesting an immediate reply. Having to make the callback rather than answering in the first place is a way of emphasizing his own situation when a male voice complains that Takashi's translation has missed a line: "'Man endowed with little experience . . .' Then?" Accordingly, at this point, the phone line cuts off, and when it immediately rings again, instead of the client's voice, we hear Akiko crying and barely able to speak.

Takashi rushes down four flights of a dark-gray stairway, the narrowness of which conveys the way that circumstance has suddenly cut off the freedom of his unencumbered life. The randomness of tragedy that the old man in *And Life Goes On* refuses to blame on God instantly appears when Takashi, backing his Volvo out of the narrow alley, barely misses a woman looking the opposite way with two small children holding each hand (evoking his relationship to Akiko). Once again, we see Takashi driving behind the cloudy, blue glass, followed by a shot from inside of an affluent, young couple who look like fashion models, just before we see Akiko sitting on a stoop in an alley, holding a handkerchief to her face. Inside the iron shell of his car, Takashi's danger from the outside world is signaled by a hostile horn, and after he leaves the car to run to Akiko, its unremitting blare forces the old man to keep his head and run back to the car, where once again the windshield glass reflects the lives of others impinging on private concerns, until he can park in a vacant spot.

As the sound track emphasizes the footsteps of indifferent anonymous pedestrians, Takashi focuses on the now-supreme object of his own life, acting swiftly and efficiently as if he were a much younger man and as if he has cared for Akiko since birth. He is now not just *like* someone who loves; he has entered into the role of the moment as James and Elle do in *Certified Copy* and as a spectator does in any compelling film. Authentic feeling is an experience of empathy and doesn't need an "original" excuse. The view of the street from inside the car remains cloudy, but once inside, Akiko's traumatized face and bloody handkerchief are crystal clear, and we care for her as much as for the AIDS children in *ABC Africa*. All children matter; blood, race, religion, or nationality do not, and just before Takashi pulls into his narrow alley, a man holding the hand of a little boy stops on the sidewalk, and just after, a woman with a baby stroller walks back the other way.

As Takashi helps Akiko out of the car, the screen becomes cloudy again because we are now looking through the gauze curtain of the neighbor across the street. While Akiko sits outside on the apartment steps holding her face and Takashi goes to the pharmacy to buy antiseptic, the woman fills in her own version of Takashi's past. She had hoped someday that they would marry, but instead he married a colleague from the university whom he chose, the woman believes, because she was pretty and tall: "You know how men are," she says to console herself. They had a daughter, but something she doesn't specify broke up the marriage, and she assumes that Akiko is a granddaughter who has come to visit, perhaps along with her mother: "Children don't visit their elders anymore," she complains, echoing the presence of Akiko's grandmother at the beginning and both grandparents in Yasujiro Ozu's *Tokyo Story* (1953).

Her lifelong burden of caring for an invalid brother as well as the red-bricked setting also echoes Raymond Burr's salesman in Hitchcock's *Rear Window* (1954).The most salient resemblance to *Rear Window*, however, is in the closing of the gap between distanced observation of the world and the intrusion of real-life danger that the James Stewart character romanticizes through the action photographs he provides for a magazine. It is the Grace Kelly character, however, who most resembles Takashi because her social position is equally insular and elevated and because she risks danger out of love rather than inclination, while the Stewart character, like the fan of action films, thinks he loves peril until it comes close enough to make him value what he has.

These oblique allusions to Ozu and Hitchcock are another way of expressing Kiarostami's view that a work of art should be a unique variation on innumerable precursors rather than an absolute original, and although he frequently said that his films are not derivative, he admits here and through *Certified Copy*'s similarity to *Journey to Italy* that films can resemble each other but that the best are never put together in the same way. The woman in the alley is indicative of modern people, for whom the lives of celebrities seem more intensely vital than their own: "Myself, I'm not married, and I have no children, so that's why. I spend my time looking out the window. It's my only distraction." Therefore, the window she appears in is barely bigger than her head, and the world she sees outside reflects an imagination limited to clichés.

There is a sense of confusion between being trapped and being safe in *Someone*'s final scene, and there is an affirmation of spiritual escape, despite what Kiarostami called the "odd prank at the end." After Takashi returns from the pharmacy, he urges Akiko to come inside because "it's cold," but at the very moment he says the words, we hear the invalid brother cry out as if he were in pain. The unnerving sound suggests the varied kinds of physical and social suffering Takashi has not had to face, and the limitation of that experience is suggested as he and Akiko are momentarily framed in the same small mirror we saw on Akiko's first entrance just to the right of the door.

Takashi heats milk for Akiko, who remains mute from this point on, and the metaphor of warmth resembles restoring the sanctuary of a small child who has just skinned her knee: "I will reheat the soup. No, you said you don't eat soup. Do you prefer some milk? I will warm it for you. Do you drink milk? Let's see if I have any. I do. I will heat it for you. It won't take long." But this comfort is mitigated by the imagery of glass, which neither reveals nor ultimately protects and which is the dominant visual motif as the camera emphasizes the reflections on the bookcase glass that hide the books inside and the placement of the windows that do not offer a clear outside view.

The language Takashi uses while tending to the wound also describes the social wounds his book on violence in society has been unable to heal. He starts by asking her to move her hand so that he can see the problem and thereby clean it to prevent infection and swelling. Then, he tells her not to be afraid because "it won't sting." But when he repeats, "You're not scared, right?" she shakes her head in resistance, keeping the cloth on her cheek, as do people in general who just want to avoid pain rather than understand it.

At this point, the doorbell rings, and his question—"I wonder who that could be?"—has a tinge of fairy tale horror because the wolf is at the door. "Just a minute," he tells her, as if to get this annoyance over quickly, but the face in the small security camera is that of Noriaki. He appears in the lower corner almost out of frame, perhaps because the characters and the audience have not yet conceived quite how dangerous he can be, and the screen's bluish tone matches the predominant color of the outside world that Takashi has encountered after leaving his apartment.

But if Noriaki's understanding is tiny, as suggested by his image on the wall, Takashi's awareness of danger is still limited, as suggested by his own image appearing again in the small vestibule mirror as he turns to double-lock the door. Though Takashi, or anyone else for that matter, may have no more than a limited understanding of why murderous violence continually threatens the world, he does have the loving courage to resist it. As Noriaki's voice barks and growls about being lied to, Takashi becomes the alert defender, searching for the threat by moving back and forth to the windows while keeping an equal focus on comforting Akiko. But the side window only reveals windows exactly like his own in the facing apartments, and we do not see what he is trying to locate by peeking through the white curtain of the big window in front. Akiko cannot be comforted at all, and she hides her face in the pillow, just before the situation becomes more dire, when loud footsteps on the stairs are followed by three thunderous raps on the apartment door.

While Takashi here acts as the archetypal defender, Noriaki now becomes a generalized figure of violent rage arising from baffled pain. His demands that they "Open up!" cannot be answered because he is now unleashed, and his rage is too deeply ingrained in human nature for social theories to fathom. Noriaki may or may not be frustrated because of his social rank, but that may only be the catalyst for the violence with which he responds to that frustration, as suggested by his slugging his employee for teasing him about Akiko and later punching Akiko herself. Not everyone with a social excuse becomes a killer, just as in *Journey to Italy*, not every Roman emperor was like Nero or Caligula nor every modern leader like Hitler or Mussolini. But the world is never without variations of these aggressors in various forms on various levels. Ahriman is always attacking, and Ahura Mazda, aided by innumerable fravashis, one of whom is now Takashi, is always fighting back (see chapter 3).

This sense of ever-present internal conflict is initially suggested when a soft, mysterious ring briefly intrudes on the sound track after Noriaki appears on the intercom. As in the intervals between wars, there seems to be a respite after the loud footsteps are heard retreating down the stairs, but then, the voices of children who have been heard throughout the scene are interrupted by a loud car horn, echoing the horns heard when Takashi fell asleep at the wheel and when he was interrupted trying to get to Akiko in the alley. On a thematic level, these children are as endangered as Akiko, the potential collateral damage of crime or terrorist attacks that, in the long view, seem to be as inevitable as the earthquake in *And Life Goes On*, which the wise old man compares to a hungry wolf. When Takashi bends down to look out the side window, he is flanked on his left by the two tall bookcases in which the books cannot be seen because the glass doors of the cases can only reflect the light, the actuality of experience rather than its meaning.

As Takashi looks down, the falsely reassuring hum of steady traffic and the even level of the children's voices are superseded by a loud female voice. She could be someone arguing with Noriaki or agreeing with him based on what he told her. We don't know why the tone has changed because hostility and conflict generally bubble to the surface before causes are invented to excuse them. The playing children are ever-present in the world, and as we have seen in Noriaki after his affable farewell at the auto shop, their unpredictable switching to monstrous rage always threatens every civilization that the book-lined study represents.

When Takashi turns back from the window, Akiko is seen again in close-up, holding the blood-soaked handkerchief and putting the pillow over her face in the center of the frame. Now he moves to the large picture window with its opaque curtain, resembling the ones in old-fashioned theaters, and while the excitement of a crime or war film usually remains safely vicarious, Kiarostami suddenly breaks this unbreakable fourth wall. Just after the old man bends to look through the gauze and then shifts position to look again, the whole right side of the glass explodes with a loud, startling sound. As the right half of the curtain blows inward, Takashi falls on his back to the left and vanishes from the frame. Then, an instant after we hear the shards hit the floor, the children's voices are replaced by Ella Fitzgerald singing "Like Someone in Love" while the closing credits roll.

Though the curtain can no longer keep the beast outside the frame, the courage of protective love is just as constant. There can be no conclusive end to a film that unblinkingly portrays these opposites, just as so far there has been no end to this internal war in our collective life. By telling the truth as he saw it, Kiarostami always tried to strengthen the souls of his viewers. And he dedicated himself to the arts of film, poetry, and photography because he wanted to share what he felt, like someone in love—with life.

NOTES

1. Abbas Kiarostami, in "Making of *Like Someone in Love*," directed by Morteza Farshbaf, 2012, special feature on *Like Someone in Love*, directed by Abbas Kiarostami (2012; Hartsdale, NY: Criterion Collection, 2014), DVD.

2. Emile Durkheim, *The Division of Labor in Society*, trans. W. D. Halls (1893; New York: Free Press, 1984), 208; quoted in William R. Catton Jr., "Has the Durkheim Legacy Misled Sociology?" in *Sociological Theory and the Environment: Classical Foundations, Contemporary Insights*, ed. Riley E. Dunlap (Lanham, MD: Rowman & Littlefield, 2002), 95–96.

3. Kiarostami, in "Making of *Like Someone in Love*."

4. Kiarostami, in "Making of *Like Someone in Love*."

5. See Graham Fuller, "*Like Someone in Love*: Kiarostami's Beguiling Japanese Conundrum," Blouin Art Info, February 13, 2013, https://www.blouinartinfo.com/news/story/866970/like-someone-in-love-kiarostamis-beguiling-japanese-conundrum.

6. Kiarostami, in "Making of *Like Someone in Love*."

Further Reading

In addition to the notated sources, readers should consult the following uncited articles by Geoff Andrew, Godfrey Cheshire, and Jonathan Rosenbaum, each of whom knew Kiarostami personally, as well as the recent book by Matthew Abbott, *Abbas Kiarostami and Film-Philosophy* (Edinburgh, UK: Edinburgh University Press, 2016), and the invaluable summary by Mehrnaz Saeed-Vafa, "Kiarostami, Abbas," *Senses of Cinema*, May 2002, http://sensesofcinema.com/2002/great-directors/kiarostami/.

GEOFF ANDREW

"Return to Uncertainty: Geoff Andrew on Kiarostami." Interview by Ebsan Khoshbakht. Notes on Cinematograh. July 4, 2016. http://notesoncinematograph.blogspot.com/2012/02/return-to-uncertainity-geoff-andrew-on.html.

"Abbas and Me: Geoff Andrew Remembers the Private Side of the Late Abbas Kiarostami." *Sight & Sound*. July 8, 2016. http://www.bfi.org.uk/news-opinion/sight-sound-magazine/comment/obituaries/geoff-andrew-remembers-abbas-kiarostami.

GODFREY CHESHIRE

"Poetry and Sufism." *Independent Weekly*, December 13, 2000. http://www.firouzanfilms.com/ArticlesAndEssays/Articles/GodfreyCheshire_PoetryandSufism.html.

"*Close-Up*: Prison and Escape." Criterion Collection. June 22, 2010. https://www.criterion.com/current/posts/1492-close-up-prison-and-escape.

"Godfrey Cheshire on Knowing Abbas Kiarostami through His Films and Friendship." RogerEbert.com. July 5, 2016. http://www.rogerebert.com/balder-and-dash/godfrey-cheshire-on-knowing-abbas-kiarostami-through-his-films-and-friendship.

"How Abbas Kiarostami Changed My Life: Godfrey Cheshire Reflects on a Master Filmmaker." IndieWire. July 4, 2017. http://www.indiewire.com/2017/07/after-kiarostami-close-up-24-frames-1201850513/.

JONATHAN ROSENBAUM

"From Iran with Love." Review of *Homework* and *Through the Olive Trees*. *Chicago Reader*, September 29, 1995. http://www.jonathanrosenbaum.net/1995/09/from-iran-with-love/.

"Fill in the Blanks." Review of *Taste of Cherry*. *Chicago Reader*, May 29, 1998. https://www.jonathanrosenbaum.net/2017/06/fill-in-the-blanks/.

"The Universe in a Cellar." Review of *The Wind Will Carry Us*. *Chicago Reader*, December 10, 2000. http://www.chicagoreader.com/chicago/the-universe-in-a-cellar/Content?oid=904119.

"Spoiler Alert." Review of *Roads of Kiarostami*. *Chicago Reader*, June 8, 2006. https://www.chicagoreader.com/chicago/spoiler-alert/Content?oid=922348.

"Watching Kiarostami Films at Home." *PBS Frontline*. January 4, 2011. https://www.pbs.org/wgbh/pages/frontline/tehranbureau/2011/01/watching-kiarostami-films-at-home.html.

Index

Abbas Kiarostami (Saeed-Vafa and Rosenbaum), 1
ABC Africa (film): adoption in, 139, 140, 142; AIDS and, 137, 138, 140, 218, 229, 261; beauty and ugliness in, 146; darkness in, 122, 138–139; DVD, 2, 100; human nature depicted in, 140–141; journalism and, 137, 143; marriage and, 229; music in, 142; nature and, 142–143; soul and, 142; United Nations and, 137
Abu Bakr, 4
academics, persecution of, 201
Accademia Gallery, 231
acting: art and, 91; Binoche on, 222, 225; naturalness and, 51–52, 86, 225; torture and, 64
adoption, 139, 140, 142
Ahmadinejad, Mahmoud, 201, 202
Ahmadpur, Ahmad, 29, 30, 45, 179, 191
Ahmadpur, Babak, 179, 191
Ahriman. *See* Angra Mainyu
Ahura Mazda, 49, 50, 52, 75, 103, 264
AIDS, 123, 137, 138, 140, 164, 218, 229, 261
Akhavan-Sales, Mehdi, 234
alienation, 75; *Like Someone in Love* and, 251; *Ten* and, 147
Ali ibn Abi Ṭalib, 4, 5, 11
altruistic suicide, 200

And Life Goes On (*Life and Nothing*) (film), 37; children in, 7; on DVD with English subtitles, 1–2; God and, 19, 25; guides in, 38–39; nature and, 99–100, 146; on-screen spectators and, 199; present awareness and, 100, 145; *Through the Olive Trees* and, 167–168; trees in, 107; "wise old man type" in, 100, 264
Andrew, Geoff, 1, 17, 150, 164
Angra Mainyu (Ahriman), 49, 54, 75, 103; as attacking, 61, 208, 234, 264; destruction and, 54, 248; victory over, 50, 129
animals, 27, 32, 54, 66, 110, 112; Muhammad and, 218; sounds of, 116, 120, 121, 124, 180, 190; *Taste of Cherry* and, 113; visual poetry of, 205–206
anomic suicide, 200
anti-Semitism, 201
Arabization, of Iranian culture, 54
Armstrong, Louis, 71, 76, 133
art: acting and, 91; beauty and, 58, 171, 214, 228; death and, 67, 68; forgeries, 230; *Like Someone in Love* and, 253, 254; love and, 218, 231, 232; movies and, 28; nature and, 20, 85, 171, 211, 227; purpose of, 234–235; role of, 19, 111; soul of, 221–222; Tolstoy on, 91; treasures, 224; value of, 231

artists, 42, 43, 113, 176, 204; credo in *Ten on Ten*, 28; God as, 58; persecution of, 201, 202; with process, 89; as prophet, 27; role of, 79, 92, 100, 113, 116, 173, 213; subject and relationship to, 57; window and, 124
Attar, Farid ud-Din, 25, 109; *The Conference of the Birds*, 23–25, 37, 38; death of, 26
auteur, 52, 232
Auty, Peter, 166

baby, sounds of crying, 183
Bach, Johann Sebastian, 134
Barks, Coleman, 25, 26
battlefield death, 200–201
Battle of Karbala, 172
Beard, Michael, 17, 26
beauty, 67, 72, 84, 240; *ABC Africa* and, 146; art and, 58, 171, 214, 228; cameras and, 27, 33, 53, 54, 94, 95, 193; God and, 19, 21, 25, 185; identity and, 146; love and, 146; nature and, 107, 130, 131, 191, 213, 259; spiritual, 147; *Ten* and, 151, 164; ugliness and, 105, 146, 147
bells: *Certified Copy* and tolling, 226, 228, 233, 235, 238–239, 242–243; *Like Someone in Love* and tolling, 257; sounds, 147
Bergala, Alain, 108, 122
Bergman, Ingrid, 224
Berlin International Film Festival, 202
bijar (tree of life) carpet, 54
Binoche, Juliette, 203, 215, 222, 236; on acting, 222, 225; Kiarostami and, 222, 240, 241
"Bismillah" (Rumi), 66
Blake, Howard, 166
blessing, love as curse and, 207
blindness metaphor, 214–215
Bordwell, David, 1, 202
Bresson, Robert, 147
Buddha, 216
Buddhism, 26, 28, 56, 57, 217
burial, in *The Wind Will Carry Us*, 101–102
Burr, Raymond, 262

Cahiers du Cinema, interview in, 23
cameras: beauty and, 27, 33, 53, 54, 94, 95, 193; in *Close-Up*, 87; close-ups to capture souls, 223; digital, 75, 147; as God, 52; movies with intimacy and, 52; in *Rug*, 54–56; in *Taste of Cherry*, 76–77; in *Ten on Ten*, 51–53, 56
Cannes Film Festival, 2, 80, 148, 202, 219n27, 223
cars: driving metaphor, 161; as egoic shell, 109–110, 111, 127; with inner nature of humans, 146; sounds, 150, 160, 260, 261, 264; traffic metaphor, 150. *See also Ten*; *Ten on Ten*
casualties: Iran-Iraq War, 3, 6; Vietnam War, 3
censorship, of movies, 105, 107, 202
Center for the Intellectual Development of Children and Young Adults. *See* Kanun
Certified Copy (film), 1, 104, 252; with art, value of, 231; Binoche and, 222, 225, 236, 240, 241; with copies of life, 240; Cupid and, 227; darkness in, 227, 234, 241–242; doors, 238; DVD, 2, 222, 236, 240; with family, forming of, 229, 232, 233; flowers and, 240; influences on, 223, 225; language and, 233, 237, 238, 239, 253; with love and art, 231; with love and souls, 226; marriage and, 229, 232, 233, 237–238; *Musa Polimnia* and, 230; plot of, 221, 225; sex in, 17–18; Shimell and, 222, 225; soul of art and, 221–222, 232; sounds of bells tolling in, 226, 228, 233, 235, 238–239, 242–243; suicide and, 101, 223, 228, 242; trees in, 228; water dripping sounds in, 242; windows and, 232, 238, 241; women with intellectual equality in, 228
César Award, 222
Cheshire, Godfrey, 102; on suicide, 64
childhood, movies reflecting, 85–86
children: adoption and, 139, 140, 142; *And Life Goes On* and, 7; Center for the Intellectual Development of Children and Young Adults, 7; with death, 65–66; in *Homework*, 7–14, 180; on Hussein, 10; identity and wisdom of, 149; illiteracy and, 9; Kanun, 7, 9, 14,

99, 100, 179; *Like Someone in Love* and, 252, 253–254, 264; as martyrs, 11; potted plants and, 179; suicide and, 12; *Through the Olive Trees* and, 27, 181–182; in *The Traveler*, 7, 12, 27; violence and, 9–11; in *Where Is the Friend's House?*, 7, 12, 18, 19, 27, 28–29; in *The Wind Will Carry Us*, 7; wisdom and, 254. *See also ABC Africa*
Chittick, William, 27–28, 109
Christianity, 11, 21, 28, 49, 71, 168; birth of, 178; Jesus Christ and, 4, 178, 179, 208
Cimarosa, Dominic, 195
Ciment, Michel, 1
The Cinema of Abbas Kiarostami (Elena), 1
The Circle (Panahi), 114
climate change, 58, 130, 259
Close-Up (film), 40; cab ride in, 81–85, 86, 93; camera and, 87; on DVD with English subtitles, 1; establishing shot in, 81; flowers and, 76, 82, 85, 94–95, 97; frame size in, 94; Iran-Iraq War and, 6; journalism and, 79–80, 81–82, 126; Kiarostami on, 204; living room scene and, 88–89; music in, 95; nature and, 89; poetic cinema and, 92; Sabzian in, 79–82, 84–97, 113, 129, 200, 217, 229; in *Sight & Sound* top films poll, 1; soul and, 79, 80, 88–89, 90, 91–92; sound in, 93
colors: of creation, 171; evil and, 71; of fertility, 181, 183, 187; of lingam symbol, 171, 185; opening titles of *Shirin* and royal, 205
Communism, 223
Concerto for Trumpet in C Major, 195
The Conference of the Birds (Attar), 23–25, 37, 38, 109
conscripts, 5, 84
Coombes, Belinda, 1
copies: of life, 240; originals and, 221, 225, 226, 229–230, 231
creation, colors of, 171
"The Creed of Love" (Rumi), 51
Crimson Gold (film), 40, 202; physical violence in, 200

critics: with negative reviews, 64; with positive reviews, 1
culture: Iranian, 23, 54, 234; Italian Culture Ministry, 231; language and, 233
Cupid, 227
curse, love as blessing and, 207
The Cyclist (film), 88, 89, 90, 91
Cyrus the Great (King of Persia), 49

Dabashi, Hamid, 22, 28, 50
Darbandi, Afkham, 23
darkness: in *ABC Africa*, 122, 138–139; in *Certified Copy*, 227, 234, 241–242; in *Ten*, 148, 155, 159, 160; in *The Wind Will Carry Us*, 122–123, 126, 133
Darwin, Charles, 7, 248
David statue (Michelangelo), 231
da Vinci, Leonardo, 230
Davis, Dick, 23
Day, Doris, 260
Day for Night (film), 171
the dead: power of, 186; sounds of, 185
death: art and, 67, 68; of Attar, 26; battlefield, 200–201; cavalier attitudes toward, 117; children with, 65–66; as ever present, 105; nature and, 22–23; terracidal, 63, 66, 202; with war as familicides, 206; war casualties, 3, 6
"Departure" (Rumi), 37
digital camera, 75, 147
dissidents, torture of, 201
divorce: family and, 149–150, 156, 159; Kiarostami and, 145. *See also* marriage
doors: *Certified Copy* and, 238; symbolism of, 29–30, 33, 35–36, 40–41, 44, 217
Doors without Keys (Kiarostami), 102, 139
"Door without Keys" (Kiarostami), 39
Dostoyevsky, Fyodor, 80
The Double Life of Veronique (film), 223
Dreyer, Carl Theodor, 1
driving metaphor, 161
Durkheim, Emile, 7, 248; on suicide, 100–101, 200
DVDs: *ABC Africa*, 2, 100; *And Life Goes On*, 1–2; *Certified Copy*, 2, 222, 236, 240; *Close-Up*, 1; interviews on, 101; *Like Someone in Love*, 2, 245–246, 250, 254; *The Report*, 2; *Roads of*

Kiarostami, 2; *Rug*, 2; *Shirin*, 2; *Taste of the Cherry*, 2; *Ten*, 2; *Ten on Ten*, 2; *Through the Olive Trees*, 2; *The Traveler*, 2; *Where Is the Friend's House?*, 1; *The Wind Will Carry Us*, 2

Ebert, Roger, 64
egoistic suicide, 200
Elena, Alberto, 1, 38; on suicide, 64
Encyclopædia Iranica, 118, 211
endings: Kiarostami on, 151; in *Taste of Cherry*, 69–77, 216; in *Ten on Ten*, 177; *Through the Olive Trees*, 167
evil, colors and, 71

family: divorce and, 149–150, 156, 159; forming of, 229, 232, 233; with war as familicides, 206. *See also* marriage
faravahar pendant, 50
Farhadi, Asghar, 17, 193
Farrokhzad, Forough, 104, 105, 111, 124, 131, 137
fertility, colors of, 181, 183, 187
Film Comment poll, 1
film conventions, *Taste of Cherry* and, 51–54
First Graders (film), 8
Fitzgerald, Edward, 21, 22
Fitzgerald, Ella, 256, 264
Five Dedicated to Ozu (Kiarostami), 204
flowers: *Certified Copy* and, 240; *Close-Up* and, 76, 82, 85, 94–95, 97; *Where Is the Friend's House?* and, 76
forgeries, art, 230
The 400 Blows (film), 80
frame size, in *Close-Up*, 94
France, 3, 229
Francis (Pope), 58, 130
fravashis, 49, 50, 55, 75, 264
funerals: *Through the Olive Trees* and, 183; in *The Wind Will Carry Us*, 102–103

Ganjavi, Nizami, 108, 202, 203
gardens, Zoroastrianism and, 54
global warming, 58
Gnostics, 28, 55, 174
God, 153; *And Life Goes On* and, 19, 25; as artist, 58; beauty and, 19, 21, 25, 185; camera as, 52; *The Conference of the Birds* and, 23–25; *Homework* and, 67–68; humanity and, 103; Islam and, 172, 221; Man-God, 172; Muhammad and, 23; natural disasters and, 19–20; nature and, 27, 58, 134; *Rubaiyat* and, 23; Rumi and, 204; souls and, 217; Sufism and, 18, 28, 103, 106; treasure and, 109; trees and, 106; in *Where Is the Friend's House?*, 19–20; in *The Wind Will Carry Us*, 19, 21–22, 102–103; wishes and, 155
Golbou, Farrideh, 203, 208
Green Film Festival, South Korea, 58
Green Revolution, 202
growth metaphor: nature and, 234; in *The Wind Will Carry Us*, 111–112
guides in *And Life Goes On*, 38–39

haiku, 29, 53, 58, 59, 60, 73
Hakkak, Ahmad Karimi, 17
Al-Hallaj, Mansur, 51
Hazrat Ali, 11
Hazrat Fatima, 11
heart, open, 25–26
hegira, Islam and, 178
Hinduism, 26, 28, 169–170, 172, 173, 179, 181; Shiva and, 180
Hiratsuka, Unichi, 56
Hitchcock, Alfred, 29, 200, 205, 260, 262
Hollywood, 52–53, 255
Holocaust, denial of, 201
Homer, 153
Homework (documentary), 81; children in, 7–14, 180; God and, 67–68; literacy and, 9; mental violence and, 199; religion in, 18
homosexuality, 70
The House Is Black (film), 105, 111, 137
humanity: God and, 103; hope for, 229; religion and, 158; Rumi and, 26–27; *Through the Olive Trees* and, 179
human nature: *ABC Africa* with depiction of, 140–141; cars with interior of, 146
Al-Husayn ibn Ali, 4, 5, 172, 180
Hussein, Saddam, 3; children on, 10; supporters of, 8

ibn Affan, Uthman, 4

ibn al-Khaṭṭab, Umar, 4
identity: beauty and, 146; transformation of, 148; wisdom of children and, 149
Iliad (Homer), 153
illiteracy, 71; children and, 9; Gnostics and, 55; literacy and, 9, 115, 187, 223; marriage and, 168, 179, 183, 187, 194
ingratitude, martyrs and, 68
intellectual equality, women and, 228
interviews: in *Cahiers du Cinema*, 23; on DVDs, 101; in *New York Times*, 17; at San Francisco Film Festival, 66
intimacy, movies with camera and, 52
Iran: Islam and, 28; with martyrs, 5; national anthem, 5
Iranian culture: Arabization of, 54; deterioration of, 234; negativity and, 23
Iran-Iraq War: casualties, 3, 6; conscripts in, 5; Kiarostami, Abbas, on, 6–7
Islam: colors associated with evil in, 71; God and, 172, 221; hegira and birth of, 178; Iran and, 28; Sufism and, 66; suicide and, 67
Israel, 5, 49, 172, 201
Is There a Place to Approach. See *Rug*
Italian Culture Ministry, 231

Japan, 12. See also *Like Someone in Love*
Jesus Christ, 4, 178, 179, 208
Jews, 5, 24, 28, 49, 201
jihad, 5, 49, 200, 201
Johns, Jasper, 228
journalism: *ABC Africa* and, 137, 143; *Close-Up* and, 79–80, 81–82, 126; power of, 80
journeys: importance of, 105–106; *Like Someone in Love* in, 250–252; of Rumi, 172; *Through the Olive Trees* and, 192
Journey to Italy (film), 223–225, 262, 264

Kanun (Center for the Intellectual Development of Children and Young Adults), 7, 9, 14, 99, 100, 179
Karbala, 4, 5, 82, 103, 172, 200
Karimi-Hakkak, Ahmad, 26
Kelly, Grace, 262
Khamenei, Ali, 26, 202
Khan, Genghis, 26
Kharijites, 172

Khayyam, Omar, 19, 50, 107, 132; with nature and death, 22; *Rubaiyat* and, 21–22, 23
Khomeini, Ruhollah (Ayatollah), 3–4, 5, 8, 212; loyalty to, 5–6, 11; religion and, 26
Khosrow and Shirin (film), 203
Khosrow and Shirin (Ganjavi), 202
Khosrow and Shirin legend, 205, 211, 214. See also *Shirin*
Kiarostami, Abbas: Binoche and, 222, 240, 241; on body of work, 2; on *Close-Up*, 204; as director, 25, 51–54; divorce and, 145; "Door without Keys," 39; on endings, 151; influences on, 3, 7, 223; on Iran-Iraq War, 6–7; *The Leafless Garden*, 234; legacy, 4, 17; with onscreen sex, 217; on originals and copies, 221; on patriotism, 201; publicity photo, 2; *24 Frames* and, 218. See also *ABC Africa*; *And Life Goes On*; *Certified Copy*; *Close-Up*; *First Graders*; *Five Dedicated to Ozu*; *Homework*; *Like Someone in Love*; *The Report*; *Roads of Kiarostami*; *Rug*; *Shirin*; *Taste of Cherry*; *Ten*; *Ten on Ten*; *Through the Olive Trees*; *The Traveler*; *Walking with the Wind*; *Where Is the Friend's House?*; *The Wind Will Carry Us*
Kieslowski, Krzysztof, 222; influence of, 239; on making movies, 223; suicide and, 223
King Lear (Shakespeare), 203
Kundera, Milan, 148, 223

Ladanian, Tahereh, 168, 174, 177, 180
language: culture and, 233; *Like Someone in Love* and, 253, 256, 263; symbolism of, 237, 238, 239, 253; with vocabulary diminished, 148
lateness motif, in *Where Is the Friend's House?*, 30–31
Laudato Si (Pope Francis), 58
Lavizan Air Force Base, 83, 199
"The Leafless Garden" (Akhavan-Sales), 234
The Leafless Garden (Kiarostami), 234

life: copies of, 240; loss and, 160; love and, 155, 265; movies and progression of life, 147; as option, 67–68, 74–75; Sufi Friend and, 223; with time spent, 106, 112, 120; work and, 114–117, 128, 130. *See also* death; suicide
Life and Nothing (film). *See And Life Goes On*
"Like Someone in Love," 256, 264
Like Someone in Love (film), 7, 40, 104; alienation and, 251; art and, 253, 254; bells tolling in, 257; car sounds in, 260, 261, 264; children and, 252, 253–254, 264; DVD, 2, 245–246, 250, 254; journey in, 250–252; language and, 253, 256, 263; life and love in, 265; with love and souls, 226; marriage and, 247, 262; music in, 252, 256; opening scene, 248; prostitution and, 249, 255–256; sex and, 245–246, 247, 249, 255–256; social contract and, 247; soul growth and, 246, 247; suicide and, 101, 223, 248; violence and, 248, 257, 259, 263–264; windows and, 251, 256, 257, 260, 261, 263, 264; work and, 246–247
lingam symbol: color of, 171, 185; Shiva and, 170, 180; yoni and, 170, 190
literacy, 9, 115, 187, 223. *See also* illiteracy
Loggins, Kenny, 166
loss: life and, 160; strength and wisdom from, 145
love: art and, 218, 231, 232; beauty and, 146; as blessing and curse, 207; Cupid and, 227; idealized, 209; life and, 155, 265; personified, 208; Rumi and, 172; souls and, 226; of Sufi Friend, 68, 192; Sufism and, 105; suicide and romantic, 203; survival of, 224; triangle, 210–215; war and, 223; *The Wind Will Carry Us* and, 118–119, 132. *See also Like Someone in Love*; *Shirin*; *Through the Olive Trees*
lunar hegira, 178

Mahdi (Imam), 201
Makhmalbaf, Mohsen, 4, 26; with *Close-Up*, 79, 80, 88; *The Cyclist* and, 88, 89, 90, 91; with *Marriage of the Blessed*, 67, 81, 205
"Making of *Like Someone in Love*" featurette, 245–246, 254
Man-God, 172
Mani (prophet), 174, 207, 208, 210, 212, 214, 215
Manichaean King of Light, 208
Manichean, 28, 55, 208
The Man Who Knew Too Much (film), 260
Marrakech Film Festival, 85–86
marriage: *ABC Africa* and, 229; *Certified Copy* and, 229, 232, 233, 237–238; divorce and, 145, 149–150, 156, 159; illiteracy and, 168, 179, 183, 187, 194; *Like Someone in Love* and, 247, 262; *Shirin* and, 213; *Taste of Cherry* and, 228–229; *Through the Olive Trees* and, 187–188
Marriage of the Blessed (film), 67, 81, 205
Martin, Adrian, 1
martyrdom, rejection of, 205
martyrs: altruistic suicide and, 200; children as, 11; ingratitude and, 68; Iran with, 5
Mecca, 5, 174, 178, 217
Medina, 4, 5, 178
meditation, nature and, 17
mental violence: *Homework* and, 199; Nietzsche and, 67
metteur en scène, 52
Michelangelo, 231
MK2, 223
Mohammad, teachings of, 28
Mona Lisa (da Vinci), 230
Mongol dynasty (1256–1353), 28
Mosaddeq, Mohammad, 234
movies: art and, 28; with camera and intimacy, 52; censorship of, 105, 107, 202; childhood reflected in, 85–86; Kieslowski on making, 223; poetic cinema and, 92, 113, 189, 206; with progression of life, 147; role of, 29. *See also specific films*
Mozart, Wolfgang Amadeus, 195
Muawiyah (Umayyad ruler), 172
Muhammad, 4, 5, 179; animals and, 218; God and, 23; persecution and, 178; Shia Islam and, 180
Mulvey, Laura, 1

Musa Polimnia, 230
music: in *ABC Africa*, 142; in *Close-Up*, 95; in *Like Someone in Love*, 252, 256; in *Shirin*, 206; in *Taste of Cherry*, 66, 71, 76; in *Ten*, 165–166; in *Ten on Ten*, 66; in *Three Colors: Blue*, 223; *Through the Olive Trees* and, 178, 195; in *The Wind Will Carry Us*, 134

national anthem, Iran, 5
natural disasters: God and, 19–20; war and, 223. *See also And Life Goes On*
naturalness, acting and, 225
nature: *ABC Africa* and, 142–143; *And Life Goes On* and, 99–100, 146; animals, 111, 113, 116, 120, 121, 124; art and, 20, 85, 171, 211, 227; beauty and, 107, 130, 131, 191, 213, 259; climate change and, 130, 259; *Close-Up* and, 89; death and, 22–23; global warming and, 58; God and, 27, 58, 134; growth metaphor and, 234; meditation and, 17; photography and, 57; *Roads of Kiarostami* and, 57–61; role of, 27; snow scenes and, 147; Sufism and, 57, 118, 217; trees, 17, 106–107, 117, 118, 126, 202, 234; Zoroastrianism and, 54–56, 57
negativity, Iranian culture and, 23
New York Times (newspaper), interview in, 17
Nietzsche, Friedrich, 67
Nowruz, 50

Okuno, Tadashi, 246
"Only Breath" (Rumi), 26
on-screen spectators, 199, 213
originals: copies and, 221, 225, 226, 229–230, 231; etymology of, 226
Ozu, Yasujiro, 1, 204, 262

Paige, Elaine, 166
Palme d'Or, 2, 64
Panahi, Jafar, 114, 200, 202, 203
patriotism, 5, 17, 81; Kiarostami on, 201; suicide and, 200
persecution: of academics, 201; of artists, 201, 202; Muhammad and, 178; of Sufism, 51

photography, nature and, 57
physical violence in *Crimson Gold*, 200
poetic cinema, 92, 113, 189, 206
poetry: animals and visual, 205–206; as religion, 105; in *Rug*, 204; Sabzian and, 103; transformative power of, 104; *Where Is the Friend's House?* and, 107; *The Wind Will Carry Us* and, 103–105, 123, 124, 129
potted plants, 126, 240, 253; children and, 179; in *Through the Olive Trees*, 192
present: *And Life Goes On* and awareness of, 100, 145; *Like Someone in Love*, prostitution and, 256
projector sounds, 147
prophet, artist as, 27
prostitutes: *Like Someone in Love* and, 249, 255–256; in *Ten*, 155–157, 159

Al-Qaeda, 49

Rahmanian, Mohammad, 203, 208
réalisateur, 52
Rear Window (film), 262
religion: criticism of, 203–204; in *Homework*, 18; humanity and, 158; Khomeini and, 26; organized, 154; poetry as, 105; Rumi and, 26; war and, 26. *See also specific religions*
Renoir, Jean, 1
The Report (film), 2
reviews, *Through the Olive Trees*, 1
Rezai, Hossein, 168, 174, 180–181, 184
Richard, Cliff, 166
Roads of Kiarostami (film): on DVD with English subtitles, 2; influences on, 56; nature and, 57–61; suicide and, 63; terracidal death and, 63, 66, 202
romantic love, as suicide, 203
Romeo and Juliet (film), 207, 212
Rosenbaum, Jonathan, 1
Roshanravan, Kambiz, 95
Rossellini, Roberto, 223, 224, 225
royal colors, 205
Rubaiyat (Khayyam), 21–22, 23, 132
Rug (*Is There a Place to Approach*) (film): camera in, 54–56; on DVD with English subtitles, 2; nature and, 54–56, 58; poetry in, 204; Sufism and, 54

Rumi, Jelaluddin, 25, 37, 89, 251; "Bismillah" and, 66; God and, 204; humanity and, 26–27; influence of, 26, 105; influences on, 26; love and, 172; with open heart, 25–26; religion and, 26; Shams of Tabriz and, 39–40; Sufism and, 51; treasure and, 108, 109

Sabzian, Hossein, 6, 96; *Close-Up* and, 79–82, 84–97, 113, 129, 200, 217, 229; poetry and, 103
Saeed-Vafa, Mehrnaz, 1, 105
Safavid dynasty, 4
Safi, Hamid, 25–26
Safi, Omid, 25
San Francisco Film Festival, 66
Sarshar, Houman, 56–57, 60–61
Saudi Arabia, 3, 5, 23
scarification rites, 102
Schopenhauer, Arthur, 201
self-flagellation, 5, 103
Sepehri, Sohrab, 38, 56–57, 59, 107
sex: in *Certified Copy*, 17–18; fantasies, 121; homosexuality, 70; Kiarostami with onscreen, 217; *Like Someone in Love* and, 245–246, 247, 249, 255–256, 256; *Shirin* and, 211, 212, 213
Shakespeare, William, 203
Shams of Tabriz, 26, 39–40
Shariati, Ali, 200–201
Shia Islam, 5; Muhammad and, 180; as state religion, 4
Shimell, William, 222, 225
Shirin (film), 106; art and nature with, 211; blindness metaphor in, 214–215; on DVD with English subtitles, 2; idealized love in, 209; Iran-Iraq War and, 6; love personified in, 208; love triangle in, 210–215; marriage and, 213; with martyrdom, rejection of, 205; music in, 206; on-screen spectators and, 199; with royal colors and opening titles, 205; sex and, 211, 212, 213; suicide and, 101, 210; supreme elevation and social destruction in, 205–215; treasure and, 108; visual poetry in, 205–206; with war as familicides, 206; war sounds in, 210; "Where Is My Romeo?" and, 219n27;

women and, 202–203, 206, 210, 215–216; with women and intellectual equality, 228
Shiva, 181; Hinduism and, 180; lingam and, 170, 180; Sufi Friend and, 174; symbolism, 171
Sight & Sound top films poll, 1
silence, sound and, 92
The Snowman (animated cartoon), 166
snow scenes, nature and, 147
social contract, *Like Someone in Love* and, 247
social destruction, supreme elevation and, 205–215
solar hegira, 178
Solaris (film), 134
souls: *ABC Africa* and, 142; of art, 221–222; *Close-Up* and, 79, 80, 88–89, 90, 91–92; close-ups to capture, 223; God and, 217; *Like Someone in Love* and growth of, 246, 247; love and, 226; *The Wind Will Carry Us* and, 120
sounds: of animals, 111, 116, 120, 121, 124, 180, 190; bell, 147; of bells tolling, 226, 228, 233, 235, 238–239, 242–243; cars, 150, 160, 260, 261, 264; in *Close-Up*, 93; of crying baby, 183; of the dead, 185; projector, 147; silence and, 92; of war, 210; of water dripping, 242; in *Where Is the Friend's House?*, 30; yin-yang, 180. *See also* music
South Korea, 58
Spain, 3, 27
spiritual beauty, 147
spiritual patriotism, 5–6
spiritual quest, in *Where Is the Friend's House?*, 31–35
"Spring Is Christ" (Rumi), 27
Sterritt, David, 39, 92
Stewart, James, 262
"St. James Infirmary," 71, 76, 133
"St. Matthew Passion," 134
strength, from loss, 145
subject: artists and relationship to, 57
Sufi Friend, 34, 107, 118, 139, 181; life and, 223; love of, 68, 192; Shiva and, 174
Sufism, 113; God and, 18, 28, 103, 106; influence of, 54, 56; Islam and, 66; love

and, 105; nature and, 57, 118, 217; persecution of, 51; popularity of, 51; *Rug* and, 54; treasure and, 108
suicide: *Certified Copy* and, 101, 223, 228, 242; children and, 12; Durkheim on, 100–101, 200; Islam and, 67; Kieslowski and, 223; *Like Someone in Love* and, 101, 223, 248; with love and victory, confusion between, 210; patriotism and, 200; *Roads of Kiarostami* and, 63; romantic love as, 203; Romeo-like, 212; *Shirin* and, 101, 213; *Taste of Cherry* and, 63–64, 66–67, 68, 101, 200, 223, 224, 228; *Three Colors: Blue* and, 223; types of, 200; violence and, 248; as war metaphor, 64, 224; *The Wind Will Carry Us* and, 101, 223
Suicide (Durkheim), 200
Sunni Islam, 5, 9
supreme elevation, social destruction and, 205–215
symbolism: of doors, 29–30, 33, 35–36, 40–41, 44, 217; of language, 237, 238, 239, 253; of windows, 217

Tahereh's Dreams, 199, 200
Tahirih, 174, 177, 178
Taize (Kiarostami), 202–203
Takanashi, Rin, 246, 250
Taoism, 56, 57, 217
Tarkovsky. Andrei, 134
Taste of Cherry (film), 22, 23, 24, 57, 59, 69, 70; animals and, 113; camera in, 76–77; with children and death, 65–66; as cinematic hymn, 64, 66; on DVD with English subtitles, 2; ending in, 69–77, 216; film conventions and, 51–54; Iran-Iraq War and, 6; Kiarostami, Abbas, publicity photo for, 2; with life as option, 67–68, 74–75; marriage and, 228–229; music in, 66, 71, 76; Palme d'Or winner, 2; poetic cinema and, 92; review of, 64; suicide and, 63–64, 66–67, 68, 101, 200, 223, 224, 228; *Ten* and, 146
Tavernier, Bernard, 1
taxidermist, 63, 65, 66, 68, 69, 71, 75, 108

Ten (film), 1, 40, 104; alienation and, 147; beauty and, 151, 164; bell and projector sounds in, 147; at Cannes Film Festival, 223; car interior and, 146; cars sounds in, 150, 160; darkness in, 148, 155, 159, 160; divorce and family in, 149–150, 156, 159; driving metaphor and, 161; on DVD with English subtitles, 2; episode 1, 165; episode 2, 162–165; episode 3, 160–162; episode 4, 159–160, 163; episode 5, 158–159, 161, 165; episode 6, 157–158, 164; episode 7, 155–157; episode 8, 154–155, 160; episode 9, 151–154; episode 10, 148–151, 158, 160, 161; with identity transformed, 148; with life and loss, 160; with life and love rejected, 155; music in, 165–166; with progression of life, 147; prostitute in, 155–157, 159; *Taste of Cherry* and, 146; traffic metaphor and, 150; ugliness and, 147, 155; with vocabulary diminished, 148; windows in, 148, 155, 157; wisdom of children and identity in, 149; with women and intellectual equality, 228
Ten on Ten (film), 79, 106; art and, 28; artist credo in, 28; camera in, 51–53, 56; car exterior and, 146; on DVD with English subtitles, 2; ending of, 177; music in, 66; Nietzsche and, 67; Zoroastrianism and, 51
terracidal death, 63, 66, 202
theocracy, 5, 25
Three Colors: Blue (film), 222, 239; music in, 223; suicide and, 223
Three Colors: Red (film), 223
Three Colors: White (film), 223
Through the Olive Trees (film), 42, 184, 209; *And Life Goes On* and, 167–168; animal sounds in, 180, 190; children and, 27, 181–182; with crying baby, sounds of, 183; with the dead and, 185, 186; on DVD with English subtitles, 2; ending of, 167; funerals in, 183; humanity and, 179; journey in, 192; lingam symbol and, 170, 171, 180, 185, 190; marriage and illiteracy in, 168, 179, 183, 187, 194; marriage in, 187–188; music in, 178, 195; with

nature and art, 171; on-screen spectators and, 199; potted plant in, 192; reviews, 1; Sufi Friend and, 174, 181, 192; treasure in, 172; *Where Is the Friend's House?* and, 179; yoni symbol and, 170, 190
Tokyo Story (film), 262
Tolstoy, Leo, 91
torture: acting and, 64; of dissidents, 201
Toubiana, Serge, 1, 23
traffic metaphor, 150
Training a Parrot, 253, 254
The Traveler (film), 218; children in, 7, 12, 27, 130; on DVD with English subtitles, 2
treasures: art, 224; God and, 109; Khosrow and Shirin legend as national, 205; Rumi and, 108, 109; *Shirin* and, 108; Sufism and, 108; *Through the Olive Trees* and, 172; *The Wind Will Carry Us* and, 108
tree of life carpet. *See* bijar carpet
trees: *And Life Goes On* and, 107; in *Certified Copy*, 228; God and, 106; in *The Leafless Garden*, 234; transplanting, 17, 202; in *Where Is the Friend's House?*, 106, 107, 117, 118; *The Wind Will Carry Us* and, 117, 118, 126. *See also Through the Olive Trees*
Truffaut, François, 80, 171
24 Frames (film), 218

ugliness: *ABC Africa* and, 146; beauty and, 105, 146, 147; *Ten* and, 147, 155
The Unbearable Lightness of Being (Kundera), 223
United Nations, 137, 201
United States, 3, 25, 70, 74

Van Gogh, Theo, 246
Van Gogh, Vincent, 246
Venice Film Festival, 222
Vertigo (film), 205, 207
Vietnam War, casualties, 3
violence: children and, 9–11; *Like Someone in Love* and, 248, 257, 259, 263–264; mental, 67, 199; physical, 200; suicide and, 248; Zoroastrianism and, 248

vocabulary, diminishing of, 148

"Walking in the Air" (Blake), 166
Walking with the Wind (Kiarostami), 17, 26
war: casualties, 3, 6; as civil war, 140; as familicides, 206; love and, 223; natural disasters and, 223; religion and, 26; sounds of, 210; suicide as metaphor for, 64, 224
Warhol, Andy, 228
water dripping sounds, 242
"Where Is My Romeo?," 219n27
Where Is the Friend's House? (film), 49, 85, 178; children in, 7, 12, 18, 19, 27, 28–29; on DVD with English subtitles, 1; flowers and, 76; God in, 19–20; lateness motif in, 30–31; with nature and art, 20; poetry and, 107; sound in, 30; spiritual quest in, 31–35; symbolism in, 29–30; *Through the Olive Trees* and, 179; trees in, 106, 107, 117, 118; windows and, 28, 30; "wise old man type" in, 100
window, artists and, 124
windows: *Certified Copy* and, 232, 238, 241; *Like Someone in Love* and, 251, 256, 257, 260, 261, 263, 264; *Rear Window*, 262; symbolism of, 217; in *Ten*, 148, 150, 155, 157; *Where Is the Friend's House?* and, 28, 30
"The Wind Will Carry Us" (Farrokhzad), 104
The Wind Will Carry Us (film), 114, 115, 132; animal sounds in, 111, 116, 120, 121, 124; burial in, 101–102; car as egoic shell in, 109–110, 111, 127; censorship of, 107; children in, 7; darkness in, 122–123, 126, 133; on DVD with English subtitles, 2; fravashis and, 50, 55; funerals in, 102–103; God in, 19, 21–22, 102–103; growth metaphor in, 111–112; with journey, importance of, 105–106; life and work in, 114–117, 128, 130; love and, 118–119, 132; with love and souls, 226; music in, 134; open heart in, 25; poetry and, 103–105, 123, 124, 129; scarification rites in, 102; soul and, 120;

suicide and, 101, 223; treasure and, 108; trees and, 117, 118, 126; "wise old man type" and, 128

wisdom: children and, 254; of children and identity, 149; from loss, 145

"wise old man type": *And Life Goes On* and, 100, 264; in *Where Is the Friend's House*, 100; *The Wind Will Carry Us* and, 128

wishes, God and, 155

women: intellectual equality and, 228; repression of, 202; *Shirin* and, 202–203, 206, 210, 215–216

Wood, Robin, 1

woodblock printing, 56–57

work: life and, 114–117, 128, 130; *Like Someone in Love* and, 246–247

The World of Persian Literary Humanism (Dabashi), 28

Yazdanian, Peyman, 134
yin-yang sounds, 180
yoni symbol, lingam and, 170, 190
Young, Deborah, 202–203

Zanadiqa, 50
Zarathustra, 49
Zeffirelli, Franco, 207
zigzag road more?, 30
Zoroastrianism, 28, 103, 234; bijar carpet and, 54; *faravahar* pendant and, 50; garden and, 54; history and popularity of, 49–50; influence of, 51, 54; Mani and, 208; nature and, 54–56, 57; violence and, 248

About the Author

Julian Rice, now retired, was professor of English at Florida Atlantic University. He has published widely in literature and film. His books include *Black Elk's Story* (1991); *Deer Women and Elk Men* (1992); *Before the Great Spirit* (1998); *Kubrick's Hope* (2008); *The Jarmusch Way* (2012); and *Kubrick's Story, Spielberg's Film* (2017).

www.ingramcontent.com/pod-product-compliance
Lightning Source LLC
Chambersburg PA
CBHW022010300426
44117CB00005B/116